THE COMPANION GUIDE TO
The Shakespeare Country

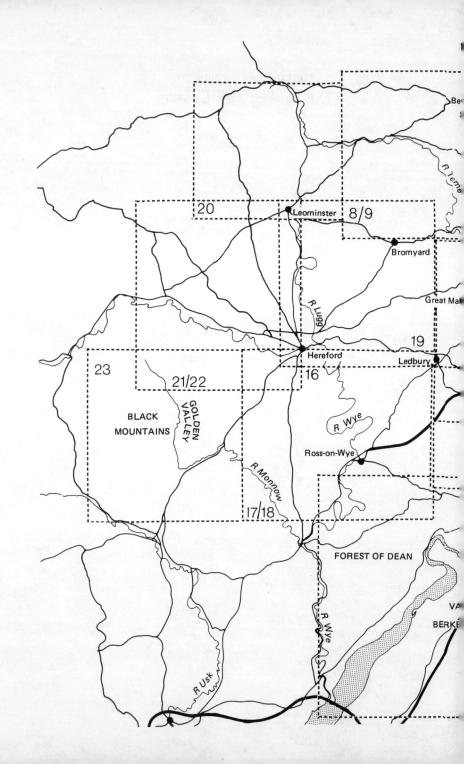

THE COMPANION GUIDES

GENERAL EDITOR: VINCENT CRONIN

*It is the aim of these guides to provide a Companion
in the person of the author, who knows intimately
the places and people of whom he writes, and is able to
communicate this knowledge and affection to his readers.
It is hoped that the text and pictures will aid them
in their preparations and in their travels, and will
help them remember on their return.*

LONDON · THE SHAKESPEARE COUNTRY · OUTER LONDON · EAST ANGLIA
NORTHUMBRIA · THE WEST HIGHLANDS OF SCOTLAND
THE SOUTH OF FRANCE · THE ILE DE FRANCE · NORMANDY · THE LOIRE
SOUTH WEST FRANCE
FLORENCE · VENICE · ROME
MAINLAND GREECE · THE GREEK ISLANDS · YUGOSLAVIA · TURKEY
NEW YORK

In Preparation
OXFORD AND CAMBRIDGE · PARIS

THE COMPANION GUIDE TO

The
Shakespeare Country

✤

JONATHAN KEATES

A SPECTRUM BOOK

PRENTICE-HALL, INC.
Englewood Cliffs, N.J. 07632

COLLINS
St. James's Place, London

Library of Congress Cataloging in Publication Data

Keates, Jonathan, 1946-
  The companion guide to the Shakespeare country.
  "A Spectrum Book."
  Bibliography: p.
  Includes index.
  1. Warwickshire—Description and travel—Guide-
books. 2. Hereford and Worcester—Description and
travel—Guide-books. 3. Gloucestershire—Description
and travel—Guide-books. 4. Literary landmarks—
England—Guide-books. I. Title.
DA670.W3K42 1983   914.24   82-20493
ISBN 0-13-154625-2
ISBN 0-13-154617-1 (pbk.)

ISBN 0-13-154625-2

ISBN 0-13-154617-1 {PBK.}

First published 1979
Hardback ISBN 0 00 216121 9
Set in Monotype Times Roman
Maps by Les Robinson
Made and printed in Great Britain by
William Collins Sons & Co Ltd, Glasgow

U.S. Edition © 1983 by Prentice-Hall, Inc.,
    Englewood Cliffs, N.J. 07632

A SPECTRUM BOOK

Printed in the United States of America

10 9 8 7 6 5 4 3 2 1

Prentice-Hall, International, Inc., *London*
Prentice-Hall of Australia Pty. Limited, *Sydney*
Prentice-Hall of Canada, Inc., *Toronto*
Prentice-Hall of India Private Limited, *New Delhi*
Prentice-Hall of Japan, Inc., *Tokyo*
Prentice-Hall of Southeast Asia Pte. Ltd., *Singapore*
Whitehall Books Limited, Wellington, *New Zealand*
Editora Prentice-Hall Do Brasil Ltda., *Rio de Janeiro*

Contents

◆

List of Illustrations

�’

photographs by David Hibbert

List of Maps and Plans

❧

Acknowledgements

❧

Five members of my family have involved themselves in varying degrees with the fortunes of this book, and to them go my first thanks. Its dedication is to my brother Timothy, whose knowledge of England is matched only by his love for it. My sister-in-law, Dr Mirella Cigarini Keates, was a long-suffering fellow pilgrim to remote churches, and my mother buoyed up flagging spirits with her usual supply of optimism and good meals. My cousins Hermione and Charlotte Gulland gave valued help in the Vale of Berkeley.

Most of the journeys described were made possible through the patience and generosity of Mrs Janet Hibbert. Her son David Hibbert showed a comparable tenacity in negotiating angry landowners, mercenary clergy, locked churches, nettlebeds and savage dogs, to take the accompanying photographs. Both provided continual encouragement.

For various kinds of assistance and inspiration, thanks are due to the following: Mrs G. Fallows, Miss K. Attenborough and Miss E. Lustig, Robin and Louisa Lane Fox, William and Angela Wood, Peter and Elizabeth Warren, James and Sue Pettifer, Elisabeth Whipp, Margaret Gardiner, James Fenton, Gervase Jackson-Stops, Sam Beadle, Michael Turner, Mark Elder, Martin Cullen and Gianni Guidetti. I am grateful also for the unfailing courtesy displayed by the staff of Malvern, Worcester, Hereford and Gloucester public libraries, of the London Library and the Library of the Society of Antiquaries, and by the incumbents of the various parishes visited on my travels. Special thanks go to Elizabeth Walter of Collins, who read my text with an expert's eye and provided a series of useful emendations.

Introduction

✤

Only the vaguest homogeneity can be imposed on the area covered by this book. My original plan was for a guide to the country surrounding the 'Three Choirs Cities' of Gloucester, Hereford and Worcester, which would take in, as a partial continuation of the Welsh Marcher country covered in the Herefordshire section, the entire southern half of Shropshire as far as Shrewsbury. For reasons both practical and aesthetic, however, I have omitted the last altogether, preferring to substitute the area of Warwickshire around Stratford, known inevitably as 'the Shakespeare Country'.

Shakespeare certainly knew more of these counties than his own corner of Arden. Hereford, Worcester, Berkeley and Tewkesbury are all mentioned in the plays, several of the dramatist's friends lived here, and so, of course, did various characters featured in the great history cycles. This is a weak excuse for lumping together such hugely varied landscapes as the Malvern Hills and Black Mountain, the Forests of Dean and Wyre, the valleys of Avon and Monnow, and Evesham and Berkeley Vales.

A better reason is that 'in-betweenity' which has saved most of this countryside from being too heavily trodden over by tourists and commuters. Rich river valleys, prime grazing, alluvial soil and extensive tracts of forest are all factors which have helped towards maintaining equilibrium between man and land in these south-Midland shires. The area is not the Cotswolds, neither is it Wales or the Black Country, yet nearness to all three has had an influence on the formation of its singular character. History, too, has accorded a certain nebulous unity. The Industrial Revolution, for example, visibly marked the Forest of Dean and northern Worcestershire at almost identical moments. On a more romantic plane, Fair Rosamund is said to have been born either at Frampton, beside the Severn, or at Clifford, above the Wye. This, what is more, is the great Civil War battleground, more violently marched over, fought upon and tussled for than any other in England.

I have tried to arrange the book in a series of tours through each county. Warwickshire journeys will, of course, take off from Stratford, and a good day may be had exploring the villages on the south-western fringe of the Forest of Arden. Warwick itself deserves a morning at least in the town (with, by the way, the best secondhand bookshop in the Midlands) and an afternoon at the castle.

Cheltenham, rather than Gloucester or Bristol, is probably the ideal spot for starting a Gloucestershire tour, although outside the scope of this guide, since here we can best appreciate the country's singular language of contrasting landscapes. The Cotswolds lie directly to the east, and the Vale of Tewkesbury spreads westwards to merge into the purlieus of the Forest of Dean. South-west are Gloucester and the dairy pastures of Berkeley Vale. Historically this is mostly 'poor' Gloucestershire as opposed to the richer parts around Cirencester, Tetbury and Chipping Campden, and it is no accident that the area sent droves of colonists to the plantations of early-seventeenth-century America. The villages are thus, I think, more interesting to look at than anything in the Cotswolds, variegated, straggling and touched with surprises. Highly recommended is a tour westwards across Tewkesbury Vale, taking in Tewkesbury itself, Deerhurst, Upleadon and Newent. As for the Forest of Dean, this is altogether another world.

This book attempts a general description of the two counties of Worcestershire and Herefordshire. Tours in the former are based on Worcester, as being centrally placed, though the city is now an absorbing study in systematic self-destruction. Few counties have more in them of what is commonly conceived as 'English'. Heavily wooded until the early 1600s, Worcestershire built freely and inventively in timber, and black-and-white is found throughout in cottages, barns, pigsties, manorhouses and church towers. The churches themselves are never without interest, and wonderful architectural contrasts are offered by, say, Norman Rock and rococo Great Witley, or by the varieties of Gothic in Bredon and Pershore Abbey. The terrain, too, provides powerful contradictions – which, for example, is the more fulfilling, Evesham Vale, with its conventional allures of blossom and fertility, or the romantic, almost lascivious curves of the hills along the Teme valley?

Herefordshire's closeness to Wales, a land where religion is less of a mere tradition than a positive instinct, has brought a striking godliness, with few redundancies among the enormous number of churches. Villages in the English sense are comparatively few: the typical scene in the valleys of Wye, Lugg and Arrow is that of a parish church between two farmyards in a landscape of hopyards, orchards and cornfields. There is a good history behind this. Hereford is a border town in the Marches, a land never without warfare from the Saxons to the Tudors, sturdily defying both the Welsh and the crown with a rash of castles over valleys and hillsides. Seclusion meant security here, and attempts by the Mortimers and others to populate the region more thickly were doomed to constant failure. Instability both of tenure and livelihood effectively ruled out the growth of big villages, and rich agriculture and bad roads prevented any of the towns from having to outgrow its function as a local market.

Farming is Herefordshire's life and the relationship between building and landscape is remarkably close and continuous. The fast-dwindling number of oast-houses in the hop country of the Lugg and Frome provides a good example of this, as do the magnificent wattle and brick barns of the upper river plain of the Wye. Hereford itself has profited most recently from this co-operation in the form of gifts to the town and cathedral from the great cider firm of W. P. Bulmer.

I find it hard to take seriously the recent local government re-organization which has tidied Berkeley Vale into 'Avon' and scrambled two counties into Herefordandworcester. The strange sing-song Worcestershire accent keeps up its strong contrast with the deeper notes of Herefordshire, and, despite the bureaucrats, each of the counties retains its individuality, proclaimed in its towns, villages and patterns of local life. There is, too, an unashamedly conservative continuity in such elements as the survival of the west-Midland squirearchy, farmers rather than aristocrats. There are still Lechmeres at Hanley, Scudamores at Kentchurch, Harleys at Brampton Bryan, Sandyses at Ombersley and Lytteltons at Hagley.

Wherever possible, I have tried to emphasize topographical character, to fill out regional history with details, and to celebrate local worthies. Omissions are several and I have been, in such places as Tewkesbury Vale, unrepentantly selective. Certain personal interests have shown through. Fondnesses for the seventeenth century, church monuments, plain church glazing and plastered walls, and penchants for prospects, rivers, spires, anecdotes and cream teas have all been given free rein. There are many who, not having written this book, will wish that they had done so, and carp accordingly. My apologies for inaccuracy are offered, not to them, but to those who, like me, love these counties, their history and their landscapes. My guiding principles should perhaps have been those of a Herefordshire poet, formulated in 1794:

15

INTRODUCTION

How best to bid the verdant Landscape rise,
To please the fancy and delight the eyes;
Its various parts in harmony to join
With art clandestine and conceal'd design;
T' adorn, arrange; – to sep'rate, and select
With secret skill and counterfeit neglect.

Richard Payne Knight: *The Landscape*

CHAPTER ONE

Stratford-upon-Avon

⚜

After London, Stratford is the most heavily tourist-visited place in England. Those who have never seen Wells or Windermere, Norwich or Newark, will always somehow have managed to see the Birthplace or the Memorial, gone out to Shottery and Wilmcote for the afternoon and back to dinner and a play at the Theatre. Few, perhaps, appreciate the central fact of the place – that even if Shakespeare made Stratford, it was Stratford which produced Shakespeare. It is maybe harder to realize this given the number of times his name features in the most incongruous places all over the town. For this reason, one has to look at Stratford streets twice over: at first glance, a rash of Shakespeareana and what a charmingly vague tourist once described to me as 'old Tudorian houses': blink, and look again at a prosperous and busy Warwickshire market town, with its shops, banks and inns, not so very unlike Shipston, Warwick or Nuneaton, none of which had anything to do with Shakespeare.

By the time of his birth in 1564, Stratford had been an incorporated borough for eleven years, with a bailiff, fourteen aldermen and fourteen capital burgesses, and long before that, since its beginnings as a Roman way-station and Saxon monastic settlement, it had been the natural centre for the horse-breeders of the Vale of Evesham. A market was established in 1196 and fairs were held, one of them, Stratford Mop, the old hiring fair, still going strong. Twenty years after Shakespeare's death William Sandys of Fladbury made the Avon navigable for thirty-ton vessels and Andrew Yarranton, Worcestershire's technological wizard, dreamt of making Stratford 'to the West of England . . . as Dantzick is to Poland', with industrial colonies of weavers and brewers. Though his scheme failed, Stratford went on exchanging Bristol sugar and tobacco for Warwickshire corn and malt.

> *Stratford her spacious magazines unfolds*
> *And hails th'unwieldy barge from western shores,*

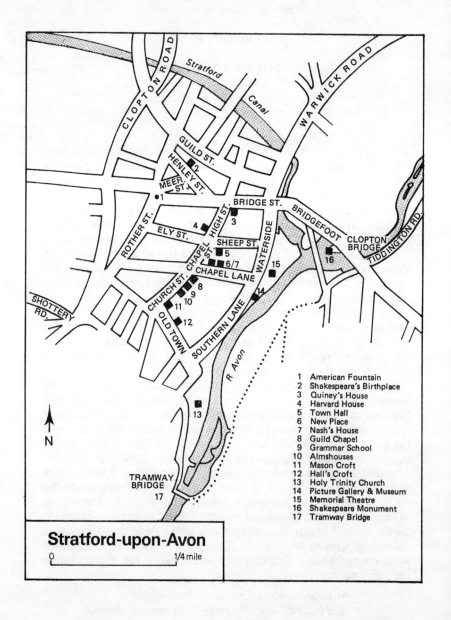

1 American Fountain
2 Shakespeare's Birthplace
3 Quiney's House
4 Harvard House
5 Town Hall
6 New Place
7 Nash's House
8 Guild Chapel
9 Grammar School
10 Almshouses
11 Mason Croft
12 Hall's Croft
13 Holy Trinity Church
14 Picture Gallery & Museum
15 Memorial Theatre
16 Shakespeare Monument
17 Tramway Bridge

Stratford-upon-Avon

0   1/4 mile

With foreign dainties fraught, or native ore
Of pitchy hue, to pile the fewell'd grate,
In woolly stores, or husky grain repay'd,

says Richard Jago, the eighteenth-century Warwickshire poet. In 1816 the Stratford-upon-Avon canal was opened. After having lost out to the railway, in shape of a branch line of the 'Old Worse & Worse' (Oxford, Worcester & Wolverhampton Railway) and an LMS terminus, it was re-opened as a navigable waterway in 1964.

Stratford's town plan is basically a medieval grid, bounded by the river to the south-east and Rother Street to the north, and we can begin our tour in the Rothermarket at the **American Fountain**. 'Hreothr' is Old English for a bullock, and many 'a good yoke of bullock' was sold in this broad square. Shakespeare, as local cicerones always point out, used the word in *Timon of Athens* ('it is the pasture lards the rother's sides') and a quotation from the same play adorns the fountain, given by George W. Childs, a Philadelphia journalist, in 1887, and unveiled by Henry Irving, who drank the first cupful after reading a specially composed poem by Oliver Wendell Holmes. Singularly horrible, in the worst institutional taste, it is now badly in need of a memorial scrub.

From here, down Meer Street, it is a short walk to Henley Street and **Shakespeare's Birthplace**. Of the various properties owned by the Birthplace Trust this often seems the least interesting because the most visited. Built of Arden timber on a Wilmcote stone base, it did duty as a house and shop for the glover John Shakespeare, who bought the eastern end in 1556 and rented the western end, where William was born on 23 April 1564. Soon after John died in 1601 it was leased as the Swan & Maidenhead Inn, and it stayed in the family (through his daughter Joan Hart) until 1896. After an almost complete change of outward appearance, it was acquired by the Trust in 1891 and restored to something like its original form.

On the west side are rooms furnished in period style: a stone-flagged parlour with plain timber-studded walls, John Shakespeare's shop with an exhibition of Birthplace history, and the kitchen, with its big open hearth and spit. Upstairs, further exhibits include the New Place purchase deed, and the famous Quiney Letter, the only known letter addressed to the dramatist, in which Richard Quiney, a Stratford mercer, asks Shakespeare for the loan of £30. The Birth Room has no documentation behind its claim to celebrity, but conversely there is no reason to doubt the idea that William Shakespeare was very probably born here. Belief has confounded scepticism, and on the window panes of the simple, low-pitched room can be seen the diamond-scratched signatures of, among others, Tennyson, Scott, Carlyle, Irving and Ellen Terry. The garden, leading out into Guild Street, is one of two in Stratford planted with a Bardic botany, Ophelia's pansies and rue, Iachimo's cowslip, Volumnia's mulberry, Lucio's 'rotten medlar' and others, including the 'streaked gillevors' which that good gardener Perdita refused to plant.

Bridge Street tosses international flags aloft in the high tourist season. The elegant white bank building at its junction with Wood Street was a Regency market hall. Facing it is **Quiney's House**, once the home of Shakespeare's daughter Judith, whose husband, Thomas Quiney, set up here as a wine merchant, and later to become 'The Judith Shakespeare Tearooms', recalled from childhood matinée visits. Thankfully it now enjoys a more dignified existence as a tourist information centre. Turning into the High Street here we reach, on the right, **Harvard House**, part of a distinguished half-timbered group including the Garrick Inn and Tudor House, which belonged to the Wolmer family, prosperous *commercants* and city fathers surely known to Shakespeare. Thomas Rogers, too, builder of Harvard House in 1596, must have been more than a name to the poet. He was a butcher, and there is a tradition that young William was once a Stratford apprentice to the trade. More notably he was the grandfather of John Harvard, founder of the university to which the house, with its ornate façade (note the lions' masks, the bull's head and bear-and-ragged-staff) now belongs. Its somewhat over-restored character, both inside and out, is partly due to the zeal of its first American purchaser, Edward Morris. Having bought it at the instigation of the novelist, Marie Corelli, he gave it to Harvard in 1909.

Almost immediately opposite, on the corner of Chapel Street, is an immensely impressive mid-Georgian piece, Robert Newman's **Town Hall** of 1767. Built of reddish-yellow Cotswold stone, it replaced an earlier building damaged during Stratford's rather stormy passage through the Civil War, and its lower arches were originally open, sheltering a cheese market. The list of bailiffs in its council chamber features, of course, John Shakespeare for 1568, and the first-floor ballroom has some good canvases, including Garrick as Richard III by Nathaniel Dance. Shakespeare's statue, on the outside wall, was the actor's gift during the 1769 Jubilee: by John Cheere, it is a copy of Scheemakers's statue in Westminster Abbey.

The Jubilee was a distinctly rum affair. Of all eighteenth-century egos, Garrick's was certainly the mightiest, and the programme for the occasion reminds one of the 'Speech by Toad – Song by Toad' ending to *The Wind in the Willows*. Heralded by gunfire, the celebrations began on 6 September with a public breakfast in the new Town Hall, Garrick much in evidence, and after that a performance of Arne's *Judith*, conducted by the composer. Then came 'a grand and sumptuous public ordinary', followed by an assembly, with minuets and country dances, and Mr Angelo's fireworks. Day Two kicked off with the Dedication Ode and Garrick and Arne posturing before the Bard in effigy: the Birthplace was covered with 'a curious emblematical transparency', there was a masquerade, attended by Boswell dressed as Paoli, the Corsican patriot and 'a person dressed as a devil . . . inexpressibly displeasing', and Garrick was as ubiquitous as Puck. Day Three brought the proceedings to a rainwashed close, though a groom called Pratt won the fifty guineas Jubilee Cup on Shottery racecourse, and the shenanigans ended with the inevitable assembly, Garrick, of course, figuring admirably in the minuets. Not a word of Shakespeare had been uttered during the entire occasion.

Chapel Street brings us to New Place, via the long range of the Shakespeare Hotel, mostly authentic Tudor and Caroline timberwork, with agreeably low ceilings and what estate agents call 'a wealth of exposed beams'. Shakespeare bought **New Place**, a house, barns and gardens, in 1597 for £60, but only completed the purchase in 1603. After various adventures, including a visit in 1643 from Queen Henrietta Maria, coming to rendezvous with her nephew, Prince Rupert, and stopping with the poet's granddaughter, Susannah Hall, it was bought in 1753 by the Reverend Francis Gastrell, who, though only an occasional resident, was sufficiently irritated by tourist enthusiasm for Shakespeare's mulberry tree and irked by borough rate assessments, to pull down both tree and house together. In fact the loss was perhaps not all that shattering, since much of Shakespeare's 'praty house of bricke and tymbre' had already gone in rebuilding. Now only eloquent foundations remain and an Elizabethan garden, with a later mulberry, where the dramatist surely meditated the hermetic wonders of the late plays. Next to it is **Nash's House**, home of Shakespeare's granddaughter, Elizabeth, who married Thomas Nash in 1626. Their supposed portrait hangs in the staircase passage between broad rooms opened up from smaller ones as part of a display of Jacobean life, all roasting-jacks and joint-stools and knobbly-looking tables and chairs, their moulding like clenched fists. Upstairs, a small museum describes

Roman and Saxon Stratford and the town's early making. The seven fourteenth-century angels, hovering in dark oak, came from the Guild Chapel roof.

This Guild of the Holy Cross was in existence by 1269, when the Bishop of Worcester authorized its raising of a chapel and a hospital. Both of these survive in Chapel Lane and Church Street respectively, together with the old grammar school incorporating the former Guildhall. The **Guild Chapel** is a fifteenth-century remodelling of an Early English original. The work was paid for by Hugh Clopton, a Stratford mercer who, though Lord Mayor of London in 1491, never forgot his home ground. His arms, a lion quartering a cross formy fitchy, are sported by an angel in the north doorway, under a porch with recently restored gargoyles. Within the chapel, which sustained hard post-Reformation usage from the vicar, Thomas Wilson, who allowed 'his children to playe at Bale . . . his servantes to hange clothes to drye in it . . . his pigges and poultrie to lye and feed in it . . . and also his dogge to lye in it', are traces over the chancel arch of a great painted Doom below the place of the former Rood, with its attendant saints. To the right, the favoured, nude and bareheaded (save for a clearly identifiable pope and bishop) enter Heaven. On the left devils hurl the damned into the flames or roast them in cauldrons.

This would have been piously whitewashed by the time William Shakespeare attended morning service here as a pupil at the **Grammar School**, to the south-west of the chapel. A two-storeyed L-shape, it was built in 1473 as the Guildhall, in fact a pair of half-timbered halls, in the lower of which Shakespeare would have watched his first play, performed by one of the travelling companies under the protection of great noblemen. The Over Hall above was used as a schoolroom from 1553, and since education at the school, an ancient medieval foundation, was free to the sons of burgesses, Shakespeare would have attended classes here – though no contemporary list of pupils survives. Between 1570 and 1580 there were four school-masters, one of them being, maybe, a model for Holofernes in *Love's Labour's Lost* and another perhaps for the dignified Euphronius in *Antony and Cleopatra*. For my money, this schoolhouse, with its close studding and rounded overhang, running into the still flourishing **Almshouses** of 1427, is worth twenty Etons or Winchesters, its building functional, muscular, unassuming, still a school and still a part of Stratford.

Before we turn the corner into Old Town, a nod towards **Mason**

Croft, now the Birmingham University Shakespeare Institute, but once the bower of Marie Corelli. Like Harriet Smith in *Emma*, she was 'the natural daughter of somebody', probably Dr Charles Mackay, who encouraged her as a musician, a career she abandoned for fiction in 1866 with *A Romance of Two Worlds*, after which, as they say, she never looked back. Her novels, sensation-seeking, ever so faintly naughty, and full of half-baked metaphysics, attracted a wild popularity. The elderly Gladstone and Tennyson were among her fans, and Queen Victoria solemnly announced to an appalled Empress Frederick that she supposed Marie Corelli would be remembered when novelists like Dickens and George Eliot were forgotten. She is indeed still widely read in the Far East. Settling at Mason Croft in 1899, she became self-appointed doyenne of Shakespeareland, philanthropic but managing and litigious. On the Avon she was punted in a gondola called 'Dream', in the town she drove Shetland ponies four-in-hand, and her voluminous décolletage was one of the sights of the Festival.

Hall's Croft in Old Town is the most rewarding of the Birthplace Trust's Stratford Houses. It belonged to Dr John Hall, a Puritan physician renowned in the Midlands, who married Shakespeare's daughter, Susannah, in 1607, and brought her to live in this triple-gabled house, with its deeply-chamfered ceiling beams and a stair-case with moulded balusters, probably added by Hall himself at some time before 1616, when he and Susannah moved to New Place. His *Select Observations on English Bodies*, a collection of successfully treated cases published after his death, is among exhibits displayed here, and his dispensary, with its service hatch looking on to the front parlour, is fascinatingly tricked out with the jars and manuals of a Jacobean surgery. One flask, still holding its castor oil, was apparently unearthed in the garden, as winning a walled plot as those at the Birthplace or Shottery.

At the foot of Old Town is the entrance to the lime-shadowed walk (twelve left-hand trees for the Tribes, eleven right-hand for the Apostles) leading to the north porch of **Holy Trinity Church**. By a favouring coincidence, Shakespeare's birth town has one of the country's stateliest medieval churches. Archbishop John de Stratford's foundation of a chantry in 1331, in a south-aisle chapel dedicated to Thomas à Becket, led to its confirmation as a college by Henry V in 1415, Agincourt year, and until the Reformation it enjoyed comparable status to that of St Mary's at Warwick. Though its collegiate role was swept away, the name clung to the E-shaped medieval house west of the church, not finally destroyed until 1799.

The fifteenth-century porch was probably added by Dean Ralph Collingwood at some period after 1491. Its inner doors into the nave were hung in 1480 by Dean Balsall, buried in the church and responsible for building the chancel. The nave itself, six bays long, is of the fourteenth century, with rather severe detailing on pillars and arches rising to a Perpendicular clerestory with ogee-headed windows. The shafts here rest on slender angel corbels. In the aisles below is richly assorted glazing, most of it modern and much of it good. What medieval glass survives at this end of the church is to be found in the Clopton chapel, at the north aisle's eastern end.

Hugh Clopton, builder of the bridge and refurbisher of the Guild Chapel, is, though buried in London, commemorated here by an altar tomb whose canopy carries the arms of Clopton, the Wool Staplers' Company and the City of London. His descendant, William, lies next to his wife, Agnes, on a late Elizabethan tombchest, with their seven children, whose names include the eloquently 'period'-sounding Lodowicke and Joyce, each, rather unusually for this type of monument, figuring at his or her proper age. Edward Marshall, master mason to Charles II, carved the exuberant piece commemorating Joyce, who died in 1635, and her husband, George Carew, Earl of Totnes. Despite its arresting lower relief of cannon and powder-kegs (Totnes was a doughty fighter for the Queen's peace in Ireland) I am not persuaded that this, a more or less routine morsel of Caroline cake-decoration, is, as the official guidebook claims, 'the finest Renaissance tomb in Europe'. Come now! Is the helm above, by the way, the Earl's?

Across the north transept runs the fifteenth-century ogee-headed oak screen, formerly marking off the chancel. The south transept holds the 'American Window', a gift in 1896 from the United States ambassador showing English and American worthies venerating the Virgin and Child. Lutyens's little memorial here to the First War's theatrical dead bears a Kipling quatrain:

> *We counterfeited once for your disport*
> *Men's joy and sorrow; but our day has passed.*
> *We pray you pardon all where we fell short –*
> *Seeing we were your servants to the last.*

The crossing, which heaves up the tower surmounted by William Hiorn's 1763 spire (stone to replace wood), and the five-bay chancel beyond it, are at a northward tilt to the nave, though whether this indicates a so-called 'weeping' plan, to simulate Christ's head on the cross, is debatable. What can hardly be disputed is the success of

Dean Balsall's magnificent Perpendicular lantern with its sevenfold east window and four-light transomed side-windows, between which rise the big hammerbeam roof trusses borne on corbels showing busts of kings. Each beam curves to a cloudy angel holding a shield – these were painted in 1835.

Here, of course, is the church's major attraction, though frankly I always think it a bathetic experience. Gerard Johnson's peepy-eyed, tufty-whiskered, baldpate **Shakespeare** looks at us out of the window formed by Corinthian columns with ugly cherubs asprawl on the entablature. Its Latin inscription means: 'In judgement a Nestor, in wit a Socrates, in art a Virgil'. The quill is, and always was, real. This is no more W.S. than Droeshout's enigmatic First Folio mask. More eloquent is the floor-slab beyond the altar rails, whose inscription sounds so Shakespearean, cursing would-be desecrators and invoking friendly respect in measured tetrameter. He was entitled to a chancel burial through his purchase of a moiety of the Stratford tithes, which made him partly responsible for upkeep of the fabric. Near him lie his wife, daughter Susannah, and son-in-law John Hall. Both his funeral and baptism are noted in the parish registers.

From the church we can cross Avonbank Gardens, scene in 1960 of a memorable open-air season of plays by Shakespeare's contemporaries, mounted by Oxford collegiate drama groups. Southern Lane is the home of the RSC's more intimate presentations at 'The Other Place' and further along is the popular pub, the Black Swan, known as 'the Dirty Duck'. Facing this is the recherché-looking French Gothic **Picture Gallery and Museum**, last surviving fragment of an astonishing piece of peppermint humbug, part-Glamis, part-Elsinore, part-Moated Grange, designed as the Memorial Theatre in 1879 by the firm of Dodgson & Unsworth. The picture collection here is a must for hunters of the artistic-obscure. Some of it is actually good: Sickert's Fabia Drake as Lady Macbeth, Laura Knight's Paul Schofield playing (well, we must all begin somewhere) the Clown in *The Winter's Tale*, a wonderfully jagged trio of Fuseli witches. Some of it, such as George Carter's *The Immortality of Garrick*, is strictly for the stagestruck. There are also Shakespeare portraits and what is said to be a pair of his gloves – a present from the inevitable Garrick to the Stratford burgesses.

The **Memorial Theatre** was destroyed by fire in 1926 and the present brick building, deemed architecturally a bit fast in its day, was designed by Elizabeth Scott, relative of Sir Gilbert, and opened in 1932. What was all the fuss about? It not only does a good job very well, but, especially in the evening, its terraces and porches lit up, actually looks exciting as theatres ought. Its record of great performances is as distinguished as the occasional epic flops to which it has played host. The company style has changed since the Ashcroft, Redgrave and Gielgud days, via the triumphs of David Warner, Ian Holm and Judi Dench, to today's Mirrens, Howards and Fleetwoods, engagés and cerebral in a manner perhaps undreamt of in the era of Edith Evans and Godfrey Tearle, though at the expense of a romanticism and a discriminate reverence which most of us who watched 1973's dreadful custard-pie *Shrew* or the shamelessly revamped *King John* the following year, pined for unrepentant.

Across the Bancroft Gardens is Lord Ronald Sutherland Gower's magnificent **Shakespeare Monument**, sixty-five bronze tons on stone plinths, showing the seated dramatist surrounded by Prince Hal with the crown, Hamlet holding Yorick's skull, Lady Macbeth sleepwalking, and Falstaff. It looks very *fin-de-siècle* French, and was indeed cast at Paris in 1888. Originally it stood behind the Memorial Theatre, and its unveiling ceremony included speeches by George Augustus Sala and Oscar Wilde.

From here, with the Stratford Hilton opposite us trying hard not to look too obvious, we come on to **Clopton Bridge**, which Shakespeare crossed on his way to and from London. This fourteen-arched stone causeway, given by Sir Hugh Clopton in the late fifteenth century, brought renewed prosperity to the town. Further downstream is the brickbuilt **Tramway Bridge**, a substantial relic of a horse tramway to Moreton-in-Marsh and Shipston-on-Stour, built in 1823 by William James of Henley as an ancillary venture to his Stratford canal. The lines were completed in 1836 and at the north end of the bridge stands one of the original wagons, in good shape, with its plump cast-iron wheels and long handbrake. It is possible to follow the tramway course as a walk across the Avon meadows on the opposite bank.

Stratford, its growth admirably contained, is ringed with good country mansions. We may even have a good word to throw at **Welcombe**, of 1869 and now one of the county's better hotels, below a granite obelisk erected by a Mr Robert Philips to his brother Mark. Good walking is to be had among its wooded dingles, and Shakespeareans will know of the poet's involvement in a local controversy here over projected enclosures. **Clopton**, next door to it, was Sir Hugh's ancestral estate. His Tudor descendants built the present house, enlarged in the 1660s, a brick-and-timber rectangle with Georgian additions on the south front, and tall panelled chimneys. The main porch, with its pilasters and lion-head keystone, is sophisticated Renaissance, the whim of a Clopton traveller perhaps. Inside are a set of first-floor rooms with plaster swags, cartouches in the frieze, and moulded panels.

Discarding doubtful Bardic associations (for this just had to be the Lord's house in the Induction to *The Taming of the Shrew*, and poor drowned Margaret Clopton had to be pretty Ophelia) two facts here deserve noting. In 1605 Ambrose Rookwood, Gunpowder Plotter, rented Clopton to be near Coughton, Huddington and Lapworth, home of Robert Catesby, and after its use as a conspirators' rendezvous it was assiduously searched by a bailiff's posse. In 1564 arises the tale of Charlotte Clopton who, buried prematurely, was found standing at the entrance to her vault – and here we are with a Bardolatrous background to Juliet in the Capulets' tomb.

Two other shrines merit a pilgrimage, and there is no reason why we should not walk to both of them. Among Stratford's virtues are its rural escape routes. **Shottery** may be something of a brickish skirt now, but **Anne Hathaway's Cottage** (*sic*) has an unfailing charm, the thatched cot to end them all and none the worse for looking a trifle precious under its straw tea-cosies. Cottage it is not, rather a yeoman's homestead, for long known as Hewlands Farm and dating from the early sixteenth century. Anne's grandfather, John, rented it in 1546, and after her brother Bartholomew's 1610 purchase of the property, the family stayed here until 1892, when the Birthplace Trust was able to buy it with some of its original furniture, including the Hathaway bed, a dark oak four-poster.

Shakespeare, you recall, left Anne his second best bed, and some take this to imply an unhappy marriage. Perhaps they were no more than conveniently wed, alderman's son to farmer's daughter, but then how many Elizabethans actually married for love? The cottage, by the way, was restored after severe fire damage in 1969.

The right places for fire make some of the best features of these rambling Midland forest farmhouses. Hewlands Farm has its big, soot-blackened fireplaces and bread oven, into which loaves were put on a long-handled shovel called a 'peel', and so has Mary Arden's House, **Wilmcote**, the Trust's most interesting property. A walk to Wilmcote along the canal towpath is a genuine delight, and the village itself, scattered down a long lane, many of its cottage doors opening directly into the roadway, is nicest on one of those dusty ends to hot days, when waistcoated codgers pedal home from ditching, and there is a lot of watering and raking going on in the garden plots.

Wilmcote was long famous for its stone quarries, and it was to save the quarrymen's souls that the Reverend Francis Fortescue Knottesford, a pious and dedicated Tractarian, built the church in 1841, using Butterfield's designs. He was presumably also responsible for the vicarage and school building. The church, inspired by the Oxford Movement, attracted a great deal of clerical attention, and was the first in which the Sarum use of vestments was revived. Wilmcote was also (1847–8) the earliest Anglican retreat centre.

Mary Arden's House belonged to Shakespeare's mother's family, yeomen of the district. Mary herself married John Shakespeare of Snitterfield in 1557. At her father's death in 1556 a detailed inventory was taken of his goods, and this has been the basis for furnishing a typical Warwickshire farmhouse and developing a museum of English rural life. Since it remained a working farm until 1930 its yards and barns have not been allowed to lose their essential character.

Beams, mullions and lead lights apart, what engage in this place are the actual colours and construction of the low-gabled house, its huge pegged uprights and verticals with their adze-roughened surfaces, the pinkish-grey shading of the kitchen flags, the crazy pitch of the bedroom floors, their timbers a smooth tobacco brown like the coat of an Alderney cow. Everything here seems less ersatz than the gathered objects of the Birthplace or Hall Croft, less determined to impress us with a borrowed authenticity, though the furniture is the same solid farmhouse ware.

Outside is an encyclopedia of good farm building, a square dovehouse, a cider mill, high-gabled barns of lias and brick, and the best farming museum in England. In the stable saddles and horsecollars gleam amid the blacksmith's tools, in the rickyard carts stand idle, their owners' names fading on the sides and wanting a Gabriel Oak to repaint them, there are drills and dibbles, a dreadful breastplough with its enormous shaft ending in a tiny shovel, tools for the cooper, the carpenter, the wheelwright and the poacher – note his flanged eelspears and the mantraps and spring-guns to catch him. In a way which Stratford can never manage, this empty farmyard captures an essence which it may not be too extravagant to call Shakespearean.

CHAPTER TWO

The Shakespeare Villages

❦

Of all the country covered in this book, these few square miles of Arden and Feldon, even more than central Worcestershire, the Wye valley or Tewkesbury vale, are quintessential England, with a beauty almost magically apposite to the spirit of the plays and poems it nurtured. Inevitably, much romantic clutter surrounds Shakespeare, some of it tenacious, much of it easily disposed of, but even the most prosaic Shakespearean cannot fail to sense, in the nature poetry of the late plays or the description of the hare hunt in *Venus and Adonis*, touches that are pure Warwickshire.

Thomas Fuller in his *Worthies of England* was perhaps echoing *Richard II* when he said that 'from Edgehill one may behold it another Eden'. Henry James, in *English Hours*, saw an overstated, almost threatening allure in its rolling pastures and elm copses. The 'Dutch' disease has decimated the tall fieldside clumps, opening up, not altogether disastrously, more vistas in a county of magnificently infinite prospects. But the gentle hills and neat villages, smooth-purling streams, and one or two of the old mills, all remain, and the Avon still prodigiously meanders.

A tour of this country from Stratford can either follow the main A46 to Warwick or take the B4086 out past the golf course along the left bank of the river towards **Charlecote Park**. This is the second oldest of a trio of great houses open to the public in west Warwickshire – and here we come up sharply against a Bardolatrous whopper. The broad park, its three sections converging on the Avon and the little river Dene, is stocked with fallow deer (remarkably tame and obligingly photogenic) grazing under its fat oaks and chestnuts. Capability Brown made one or two tactful alterations here in 1769, including changing the course of the Dene (the bridge opposite the entrance is by David Hiorn, 1755) but was forbidden to cut down the seventeenth-century avenues to the house. So far, so good: however, it was perhaps during this period, with Stratford Bard-worship going full pelt, that an old tale was lugged out about a young scamp named Will Shakespeare poaching deer in Charlecote Park and making the

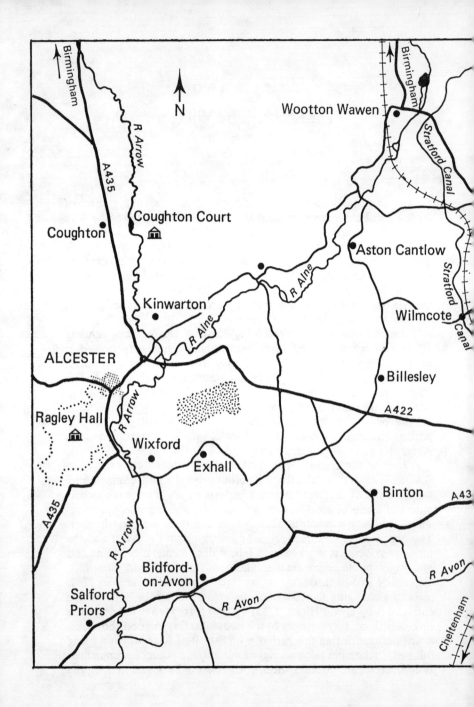

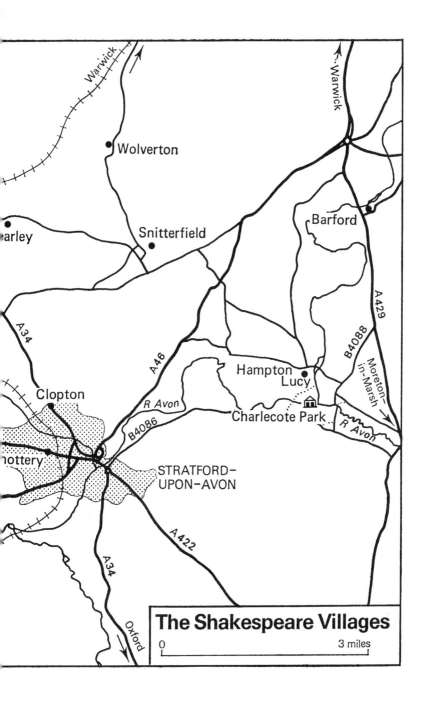

The Shakespeare Villages

0   3 miles

owner, Sir Thomas Lucy, into his Justice Shallow. Was this the reason for his flight to London and immortality? Far more attractive than the real cause, which seems to have been his father's material and psychological collapse. Thus stories start and thus they grow, and this one, with absolutely no foundation in fact (there were apparently no deer for the poor lad to steal anyway) is in rude health.

Charlecote has more to it than mere taradiddles. Lucys have lived here since the Middle Ages, with one or two genealogical loops, quietly and steadily. Few sights in England parallel that first glance along the avenue towards the Tudor gatehouse, built in 1551 by the first Sir Thomas Lucy. Rose-pink marbled with lichen, it blends Gothic with sinuous Renaissance in its cupola'd angle-towers and rib-vaulted arch. Beyond this is the broad forecourt, with steps to the right leading up to the gardens. The lead shepherd and shepherdess are by John Nost (1718), and the wrought-iron gates are of 1722, by Thomas Paris, of a noted family of local craftsmen.

The house itself is substantially of two periods: Elizabethan in the projecting entrance porch and its general outline, but generally a reconstruction, in remarkably good taste, during forty years from 1826. George Hammond Lucy and his wife, Mary Elizabeth Williams, of Bodlewyddan, understood perfectly the spirit they were trying to recapture and fuse with the taste of a generation reared on Scott and Harrison Ainsworth, and in this they were ably assisted by the heraldic glass artist, Thomas Willement, and the architect Charles Smith, a pupil of Wyattville.

Inside, the rooms are more or less as they were in the nineteenth century. George and Mary Lucy were collectors (he was also a talented amateur designer) and their taste is plainly revealed in the display of furniture and paintings. The Great Hall is, indeed, arranged as a gallery, centred on the bust of Queen Elizabeth over the fireplace and bringing together a pleasing 'baronial' ensemble of portraits, weaponry and stags' heads, over a Venetian marble floor and the enormous *pietre commesse* table from the Borghese palace, bought in the sale of contents at Fonthill House, Wiltshire, in 1823.

Willement decorated the Dining Room and the Library in the Tudor Revival style between 1829 and 1834. Both have enriched ceilings and bay windows seemingly designed as showcases for perfect landscape views, and Willement's (and his patrons') attention

Shakespeare Monument, Stratford, by Lord Ronald Sutherland Gower

to detail can be noted in the matching wallpaper and Axminster carpet in the Dining Room and the woodwork and chair covers in the Library. Perhaps most remarkable of all the objects shown in the former room is the heavily-carved 'Charlecote Buffet', by Willcox and Kendall of Warwick, bought by the widowed Mary Elizabeth in 1858. It had been offered to Queen Victoria, who described its tumid display of the bounties of nature and farming as 'a masterpiece of genius and skill', which it surely is.

The Library window has what is certainly the finest view from the house, of the gardens falling down towards the slick curve of the Avon. The supposed portrait of Shakespeare may only be an anonymous seventeenth-century Italian, and the lounging Garrick beside a bust of the poet replaces a Gainsborough original, destroyed at Stratford in 1947. It is refreshing, after the somewhat ponderous effect the room gives, to cross the hall again, this time past a fine, leaping late seventeenth-century staircase at the northern end, into the Ebony Bedroom. This is really a billiard room, used to show furnishings from upstairs, including the amazing ebony bed, converted from an Indian divan by William Beckford at Fonthill and bought by George Lucy in 1823. The surrounding lacquer and marquetry furniture is arranged to match, and the delicacy of these and the eighteenth-century Italian gouache views on the walls contrasts interestingly with the decorative scheme of the rooms we have already seen.

Of the pictures in the house, my favourite hangs in the Drawing Room. Charlecote is full of good portraits – the seventeenth-century Richard Lucy, for example, in the Great Hall – but none matches the assured opulence of the portrait of George Lucy, painted in 1758 in Rome by Pompeo Batoni. George had made the tour with his secretary, Mr Dobson, who remarked on the many sittings demanded by the artist. Batoni still has to find his deserved niche among the better eighteenth-century masters, and this, with its luminous blue background and exquisite detailing, is a perfect example of his work as the most sought-after portraitist by noblemen on the Grand Tour.

Outside, the kitchens, brew-house and coach-house have all been lovingly reconstructed with their original equipment. In the coach-house stands the travelling carriage, in black and green, which carried George and Mary (another carriage took tutor, footman,

Warwick: Lord Leycester Hospital
Warwick: Shire Hall, by Sanderson Miller

nurse and courier) on their tour of France and Italy in 1841. It was in this that the little Edmund Davenport Lucy died in his mother's arms as they crossed the Mont Cenis in heavy snow. She clutched him to her breast throughout the eleven-hour descent to Turin, reached at three in the morning.

Charlecote church was rebuilt by Mary Elizabeth in 1853, using John Gibson as architect, to contain the fine Elizabethan and Jacobean family monuments, amid rich stained glass, a new organ and the novelty of central heating. Read the epitaph on Lady Joyce Lucy's tomb, composed by her husband in 1595. Nothing is more moving than the close to this prolonged account of her virtues: 'Set down by him that best did know what hath been written to be true – Thomas Lucy'. Best, indeed artistically superlative, is the tomb of Sir Thomas III, who died after a fall from his horse in 1640. Next to his wife, Alice, and holding his sword, he lies beneath a shelf of books from his library with their Latin titles and a music book, *Winters Ayres*, with a relief showing him riding across a Warwickshire field. The entire composition, attributed to John Schurman, pupil of Nicholas Stone, makes a perfect reflection of that gentlemanly Caroline calm soon to be shattered by the nagging tedium of civil war.

Across the river, **Hampton Lucy** is something of a model village, much of it having been rebuilt in the early nineteenth century, presumably under George Lucy's direction. Of several older houses, the handsome old rectory, south of the church, is probably the best. Its grandeur is perhaps explained by the fact that the rector, until 1858, also held jurisdiction over the parishes of Wasperton, Alveston and Charlecote. The early Georgian house, with a strong Smith of Warwick cast, has quoins and keystones, a round pedimented doorway on the south front and a balustraded parapet. The church is a Gothic Revival masterpiece, built in 1826 by that wizard of the style, Thomas Rickman. Trim of line, jokily ogival and crocketed, it is, for me, worth ten of the more sombrely academic mid-Victorian efforts. Gilbert Scott must have thought so, too, since he remodelled the apsidal east end to match the rest in 1858. The windows illustrate scenes from St Peter's life, though they are more or less impossible to see, since the church is locked with no clue as to a key.

Crossing back over the Avon to the B4088 by a single-span iron bridge built at his own expense by the Reverend John Lucy, rebuilder of the church, using cast iron from Shropshire, we move north to **Barford**. The church here is another Gothic Revival job (the Perpendicular tower is original) by R. C. Hussey, paid for by a Mrs

Ryland, who lived at Sherbourne nearby. An earlier building presumably saw the Sunday devotions of the young pupils of the Misses Byerley at Barford House, among whose number was Elizabeth Stevenson, later Mrs Gaskell, the novelist. Here, during happy schooldays, *Cranford*'s author was given a surprisingly broad education, including French, Italian, Latin, English Literature and Dancing.

Some visitors may wish to go on to Warwick at this point (see p. 44). Or, instead, we can take the main road as if back towards Stratford, turning off south of Fulbrook to visit Snitterfield, Wolverton and Bearley. This is Shakespeare's native soil *par excellence*, since his grandfather, Richard, settled in **Snitterfield** in 1535 as a farmer, dying there in 1560. The Shakespeares were always a somewhat mercurial lot, and neither of his two sons, Henry, who stayed farming here, and John, who left for Stratford, seems to have been a steady character. Records of their connection with the parish are shown in the appropriately-named church of St James the Great, with a long fourteenth-century chancel and tall aisled nave, its exceptionally sturdy-looking roof said to have come from the demolished castle at nearby Fulbrook. Vicar here from 1751 to 1784 was Richard Jago, whom anyone lucky enough to possess a *Chalmers's English Poets* will recall as the author of the still readable *Edgehill: A Poem*.

Wolverton church is entered through a Perpendicular south porch, though most of the fabric is of the thirteenth century. There are excellent glass fragments here: the east window obviously held a Doom with trumpeting archangels and awakening dead, the northwest chancel window bears the arms of Richard Neville, Earl of Warwick, to whom the manor belonged, and the nave windows have a jumble of fifteenth-century pieces, including a kneeling donor, John Walford and his wife. The south-east chancel window has been variously given to Morris or Burne-Jones.

This is high, hilly country, with glorious views towards distant Cotswolds and Malverns. Hunting country, too, and at Edstone, to the right of the Wolverton–Bearley road, lived another minor Warwickshire Augustan muse, William Somerville. Somerville (1675–1742) was a fellow of New College, Oxford, who settled down at Edstone to hunt and scribble cheerful verse which earned him an urn in Shenstone's park at Halesowen. Stimulated with rum mixed with blackcurrant jelly and water, he produced the delightful Miltonic burlesque *Hobbinol*, and *The Chase*, an entirely successful attempt to write a poem on his favourite sport with the idea that it should be both practical and imaginative.

He is buried at **Wootton Wawen** (pronounced Wootton Warn), whose church is by far the most interesting in an ecclesiologically dull countryside. It consists of a big Norman nave, with a Perpendicular clerestory, embattled and crocketed above, and a south aisle of the same period, with a timber porch. The lower storeys of the tower are late Saxon work, perhaps by Wagen, lord of the manor before the Conquest, coming down in stumpy round arches to the building's very core. In 1635 Charles Smith, Lord Carrington, a local recusant who was murdered by his valet at Pontoise in 1655 after years of Royalist exile, raised the chancel walls, and the parallel south chapel was given over to the Smith and Somerville families.

The walls of this chapel contain faint traces of wall-painting, showing St John the Baptist preaching, and some of the Seven Deadly Sins (Pride, Sloth, Greed and Lechery). Here also lies Francis Smith, on a canopied table tomb of 1605, and round him are genealogically complicated tablets to members of the Knight family, earls of Catherlough, whose most famous member was the blue-stocking Lady Luxborough of Barrels Hall, north of Henley-in-Arden. She, too, put up a garden urn to Somerville, whose own Latin memorial inscription here says: 'If you find anything good in me, imitate it: if anything bad, avoid it as best you can'. The marble altar tomb in the chancel is of the knight, Sir John Harewell (note the hare's head crest on the helm), who died in 1428. His great-great grandson, John (1505), lies nearby as an armoured brass, beside his wife, Lady Anne Grey, who has a pomander on her girdle.

Wootton Hall, a grand emparked affair behind the church, is highly sophisticated work of 1687, built by Francis Smith, second Lord Carrington, its architect anonymous. The village, though pretty enough, has always been too uncomfortably close to Birmingham, a commuter bijou on the trundle-train to Stratford, so let us move quickly south, down the lush valleys of Alne and Arrow, safely rural in a country of gentle slopes, cornfields and flower mills.

There is not much to detain us at **Aston Cantlow** beyond the chancel roof of the church in an attractive churchyard, a spread of good village houses, which includes the old Guild House, opposite the King's Head Inn, with late medieval half-timbered overhang (the Guild, founded in 1469, was dissolved at the Dissolution) and hummocky traces of a castle of the Cantelupes (hence Cantlow). In 1557 Shakespeare's father, John, married Mary Arden here, and she herself was probably christened in the font.

Nearly every Warwickshire village is a compendium of good

domestic building, whether in Arden timber, Wilmcote stone or the warm, ochre-coloured local brick – though I confess to an acute dislike of the colour and texture of grey lias, mournful and diseased-looking material for farms and cottages in this area. Particularly fine are the surviving mills hereabouts: the best is off the road from Aston Cantlow to Great Alne, where the smooth-sliding, willow-fringed stream skirts the ridge of the Alne Hills.

South-west of Great Alne, **Kinwarton** is a tiny parish, deserving a visit for its medieval dovecote, a National Trust property. This round stone drum, topped by a lantern, stands in a field north of the church. Entered by a low ogival door, it has six hundred nesting boxes and retains its original central ladder for reaching the nests. As the columbarium of a medieval grange of Evesham abbey, it was probably built for Abbot William de Boys in about 1350. Forty years before, the little church of St Mary was consecrated by Walter de Maidstone, Bishop of Worcester. Its wooden bell turret is probably seventeenth-century work. Notice, on the font, the Tudor bar and staple attachment for locking the lid. The medieval south chancel window shows the Virgin carrying the Child and waving a lily, above a yellow-winged dragon. The figures are surrounded by an ornate pinnacled niche, with kneeling saints and the donors' names, William and Lettice Attwood, below.

Kinwarton is really a suburb of **Alcester**, whose newer parts lie in the mesopotamia of Alne and Arrow, which it joins north of the A422. The name indicates a Roman settlement and occupational traces suggest some sort of posting station at the junction of the Ryknild Street, which can be followed right across through Wixford to the county border south of Bidford, with the 'street' which fords the Avon at 'Strat-Ford'. Parking behind the High Street, we can walk up into it through one of the narrow alleys known here as 'cheweries'. Like all the town's main thoroughfares, this has examples of good building in various styles, mostly carrying those market-town Georgian fronts so typical of west-Midland streets. Leading off it are Church Street and Henley Street, with some Tudor timber-framing, and the pretty little alley of Butter Street, squeezing in at the churchyard's west end.

St Nicholas's Church, basically medieval but rebuilt in 1729–33 by the Woodwards of Chipping Campden, is something of a disappointment. Inside, the Doric columns and coved ceiling have peeled and form a dismally tatty setting for the altar tomb of Fulke Greville's father (d. 1559) and his wife, Elizabeth Willoughby, and for Chantrey's reclining effigy of Francis, second Marquis of Hertford

(1822). An altogether more interesting building is the **Town Hall,** on the north-east side of the church. Its top storey is timber-framed, its lower stages of stone (the arches were filled in 1873) and it was largely the gift of Fulke Greville in 1618. Inside, on the upper floor, is a long hall with a hammerbeam roof and lists of the bailiffs of Alcester borough. Though its borough status, dating from the early twelfth century, has been considerably modified it still maintains a ceremonial Court Leet, with High and Low Bailiffs, Breadweighers and Aletasters, all appointed at the time of the Mop Fair on the first October Tuesday. A seventeenth-century bailiff, Thomas Lucas, built the grand brick **Churchill House** (1688) opposite the Town Hall. On the other side of the street, down an entry, is a distinguished-looking grey **Victorian Baptist Chapel** of 1859, with a winningly modest little brick meeting-house behind.

Alcester, a strongly Protestant borough under the tutelage of the Conway family at nearby Ragley, had its industrial fringes. According to the medieval Evesham chronicler, Abbot Ecgwin, preaching to wealthy Alcestrians, was silenced by the hammerings of blacksmiths and invoked God's wrath on the town. Malt Mill Lane, with its timber-gabled Malt House, recently restored, tells its own story: there were once seven malting kilns at Alcester. There were also glovers, needlers and gunmakers, and some of these were among the angry mob of mechanicals who on 3 December 1688 raided and sacked the house of the Catholic Throckmorton family at **Coughton Court,** immediately to the north of the town, on the Birmingham road.

One of England's great recusant clans, the Throckmortons, originally from Worcestershire, came to Coughton in 1412 when Sir John married Eleanor Spiney, daughter of the lord of the manor. Their religious loyalties were severely tested in 1605 when the Gunpowder Plotters, many of them family relatives, used the house as a rallying point where their womenfolk and the Jesuits, Garnett and Tesimond, could await news (ultimately fatal as it proved). In the Civil War the Parliamentarians occupied the building until scared away in 1644 by the approach of the royal army.

The house was formerly a quadrangle, whose east wing, damaged in the 1688 raid, was finally demolished in 1780. North and south ranges now centre on a superb early Tudor gatehouse with octagonal angle-turrets and a double oriel flourishing the royal arms of Henry VIII and those of Throckmorton, with their elephant's-head crest over a shield gules a chevron argent with three gimel bars sable. This family shield fell down and was broken on the day in 1916 that

Colonel Courtenay Throckmorton was killed fighting in Mesopotamia. Attractive Gothic wings of 1780 flank this west gateway front. On the east side, the courtyard ranges have timber upper storeys of the sixteenth and seventeenth centuries.

Entering by the fan-vaulted front hall (the gatehouse ground storey) with its access to two priestholes, we climb the stairs to the Drawing Room. On the red staircase walls falls a cascade of outstanding portraits, among them a Vanderbank of Catherine, Lady Throckmorton, painted in 1737 and one of two portraits by Batoni. In the Drawing Room are two canvases of 1729 by Nicholas de Largillière, one showing Anne Throckmorton as a nun, the other of Sir Robert Throckmorton in an embroidered coat and cuirass, with a magnificently ornate French frame. The family's patronage of Largillière was an inevitable upshot of the Continental links maintained by all the recusant gentry throughout this period. A collection of miniatures includes several Actons, with whom, in the slightly parochial atmosphere of the English Catholic *gratin*, the Throckmortons married on various occasions.

As well as Actons in the family there were also connections with the Catholic Pakingtons at Harvington and with the Yates, represented in the Little Drawing Room by Cornelius Johnson's Mrs Pakington and Lely's Apollonia Yate – she is buried in Chaddesley Corbett, Worcestershire. Her sister Mary's 1680 passport survives, permitting her 'to imbarque with her trunkes of apparell', but with the proviso 'that she will not repaire to the city of Roome'.

The Tower Room was once a chapel, from which priests could disappear into a secret chamber down the shaft of the north-east turret. Showcases here have a changing display, based on the Throckmorton family papers, showing different aspects of life in a great house.

In the south range are the broad Dining Room, with its Caroline panelling and black and white marble chimneypiece, and the Tribune with Catholic Stuart relics such as Mary Queen of Scots's Fotheringhay chemise, Bonnie Prince Charlie's garter and the Old Pretender's glove. The Dining Room contains a chair made from Richard III's Bosworth-night bed, and the Dolegate of Denny Abbey, of which Elizabeth Throckmorton was the last abbess. The Tribune, where she and two of her nuns spent their last days, looks out on to the Saloon, a private chapel during the early nineteenth century, which contains a staircase from Harvington and the famous Throckmorton Coat. On 25 June 1811 Sir John Throckmorton, eager to prove the superiority of British wool and cloth, had two Southdowns shorn in the morning and during the rest of the day a coat 'of the admired dark Wellington colour' was made up under the direction of Mr Coxeter, a Newbury weaver, ready for Sir John to wear at a dinner for five thousand people that night. A picture here tells the tale.

Coughton Church, mainly Perpendicular, has good glazing, mainly as a result of a Tudor Sir Robert's legacy. He died in 1518, on a pilgrimage to Jerusalem, leaving instructions as to a Doom in the east window, the seven Sacraments in the north chapel, and the seven Works of Mercy in the south. Much of this has been jumbled over the years, but three Sibyls still remain in the east window, with rich gowns of blue and green, and in the two chapels are twelve apostles and four evangelists (St Thomas unnamed and Saints Jude and Matthias in fragments). Some of the woodwork, too, belongs to this period, including the chapel screens and much of the seating in the nave and choir.

Though Papists, the Throckmortons presented to the living until 1917 and the church holds a number of family memorials. The pilgrim Sir Robert's altar tomb in the nave was not actually used until 1790, for a later Sir Robert. On the chancel north side are the brasses of Sir George (d. 1552) and his wife, Katherine Vaux, with their brood of eight sons and eleven daughters around the tomb-chest. Up by the altar, Sir John, Queen Mary's Master of the Court of Requests (d. 1580) lies robed as a judge in monumental alabaster beneath a canopy with a massive architrave over six Corinthian columns.

Alcester is framed between two great estates, for on its southern side is **Ragley Hall,** belonging to the Marquis of Hertford. This is part of the manor of Arrow, whose church, down a drive off the A435, has a Gothic tower of 1767 said to have been designed by Horace Walpole: the rambling rectory opposite seems to fuse every style from late medieval to cottage *ornée* Victorian. The estate passed from the Conways to their Seymour cousins, descended from Protector Somerset, in 1683, but by then Ragley Hall had been substantially completed for Edward, Lord Conway, by Robert Hooke, rival of Wren and author of *Micrographia,* the first English treatise on microscopes. Hooke, not always the most imaginative artist, took enormous care here over proportions. Though his original projecting wings were swept away in 1780 and a portico added in 1813 by Wyatt, the body of the house is still a sizeable late-Restoration villa of great formal interest.

To approach it through the park on a summer day makes an agreeable walk. Brown was responsible for the layout, under the direction of Francis, first Marquis, Ambassador to Paris and Lord-Lieutenant, a man described by a contemporary as 'negatively good'. Ragley's charm as a house is that its owners so obviously inhabit every room. The Study has the first of a series of decorations by James Gibbs, who remodelled ceilings and fireplaces in 1750. Portraits here include Anne, Lady Conway, a Protestant *dévote* whose friend Henry More, the Cambridge Platonist, had her 'preserved in her coffin above ground with spirits of wine, having a glass over her face, that he might see her, before her interment'. In the Library, notice the Grinling Gibbons swags above the doors and the Gothic frieze on the bookcases. The portrait over the fireplace, one of a number of outstanding Reynoldses in the house, shows a pensive Horace Walpole among his books.

The Great Hall is the most splendid example of mid-Georgian decorative art in the west Midlands. Corinthian pilasters rise towards an entablature and frieze decorated with oak-leaves and a moulded cornice marking the original second-floor level. Over this is the rococo vaulting added by Gibbs, hoisting up a forty-foot ceiling with a centrepiece showing Britannia urging on a chariot drawn by winged lions. The two busts of the Prince Regent (Nollekens) and the second Marquis (Count Gleichen) were added in the nineteenth century. The Blue Room's self-conscious femininity, with its slender-limbed Empire furniture, is emphasized by Wissing's William-and-Mary portraits of white-breasted beauties. The Dining Room, all gleaming silver plate and Paul Storr salt cellars, was only restored to its former use in 1973 after some sixty years' neglect. Portraits here are mostly of members of the royal family, though to the right of the fireplace is a fine full-length of Sir Edward Seymour, robed as Speaker of the Long Parliament.

With a good deal of audacity the present Marquis has splashed a gigantic Ceri Richards abstract across the staircase hall. Here, too, is a collection of family impedimenta – a sedan chair, a Coronation robe, a captured German machine gun. The Mauve Drawing Room, with its coved ceiling by Benjamin Wyatt, has an agreeably Frenchified grace, reflected in Vernet's southern Italian landscape, the Chinese Chippendale looking-glass, and the same master's little Gothic bureau. Wyatt's hand is again prevalent in the decoration of the Red Saloon, where Sebastien Bourdon's *Entry into Jerusalem* of 1670 crowns a display of minor seventeenth-century masters.

In the Green Drawing Room hangs a little display of the best Reynoldses, their faces full of that misty-eyed pensiveness which belies all charges made against the artist of being facile or inexpressive. The Prince Regent's Bedroom contains the tall valanced sleeping pavilion specially designed for the visiting Prinny: here he awoke to the news of Princess Charlotte's death. Finally out via the South Staircase Hall to the gardens – gloriously empty when I last saw them in early summer, with a cuckoo piping from high woods to the west. This Staircase Hall, by the way, is so completely unlike anything else in the house that it deserves to be kept a secret, its visual surprise unspoilt.

We can return to Stratford via **Wixford** and **Exhall**. The former is simply a hamlet with a small church lying up a dead-end lane, actually part of the Ryknild Street, which you can follow as far as the river. From the churchyard, loud with spring chaffinches, there is an exhilarating sweep of vista over the rolls of countryside. The church is locked but contains a superlative fifteenth-century brass on the tombchest of Thomas de Cruwe, attorney to Margaret, Countess of Warwick, and his wife, Juliana de Morehall. He wears full armour, and she is in an exquisitely pleated gown with a lapdog looking up at her. Another brass commemorates little Rice Griffin of Broome, who died in 1598 'being but three quarters olde'.

Exhall is full of timber-framed cottages. Its church is a curious mélange of every style from Norman to Victorian. Most of the Norman work is in the nave; the thirteenth-century chancel has brasses to John Walsingham and his wife, Eleanor Ashfield, of 1566. They were distant relatives of that dour and rather sinister Elizabethan, Sir Francis.

South of these villages, on a bleak, treeless upland, surrounded by yawning fields of market gardening spilt over from the Vale of Evesham, lie Salford Priors and Bidford-on-Avon. **Salford Priors** belonged to Kenilworth Priory and its outlier, Abbots Salford, to Evesham. Salford Hall, a big stone Elizabethan house approached through a timbered gateway, was built by John Alderford in 1602. His son-in-law, Charles Stanford, was a recusant and his family converted a northern ground-floor room to a chapel in 1727. From 1807 to 1838, during which the property passed to the Spetchley Berkeleys, the house was used by English Benedictine nuns from Cambrai. It is now a hotel.

The church has a stair-turret in the tower reaching over the south aisle roof, apparently intended for a beacon to guide travellers across the Avon. The jolly gargoyles include a woman riding a monster, a man clutching at his beard and what the County History discreetly calls 'an erotic woman'. In 1633 the tower was refurbished by Sir Simon Clarke of nearby Broom Court, whose monument, on the chancel north side, sprouts a rash of heraldry to prove that the Clarkes came over with the Conqueror. In the centre of all this armorial pomp is the tiny recumbent figure of his first wife, Margaret. Dorothy, his second wife, reclines opposite: a daughter of Hobson, the Cambridge carrier, of Hobson's choice fame, she died in 1669. Perhaps she composed the affecting epitaph to her little grandchild, Margaret, on the north wall:

As careful nurses to their bed do lay,
Their children which too long would wantons play,
So to prevent all my insuing crimes
Nature my nurse laid me to bed betimes.

Bidford-on-Avon is a dusty, tatty, main-road affair, but its medieval bridge on the Avon is noble enough. In 1449 Bishop Carpenter of Worcester offered a year's indulgence to all contributors to its maintenance. It was rebuilt after Charles I, retreating to Oxford, knocked it about in 1644.

Binton's connections with Captain Scott, married to the Rector's daughter, Kathleen Bruce, are perpetuated in a remarkable west window, showing the expedition's discovery of Amundsen's Norwegian flag, Captain Oates walking out for 'rather a long time' into the blizzard, and the search party setting up a cairn. **Billesley**, to the north, was a decayed village by 1450. It is now an impressive group of gabled sixteenth-century hall, a barn and a seventeenth-century church approached through a farmyard. This was built in 1692 by Bernard Whalley, lord of the manor, using some original walling, but superimposing a contemporary look with a louvered bell-turret, urns over the gables, and a gallery and box pews. In an earlier church Shakespeare's granddaughter Elizabeth married Sir John Barnard in 1649.

CHAPTER THREE

The Town of Warwick

❧

Warwick is the most uniformly handsome town of any size in the west Midlands. It is, for a start, perfectly sited along a low hill above the Avon, which gave the town its name, 'Waerinc-Wic', village by the weir. Its townscape gives primacy to the soaring baroque Gothic church tower which beckons for miles across the fields along the Stratford road and gives expectations of beauty which a closer look cannot disappoint. Begun as a Saxon 'burh' by Alfred's daughter Aethelflaed, it was a flourishing walled town in the Middle Ages, with a castle founded in 1086 by William the Conqueror and built up most impressively in the last quarter of the fourteenth century by two successive Earls of Warwick named Thomas Beauchamp. Queen Elizabeth was twice a visitor, first in 1566 and then six years later, when the Recorder, Mr Aglionby, gave her a long and erudite harangue. Obviously rather overcome by his own audacious eloquence, Aglionby stood trembling as the Queen then received a purse of twenty gold pieces, but with her unmatched ability to make people eat out of her hand, she called to him, 'Come hither, little Recorder. It was told me that you would be afraid to look upon me or to speak so boldly, but you were not so afraid of me as I was of you.'

The most far-reaching event in the creation of Warwick's unique character was still to come. On 5 September 1694 a disastrous fire broke out in the town, causing some £120,000 worth of damage and making 250 families homeless. With 460 buildings destroyed and the entire town centre gutted, there was a chance for a planned recon-struction which Warwick, following Northampton's example of nineteen years earlier, was quick to seize. Houses were to be of brick or stone, roofed with tile or slate, and where sufficiently strong walls survived, they were to be refaced. The nucleus of the whole design was the crossroads formed by the High Street, Church Street and Castle Street.

Rebuilding was slow but consistent, throwing up what might almost be termed a 'Warwick School' of architect-masons in Francis

Smith, David and William Hiorn and Thomas Johnson, and calling in such first-rate outsiders as Sanderson Miller. Most of their work has survived in a town of broad, bright streets, whose houses preserve an almost miraculous uniformity of scale. Warwick is the only west-Midland town which stands firmly in the country yet never looks or feels provincial.

We may as well begin with what most visitors come to see – **Warwick Castle**. Despite the name 'Ethelfleda's Mound', picturesquely given to it in 1893, the earthworked south-western keep is Norman and the earliest masonry dates from the fourteenth-century Beauchamp reconstruction. What now survives is one of the largest continuously inhabited castles in England.

We enter from the lodge gates on Castle Hill and follow the drive up to the Barbican and Gatehouse, with its original portcullis. To left and right of the Gatehouse, the Beauchamps stacked two huge towers: Caesar's Tower, nearest the river, probably the later of the two, is very French in style, with a machicolated walk embracing a small turret; Guy's Tower to the west is altogether simpler. Inside the ward is a broad green court, with two further towers, Clarence and Bear, continuing the western walls. These are part of an attempt by 'false fleeting perjured Clarence', brother of Richard III, to erect a new defensive work here during the Wars of the Roses.

After Queen Elizabeth's 1572 visit, when she had watched the country folk dancing in the courtyard and been treated to a firework display whose centrepiece of a flying dragon made of squibs nearly set the town alight, the castle fell into decay until Fulke Greville, distantly related to the Beauchamps, acquired the estate in 1604. Little of his £20,000 refurbishment survives, and in any case his descendants had to make ready for defence in the Civil War, when the castle was a Parliamentarian stronghold.

The fittings of the state apartments on the east side of the courtyard are therefore very much of two later periods – baroque and late Georgian. In 1670 William and Roger Hurlbut, local men, were employed to redesign the rooms (the former had been sent to look over Kingston Lacy House in Dorset for reference) and their work, strongly allusive to the best in the Wren-Gibbons tradition, can be seen in the Cedar Room's gorgeous ceiling moulding and panelling festoons falling from shields on either side of the fireplace, carrying the Greville arms of an engrailed cross with five pellets. Similar fruity swags and leafy garlands sprout from the ceilings and overmantels of the Blue Boudoir and the Green Drawing Room, all spanking new for William III's visit here on 4 November 1695, when

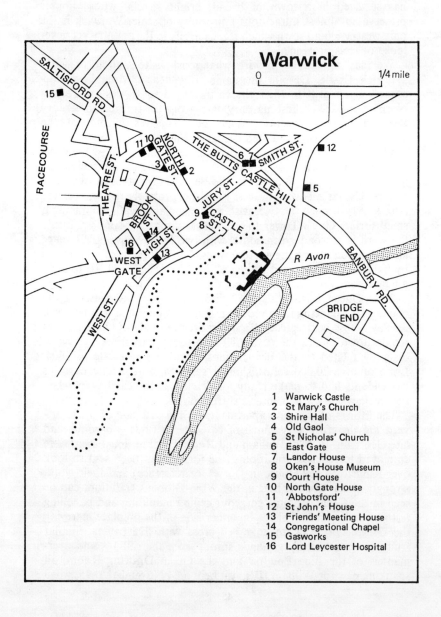

Warwick

0   1/4 mile

RACECOURSE
SALTISFORD RD.
15
THEATRE ST.
11 10
GATE ST.
NORTH
3
2
THE BUTTS
6 7
SMITH ST.
12
CASTLE HILL
5
BROOK ST.
JURY ST.
CASTLE ST.
9
8
14
HIGH ST.
16
13
WEST GATE
1
R Avon
BANBURY RD.
WEST ST.
BRIDGE END

1   Warwick Castle
2   St Mary's Church
3   Shire Hall
4   Old Gaol
5   St Nicholas' Church
6   East Gate
7   Landor House
8   Oken's House Museum
9   Court House
10 North Gate House
11 'Abbotsford'
12 St John's House
13 Friends' Meeting House
14 Congregational Chapel
15 Gasworks
16 Lord Leycester Hospital

the townsfolk in the courtyard drank a hundred gallons of punch.

Some fifty years later the energetic Francis Greville, soon to unite title and estate as first Earl of Warwick of the fourth creation, began a more ambitious overhaul, continued by his son George at a cost which brought him to bankruptcy in 1804. Francis made a new dining room, with a ceiling by a highly-skilled local plasterer, Robert Moore, and a Gothic porch by Thomas Lightoler. The poet, Gray, writing to the antiquary, Dr Wharton, in 1754, says of Greville's improvements, 'he has sash'd the great Appartment, that's to be sure . . . and being since told that square sash-windows were not Gothic, he has put certain whim-whams withinside the glass . . . he has scooped out a little Burrow in the massy walls of the place for his little self & his children, which is hung with Paper & printed Linnen, & carved chimneypieces, in the exact manner of Berkeley-Square or Argyle-Buildings. What in short can a Lord do now a days that is lost in a great old solitary Castle, but sculk about, & get into the first hole he finds, as a Rat would do in like case.'

There were also new stables and coach-houses, a library, and a spiral staircase outside the Green Drawing Room. In 1788 the second Earl created the present entrance to the castle grounds by siting a new bridge to the north-east to carry the Banbury Road. This was designed by William Eborall of Warwick, who had already created a greenhouse to hold the Earl's newly-acquired white marble vase. Decorated with silenus-heads, it was found on a lake bed near Hadrian's villa at Tivoli and sent to England by Sir William Hamilton.

The last burst of restoration brought in the Victorian gothicizer, Anthony Salvin, to give the river front its 'silver-fork' grandeur and to supervise a pleasing reassembly of the Great Hall, gutted by fire in 1871. This contains some magnificent suits of tilting armour, and part of a good portrait collection. Holbein's puffy-faced Henry VIII hangs in the Blue Boudoir. Another king, Edward VII, was a frequent visitor at Warwick: the radical Countess Daisy had splendid riverside grounds to walk in. Laid out by Brown in 1753, they incorporate a mill by Lightoler and a Gothic hunting lodge, and make a singular feature, walled off as they are between town and river, in the already unique openness of Warwick.

St Mary's Church is the other great wonder of the town. Grand as a small cathedral, it was made collegiate in 1123, served by a Dean and canons, who lived in houses round the churchyard, fronting a path formerly known as Canon Row and now (why?) called the Tink-a-Tank. Nothing of Earl Roger de Newburgh's Norman building survives except the crypt: and what stands above ground is substantially of three later periods – a late fourteenth-century choir, the florid Perpendicular Beauchamp Chapel, and the tower and nave restored in majestically sober Gothic after the 1694 fire.

We enter under the portico of the west tower, built across the pavement at the top of Church Street. The baroque town plan allows us to appreciate this remarkably successful fusion of styles from whatever direction we approach, and it comes as no surprise to learn that its design was attributed to Wren. Of course it isn't his. The town commissioners, armed with a grant of £11,000 plus another £1000 from the Crown, had applied to him, but then called on Sir William Wilson of Sutton Coldfield, self-made son of a Leicester baker. Wilson's best work is probably here in Warwick, where he was assisted by the Smiths and by Samuel Dunkley, a Particular Baptist minister. Advice from Edward Strong, Wren's master-mason at St Paul's, saved the tower from crashing into the nave and prompted its re-orientation towards Old Square. One hundred and seventy-four feet high, it carries a ring of eight bells by Rudhall of Gloucester.

On the south side of the entrance, notice the monument to Walter Savage Landor, born in Warwick in 1775. Above the door is the four-manual organ, whose casework is by Thomas Swarbrick, one of the 1694 commissioners' local team. Swarbrick worked for the great organ-builder, Renatus Harris, and encouraged a story that he himself was German so as to boost Harris's rivalry with the famous Bernhardt Schmidt – 'Father Smith'. His is the carved trophy panel of recorders, hautboys, citterns, violins and a harp, about which he sent his employers a pathetic scrawl: 'I hope you gentmen, by this time to some reselyshom to setel a salreay, and to consider that I cannot alwayes worke for nothing'. The mayoral mace-rests on the front pews are by another Warwick craftsman, Nicholas Paris, whose work was in considerable demand throughout the Midlands. Before leaving the nave, note the bread-shelves on the southern side, from which loaves were given to thirty-two poor men and women.

Earls Thomas I and II Beauchamp built the choir between 1362 and 1400. High in the leaping vaults, airy and audacious, angels hover with the family arms. The vestry, on the north side, retains some of the former east window glass and carries a Watching

Orchards in the Vale of Evesham
Croome Court, near Upton-on-Severn, ascribed to Sanderson Miller

Chamber, which allowed a guard to be kept on the holy relics. They included a piece of Mount Calvary, some of the Blessed Virgin's hair and bones of the Holy Innocents. There is also a polygonal chapter-house holding Sir Fulke Greville's monument, a massive black sarcophagus with its famous inscription 'Servant to Queene Elizabeth, Conceller to King James, and Friend to Sir Philip Sidney'. This apart, Greville was one of the most versatile of poets, purveying a kind of personal gloom in his sonnets and love lyrics which found a more extended outlet in *Mustapha* and *Alaham*, dramatized politico-philosophical treatises set in exotic Eastern locales, but with a strongly Senecan flavour. It was not enough to be servant, councillor and friend, or even ranger of Wedgnock Park at twopence a day, with rights of herbage and pannage: he must have seen his end coming – in 1628 he was stabbed by an old servant to whom he had refused a pension.

Thomas Beauchamp I, with his wife Katherine, lies before the high altar of the choir he began with French ransom money from Poitiers. His grandson Richard's tomb is the focus of one of the most gorgeous English decorative schemes – the **Beauchamp Chapel**. This was the brave warrior against the French at the close of the Hundred Years War, whom Shaw makes such an inimitably English figure in *Saint Joan*. He died at Rouen in 1439, and the chapel, costing £2784, was built in fulfilment of his will, from 1442 to 1462. Its nave entrance porch is a brilliant pastiche by Samuel Dunkley (a contemporary guide calls it 'that August Frontispiece') betrayed only by its classical cornices. Within is a treasure-house – vaulting whose tracery centres on octagonal panels of the Virgin and the arms of Beauchamp and Newburgh, a pretty little gallery over the porch, a symphony of angel musicians, God in glory and all His angelic host round the east window, carved stalls, a Last Judgement on the wall, a patchwork of glass fragments, and a Georgian plaster reredos.

Much of this work constitutes the original late Gothic decorative plan. The stone carving in the mullions is by John Massingham, the woodwork was made in London by Richard Byrde and John Haynes, and the glazing belongs to King Edward IV's glazier John Prudde of Westminster. It is all satisfying enough not to make us want to quarrel too much with intrusive features like Robert Bird's Michelangelesque 1678 repainting of an earlier Last Judgement or Thomas Lightoler's 'fine bas relievo' reredos, carved by William Collins, a

Strensham: monument to Sir Francis Russell, 1705, by Edward Stanton pupil of Henry Cheere who specialized in chimneypiece reliefs. Even the ostentatious tombs of the parvenu Dudleys, with effigies coldly pompous as their originals, cannot spoil the show. I share Froude's view of Robert, Lord Leicester: 'without courage; without talent; without virtue', a formidably unattractive figure, on whom Ben Jonson had the last word:

> *Here lyes a valiaunt warrior who never drew a sword,*
> *Here lyes a noble courtier, who never kept his word,*
> *Here lyes the Earle of Leicester who govern'd the Estates*
> *Whom the earth could never, living, love, and the just heaven*
> *now hates.*

His three marriages were loveless, and Countess Lettice, who brought him Essex as a stepson, is said to have poisoned him before marrying Sir Christopher Blount. She died in 1634, a tough old beldame of ninety-five, and a jejune row of verses here celebrates her presumed virtues. Robert's brother Ambrose, Earl of Warwick, dullest of the Dudleys, lies nearby, and an infant son, 'the noble impe' who died at three years old in 1584, is also buried here.

These are vanities beside the breathtaking calm on the gilt bronze face of Richard Beauchamp, lying on a Purbeck marble chest, his hands awesomely lifelike in the detailing of veins, knuckles and nails. The mid-fifteenth-century effigy, perhaps designed by the carver Massingham, was cast in London by William Austen and engraved and gilded by a Dutch goldsmith, Bartholomew Lambespring. It is interesting to note that Roger Webb, Warden of the Barber Surgeons' Company, was called in for anatomical advice. On the tombchest mourning relatives and friends surmount their appropriate arms, family names from the cast of Shakespeare's *Henry VI* trilogy, Staffords, Nevilles (the King-Maker himself on the south side) and Beauchamps (the widowed Countess raises a hand to her face). Under the hooped guard of gilt copper, Earl Richard's composed features are turned upwards to meet the figure of the Virgin in the vault above.

Out into the streets after, maybe, a stroll round the Tink-a-Tank path. Warwick is a lexicon of good English building. Up from the church on the corner of Northgate Street is the **Shire Hall**, 1753–8, built for Sanderson Miller by Job Collins and the two Hiorns, as a pilastered red sandstone frontage to an enormous ninety-foot room, whose decoration cleverly repeats the exterior design. Miller was so pleased with the two octagonal court rooms behind that a friend of his twitted him with preferring them to his sweetheart, Miss Bankes.

The Kent and Burlington style of all this is in sharp contrast to the façade of the **old gaol**, rebuilt in 1777–83 by Thomas Johnson, after a visit by the reformer, John Howard, had disclosed bad conditions. Simple, severe, crushingly neo-classical, it is pure *Fidelio* against the Mozartian spring of the Shire Hall. Beneath it is the original round dungeon of 1680, where the prisoners were chained by the feet to a central block.

Johnson's highly original talent can be further appreciated in **St Nicholas's Church**, nearly opposite the castle entrance. By 1779 this was a decayed medieval foundation, and Johnson built the new church as a Gothic pavilion, with a lantern cupola. The chancel was added a century later by John Gibson, a pupil of Barry, whose speciality was National Provincial bank buildings. The church retains its west gallery, and the churchyard has a tree planted by members of the TUC in 1934 to commemorate the Chartist incumbent (from 1811 to 1845), Arthur Wade.

Wandering down to the river and crossing Eborall's 1793 bridge, we come to **Bridge End**, a snatch of Warwick as it must have looked in pre-fire days, rows of low-pitched brick and timber houses with tall chimneys. Grander Tudor pieces line the eastern side of Mill Street, which runs under the castle walls to the ruins of the earlier bridge, deliberately left by the second Earl George to become romantically weed-grown. At the top of Castle Hill, at the junction with Jury Street, is the fifteenth-century **East Gate**, containing a chapel built in 1788 by Francis Hiorn and now part of the Girls' High School. The school also occupies the house on the east side built two years before the fire, in that nice plump, jowly, well-hipped Restoration style, for Dr William Johnston by Roger Hurlbut, and known as **Landor House**, since here the poet was born. There is an excellent second-hand bookshop further down on the opposite side of the street.

Jury Street itself is named from a small medieval Jewry, which included 'Magister, father of Herla, a scholar', and 'Vives le Romaunzur, a ballad singer'. It features some of the best of the 1694 rebuilding, and most of the town's principal inns and hotels. Warwick has two museums, the more recondite of them lying down to the left in Castle Street at **Oken's House**. Thomas Oken, who died in 1573, was one of those open-handed benefactors in whom Tudor and Stuart England was so rich. A wealthy mercer, he left his property to the poor of the borough, by whom it has been enjoyed ever since. Following a sermon at St Mary's, a yearly feast concludes with a toast to his memory and that of Joan his wife. The high-gabled timber-framed house, with its wildly sloping floors and sudden steps, now holds a display of dolls and toys collected by Mrs Joy Robinson. This is one of the largest such private collections in England, and it affords a bizarre, sometimes almost macabre treat to return the glassy-eyed, waxen-cheeked stares of dolls ranging from the little limp husband-and-wife 'babies' of Hanoverian days to the fussy, flouncy, pert, proud misses of the Victorian nursery.

Back on the corner of Jury Street stands the fine **Court House**, built at great expense to the corporation by Francis Smith between 1725 and 1730. Its lower storey contains a Mayor's Parlour and Magistrate's Court (currently being reorganized) and behind the long windows and Doric pilasters of its upper storey, framing a statue of Justice by Thomas Stayner (1668–1731, best work at Stowe–Nine Churches, Northants.), lies one of those big assembly rooms in which, at race balls and routs, the squirearchy footed country-dances under the wax-lights and shuffled their daughters towards a good jointure.

Other fine houses lie on the fringes of the town. Don't miss a look at **Northgate House** up the street beyond the Shire Hall, very good 'Queen Anne' (1698 actually) with a sundial in the pediment overhanging the double doors of a carriage entrance to what is in fact an early example of semi-detached living. The boring new county offices in the Market Place have been tacked on to **'The Abbotsford'**, a very grand affair of 1714, whose architect is unknown, but which looks, with its tall Corinthian pilasters and volutes to the central window, exactly like some Bavarian nobleman's palace. **St John's House**, on the way out towards Coventry, is a five-bay Jacobean and Caroline mansion built by Anthony and Nathaniel Stoughton on the site of a travellers' hospice, with graceful alternation in the straight and curved lines of the gables. This is now a folk museum and on the first floor is a display of exhibits connected with the Royal Warwickshire Regiment, founded in 1673 as part of an English division to assist the Dutch against Louis XIV. The regiment went on to win honours at Barcelona, in the '45, and against 'the refractory Charibees of St Vincent', and retreated to Corunna with Sir John Moore. Its regimental badges are the antelope and rose-and-crown, and its motto *'Nec aspera terrent'*.

Space prevents more than the briefest mention of other delights: the old **Friends' Meeting House**, off the High Street, 1695 but very sober in its garden, the **Congregational Chapel** near by in Brook Street, stuccoed Regency by Thomas Stedman Whitwell, author of an early treatise on central heating, and designer of the disastrous iron-roofed Brunswick Theatre, London, which collapsed in 1828 only two nights after its opening: the pretty white octagons of the 1822 **Gasworks**, down in Saltisford near the great racecourse: **Theatre Street**, commemorating a vanished playhouse, where Macready acted Othello, Kemble played Falstaff, and Kean was Shylock and Richard III.

Our tour of Warwick can fittingly close with the last of its trio of wonders: the **Lord Leycester Hospital** (for unaccountable reasons, that precious 'ye olde'-looking 'y' is retained). Beside the town's West Gate, a medieval rock-tunnelling, is a big half-timbered quadrangle, forming what was until 1546 the hall of three guilds, Holy Trinity, St George and the Blessed Virgin. After a brief spell as a home for the Grammar School (still flourishing as an independent day school) it became in 1571 a hospital for a Master and twelve poor old soldiers, preference to be given to natives of Warwickshire and Gloucestershire and tenants and servants of its founder, Robert, Earl of Leicester.

The timbering, all dating from the turn of the fifteenth and sixteenth centuries, is among the best of its period, and all the more significant in having escaped the fire. Entering the courtyard under an arch, we find the Great Dining Hall on our left, where Fulke Greville entertained King James in 1617, and to our right the Guildhall, reached up stairs giving directly on to the yard. Both rooms have admirably sturdy roof timbers, and the Guildhall has the additional interest of an upper room looking out from the gatehouse, part of a former Master's Lodging. This lodging was later transferred to the opposite side of the courtyard, best Victorian Friesian-Cow-Tudor (the jolly blue porcupine, by the way, is for the Sidney family) with beams as faked as a Payne Collier Shakespeare forgery. The beautifully overhung gallery gives on to the Chaplains' Dining Hall, and in the old kitchens below we can eat a very good cream tea, with homemade cakes.

CHAPTER FOUR

The Vale of Evesham

❧

'Many counties, I believe, are called so,' Jane Austen's Emma coolly remarks to Mrs Elton's insistent claims for Surrey as the garden of England. She might just as easily have named the Vale of Evesham, the lush alluvial plain of the Avon, in which nothing won't grow, and where a fence-post or a walking stick may sprout green leaves and start fruiting. Since the Middle Ages, when the great abbey of Evesham farmed the land, the Vale has grown the best fruit and vegetables in the west of England, and indeed perhaps not even Kent or the East Anglian growing areas can match the tireless fertility of its dark soil. Aesthetically the result is a variegated landscape, where a continuing green, of leeks, cabbages, asparagus, currant bushes, gooseberries, and now maybe a vineyard or two, is powdered in spring with a froth of blossoms and contained within the changing colours on the slopes of Bredon, the Cotswolds and the distant Malverns. There is money in the Vale and a smart, sometimes positively meretricious village look to show for it. None of your scattered Temeside hamlets or dusty forest farmsteads here: this is Shakespeare's Worcestershire, a commuter's reach from Oxford, Reading and Paddington, a world of tweed caps and Hush Puppies, headscarves and retrievers, purring Jaguars and glossy geldings, every stable-door well creosoted, every verge well trimmed, the manorhouses, rectories and cottages, the very pigsties, undeniably, almost unctuously beautiful.

Pershore, the fairest town in the Vale, lies flat out on its water-meadows in one of the Avon's countless meandering loops. The settlement grew up around a Benedictine monastery, refounded in 972 from an earlier secular community, and dedicated to, among others, St Eadburh, King Alfred's granddaughter, relics of whom the abbey bought for £100. Eadburh's life has the engaging homeliness typical of Saxon saints. She used to clean her sisters' shoes and wash their stockings while they were asleep, before slipping off to pray in the chapel. Henry III granted Pershore a fair on her day (26 June), which is still held, and an old Worcestershire rhyme connects this with the last summer cuckoos:

The cuckoo guz ter Parsha fair
And then 'er hops it off from there.

Pershore had been carved up, by a legal fiddle immediately before the Conquest, between its own abbey and that of Westminster, which got most of the town and the best of the deal. This explains St Andrew's church, now a parish centre, formerly serving the Westminster tenants. Of the **abbey** itself what survives, though only the choir, the crossing tower and a south transept, is impressive enough to convey the idea of a more substantial church. None of the monastic buildings, originally spreading southwards, remains, though two recently restored pieces of timber-framing on the northern side of the big green may represent an abbey almonry.

We enter under the tower, fourteenth-century work, built after a fire in 1288, and possibly the work of masons from Salisbury, with whose cathedral tower it has certain affinities. The distinctive pinnacles were only added in 1871. Buttressing replaces a vanished north transept. The font on this north side, with its rows of saints in interlocking arches, is clearly Norman, though much weathered. Note the small fragment of a wooden screen, whose inscription dates it to 1434, during the abbacy of William Newton.

On the south side of the church, the abbey's history can be followed in a detailed series of forty-eight panels by Hardman, of 1870. The western end of the south aisle formerly opened on to St Eadburh's chapel, where her miraculous relics were venerated. In the south transept is the oldest work in the abbey, early Norman, grandly monolithic. Abbot Newton's rebus, with a tun (barrel), can be seen on a boss in the vaulting on the south-west side, and another abbot lies pillowed on his mitre below. Our best view of the monastic choir (its Lady Chapel gone, and replaced by rather apologetic apsing) is from under the arcaded lantern of the tower. Noteworthy are the clever sandwiching of clerestory and triforium, the Purbeck shafts (as at Worcester) in the sanctuary, and the spring of ribs to huge bushy bosses – the word 'vault' was nowhere better given.

Pershore Abbey was surrendered by its close-fisted Abbot, John Stonewell, on 21 January 1540, much of its land being bought up by the Dean and Chapter of Westminster, the building stone going to local houses. Little else specifically medieval remains in the town, though the quintessentially Georgian character of its façades in the piazza of Broad Street, its T crossed by High Street and Bridge

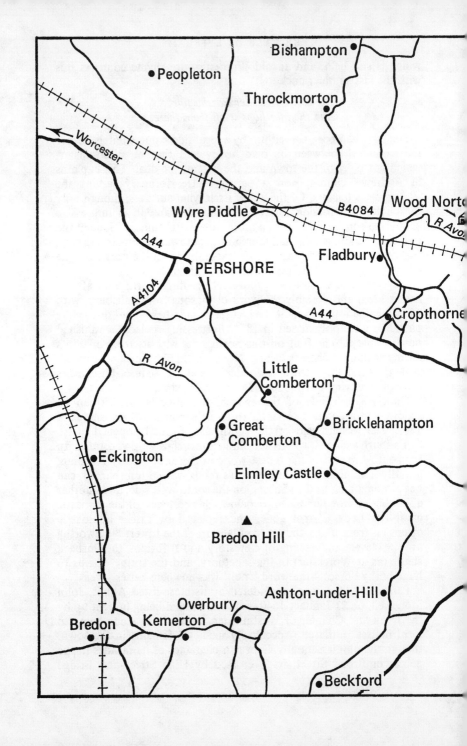

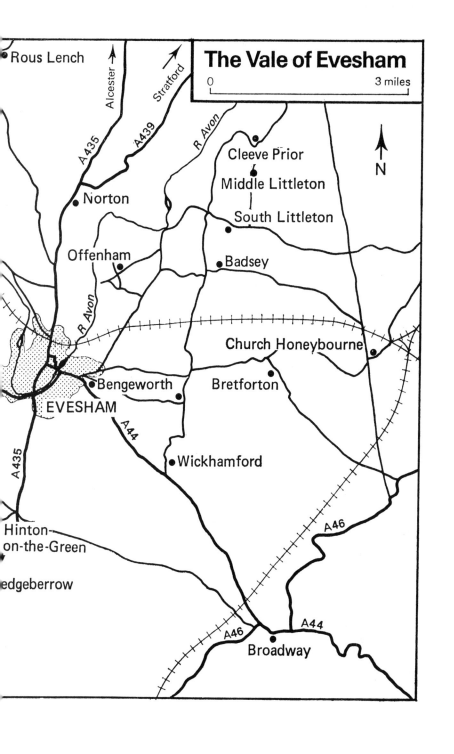

Street, is often deceptive. No. 19 High Street, for example, resembles several other Pershore buildings in masking older workshops and warehouses with a smart street front. Many houses have garden plots backing on to the river. Outstanding among them is **Perrott House**, almost opposite the Regency verandah of the Three Tuns. Perrott House was built in 1760 for a leading Worcestershire judge, Sir George Perrott, whose family later acquired Craycombe near Fladbury. As Robert Adam was then working for Lord Coventry at Croome, it seems reasonable to detect his hand here. Certainly the profusion of garlanded plasterwork, the Venetian windows of the main hall and drawing room, and the enriched decoration of ceilings and mantelpieces, give the house a startling sophistication, nicely complemented by its function as a showroom for Georgian antique furniture. Immaculately maintained gardens stretch away to the Avon beyond.

A sharp right turn past Pershore bridge (on the old bridge close by the post-Civil War rebuilding of the damaged central arches is clearly marked) signposts to 'The Combertons', sounding like the title of some Victorian three-decker novel. Both **Great** and **Little Comberton** have lately tended to become bijou overspills for Evesham and Pershore, with some of their new housing built in a violent local stone needing a century of weathering to become attractive. Both have good gargoyled Perpendicular towers to their churches, and St Peter's, Little Comberton, has the additional interest of a north porch built in 1639. Note here also the dovecote at the farm north of the church: its shape, a buttressed stone round, suggests medieval origins.

South-west of these, on the peninsula made by one of the Avon's capricious windings, is **Eckington**, lying on the site of a Roman villa. A main road from Pershore slices rather uncomfortably through the village and the church stands right on it, a grand, dark Norman building, with a Perpendicular tower on the south side and an excellent fifteenth-century nave roof, whose cross-pieces carry carved figures and decorative patterns. The monument to John Hanford and his wife, Anne Rake, facing one another across a prayer desk, dates from 1616 and has been attributed, from the delicacy of its carving, to Epiphanius Evesham, that Inigo Jones of monumental sculptors, to whom everything is sooner or later ascribed. A tablet to Christianus Kendrick, however, is signed by Richard Squire (1700–86) whom Pevsner doggedly persists in calling an architect, which he never was.

In the old days, Eckington church had, not a band, but a proper little orchestra of two violins, two 'cellos and double bass, flutes, clarinets, bassoons, trumpet and trombone. The churchwardens' sedulous accounts are eloquently misspelt: we have entries for 'Geten the Stones oute of the Rifor', 'Gunpowder Treason Eale', 'for Burds egs and urchins' (hedgehogs), 'too Kees', 'Eliz, Willks in want. Bleeding Do.', 'Paid to a woman in a fitt', and, pure Worcestershire this, 'Fowls taters'. The 'stones oute of the rifor' may have belonged to old Eckington bridge, rebuilt from earlier materials by Robert Tayler and Thomas Wilkinson, Worcester masons, in 1728-9. On the outer cutwaters of its five arches you can still see the marks made by ropes used for bowhauling Avon barges underneath, which moved Arthur Quiller-Couch to not especially good poetry.

Like all the other villages round about, Eckington is dominated by **Bredon Hill**, that ineluctable fact of the county landscape, whose broad, low, scrubby dome can be seen for miles and has been immemorially used as a weather gauge in the rhyme:

When Bredon Hill puts on his hat,
Men of the Vale, beware of that.

A lias mass, with an oolitic limestone cap, its scarps relate it pretty clearly to the Cotswolds, of which it forms an outlier. Unlike them, it is difficult to get at, its slopes heavily farmed and in places thickly wooded, but there is some good rough walking up cart tracks, over gates, fences and stiles, and across the summit's bramble-patched broken ground among the remains of Iron Age encampments. The principal fort dates from the second century BC, but its life seems to have ended abruptly in a battle, judging from the hacked skeletons of defenders found in one of the ditches. Within the rampart stands a small Georgian folly tower, built by a Mr Parsons of Kemerton. On the north side of the hill is Woollas Hall, an exceedingly handsome Jacobean piece, with fetching contrasts in the line of the gables and projecting porches and wings, built in 1611 by John Hanford and now divided into flats.

Prettiest of the hamlets ringing the hill is its eponymous village of **Bredon**, perhaps best seen from the M5 just before it crosses the river. Bredon is one of those places which are both a paradigm and a vindication of the English village. Its site, on a bluff above the Avon, is the finest in the county, its houses among the most elegant, it has one of the grandest parish churches in the Midlands and a glorious medieval tithe barn close by.

St Giles's Church probably occupies the site of a Saxon monastery, burnt by Danish raiders in 841 and rebuilt in late Norman style around 1180, perhaps by Worcester and Tewkesbury masons. Certainly the sixty-foot nave, western tower arch (its base, despite the recessed spire, is also Norman), the north porch and the two west turrets all testify to an accomplished mastery of design. The Mitton chapel on the south side was added by Sir Nicholas de Mitton in 1230, with wonderfully slender-shafted lancets, and about a century later John Trillek, later Bishop of Hereford, built the north chapel and clapped on the spire, as well as refashioning the spacious chancel. His arms can be seen among the eighty-six heraldic tiles on the chancel steps, which also feature those of England, Castile and France, and of big baronial clans such as Mortimer, Bohun, Despenser and Grandison. Look as well for those showing the months of the year.

On the north side of the sanctuary, below a medieval window showing St Mary of Egypt and St Mary Magdalen, stands a restored Easter Sepulchre, and a tomb recess on the opposite wall contains effigies of an unnamed medieval couple, with Christ in glory in the canopy above. These may be members of the Reed family. Their descendant Giles and his wife, Catherine Greville (Fulke's daughter), lie in the Mitton chapel, in a loudly sumptuous monument, a massive confection of alabaster and black and white marble, with a Latin inscription rendered into slightly old-fashioned alexandrines (the Reeds died in 1611), obelisks and fat putti bearing symbols of mortality.

Notable also is the plaque in the chancel to John Prideaux, Bishop of Worcester. Prideaux, a Devon man, became Rector of Exeter College, Oxford, in 1612, and went on to be Regius Professor of Divinity and vice-chancellor. His reputation for firm but kindly administration got him his bishopric in 1641, though shortly afterwards the Civil War robbed him of almost everything. Never a rich man, he was forced to shelter at his son-in-law's rectory of Bredon, where he lived by pawning his possessions, until he died in 1650 of a fever. The rectory itself, still substantially Elizabethan, stands north of the church. Here, during the incumbency of Henry George Cavendish Browne, a visitor was his infant cousin, Ottoline Cavendish Bentinck – though the thought of Lady Ottoline Morrell ever having been a child is a little bizarre. West of this is a fine Georgian stone manorhouse, with nice rough details, and behind it again is Bredon's second treasure, the great **Tithe Barn**. Built in Edward I's reign for the estate of the Bishops of Worcester, it measures 124 feet, with deep porches and aisles and high, sinewy rafters.

Kemerton and **Overbury** lie within spitting distance of each other, nooks of twee rusticity if ever there were. The latter's unascribed manorhouse, Overbury Court, is partly of 1735, sporting traces of work by Norman Shaw (1895), much more obviously present in the jolly estate cottages and village hall. House and village and five thousand acres around all belong to the Holland Martin family. The church has nice Perpendicular features, a gargoyled and crocketed central tower and east window among them, and the chancel's lancets, rib-vaults and carved bosses make an elegant riposte to the Norman clerestory windows in the nave. The war memorial is, originally enough, a timber lychgate over a stone block, designed by Sir Herbert Baker.

Westwards over the plain, looking across that haunting stretch of champaign towards the hummocky Cotswold outliers of Dumbleton and Oxenton, **Beckford** once held an Augustinian priory, founded in 1128 by canons from Ste Barbe-en-Auge, Calvados, under the patronage of Henry I's chamberlain, Ravel de Tancarville. Nothing survives of this but the cellar undercroft of Beckford Hall, which returned to Catholic use with its purchase by the Salesian Society in 1936. No doubt the imposing parish church, set back off the village street among mellow stone cottages, had some connection with the priory, if its arresting Norman masonry is anything to go by. The south porch has a tympanum carried on stumpy corbel heads, but its treatment of the four evangelical symbols is lumpy hobbledehoy stuff compared with the Harrowing of Hell in the corresponding north doorway. Norman, too, are the base of the tower and its westernmost arch, dotted with weird carved fragments.

This side of Bredon, a lonely back door into Gloucestershire, is its most attractive, especially late on a summer afternoon, with big shadows thrown across the cornfields between the hills. Here, too, the frontier villages have a more agreeably tousled look than posh Overbury or Kemerton. **Ashton-under-Hill's** church has a rare dedication to St Barbara; the late Jacobean chancel, built in 1624 by Sir John Franklin, carries details of his arms (dolphins and lion-heads) over the windows. **Hinton-on-the-Green** gave its name to a method of change-ringing known as Hinton Surprise Major, and the north wall of its chancel shelters the robed figure of William de Halford, bearing his pastoral staff as Abbot of Bordesley. At **Sedgeberrow** William Butterfield did the cheerful tile-and-mosaic reredos, and the east window was designed in 1878 by Mrs Barber, the vicar's wife.

From Ashton the old road hugs the hillside, bringing us round to

Elmley Castle, for two reasons the most worthwhile of Bredon villages. The first is its proper village street, complete with open water-kennels and lime trees on either side and gates giving on to the cricket field, leading up to one of the prettiest village churches in Worcestershire. The outside is pure embattled Cotswold Perpendicular, but the base of the tower and some craggy-looking interior masonry hint at an earlier church begun, maybe, by Robert d'Abitot, Norman lord of Elmley, and rebuilt by the Beauchamps. So also do the carved pig and lop-eared rabbit on the stones of the porch, and the writhing dragons at the base of the font.

Apart from an old organ, with agreeably wheezy pipes, Elmley's treasure is the pair of magnificent monuments in the north transept. On a marble chest, between his father, William, and his widow, Catherine, lies Giles Savage, to whom the tomb was raised in 1631. At his feet his four sons kneel, in cloaks, ruffs and rhinegrave boots, with their family badges. The whole is in flawlessly cut alabaster, its details, such as the crisp folds of the lady's skirt and her slender fingers clutching a swaddled infant, making it one of the most brilliant examples of Caroline sculpture. Quite as graceful, in the fall of wig, stock and full sleeves, is the nearby reclining figure of the first Earl of Coventry (1700) by William Stanton. This came to Elmley through the snobbery of the Earl's son, outraged at his father's marriage to the housekeeper's niece at Croome and furious enough at the statistician Gregory King's allusion to her, in his memorial inscription, as the daughter of a Norfolk gentleman as to challenge it in the courts with evidence that her father was 'a mean person, by trade a turner'.

The other village magnet is The Plough, one of the last really good Vale pubs to sell rough cider, drunk in mugs, with its uniquely sour flavour, like sweetened vinegar. For those who loathe beer as I do, this is in every respect an agreeable substitute, light, powerfully alcoholic and compellingly cheap. What is more, the pub's atmosphere thankfully makes no concessions whatever, in furnishings or clientele, to the blandishments of brewery kitsch. But the castle, a bristling Beauchamp stronghold on the hillside with its park and warren? Gone, alas! together with the stone manorhouse where William Savage entertained a weekending Queen Elizabeth on 20 August 1575. She arrived on a progress from Worcester in her litter, and was feasted on roast swan, lamprey pie, partridge, jellies, dates and almonds, washed down with sack. Poor William – one wonders how much it all cost!

Bricklehampton, north-west of Elmley, has the best Victorian mansion in Worcestershire bar none, well viewed from the Pershore road. It was built in 1848, by an unknown architect whose grammar was airily Italian, with big roundheaded windows and a jolly belvedere. Back on the main A44, high above the Avon valley, we pass another piece of felicitous faking, Wick Manor, 1923 timber-framed but coyly deceptive for all that. Further on, a left turn takes us down to **Cropthorne**, with its steeply falling village street of half-timbered cottages and its bizarre stories of the Dingley, or Dineley, family. Of the five sons of Eleanor Dingley and Sir Edward Goodere, three died before John succeeded to the title with his brother Samuel as heir. In 1741 the latter, fiercely jealous, contrived to have the former strangled on board *The Ruby*, the man-o'-war which he commanded, but was tried and hanged for it at Bristol. His two sons died respectively a lunatic and a pauper, desperately canvassing rich wives.

More prosperous Dingleys, Elizabethan and Jacobean, lie in the church, one of comparatively few to retain its plain windows and plastered walls and all the better for that. In the north aisle, above the painted figures of Sir Francis and his wife, Elizabeth Bigge of Lenchwicke, a pompous inscription stresses her connection with royalty while, slewed at an awkward angle across the end of the Norman nave arcade, Edward kneels opposite his black-gowned widow, Joyce Sandys. But did they die out altogether? When I last visited Cropthorne, a glance at the electoral role showed several Dingleys still in the parish – too much of a coincidence.

On a south nave window sill at Cropthorne church is a Saxon cross-head dating from the early 800s, decorated with birds and geometric designs. Its origin is unknown but it was found as part of the lower wall masonry.

Over a gentle hill and we are in the suburbs of Evesham, passing the ochre-coloured Perpendicular church at Hampton and crossing a pale green and grey concrete horror of a bridge, to the fringes of a small town whose market gardens come almost into the main streets. **Evesham**, like Pershore and Tewkesbury, grew up around its riverside abbey, but was only given its charter in 1604, after squabbles between the townsfolk, who regarded it as a free borough, and Sir Philip Hoby who had bought the abbey lands. With six fairs and a Monday market, Evesham was already noted as a wool mart in 1315, when an Italian merchant called it '*Guesame in Chondisgualdo*' (Cotswold) and of the heavy horses sold at its September fair Habington writes in his county survey (1607): 'they are often pre-ferred from the Cart and plow to the Court and the tylt, and which is most laudable, to serve in the warres.'

The abbey was the biggest in the south Midlands. Its foundation in 714 by Bishop Ecgwin of Worcester was inspired by a vision imparted to the swineherd Eoves, of the Virgin with a book in one hand and a gold cross in the other. Ecgwin in fact renounced his see to become 'Eoves-ham's first abbot and his relics, along with those of St Odulf, St Wulsy of Crowland and St Wistan (given by King Canute), were preserved in the church. The presence of its vast estates, ruled by mitred abbots (the last of whom, Philip Hawford, as Dean of Worcester, was buried in abbatial robes) can be traced all over south Worcestershire in barns, granges, dovecotes and stew-ponds, but of the church itself nothing remains save four significant fragments.

The first of these, seen in the Vale for miles, cheating the traveller with the promise of some huge fane, is the great Perpendicular bell-tower begun by Abbot Clement Lichfield in 1513. This is a final fling of exuberant abbatial splendour, heavily panelled and ogeed, though its pinnacles were added in 1717. Below this, a single arch of the Chapter House, dotted with little figures, dates from *c.* 1285 during the abbacy of John de Brockhampton, as part of his intensive rebuilding. The Great Gate, to the south-west of Merstow Green, has been absorbed into the body of a Queen Anne house, and in the half-timbered Almonry (it probably wasn't) is a small museum. Most interesting is the Norman cemetery gateway built by Abbot Reginald in *c.* 1130, its waves of blank arcading carrying fifteenth-century timber stages, and it is under this that we approach Evesham's signal mystery – two parish churches.

Why All Saints lies cheek by jowl with St Lawrence's can only be explained by the fact that one was for the cemetery and the other for the parish. The former is more absorbing, fusing Norman work at its western end with a Decorated chancel arch and a Perpendicular south transept for Abbot Lichfield: here, in a kind of late Gothic vignette, look up amid the harmony of fan-vault and quatrefoiled window for Lichfield's monogram C.L.P. (P for Prior as he then was). Loving Evesham as he did, he was not content with a chapel at All Saints but must give one to St Lawrence's, too, dedicated to his namesake, St Clement. Arguably more splendid, it enhances a dark, dull church, heavily overhauled in 1836 by Henry Eginton.

Considered as a town Evesham lacks both unity and character. Most of its old inns are appropriately in Vine Street. Its dismal, draughty High Street has one or two characterful buildings, including the grand Dresden House of 1692, built by Thomas Cookes of

Tardebigge, with a Jacobean mantelpiece in the garden, and a stuccoed Georgian summerhouse. Further on, above a shop on the same side, note the sign advertising Messrs Wheatley – Bootmaker to HRH the Duchess of Aosta. For train travellers Evesham Station, with its surrealistic piles of fruit boxes, sometimes has the pleasant evening adjunct of the Avonbank Silver Band practising in a shed beside the platform.

The Abbey's southern precincts fall down gentle lanes to the Avon, whose southern bank, reclaimed from eyots, was laid out as a river walk in 1864 by Henry Workman. On this side **Bengeworth** was once a town in its own right, boasting a bluecoat school founded by John Deacle, a London draper, whose monument in St Peter's church deserves a look. The posture of the figure, semi-recumbent, periwigged and robed as master of the Drapers' Company, suggests, in its intensely expressive hands and face, the work of Edward Stanton, already familiar from work at Strensham. Here in a laundry at the house called The Elm, in March 1832, died the composer Muzio Clementi, friend of Beethoven and Haydn and famous not only as a pianist (in 1781 a friendly competitor with Mozart) but also as a pioneer in piano technique, both through experimental sonatas such as the programmatic *Didone Abbandonata* and actual improvements to the instrument itself. He was Evesham's second musical worthy: the first, to whom he had no doubt reason to be grateful, was the monk Walter Oddington, inventor of the minim, whose *De Speculatione Musicae* was the fruit of long study here and at Oxford. I love to think of Walter charging, Rutherford-like, into the scriptorium, breathlessly to announce to the gaping brethren that he had split the semibreve.

The oldest of Worcestershire's three battlefields lies north of the town on the ridge of high ground between the A435 and the Avon. Evesham, at a river crossing, is well placed for a confrontation (Charles I is said to have wept at the loss of its Civil War garrison) and here on 4 August 1265, during a violent thunderstorm, the short fierce conflict was fought which ended the long struggle between Simon de Montfort and Henry III. The details of the story passed quickly into legend: how Simon watched the approach of the huge royal force from the abbey tower, how the king, his prisoner, was nearly killed by his own men led by Prince Edward, how Roger Mortimer picked off Simon's fleeing Welsh infantry at the bridge and sent the head of the proud, cruel, arrogant, high-principled rebel on a lance to Lady Maud Mortimer at Wigmore, who publicly reviled it.

65

Such was the murder of Evesham, for battle none it was,
And therewith Jesus Christ well ill-pleased was

says Robert of Gloucester's rhymed chronicle. Montfort's body, with those of Bohun, Despenser, Basset and others, was buried in the abbey.

The architect of nearby **Abbey Manor** seems to have taken hints from the battle for castellated Gothic and its grounds, besides an obelisk and an icehouse, contain a folly, Leicester Tower. Beyond, the B 4084 teeters between the wooded hillside and the river, passing, on its right, the gates of a later Victorian pile, **Wood Norton**. Though not of much intrinsic interest, the house is notable for having belonged to the duc d'Aumâle, fifth son of Louis Philippe and an exile in England from 1848 to 1870. Aumâle himself, to judge from his letters to his old tutor, Cuvillier-Fleury, was anything but happy among those for whom he posed as a gentleman farmer: *'L'Angleterre me pèse, et les Anglais encore plus.'* On 23 September 1863 he addressed the Vale of Evesham Agricultural Society – *'un comice agricole, avec le* speech. *Ce n'est pas gai, mais les bons rapports avec le pays sont à ce prix.'* Reported in *The Times*, it emerges as rather a banal address, ending, 'And so, gentlemen, I fill my glass with what I may call, and what I am proud to call, the agricultural produce of my own merry and beloved land (Cheers). It is a produce which Worcestershire men, with all their skill, cannot grow in their fields (Laughter). I now fill my glass, then, with what I may call a genuine countryman of my own, and I drink to the prosperity of the Evesham Agricultural Society.'

It is nice to find, in the teeth of all this Gallic sneering, that vines were in fact grown here, and the beautiful L-shaped Craycombe Hill, cultivated to its very top, lined with fruit trees and sheltering a golf course, always has for me an Italian look, a place for olives and grapes rather than apples and blackcurrants. Craycombe House, now a country club, was built for George Perrott of Pershore in 1791 by George Byfield (1756–1813), architect of various Worcester civic buildings. 'Vines still flourish and ripen well in that garden,' says Noake of **Fladbury** rectory, a house recently gutted by vandals. The village (Fleda's *burh*, but who was Fleda?) hangs high on a bluff over the Avon and is one of the valley's pleasantest, with its old mill occupying medieval foundations. The parish church has rewards both inside and out. Fabric includes Norman work on the lower tower stages (the upper part is of 1752) but a rebuilding during the 1340s gave the nave its late Decorated sophistication, culminating in the lovely buttressed and rib-vaulted porch, and we can be thankful that a good Victorian restorer left untouched the jolly Georgian ceiling raised on a brick clerestory and coved like some Oxford college dining hall.

Within is an ecclesiological picnic. First the delicious Virgin and Child in a fourteenth-century glass panel in the Lady Chapel, done with all the lyrical tenderness infusing high medieval glass painting. Then Worcestershire's best brasses on the altar tomb of John Throckmorton and Eleanor Spiney, whose marriage took the Throckmortons to Coughton. Though this is of 1445 and her husband's articulated armour-plates give him the look of an elegant wasp, Eleanor is robed with a nun-like sobriety. Other brasses among the Malvern tiles on the chancel floor recall priests of the same period.

Lastly, Dr William Lloyd, on the north chancel wall, a marble half-length by James Withenbury, done for £140 in 1718. As Bishop of Worcester, Lloyd owned Fladbury manor, and his son the rector supervised his father's lying-in-state at the parsonage. As Bishop of St Asaph, he had been one of the Seven to defy James II. The diary of his accident-prone chaplain, Francis Evans (leg crushed by a horse, fell into a lavatory, got hit on the head by a beam, etc.), reveals him as vigorous, eccentric and efficient, whether touring his diocese, scolding a slovenly Warwickshire vicar, writing with advice on the Bishop of Lincoln's piles, discussing prophecies with Pepys and Evelyn, or endowing the Oxford chair of Arabic.

As you leave the church, look for the memorial slab to the Reverend W. A. Pruen, on the right of the door, which tells us that 'he received his death stroke when in the pulpit at the Archdeacon's visitation at Stratford. His last words were "the Lord pardon this neglect of duty" '. It was of the wife of one of his predecessors that a Royalist soldier in 1644 noted: 'the parson's wife of Fladbury, a young woman often carrying a milke-payle on her head in the street – soe far from pride'.

Few of the other villages north of the Avon command quite as much interest, though none of them lacks charm. At **Throckmorton** the moated, timber-framed Court Farm was built in about 1500 by Sir Robert Throckmorton, member of a family associated with the village since the twelfth century. In **Wyre Piddle** church a Norman chancel arch complements a geometrically patterned font of a similar type to the one in St James's, **Bishampton**, whose decoration of ropes and rosettes is even more playful. **Peopleton**, in a mesopotamia of the Bow and Piddle brooks, was a manor of the Charlton

Dingleys, who still held it in 1850 – another proof (see Cropthorne) that they did not die out altogether – and its church preserves a handsomely adorned beam from a former rood screen in the nave west end.

And so out of a land of 'little bank-dividing brooks' into the wooded hill country of the Lenches – five of them in all, Rous, Church, Sherriffs, Atch and Ab, the last three little better than 'poor pelting farms' for Shakespeare's Edgar to lurk in – a lovely, lonely, hedgy, lark-singing landscape, good for walking over with its ridges and combes. **Rous Lench**, the northernmost, was once Bishop's Lench and Lench Randolph, before getting its present name from the Rous family. Sir Thomas Rous, an ardent Parliamentarian, played host in 1646 to Richard Baxter, who dedicated to him the first part of *The Saints' Everlasting Rest*, and the parish church is full of Rous monuments.

The man who did most for the village, however, was Dr W. K. W. Chafy, its energetic squarson from 1876 to 1916. Chafy was proud of his domain: 'the climate is Malvernesque in purity, and conducive to longevity. Octogenarians are common, nonagenarians not uncommon.' He it was who gave the village green its engaging mock-Tudor look, with an enormous half-timbered postbox, and built the Gothic school: 'the room is heated with Musgrave's Stove with a luminous front, and ventilated with one of Boyle's ventilators. A dado of chinese matting gives a warm aspect to the room.' As well as all this, and writing the village pantomimes and decking out the church altar with an elaborate Venetian Romanesque canopy, he added to the already handsome Rous Lench Court, right of the Church Lench road, an astonishing machicolated brick tower, pure Romagnole, and filled the garden with good topiary.

St Peter's church is basically Norman, its typically zigzagged south door bearing a fine tympanum of Christ framed in wings, suggesting a possible Northamptonshire source. Of the same period are the chancel arch and north arcade. Perhaps the two Elizabethan pulpits were given by Edward Rous, who lies beside his wife, Mary Haselrigg, under a cartouche of arms with a Moor's-head crest. No effigy, however, marks the dignified obelisk and black columns for his son John, but even better is Frances Rous's memorial, perhaps made by her father, Thomas Archer the architect. With a medallion of her husband borne by putti, she sits holding her heart beside a dove-crowned urn.

Shakespeare's son-in-law, John Hall, was the Jacobean Rouses' family doctor, but it was a beggarly local muse who produced another Sir Edward's 1677 epitaph:

If prayers, tears and sighs could have
Made ransom for him with ye grave
No eye within this Countie but
Had lent a tear to pay the shot.

Returning to Evesham through Church Lench and along the A 435 at Harvington, it is worth stopping at **Norton** church, dedicated to St Ecgwin. The lectern here, dug up in 1813 at Evesham and so presumably abbatial, is as grandly late Romanesque as Crowle's, to which it was perhaps a companion. A Jacobean pulpit and panelling complement the fluently sophisticated carving of Sir Thomas Bigg and his wife, Ursula Throckmorton, kneeling over a prayer desk and attributed rather convincingly to Epiphanius Evesham.

South-east of the Avon the true Vale country of market gardens, their teeming fields seasonally full of booted pickers and piled-up boxes, and the roads lined with stalls selling strawbs., rasps., caulis., and toms., stretches away into the bleak grey-lias upland of the Warwickshire border. Though the monks had exploited the Vale's fruitfulness, it was a seventeenth-century Genoese envoy, Francesco Bernardi, who, settling here in dudgeon at his republic's shabby treatment of him, spent over £30,000 on cultivation and began market gardening here in earnest. **Offenham**, for instance, tucked in its Avon loop, became famous for strawberries, especially the big, juicy Myatt's British Queen variety, while **Badsey**, to the south, is still the centre of asparagus-growing – the best, apparently, in England. The plant, known locally as 'gras', has given its name to a pub, The Round of Gras, on the Bretforton road. Badsey, deplorably suburban, has a big stone and timber manorhouse, formerly a convalescent home for the Evesham monks and given in 1545 to Philip Hoby of Bisham, whose son Richard's battered monument graces the dull parish church.

Bretforton, on the other hand, is a delight. Manor Farm, north of the road, preserves most of the medieval appurtenances, including dovecote, fishpond and barn, of the abbey grange at which the notorious Abbot Norreys (1191–1213) held an annual binge, getting through in a day what would have fed many monks for a year. Entering the village we pass the sprightly Gothic Bretforton Hall, with ogee windows and crenellated tower, pausing in the dark over-scraped nave of St Leonard's to look at the thirteenth-century carved capital illustrating the legend of St Margaret of Antioch. The saint, prior to her martyrdom, was assailed in prison by the Devil, who appeared as a fire-breathing dragon to swallow her up. Using the cross she carried, she prised herself out of his jaws in the nick of time.

The village boasts Worcestershire's oldest inn, The Fleece, a medieval long-house, recently presented to the National Trust after passing through generations of the same family. Among fields with Edward Thomas-like names – Porridge Yats, Bull Butts and Pumbleditch – we can turn south again over Bowers Hill to **Wickhamford**, another abbey manor, the site of whose grange may be identical with the rambling timber-framed house by the church. The latter is full of incidental pleasures: a seventeenth-century west tower, medieval lancets in the chancel and the arms of Charles II on a beam over the arch, as well as – rare joy! – box pews, a west gallery and Georgian altar rails. This perfect Anglican ensemble is triumphantly completed by a bonny tomb, laid out under a double arcade, with finialled canopy and achievements, for Sir Samuel and Sir Edwin Sandys and their wives, Mercy Culpeper and Penelope Bulkeley. Buried nearby is their relative, Penelope Washington, 'humble and chaste and wedded to Christ alone'. Dying in 1697, she was the daughter of Colonel Henry Washington, thus connected with the famous Sulgrave presidential clan.

To the north and east the Littletons and the Honeybournes. **South Littleton**, a village proper, boasts among other excellent houses the substantial and rather whimsical-looking Hathaways, a brick mansion begun, as its broad cornices show, in 1685, perhaps for the Coventrys, then lords of the manor, and extended in 1721, with a cupola and rangy-looking chimneystacks linked by open arches.

Middle Littleton is among my favourite Worcestershire places, striking in its shaggy, silent remoteness, a piece of secret England, worth all the Broadways, Burfords and Castle Combes put together. Standing amid hummocky fields and sheep-grazed orchards are a seventeenth-century stone manorhouse, with two gabled wings, built by Sir Matthew Carew, the church, with a Norman font and fluidly carved leaf spandrels over the tower arch, and a great abbatial barn, currently being restored by the National Trust. Once the buttressed stone structure had four porches, now there are two, and recent research has also given it a date approximating to the abbacy of John de Brokehampton (1282–1316).

Cow Honeybourne plays Chatham to **Church Honeybourne's**

Rochester, with only Roman Ryknild Street between them. The history of the latter's advowson reflects another pocket of Midland recusancy, since it passed from the Throckmortons to the Carylls, Dormers, Mostyns and Berkeleys. Their protégés could minister in an elegant late thirteenth-century church, to which two centuries later south clerestory windows were added, and a roof whose jack-legs rest on shield-bearing angel corbels.

On the ridge of hills above the Avon stands **Cleeve Prior**, given by King John to the Prior of Evesham for rent of one hundred marks and a palfrey. Later landlords were the Dean and Chapter of Worcester, from whom the manorhouse with its fine two-storeyed Elizabethan entrance porch was tenanted by the Bushell family. Thomas Bushell (1594–1674) was a talented eccentric, who Aubrey tells us 'was the greatest arts-master to runne in dept (perhaps) in the world'. After a spell as Bacon's protégé at Gorhambury, he went to live in a hut 470 feet above sea level on the Calf of Man 'where, in obedience to my dead lord's philosophical advice, I resolved to make a perfect experiment upon myself for the obtaining of a long and healthy life . . . by a parsimonious diet of herbs, oil, mustard and honey, with water sufficient, most like that of our long-lived fathers before the flood.' Having worked the royal silver mines in Cardiganshire and made himself expert in hydraulic engineering, he held Lundy for the King in the Civil Wars and set up a mint at Aberystwyth, spending the rest of his life as a plausible projector of fantastic technological devices.

I have to mention **Broadway**, though I would honestly rather not. It simply does not belong to Worcestershire, and it has been consistently spoilt over recent decades by too dedicated an attention to keeping it just-so. Not a stone tile, not a window frame, not a gatepost is out of place, the main street seems almost exclusively devoted to pubs and antique shops, and it is an effort to imagine what it was all like when the village was still a rural labouring community.

Taking off from the Green with its pretty Gothic pavilion at the bottom end, the High Street is a magnificent ensemble of the best in English country building from the Middle Ages down to the various Arts and Crafts offshoots of our own century. Even the banks conform. Several of the seventeenth- and eighteenth-century houses must have started life as farms, though Broad Close, smart late Georgian, was perhaps always a private residence. The street's upper end has more farmhouses, all of them now 'superior conversions' and none the worse for it, epitomizing the wealth of the Vale, of which the side of Fish Hill offers a classic prospect.

By far the most distinguished of Broadway's mansions is the tremendous Jacobean Lygon Arms, a perfect setting for the manor-house-turned-inn of *She Stoops to Conquer*, save that it is the real thing, complete with mullioned and transomed windows and decorated chimneypieces. It puts the old church of St Eadburga, down a side lane, quite into the shade, though this, too, aspires to grandeur, with a Perpendicular tower and chancel windows. Over-polished though its charms may be, Broadway, already Cotswold yet still just in Worcestershire, makes an ideal counterpart to those sections in Fuller's *Worthies* placed at the end of each county and labelled *the Farewell*.

CHAPTER FIVE

The City of Worcester

❧

Once the noblest Georgian townscape in the Midlands, a band of warm brick along the waterside from Diglis weir to Pitchcroft racecourse, a warren of lanes with names like Newdix, Dolday, Tolladine, Birdport and Pope Iron, its skyline superbly punctuated by rococo church towers, Worcester has fallen a notable modern victim to a series of dramatically inept civic developments. The cathedral should be, but isn't, the city's dominant building: pride of place has been yielded to a pair of monstrous, slab-like multi-storey car parks and to the yellow mediocrity of the Further Education College flanking (and effacing) the old Bishop's Palace. Still, Worcester's venerable age guarantees a certain resilience, so that beyond the reinforced concrete and nose-to-tail traffic along merciless ring-roads there is still a great deal to see and to admire.

The Saxons found here a small Roman market town which they called Weogornaceaster, but it was left to the Amazon Aethelflaed, Lady of the Mercians, to wall and ditch it as a fortress and found a minster on the present cathedral site. No less than three energetic Saxon church fathers continued her achievement: Oswald and Dunstan brought the Benedictine rule to the Priory of St Mary, and Wulstan rebuilt the minster entire. In 1067 Prior Ecgwin received Worcester's first Norman lord with an Old English rhyme: 'Hattest thu Urs? Haebbe thu Goddes curs!' – 'Art thou called Urs? Have thou God's curse!'

'Urs' was Urse d'Abitot, riding through the west Midlands alongside exotically named reivers such as Drogo Fitz Ponz and William Goizenboded, to build strong castles against Welsh attack. Prior Ecgwin's rage was justifiable, since Worcester castle (all gone, alas!) was set up on monastic land, cheek by jowl with the cathedral priory. God's curse, however, doesn't seem to have overtaken Urse, whose pattern of firm but fair administration was followed by a succession of barons and bishops, giving to the town, with its glovers and clothiers, a secure prosperity only to be broken by the northward-shifting Industrial Revolution.

Worcester

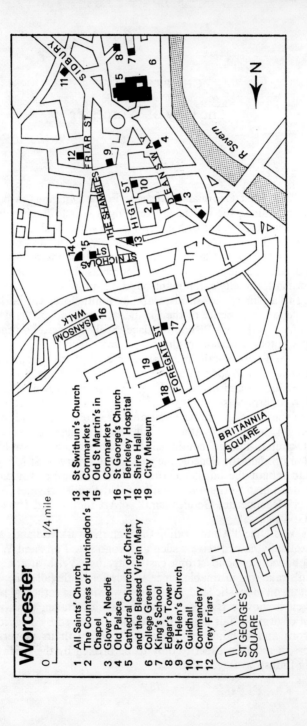

0 _____ 1/4 mile

1 All Saints' Church
2 The Countess of Huntingdon's Chapel
3 Glover's Needle
4 Old Palace
5 Cathedral Church of Christ and the Blessed Virgin Mary
6 College Green
7 King's School
8 Edgar's Tower
9 St Helen's Church
10 Guildhall
11 Commandery
12 Grey Friars

13 St Swithun's Church
14 Cornmarket
15 Old St Martin's in Cornmarket
16 St George's Church
17 Berkeley Hospital
18 Shire Hall
19 City Museum

ST GEORGE'S SQUARE

BRITANNIA SQUARE

R Severn

N

SIDBURY

FRIAR ST

THE SHAMBLES

HIGH ST

DEANS WAY

ST NICHOLAS ST

SANSOM WALK

FOREGATE ST

Royalty, too, favoured Worcester. Stephen and the hapless John kept uneasy Christmas here, Henry II wore his crown in the cathedral, and George III, Queen Charlotte and three of the royal brood patronized the Three Choirs music meeting in 1788. Most memorable visitors were a Tudor in peacetime and a Stuart fighting for his throne. Queen Elizabeth, besides founding the Royal Grammar School on her visit in 1575, fell an uncharacteristic victim to a rather obvious piece of civic dupery. Met at the bridge by the mayor and corporation in full fig, she was escorted along Broad Street to the Cross, where a mature pear tree, apparently groaning with fruit, sprouted from an enormous tub. So taken was the Queen with this, as with the fulsome Latin orations that greeted her from under its branches, that she added the fruit forthwith to the city's coat-of-arms. The pears, need it be said, were wooden ones.

Prince Charles Stuart's arrival in 1651 was at the head of a large host of English and Scots. Worcester, six-gated and 'reasonably wel-waulyd', had watched the Civil War's first skirmish at nearby Powick and had twice sustained siege. Now King Charles I's 'Faithful City' prepared again to withstand Parliament's onslaught. On 3 September, traditionally a lucky day for Cromwell, personally commanding the main force, the armies met on open ground to the south of the cathedral. Beating back the Duke of Hamilton's Scots, the Parliamentarians pressed on into the city, where the narrow streets became choked with corpses as the Royalists offered a desperate resistance. Charles himself, early giving up all for lost, got out of Judge Berkeley's house in the Cornmarket by the back door as Cromwell's soldiers came in by the front, and spurred away towards Kidderminster on the first lap of his unforgettable escape. Though Worcester paid dearly for her loyalty in plunder and indemnities, Charles, generally somewhat remiss in returning favours, was kind enough to grant the city its present motto: '*Civitas In Bello Et Pace Fidelis*'.

Renewed fame was conferred in the following century by Dr John Wall, who was born at Powick in 1708 and died in Bath in 1776. Besides helping Bishop Maddox to found the Royal Infirmary, and promoting the Malvern water cure, Wall was able to develop an interest in the fine arts (he was a talented history painter) by patronizing a small porcelain factory set up at Worcester in 1751. The typical blue-and-white 'Dr Wall' ware and succeeding types produced by the Flight & Barr factory encouraged orders from George III and Queen Charlotte for three complete services on their 1788 visit. Standards have since declined, and though Royal Worcester flourishes, commercial pressure has had perhaps rather a dire influence on design. The works and museum, south of the King's School, are open from Monday to Friday.

As for that other notable Worcester speciality, Messrs Lea & Perrins, in cloak-and-dagger secrecy, maintain production of their sauce in a factory next to Shrub Hill Station, and when the wind is in the right quarter, that world-famous, pungent, nostril-tingling smell wafts heavily across the gardens and allotments on either side of the line.

A tour of Worcester best starts by crossing the Severn over a fine five-arched bridge of 1780 by John Gwynne (architect of Oxford's Magdalen bridge) and following the road up to Deansway and **All Saints' Church** high on its bright banks of tulips and wallflowers. A Worcester church by a Worcester architect: Thomas White (1677–1748) having served as apprentice to Wren himself, returned to his birthplace to design some of the most assured baroque work in the west Midlands. At All Saints, begun in 1739, he and his assistant, Richard Squire, raised a sober classical temple on earlier medieval foundations, and though much of the church's truly Georgian character was swept away by Sir Aston Webb's unfortunate 1888 restoration, we can still appreciate, in the cool sweep of Ionic arcades, White's essential harmonies. The south aisle has one of the city's most enjoyable memorials, to a Worcester merchant named Samuel Matthew, who died in 1676: there he sits, arms folded, his smiling, rubicund face, moustache loyally modelled on Charles II's, the very picture of civic self-consequence, while hugely corpulent putti puff apoplectically over his periwigged pate. Talking of periwigs, notice, by the way, what many visitors often miss – White's tribute to his patron, Bishop Hough, a splendid round-framed bust high in the east pediment, something of a rarity for its period and position.

Across Deansway from the church is one of Worcester's truly atmospheric buildings, now perhaps doomed to the barbaric neglect which has destroyed so many of its neighbours. **The Countess of Huntingdon's Chapel** lies up a little courtyard, flagstoned and colourful with porcelain plant pots, a bizarre preparation for what lies beyond. Through the porch, with its Victorian coloured glass, and into a weirdly exuberant Evangelical interior, which, with its beige box pews, green pillared galleries, and ornate gilt balustrades to a central pulpit, can have changed little since its building in 1804.

Opposite is one of the city's landmarks, the so-called **'Glover's**

Needle' (gloving is still a leading industry here), the 155-foot spire of Saint Andrew's church. This is in fact a ruin, but the extreme purity of the spire's Gothic lines is deceptive, as it was actually the work of an eighteenth-century mason, Nathaniel Wilkinson, who created similar steeples at Ledbury, Ross and Monmouth, designing St Andrew's tapering grace in 1751. Second only to the spire of Salisbury Cathedral in height, the Needle sits uneasily next to the squat, mud-coloured College of Further Education, just as this crowds out its next neighbour, the **Old Palace**.

This is reached through tall gatepiers on the right of Deansway as the road turns up towards the cathedral. If its friable baroque sandstone façade seems a bit austere, this is only because Thomas White was faced with the near-impossible task of clapping it over an extraordinary jumble of rooms added, under Elizabethan and Jacobean bishops, to an essentially medieval foundation. Some of the earlier building, including a fourteenth-century undercroft dubbed 'the Abbot's Kitchen', can occasionally be visited, though most of what was until 1842 the episcopal town house is now a diocesan centre.

Deansway leads us out into the broad square – a sort of English *Piazza del Duomo* – formed by the modern (and for Worcester fairly inoffensive) Giffard Hotel and the cathedral precincts. Church and city here meet rather too abruptly; London-bound traffic puffs and grinds under the buttressed walls, while only a little L-shaped terrace planted with incongruous hollyhocks and gleaming with a predictable rash of solicitorial brass reminds us of the former close.

The **Cathedral Church of Christ and the Blessed Virgin Mary** began as two minsters, dedicated to the Virgin and St Peter and finally amalgamated by St Wulstan in 1084. Beyond the crypt, transepts and chapter-house, little of the Norman structure has survived. In 1175 the new tower collapsed, and fire wasted much of the rest in 1203, the year, ironically, of Wulstan's canonization. Rebuilding started in 1218, under the patronage of Henry III, and the fact that much of what exists is after this date gives the building a notable interior harmony, which a Victorian overhaul by Sir Gilbert Scott and the sensitive cathedral architect, A. E. Perkins, enhanced rather than destroyed.

Entering by the north door, under Bishop Wakefield's Perpendicular **porch** of 1386, we find ourselves in a spacious **nave** – Decorated work, elegant and refined, its north and south arcades divided in time by the advent of the Black Death. The westerly bays in both aisles are perfect late Norman, though rather uncomfortable flankers to John Hardman's over-assertive 1874 **west window**. This part of the cathedral is rich in good monuments: on the north side, Bishop Thornborough (1617–41) lies rocheted and chasubled under a canopy, while opposite him Robert Wilde, the Elizabethan merchant who gave his name to Wilde's Lane in the city, kneels beside his billycock-hatted wife. Best Georgian marmoreal shows in John Bacon jun's Colonel Ellis in the south aisle, falling plump from his horse at Waterloo into angelic arms, and Joseph Nollekens's fine staring bust of Bishop Johnson (1759–74).

Worcester has its fair share of famous dead. **John Gauden**, next to the cloister door, was perhaps author of the royalist bible, *Eikon Basilike*, once attributed to Charles I. Published in 1648, it went through fifty editions in a year, though Gauden was discreet enough not to claim authorship until after the Restoration. **Sir Thomas Lyttleton**, close by, was the first of a talented Worcestershire line. By his death in 1481, he had laid the foundations of the law of real property in England by his *Treatise on Tenures* which, with Sir Edward Coke's accompanying commentary, as *Coke Upon Lyttleton*, proved hard study for generations of budding barristers.

In the **north transept**, sternly Norman in its fashioning, are memorials to two local authoresses. **Martha Sherwood** (1775–1851), daughter of the rector of Stanford-on-Teme, wrote *The Fairchild Family*, a work which nowadays seems too blatantly improving and was probably more popular with parents than with the children at whom it was aimed. After early years in India, where *Little Henry and His Bearer* is set, Mrs Sherwood came back to Worcester to run a boarding school. **Mrs Henry Wood** (1814–87) produced a crop of lively romances, bringing her easy fame, many of her books actually being set in Worcester itself. Her chef d'œuvre is undoubtedly that great tear-jerker, *East Lynne*, distinguished both for featuring the first railway accident in fiction, and for having been turned into a melodrama which, with its imperishable curtain line 'Dead! – and he never called me mother!', held the stage until well into the present century.

The glory of this end of the cathedral is undeniably Louis François Roubiliac's monument to **Dr John Hough**, bishop from 1717 to 1743. Hough was outstanding in an age of ecclesiastical mediocrity. As President of Magdalen College, Oxford, he was involved in a dispute with King James II, who wanted to appoint a distinctly shady Papist as president and was firmly but unsuccessfully resisted by the fellows.

Biding his time, Hough returned in 1688 to his presidency and the see of Oxford, which he held together until his Worcester translation. He was a well-loved figure and stories of his natural goodness are many. My own favourite concerns a nervous curate who, in bowing to his Lordship, dislodged and broke a favourite barometer. Hough's reply was characteristic: 'Do not be uneasy, sir; I have observed this glass almost daily for upwards of seventy years, but I never knew it so low before.' Worcester's gratitude to its pastor, who died at the age of ninety-three, can surely have found no better expression than in Roubiliac's work, as grandly affirmative in marble as his contemporary, Handel's, in music. The bishop, sans wig or mitre, sprawls across a canopied sarcophagus, while the hooded figure of Religion lifts aside an edge of the pall to reveal a bas-relief of Hough's confrontation with King James. Below, a weeping cherub supports a grey medallion of his widow. Everything, drama and spontaneity in the modelling, incredible refinement of detail in the relief, and superb bravura in the composition, go towards making this the cathedral's finest single art work.

After the sobriety of the nave, the church's eastern end is rather more sprightly. The medieval bishops wanted, and got, a **choir** and **choir aisles** in which graceful forms and decorative ingenuity went hand in hand. In the five bays of the choir itself elegant octagonal clusters of sandstone columns are offset by detached shafts of black Purbeck marble, joined to the capitals with brass rings. The agility of design here, as if the cathedral were about to take off into the air, is wittily pointed by the unique double-layered triforium above, and narrow triple-light clerestory windows over all.

Here, where before the Reformation stood the shrines of Saints Oswald and Wulstan on either side of the presbytery, a modern embroidered banner has been placed to commemorate each. It was between these two shrines, as a kind of insurance policy, that **King John**, at the close, in 1216, of an increasingly disastrous reign, had asked to be buried. The tomb has the double distinction of carrying the oldest surviving royal effigy in the country and containing the first medieval king to be buried in England. Twice exhumed, in 1754 and 1797, its Plantagenet corpse was found, both in pose and accoutrements, to bear an almost exact resemblance to the black marble figure above. The body was clothed in a monkish habit, though girt with a sword as directed by the King's will, preserved (unsigned) in the cathedral library.

On the right of Sir Gilbert Scott's gaudy reredos, a royal tomb of far greater splendour holds the remains of **Prince Arthur**, eldest son of Henry VII, who died aged sixteen at Ludlow after a mere few months' marriage to Katharine of Aragon (their proxy wedding took place at Tickenhill outside Bewdley). The funeral procession, with its scores of armed knights and taper-bearing monks, must have been the most magnificent ever seen in the Midlands, and half the senior clergy of England appear to have officiated at the cathedral service. Most spectacular of all was the ceremonial presentation of young Lord Gerrard, dressed in the prince's armour and mounted upon his richly-caparisoned grey charger, to the Abbot of Tewkesbury in the choir, after which, says the chronicler, 'he had a hard heart that wept not'.

Begun in 1504, Prince Arthur's Chantry is a delicate cage of Perpendicular filigree surrounding a plain altar tomb. Though all the figures of saints and kings on the reredos were smashed by pious reformers, there is much to admire in the sculptured panels on the chapel's southern wall, a profusion of deftly-carved scutcheons, flowers, rebuses and heraldic emblems, including both Yorkist and Lancastrian badges and, a touch of the exotic, Katharine's arrows of Aragon and pomegranate of Granada. Paradoxically it was a Bishop of Worcester, Giuliano de Medici, who as Pope Clement VII forbade the divorce between Katharine and Arthur's brother, Henry VIII.

Behind the high altar the **Lady Chapel** has a higgledy-piggledy collection of monuments, including an alabaster horror to Lord Lyttelton, Gladstone's brother-in-law, who ended a full and philoprogenitive life (he had fourteen children) in depressed suicide. Izaak Walton's tablet to his wife commemorates her as 'a model of the primitive piety'. John Hardman's **east window** first figured at the Paris Exhibition of 1862 and nicely complements the Victorian-Gothic decoration of the ceiling vaults, of which Scott was so proud; both features make good examples of the discernment with which nineteenth-century restorers approached their task. Noteworthy also are the **decorated spandrels** of the arcaded aisle walls, forming an unbroken frieze of thirteenth-century panels unrivalled in their imaginative detail. Find those in the south transept, representing two crusaders fighting a lion, an angel weighing a soul with a devil pulling down the scale, Hell mouth, Devils toasting souls, the rising

---

Worcester: 'The Glover's Needle' (St Andrew's Church)
by Nathaniel Wilkinson, 1751

Dead, and an especially eloquent Expulsion from Paradise.

Returning along the south choir aisle and down the steps past Sir Thomas Brock's beetling patriarchal figure of Bishop Henry Philpott (1861-91) we descend through an arched doorway into the **cloister**. In a redder sandstone than the rest of the cathedral, this is early Perpendicular work of 1362, still retaining its original lavabo or monkish washing place, to which water was piped across the river from Henwick; its reading carrels; and one or two excellent bosses, including an extravagant Coronation of the Virgin in the south aisle. The window glass offers a lively reconstruction of the cathedral's history from Aethelflaed to George VI. On the south side the King's School hall occupies the former frater and has the mutilated outlines of a colossal carved Christ in Majesty above the dais. Other monastic remains survive outside to the west (a reredorter) and south-east (part of the guesten hall).

A whitewashed passage takes us out into **College Green**, the best place from which to view John Clyve's dignified central **tower** of 1374. Lack of a close on the north side is amply compensated for by this quadrangle of houses from all periods, forming part of the **King's School** and occupying the site of old Worcester Castle. The school is one of England's oldest, certainly existing in the fourteenth century and refounded by Henry VIII. The stone building on the east side of the Green is the seventeenth-century schoolroom, where old Wirgornians can still recall hitching their ponies to the wall, having ridden them in from the manors and vicarages of the country round. The shapely Georgian building by the gateway is the present Deanery, while the white house opposite was for many years the home of Thomas Tomkins (1572-1656) the first of Worcester's two great composers, until he was forced to leave after it was damaged by Civil War cannon and his cathedral organ smashed by the Puritans.

Out again into the city, under **Edgar's Tower** (not Edgar's, but King John's early thirteenth-century castle gateway) and up the steps on the left, past a tidy little cobbled lane of brick cottages and into the roaring square by the Giffard Hotel. On the left-hand side of the main road, just beyond the Talbot Hotel, is the entrance to Friar Street, which has a recently-opened local history museum (in course of arrangement) and, nearly opposite this, a fifteenth-century half-timbered range of the former Grey Friars. On the High Street front

---

Avoncroft Museum, Bromsgrove: Danzey Green Windmill

of the Giffard itself, a blue plaque marks the site of Elgar's father's music shop. It was as his father's assistant that young Edward Elgar first learned harmony and counterpoint by browsing through the textbook stock. In the evenings after work he would join his father at meetings of the Worcester Glee Club in the Crown in Broad Street, where part-songs and solos were given in a clubbable atmosphere of churchwarden pipes and best ale. In more serious vein he first played in the Worcester Festival in 1878, the *Froissart* overture was his earliest work to be performed here (1890), and after 1902, with the first professional performance of *The Dream of Gerontius* to be conducted by the composer, he became the doyen of succeeding festivals.

St Helen's Church, across the road, where Elgar played the opening voluntary before rushing off to do the same at St George's, now houses the county archives. The most treasured possession here is probably the simple marriage licence granted by the Bishop of Worcester to 'William Shagspere and Anne Hathwey of Stratford 28 Nov. 25 Eliz.'

My favourite Worcester building stands half-way down the High Street on the left. It is curious to think that anything so immodestly gorgeous as Thomas White's baroque **Guildhall** could possibly have been threatened with destruction, but such, during the 1950s, was the case. This is White's tribute to the city which had used him so well (he was to leave all his earnings as municipal architect to Bishop Maddox's newly-founded Royal Infirmary) and the love with which decoration has been lavished on the warm brick façade to make a truly sumptuous splash of trophies and statues (those above the pediment represent Labour, Peace, Justice, Plenty and Chastisement) is evident in every detail. The building, begun in 1721, took four years to complete, and as final evidence of the Faithful City's fidelity, manifested in the niched effigies of Charles I, Charles II and Queen Anne, White could not resist adding a weird mask on the keystone of the central porch – the head of Oliver Cromwell, nailed by the ears!

Parallel with the High Street run Friar Street and the Shambles. Just before we turn into the former from the cathedral end, it is worth going a little way down Sidbury to have a look at the **Commandery**, founded as a hospital by St Wulstan in 1085 and governed by a preceptor on lines presumably similar to those of commanderies' ruled by Knights Hospitallers. The existing building, recently restored, is late medieval, with a fine timbered great hall and ample oriel with elegant little glazed panels. An Elizabethan staircase is matched by murals of the same period in an upper room, illustrating Biblical scenes. Equally significant in a Wigornian context is the guest house of the Franciscan **Grey Friars** in Friar Street. Built in the late fifteenth century, with added Tudor wings, this is of supreme importance as one of the very few timber-framed ranges surviving from an English friary of the Middle Ages. The garden at the back is surely Worcester's most attractive.

A religious riposte to secular self-consequence, **St Swithun's Church** lies on the High Street's right-hand side, down its eponymous lane. White was for once not the architect, though he must certainly have approved the designs submitted by the brother stonemasons, Edward and Thomas Woodward of Chipping Campden. The church dates from 1736 and retains its original fittings complete – black box pews, west gallery, curlicued altar rails, and luxuriantly pompous three-decker pulpit. The Christian symbols on this last, a work of art in its own right, showing the Dove of the Holy Spirit, the Anchor of Faith and the Pelican of Piety, must have somewhat disturbed evangelical susceptibilities. Among early congregations was John Hackett, whose memorial slab records him as *'nicotianistus'* ('tobacconist'), Latin triumphantly proving its adaptability to changing times.

St Swithun's east end, with winged angel heads yoking Ionic columns, fronts the end of the Shambles, and Mealcheapen Street opposite leads down to what is left of the **Cornmarket**. Here the half-timbered town house of the Berkeley family, from which King Charles escaped, still remains, appropriately enough as a corn and seed merchant's, though neither Charles nor Anthony Keck, architect, in 1768, of nearby **Old St Martin's in Cornmarket** would recognize the surrounding dull little huddle of workshops and garages. St Martin's decent brick exterior masks unashamed High Anglicanism, gilded images and Stations of the Cross giving positively Italianate zest to Keck's restrained Tuscan columns and decorated cornices.

Skirting the car park beyond, we reach Sansom Walk, where the present **St George's Roman Catholic Church** boasted Elgar among its organists and an earlier building provided the backdrop for one of Worcester's rare exhibitions of effrontery to visiting royalty. In 1687 King James II, eagerly courting a dwindling popularity, descended on the city during a Midland progress, and having touched for King's Evil in the cathedral, insisted on going to worship at the

Catholic chapel. Surprised that Mayor Shewring and his corporation halted at the threshold, he angrily motioned them inside, to which the mayor brazenly retorted: 'I think we have followed your majesty too far already.' The Guildhall account books bear the significant entry: 'Paid in expenses at ye Green Dragon when Mr Mayor and aldermen waited for his Majesty while he was at mass in ye chapel: 2s.' Seldom can an English king have been so eloquently insulted.

St Nicholas Street leads us back into the main thoroughfares, past Humphrey Hollins's drab, featureless St Nicholas's church of 1730. A few steps further along on the south side of Foregate Street, much-needed relief is offered by the **Berkeley Hospital.** Robert Berkeley, whose family still lives at Spetchley Park on the city's eastern edge, was a diplomat at The Hague, and his 1692 rebuilding of his grandfather's charitable foundation for twelve poor old men owes a good deal to Dutch inspiration. To enter the flagged, tree-lined courtyard, with its two low brick ranges leading to a tall chapel, is like stepping into a Pieter de Hooch genre scene. The hospital is still fully administered and the chapel, with its life-size painted statue of Berkeley in scarlet coat and Steenkirk collar, may be visited (ring custodian's bell by the gate).

Beyond Foregate Street Station the city's northerly reaches take the form of quiet Regency squares and terraces (**Britannia Square,** a harmony of Doric doorways around a thickly hedged garden, and **St George's Square,** closed to the east by an Aston Webb church, are especially good). Here, between the Odeon Cinema and Day and Rose's severely neo-classical **Shire Hall** of 1834, with its alarmingly pugnacious statue of Queen Victoria, is Worcester's **City Museum,** a comprehensive historical display together with an art gallery for seasonal exhibitions by local painters. Certainly the most fascinating of the permanent collections has been formed from trophies and mementoes of the 29th/36th Foot, the Worcestershire Regiment, recently amalgamated with the Sherwood Foresters. The Worcesters, the 'Vein-Openers' or 'Saucy Greens' (from their green facings), were one of the oldest line regiments, raised in 1692 for service against the French. Their military record is a long series of triumphs, stretching from gallantry under Marlborough at Ramillies, and harrying Tippoo Sultan in such gloriously-named spots as Palghautgherry, Sattimung-lum and Nundydoorg, to heroism at Talavera earning Wellington's accolade of 'the best regiment in this army', and the truly brilliant Gheluvelt assault of 1914 which saved Ypres and halted the German advance on the Channel ports.

The amalgamation of the two regiments in 1969 was another in that apparently infinite series of blows aimed at the city's pride by recent decades, whether in stripping it of its ancient buildings and institutions or by making its centre a wilderness of car-parks. I can never contemplate its present begrimed, slovenly, almost shamefaced look without contrasting it with Cobbett's description in *Rural Rides*: 'One of the cleanest and handsomest towns I ever saw: indeed I do not recollect to have seen any one equal to it.'

CHAPTER SIX

Central Worcestershire

❧

More than any other western county, Worcestershire is a clichéd England in microcosm. It has a hilly industrial north, a watery Welsh-looking scarp, a lush southland, and in the middle a glorious roll of hedgy, oak-dotted farmland whose lights and forms are those of an eighteenth-century watercolour painter. Much of this part was once forest – with plenty of big trees still to show for it – and there is more timber-framing here, in manorhouses, churches, cottages or barns, than elsewhere in the county. This, too, is recusant country, ridden over by Gunpowder Plotters and pursuing justices, its houses riddled with priestholes and steeped in grim memories of courage and devotion.

Leaving Worcester by the north-east, on a road running almost parallel with the railway line to Wolverhampton, we reach the first of these recusant nerve-centres at **Hindlip**, which, though its old hall has now gone, preserves associations with Worcestershire's greatest Papist family, the Habingtons. Soon after John Habington, Queen Elizabeth's treasurer of the household, bought Hindlip, his son Edward was hanged for complicity in the Babington Plot. Another son, Thomas, was pardoned by his royal godmother, and his wife, Mary Morley, was said to have written the famous letter, warning of the 'terrible blow' of the Gunpowder Plot, to her grandfather, Lord Monteagle.

The house was fitted up with eleven hides by Nicholas Owen, known as 'Little John', a builder employed by Catholic gentry to make their houses ready for fugitive priests; and it was used as a refuge by the martyr Fathers Garnet and Oldcorne. Finally, having lived off marmalade and broth conveyed to their hiding place through a reed stuck into the wall, they were betrayed to the Privy Council by Humphrey Lyttelton, brought to justice with Oldcorne and hanged with him at Redhill, Worcester, on 7 April 1606. Thomas Habington, pardoned on condition that he stayed within county boundaries, settled down to write his classic survey of Worcestershire. His son William, marrying Lucy Herbert, daughter of Lord

Powis, became part of a cultured recusant coterie in the Caroline court, and in *Castara* produced a collection of elegies and love lyrics which places him among the most thoughtful and discriminating minor poets of his period. Add to this his excellent tragi-comedy, *The Queen of Aragon*, whose well-governed verse veers interestingly towards Shakespeare rather than the fashionable Fletcher, and we have a writer who merits more critical respect. Habington sketched himself in the play as Oniate, the sober country squire who wins the love of the witty lady Cleantha. Buried at Hindlip in 1654, he left the estate to his son, from whom it passed to a branch of the Compton family.

Barely a mile away at **Martin Hussingtree**, we recall an Anglican muse contemporary with Habington's – Thomas Tomkins, the Jacobean organist and composer, whose anthems and keyboard music make a poignant counterpart to his Catholic neighbour's poetry. Like Habington, he died saddened by the triumph of those for whom his art was mere vanity (though he was Oliver Cromwell's favourite composer): the organ on which he had improvised brilliant preludes and fancies in Worcester Cathedral was smashed, and he himself forced to retire here to his son Nathaniel's house at Court Farm, where he wrote his bitter *Sad Pavan for these Distracted Times*. He is buried in the churchyard, and a memorial has recently been placed in the chancel. Across the track from the church is a tall, almost reproachfully elegant Georgian rectory in richest russet brick.

A left turn off the Roman road leads to **Salwarpe**, an eponym of the nearby river, and the end of the little stretch of Droitwich Canal. Salwarpe belonged to the Talbots (see Grafton, ch. 7) who lived at the big black and white court across the canal from the church (some of the beams are mere 'ye olde' painted on brick). Lady of the manor in 1574 was Olave Sharington, on whom Aubrey is irresistible: 'her father not consenting that she should marry him [John Talbot]; discoursing with him one night from the battlements of the Abbey Church, said shee, I will leap downe to you. Her sweet heart replied, he would catch her then; but he did not believe she would have done it. She leap't downe, and the Wind, which was then high, came under her Coates and did something breake the fall. Mr Talbot caught her in his armes, but she struck him dead: she cried out for help, and he was with great difficulty brought to life again. Her father told her that since she had made such a Leap she should e'en marrie him. She was my honoured friend Col. Sharington Talbot's grandmother, and died at her house at Lacock about 1651, being above an hundred years old.'

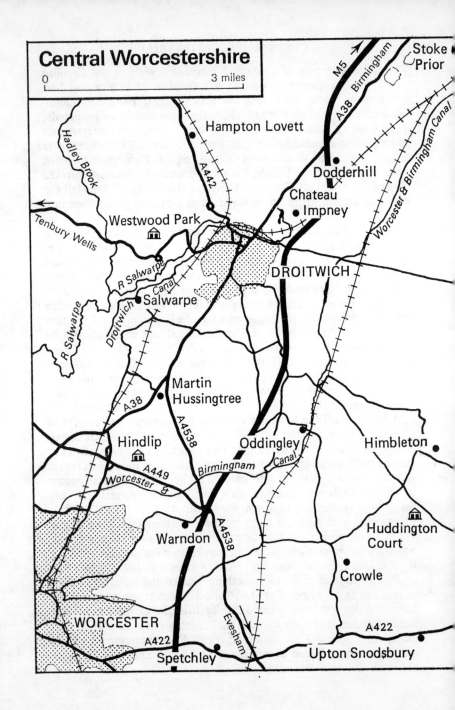

Central Worcestershire

0   3 miles

Hadley Brook

Hampton Lovett

Tenbury Wells

Westwood Park

R Salwarpe

Droitwich Canal

Salwarpe

R Salwarpe

A42

A38

Stoke Prior

M5

A38 Birmingham

Dodderhill

Chateau Impney

Worcester & Birmingham Canal

DROITWICH

Martin Hussingtree

A4538

Hindlip

A38

Worcester &

A449

Birmingham

Oddingley

Canal

Himbleton

Huddington Court

Warndon

A4538

Crowle

WORCESTER

A422

Spetchley

Evesham

A422

Upton Snodsbury

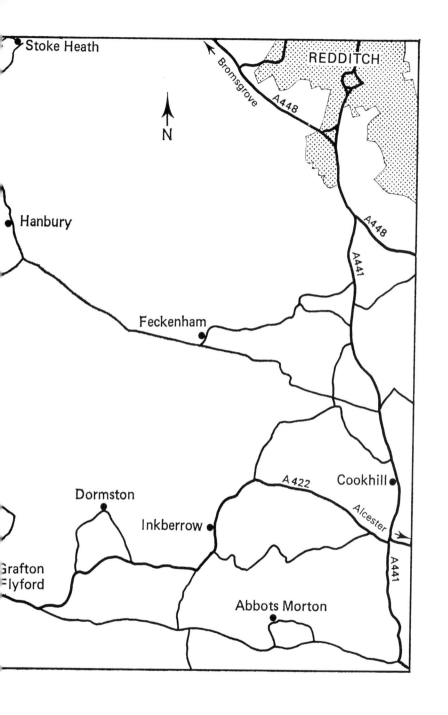

Hence to **Droitwich**, or, if it still pleases, Droitwich Spa. The first name is said to have come from the municipal rights of sac, soc, toll, team, infangtheof and frankpledge, given to the settlements of Upwich, Middlewich and Netherwich by King John in 1215. The town probably grew up over the remains of Roman 'Salinae', and salt was its livelihood until its brine cure, an 1830s cholera specific, turned it into a Victorian resort.

It has, rather exceptionally, two medieval churches: St Andrew's, the old parish church, has a thirteenth-century chancel and tower and an interesting Jacobean font of painted stone. In the nave, a trophy monument to Coningesby Norbury tells us that he was 'Captain of one of His Majesties Ships of War and Envoy from King George the first to the Court of Morocco to redeem the British Slaves'. St Peter's, in the lane of the same name, shows older material in its Norman chancel, with ornamented capitals on the principal arch. The tower is fifteenth-century work, and the clerestory deserves attention for its timber-framed brick nogging – unique, I suppose, in this part of the county. In the south transept windows is some vivid medieval glass, and below this the recumbent figure of George Wylde in his robes as a Serjeant-at-Law. He died in the same year as Shakespeare: his wife was a Huddlestone and his daughter married a Blount, so was he a secret Catholic?

Droitwich's spa days are over, and its brine baths, the largest in Europe, have lately been closed. At its centre is a cluster of old hotels – most notably the four-star Raven – some of whose timbering is genuinely antique, but much simply a rash of ye olde oake fakerie. In High Street and Friar Street a few ancient houses make a walk through the town worthwhile, and gabled St Peter's Manor near the church is a late Jacobean piece which impressed its style on Droitwich's Victorian improvers. It is not easy, however, to work up much enthusiasm for the place, particularly now that an ugly scab of new housing has broken out on its northern edge to make it a motorway overspill for Birmingham.

Edward Winslow, the Pilgrim Father, founder of Massachusetts colony and author of *Good News from New England*, was born in Droitwich in 1595 and baptized in St Peter's. The town also claims a saint, Richard 'of Chichester', commemorated in garish mosaic on the walls of the Church of the Sacred Heart in Worcester Road, an audacious piece of mock-Romanesque. Richard Wych was born here in 1197, the son of a knight. After his father's death, he worked in the family fields, then entered the church, becoming one of Oxford University's early chancellors and bishop of Chichester in the teeth of Henry III's opposition. He died in 1253 and was canonized nine years afterwards. He is best remembered today as the author of the prayer: 'Three things I ask of Thee, o God: that I may know Thee more clearly, Love Thee more dearly, follow Thee more nearly.'

Outside Droitwich is **Westwood Park**, built on lands of a Benedictine nunnery granted to the Pakington family in 1539. The house itself, now divided into flats, is an impressive transformation of a Tudor hunting lodge built by 'lusty' Sir John Pakington, a favourite of Queen Elizabeth, who maternally intervened to stop him taking part in a swimming match. The flanking towers, giving a thrusting sense of height and compactness, are remarkably conservative mid-seventeenth-century work and were formerly matched by four pavilions in the garden wall on each axis. The conical roofs, giving an oddly Baltic appearance, like those on some Danish 'slot', were added this century by Sir Reginald Blomfield.

During the Commonwealth Westwood, under the aegis of the saintly Dorothy Pakington, daughter of Lord Coventry, seems to have been very much like Great Tew as pictured in Clarendon's history, a little Anglican university where the displaced clergy could study and debate undisturbed. Here came all the great Latitudinarians of the next generation, Dr Fell of 'I do not love thee' fame, Dr Morley, later Bishop of Winchester, Hickes, the Anglo-Saxon scholar, the dedication of whose Old English grammar to Sir John Pakington contains an extravagant eulogy of Westwood, and Bishop Gunning of Ely, 'that incomparable hammer of the schismaticks'. All of them are said to have collaborated with Dame Dorothy on that anonymous bestseller, *The Whole Duty of Man*.

The death here in 1660 of Dr Henry Hammond meant the loss not only of the Westwood circle's spiritual guide, but of a man whose wise leadership might have given English Christians a greater sense of unity. He died on the day Parliament voted for the King's restoration, and is buried in **Hampton Lovett** church on the other side of the Kidderminster road. The bewilderment of a lady from whom I asked directions was understandable, since Hampton Lovett (comprising 'the manor of Thickenappletree, held at Domesday by Hugh the Ass') is a parish, not a village. The church is down a gravel track, with its east window looking straight on to the railway line. Basically Norman, with a fourteenth-century south tower, it has a Perpendicular chantry on the north side, used as the Pakington chapel, whose Elizabethan stained glass quarters the arms of Pakington, Baldwin, Arden and Washbourne. This also contains the lounging figure of Sir John Pakington (d. 1727) by Joseph Rose (one of his only two signed pieces – the other is at Reigate, Surrey). In Worcestershire politics Pakingtons played Tory to Whig Lytteltons, and Sir John, a diehard Church and King man, is often supposed, without much foundation, to have been Addison's original Sir Roger de Coverley. Dr Hammond's memorial, a feast of erudition on the south side of the church, is by Joshua Marshall, who did the pedestal of the King Charles statue at Charing Cross. To this inscription, however imposing, I prefer 'Worthies' Fuller's commendation: 'As distillers extract aqua vitae from the dregs of dead beer, so he, from the rotten writings of the Rabbins, drew many observations to the advance of Christianity!'

> Whoe'er has been to Dodderhill
> And down on Droitwich gaz'd,
> Will not, if he has been to Hell,
> Be very much amaz'd.

Dodderhill, watered by brooks called the Body and the Salty, stands on a ridge a little way out of Droitwich, of which its view is not wholly hellish. Its parish church has felt the effects of salt mining below, but Civil War damage was responsible for the rebuilding of the stolid, thickset south tower in 1708. There is no nave, simply a big north transept and a chancel with Decorated Gothic windows.

As children, my brother and I were always taught to consider **Chateau Impney**, on green slopes nearby, the very incarnation of architectural vulgarity. Flamboyantly imitative it certainly is, Second Empire Grand Siècle, built by Richard Spiers in 1869–75 to designs by Tronquois of Paris, reposing among the trees with the calculated poise of a *nouveau-riche* siren on a sofa. Vulgar? Perhaps not. It was made for John Corbett, the Droitwich salt king, and book after book on Worcestershire says that he chose the design to remind his French wife of her native Loire Valley. French fiddlesticks: Mrs Corbett, whom he married in 1856, bore the ever-so-Gallic name of Anna Eliza O'Meara and her childhood rivers were those of County Tipperary.

Corbett's enterprise was phenomenal. Son of a Staffordshire bargee, he worked his way through the Stourbridge ironworks, sold up his father's business and began to develop the saltworkings at **Stoke Prior** in 1828, leaving Droitwich to its water-cure. He lined the brine-pits with cast-iron cylinders to stop the inflow of fresh water, converted the annual output of salt from 26,000 to 200,000 tons, and established London depots as well as building up the model works with gardens, schools, a club room, a dispensary and operatives' cottages. A Victorian guide to Bromsgrove comments: 'The moral influence of these cottages was soon evident in the increased self-respect and thrift of the saltmaker.' Recent demolition has left remains of these works along the eastern side of the canal, though an older settlement lies to the north, in a loop of the Salwarpe on the B4091. Here the fabric of St Michael's church forms an intriguing mélange of Transitional and Early English, best understood from the four substantial stages of the tower, with its recessed spire, on to which a south aisle was joined about thirty years later. Good, too, of its homely kind, is the eight-sided font, hung with angels and saints.

At Stoke Heath, **Avoncroft Museum** is, as far as I know, a unique creation. Laid out amid fields and orchards from 1967 onwards, it is an astonishing display of reconstructed buildings from all over the Midlands, designed as much to show the techniques of their construction as to reflect the domestic and industrial life that went on inside them. We begin with an Elizabethan merchant's house from Shrewsbury, which later became a pub. Then comes the huge thirty-four-foot span of medieval roof timbers salvaged from the Guesten Hall of Worcester Priory. Cholstrey Barn, from Leominster, lovingly re-thatched, shows a technique, in use since the sixteenth century, of walling between the beams with woven pales of split oak. The Georgian granary opposite comes from Temple Broughton, down the road, an oddly modernistic arc perched on round brick pillars.

Most favoured by visitors is Danzey Green windmill from the Forest of Arden. This is a post mill, whose upper storey, poised on a post, can be winched round so that the sails catch the wind. The mechanism, with its gleaming cogs and grindstones of French quartz, is kept in working order, and corn is ground here annually. Opposite, behind the Cholstrey barn, are nail and chainshops, from Bromsgrove and Cradley near Birmingham. These, complete with hammers and bellows-operated furnaces, have been left in an evocative dinginess. Finally the Bromsgrove Merchant's House shows us a fifteenth-century oak frame structure, with hall screens and a timber chimneystack added in Tudor times. As a piece of practical history, the whole scatter of buildings is compulsively absorbing.

The Salt Way, a Roman road east of Droitwich, runs down to meet the Ryknild Street at Alcester. Here the country grows more suddenly hilly, and a consequent loop in the Roman straight at the Vernon Arms inn marks the turn to **Hanbury**. 'A stately seate, meete for a Kinge's pallace', Habington calls it, and the lawyer, Thomas Vernon, county MP 1715–22, seems to have taken his cue here for the building of Hanbury Hall, thirteen bays of stone-dressed brick, with pediment, cupola and decorated volutes to the central window, completed in 1701 by William Rudhall of Henley to designs by William Talman. The hall staircase has a frescoed ceiling and walls by Sir James Thornhill, famous for work at Greenwich and St Paul's, and the painting, baroque at its most expansive and expensive, can be assigned a *terminus post quem* from a uniquely satirical detail in the ceiling group of assembled Olympians – a cherub holds up a portrait of Dr Sacheverell, whose trial took place in 1710, to be torn by the Furies. Scenes on the walls are taken from the life of Achilles, and in the Dining Room, with delicate carved sprays over the chimneypiece, Thornhill added the stories of the Rape of Orithyia and Apollo and Leucothea. Plans are afoot to open more of the house to the public.

Outside to the left, silent garden walks around the Ice House, the Orangery, and a sort of covered tennis court, to a weedy little lake with a vista down the fields. Thomas Vernon has his memorial in the church (locked) on a hilltop north of the house. In wig, square-toed shoes and lawyer's gown, he reclines between Justice (l.) and Learning (r.), below looped-up curtains over an inscribed tablet. The composition (1722) is by Edward Stanton and the partner, Christopher Horsnaile, to whom he left £40. Nearby in the chancel is Roubiliac's strangely awkward-looking Bowater Vernon, with a putto holding a medallion of his wife, Jane Cornwallis. With Chantrey's Thomas Tayler Vernon of 1837, and a pair of kneeling Caroline forbears, the chancel becomes an outstanding display-case of English funereal art. The tower is 1793 Gothic by Thomas Johnson, and the interior fittings – gallery, pews and chandelier – are more or less contemporary.

The Salt Way continues towards **Feckenham**, the village and manor giving a name to the great forest, 184 square miles, spreading up from Worcester Foregate as far as Redditch and Bromsgrove. The presence of this is still apparent from the triangular lie of the main roads around it, the scattered woodland clumps, and the isolated farms in what may once have been forest clearings. Feckenham, what is more, has some notable half-timbering, in the village itself and in outlying houses such as Shurnock Court to the east, with big chimneystacks, and the White House, between Ham Green and Redditch, dating from Charles I's reign.

The manor was a perk of the Queens of England, belonging to famous consorts like Eleanor of Castile, Isabella, Philippa and the last three wives of Henry VIII, before Queen Mary settled it on the Throckmortons. As for the forest, one of whose wardens was

Geoffrey Chaucer, its days as a game preserve (wolves roamed as late as 1280) were numbered by the growth of Droitwich salt workings, involving wholesale felling of young timber for fuel. Disafforestation in 1629 was attended with the usual riots. The more enterprising new tenants tried tobacco planting in fields near the church (the chancel is by Butterfield, 1853) until prohibited by the 1675 act. Forgive the alliteration, but Feckenham was also formerly famous for fishhooks.

South along the A441, nudging the Warwickshire border, we reach **Cookhill**, site of a Cistercian nunnery refounded in 1260 by Isabel, Countess of Warwick. The Prioress and her six nuns always had difficulty in making ends meet, relying continually on diocesan exemptions and perks. Some of the chancel walls were incorporated into the chapel of the Georgian house built on the site by Sir John Fortescue, who had sailed with Anson round the world. This, a pretty meeting between brick, stone and stucco, is clearly visible from the road. A woodshore south of the priory has the strange name of 'Cank', a dialect word meaning 'natter': here the nuns came to chat with local priests and, as one local source suggests, something more besides, judging from babies' skeletons exhumed at Cookhill.

Inkberrow is one of the county's handsomest villages, full of excellent houses in forest timber and dark orange brick. Legend says that fairies called Arkubs tried to stop the village church being moved to its present site, where the circular shape of the churchyard, overlooking a green valley, may indicate pagan religious use transformed by later folk memories.

Neither sleep, neither lie,
For Inkbro's ting-tangs hang so nigh,

sang the Arkubs, but the church got put up, a swaggering Perpendicular job with battlemented north tower and gargoyles on the porch. The Gothic pulpit and the south transept are both Georgian. In the Dormstone chapel is the armoured effigy, a trifle battered, of John Savage of Emley, who bought an estate at Edgiock nearby in 1609. He had three wives, six sons and four daughters, as well as a 'supposed daughter ffrances', some of whom are featured here.

Seventeenth-century Inkberrow boasted characters and incidents that are pure Shakespeare. Besides Edward Pearce, the drunken parish clerk, who pushed the hostess into the alehouse fire and 'went abroad into the fields with two women very suspiciously', there was the Reverend Henry Mugg who, in 1675, married Jenny Reeks, Oxford apothecary's daughter and belle of the city, whose portrait as Queen Dervorgila hangs in Balliol hall. Poor Mugg, trudging between two livings, was a frequent absentee. He left the advowsons to widow Jenny; she was courted by an ex-buccaneer turned parson named Allen, who, having wheedled one of them from her, promptly produced a wife and children from Jamaica. Inkberrow, incidentally, is also said to be 'Ambridge' of the long-running agricultural soap-opera, *The Archers*, and its village pub to be the original Bull.

West of Weethley wood, where Cookhill nuns canked, **Abbots Morton** lies in delicious seclusion, a veritable museum of the timber-framer's art in cottages of all sorts. St Peter's church, on a little rise at a bend in the street, was left unfussed by Victorians, and has the agreeably tousled interior of a real country church. The main road, in returning to Worcester, passes the turn to **Dormston**, a hamlet whose timber church-tower and porch complement Moat Farm, built by John Callow, 1663, who marked his initials on the south gable and added a 700-hole dovecote. This is one house to have kept the bracketed tiles to deflect rainwater, once a more common feature hereabouts.

'John Martin of Worcester he made we 1676' says one of the five bells at **Grafton Flyford**, a place whose woods were held to be the finest foxcover in Worcestershire. The church is mostly W. J. Hopkins's 1875 re-working of medieval material, but the pinnacled and gargoyled tower is intact fourteenth-century, and inside are two Elizabethan paintings on wood of the evangelistic symbols of Mark and John. Their signs, with those of Luke and Matthew, also figure on the fifteenth-century font at **Upton Snodsbury**, where Hopkins was again at work.

Commandery Farm at **Crowle** stands on the site of a grange of Worcester Priory, though it was from Pershore Abbey that the singular lectern in the church is thought to have come. Made of limestone, with the figure of a kneeling man clinging to two vine tendrils, it dates from around 1200 and was put together, after years of neglect, by a Victorian vicar. Crowle also deserves a visit for its big medieval wooden porch, with carved fleurs-de-lys and an Annunciation in the apex of the arch.

Worcestershire's most poignant associations with the Gunpowder Plotters are preserved in the beautiful L-shape of **Huddington Court**, on the banks of the Bow brook between Crowle and Grafton Flyford. In its moat, the black and white house is perhaps a Tudor replacement of an earlier mansion, and was built for the Wyntour family,

---

Redstone Rock Hermitage, Stourport

from whom it passed at the end of the seventeenth century. The Wyntours (their Welsh name means 'white tower' and their crest shows a falcon alighting on a turret) were noted recusants, connected with all the leading Catholic families, and a cousinly loyalty seems to have brought the two eldest brothers, Robert and Thomas, into the 1605 plot. On 6 November the scattering conspirators dined here, and at three o'clock the next morning heard mass, confessed and were absolved before riding north to Hewell and Holbeache. The Wintours' names, scratched on a window pane with a diamond, can still be seen, together with the glum inscription 'Past cark, past care'. With their innocent brother John, for whose reprieve Thomas unavailingly pledged his own life, they were captured and sentenced. Huddington, of course, has its priestholes, one in the loft and one behind a false landing wall, and Robert's ghost is said to walk, carrying its head, while his wife anxiously paces the way up to the door, awaiting his return. The church has a dignified Tudor east window, with a porch and stalls of the same period. There is a good Jacobean screen and some medieval tiles.

Himbleton, too, has its timber porch, to a Norman doorway into a wagon-roofed nave. The chancel has long lancets and some fragments of early glass. In the weatherboarded belfry hangs a John Martin tenor bell, with the Worcestershire-sounding legend, 'All men that heare my rorin sound, Repent beefore you ly in ground.'

Oddingley's church seems almost wholly Victorian, apart from a doorframe in the south transept leading to a former rood-loft, but it is worth looking closely at the glass in the east and north windows. Pevsner gives the former an approximate '1500' dating, but the arms of Mortimer held by a saint in the right-hand light give a better clue, as does St Catherine on the left, sporting the royal arms impaling Neville. We know that Oddingley belonged from 1461 to 1485 to Cicely Neville, Duchess of York, mother of Edward IV and Richard III, so the kneeling figures below, of 'Dns Johnes Haryes' and 'Johannis Yarnold' and their wives, are presumably local Yorkist donors – the same, maybe, as gave the font with its Yorkist roses and fetterlocks.

Netherwood Farm, past the bend in the road where it crosses the canal and railway, was the scene of a grim and sensational double murder. On 24 June 1806 the Reverend George Parker of Oddingley

Great Witley: church ceiling fresco, originally from Canons Park, Middlesex, 1716, by Antonio Bellucci was shot and then clubbed to death. Evidence pointed to a local wheelwright, Richard Heming, as the murderer, put up to the deed by Captain Evans, a farmer incensed by Parker's niggling obsession with tithes. Heming promptly disappeared, and it was only the discovery twenty-four years later of his skeleton in a Netherwood barn which induced Thomas Clewes to make a dramatic confession at the inquest. On the day following the murder, Evans, accompanied by Clewes and a man named Taylor, had gone into the barn where Heming lay hidden, crying: 'Get up, Heming, I have got summat for thee,' and 'as he rose up, Taylor up with a blood-stick and hit him on the head two or three blows.' The hapless rector lies before Oddingley altar: the inscription on Evans's grave at Droitwich marks him discreetly as 'one whose name is connected with the double murders at Oddingley'.

Back to Worcester via **Warndon**, with its timber-framed church tower, probably medieval like the nave and chancel, its box pews and its fifteenth-century east window glass. Or we can rejoin the A 422 and visit **Spetchley**, seat of the Berkeleys, offshoots of the Gloucestershire family, who bought the estate in 1606. The present house, begun in 1811, is by John Tasker, who had worked for another Catholic family, the Welds of Lulworth, Dorset, and whose design, fronted by a huge Ionic portico, gives prominence to the chapel. Berkeleys lie grandly and comfortably in All Saints church, where the entrance under the tower has a wonderful, haunting smell of decaying woodwork, damp plaster and bird droppings. The interior walls are unscraped, and the pulpit is painted bright blue. Robert Berkeley built the Holy Trinity chapel in 1614. His father, Rowland, and mother, Katherine Haywood, have a gorgeous alabaster tomb of 1611, their effigies placed between obelisks on jutting plinths, under a canopy. Robert himself, shown in his furred robes of a Serjeant-at-Law, was one of the judges sent to the Tower for upholding Charles I's ship money claim, but got out on payment of the vast sum of £10,000. The monuments to Robert and Thomas Berkeley, of 1693 and 1694 respectively, have tell-tale details in their exquisite flower sprays, weeping putti, and cartouche of a skull with a torch and hourglass, which suggest Thomas White's hand.

Spetchley has long been noted for its twenty-eight-acre garden merging into open woodland by a lake with grebe, geese and black swans. These are open to the public in spring and summer, and match a superb Alpine garden with the sweep of broad herbaceous borders. Garden enthusiasts will in any case associate Spetchley with pioneer work on polyanthus breeding.

CHAPTER SEVEN

The Industrial North

🍂

North Worcestershire offers the frankest possible contrast to the south and west of the county. Even forgetting the spectre of Brum, with its radiating motorways and stretches of dual carriageway, and its octopus-like suburbs, we have here to acknowledge one of England's oldest continuous industrial traditions, one which has marked the landscape idiosyncratically but has never succeeded in obliterating earlier and simpler patterns of life. Thus the villages lie as islands on the grid of roads, canals, railways and works, and the market towns remain as if perpetually surprised by the encroachment of factories and strings of terraced cottages.

Bewdley, caught napping by the Industrial Revolution, is the best place from which to start a tour along the top of the county, close as it lies to Telford's Shropshire, the Staffordshire of Erasmus Darwin, and the Birmingham of James Watt. But we can take an initial rural breather at **Upper Arley**, lying to the north up in woods above the Severn, and part of Staffordshire until 1895. Here in the 1680s Henry Lyttelton, living in the family dower house of Arley Castle, used to cultivate vines giving light wines 'equal to those of France'. The castle itself passed to the Annesley family, Earls of Mountnorris, whom Lucy, heiress of the 'bad' Lord Lyttelton ('bad' only because, in comparison with his very virtuous father, he was an ordinary Georgian rake), married in 1767. Their son Henry is commemorated by a heartrending inscription in the early-fourteenth-century parish church: 'the circumstances attending his death were most affecting and awful. When bathing in the sea at Blackpool, he was borne away by the violence of the waves. The vital spark was suddenly extinguished, and his relatives were plunged in the deepest distress. His mourning Widow, overwhelmed by the waters of affliction, has erected this tablet as a token of tenderest remembrance and as a tribute to departed worth.' Over the chancel arch is an almost obliterated Doom painting. The battered knight on a tomb-chest, with sword, shield and bascinet, was probably, to judge from his *barry dancetty* arms, Sir Walter de Balun, killed in a tournament

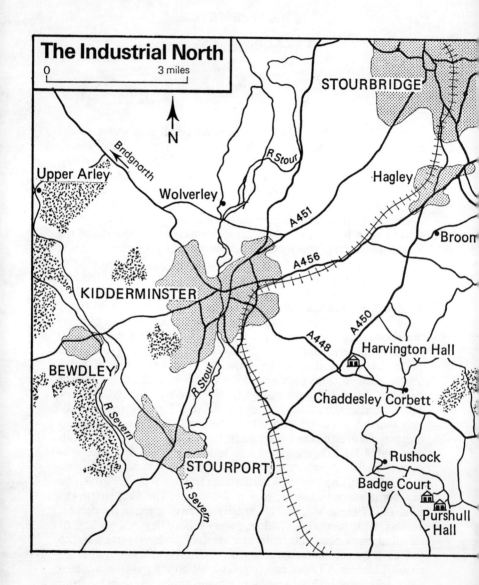

The Industrial North

0   3 miles

N

STOURBRIDGE

Bridgnorth

R Stour

Upper Arley

Hagley

Wolverley

A 451

Broom

A 456

KIDDERMINSTER

A 450

A 448

Harvington Hall

R Stour

BEWDLEY

Chaddesley Corbett

R Severn

Rushock

STOURPORT

Badge Court

R Severn

Purshull
Hall

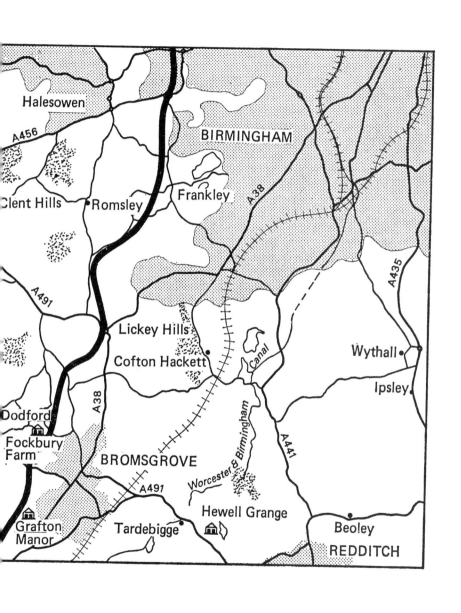

at Southampton in 1270, on the day of his wedding to Iseult Mortimer, who promptly married Sir Hugh de Audley of Much Marcle.

Rejoining the Bridgnorth road and turning right as if towards Kidderminster, we reach **Wolverley**, one of the most arrestingly placed villages in this part of the county, and idiosyncratic almost to a fault. The church, of 1772, has a memorable awkwardness about its red brick shapes, with heavy window arches and thick interior pillars. Inside, among numerous attractive Georgian monuments, is Flaxman's relief of Helen Knight at prayer. The Knights were influential ironmasters from Shropshire (see ch. 20) and their tinplate works were at Cookley near by. They lived at Knight House, the mid-eighteenth-century mansion on the hillside, and their critical interest in art and aesthetics must inevitably have affected Wolverley itself. The imposing Gothic portico of the Sebright School, forming a centrepiece to a complex of cottages and school offices, all built in 1829, is a mature expression of a taste pioneered some fifty years before by Richard Pyne Knight at Downton. Wolverley was the birthplace, in 1706, of John Baskerville, greatest printer of his age and perhaps of any other. Closely connected with the Birmingham scientific movement, he was a committed atheist and had himself buried in his own garden, from whence he was afterwards dug up and re-interred at Cradley.

Kidderminster is an enduring urban chiché for the very worst that has happened to north Worcestershire in the past two centuries, and I find it hard to be enthusiastic about any of it. More dingy than grimy, it lacks soul or centre, and is mercilessly guillotined by new roadways. In the Middle Ages it was a fortified manor, round which a market town grew up at the junction of four main roads by the river Stour, whose mineral-rich waters, excellent for fulling, could be used in the making of linsey-woolsey curtains for fourpost beds. Andrew Yarranton's navigability schemes on the river (see p. 119) increased prosperity, coal first being brought up here in 1665, and in 1749 John Broom, setting up a Brussels carpet loom, began an industrial trend which was to be the town's making.

Clothworking and weaving spell Nonconformism, and the town is dotted with chapels of different persuasions in varying states of repair. For anyone interested in this architectural aspect, these make the most obvious excuse for a walk round the town. Others are offered to industrial archaeologists by the carpet mills beside the river. Richard Baxter was a Nonconformist minister here during the Civil War and his statue stands in the town centre.

Beside the canal are a number of good warehouses – Park Butts, for example, has a tall five-storey building of 1780, now weedgrown and derelict, with a loading platform on top, and a watergate like a Venetian palace. Further up, by the bridge, is the aqueduct carrying the canal across the river.

Immediately above this, on a little hill, is **St Mary's Church**, which, with the street outside it, makes one of Kidderminster's few pre-Industrial ensembles. Most of the fabric is either Victorian or early Tudor, and there is a noteworthy late Perpendicular south-west tower, bearing figures of the Virgin and Saints Peter and Paul. Simon Rice rebuilt the chantry in 1547, which was used as a school, named in the town's 1636 charter as 'the Free Grammar School of Charles, King of England'. Its famous pupils included Edward Bradley, author, as 'Cuthbert Bede', of the popular Oxonian spoof *The Adventures of Mr Verdant Green.*

The church has a superlative array of monuments. In the south aisle is a beautiful composition of crocketed canopies over a recess holding the effigy of Lady Joyce Beauchamp, foundress of the chantry. Of more or less the same period is the brass before the altar showing Sir Walter Cokesey and Sir John Phelip beside their wife, Matilda. The Latin inscription tells us that Sir John, second of her two husbands, was the friend of Henry V, fought well at Harfleur and died on 2 October 1415, Agincourt year. Sir Walter Cokesey's son, Hugh, lies next to his wife under an arch quartering their arms, with angels holding other shields on either side. Lady Cokesey was one of the last of the great old Marcher house of Braose, a name to terrorize the Welsh border in the days of John and Henry III. Husbands and wives at Kidderminster seem to come in pairs, since in the chancel Sir Edward Blount, in best Caroline alabaster, reclines on his elbow like a sultan in the seraglio, with his two spouses, Mary Neville and Mary Wigmore.

Two parting notes on the town. The first apropos Brecknell's Charity: in 1776 John Brecknell left money to provide every child or unmarried person born or living in Church Street with a twopenny plum cake every Midsummer's Eve, with pipes, tobacco and ale for the male householders. Is it still kept up, I wonder? The second is one of several immortal comments by the local antiquary, Noake: 'this town may not inaptly be compared to a bottle, owing to the narrowness of its approaches; and for the same reason it may be likened to the Court of Chancery – when once in, it is with difficulty you can get out again.'

Noake has another lovely remark on **Broome**, the turning to which is just past Churchill and Blakedown, with their yachting lakes and golf courses for leisured Brummies. 'If we ever take to the clerical profession,' says he, 'commend us to Broome . . . No manufactures or public works, no local squire, no mansion, no Dissenters' chapel, no Fenianism or agitation of any sort.' He would probably be correct even now.

Hagley introduces us to one of Worcestershire's great paradoxes. Here, in a sort of *rus in urbe* created by Birmingham's rather half-hearted efforts to avoid muddying her skirts, there took place in the mid-eighteenth century two of the classic English attempts at taming wild nature, George Lyttelton's Hagley Park and William Shenstone's The Leasowes. The two men were quite dissimilar: Lyttelton was an eccentric and erratically brilliant nobleman, Shenstone a quiet, somewhat naïve poet. Lytteltons being the tenacious breed they are, Hagley has survived, despite a disastrous fire in 1925, pretty well intact and still belongs to one of the county's most prolific and distinguished clans. It was built between 1754 and 1760 by Sanderson Miller, in gardens laid out seven years before. The house has affinities with Croome Court, for which Miller may also have been responsible, especially in its feature of corner towers with pyramid roofs, a device presumably suggested by Wilton. The decoration of several of the rooms is noteworthy, including plaster-work by Vassali, that wizard of the genre. He was from a family of virtuoso craftsmen living in Bergamo, and more of his work may be seen in the recently restored menagerie at Horton, Northants. The medallions in the Tapestry Room ceiling are by James 'Athenian' Stuart, who also contributed the Temple of Theseus to the extraordinary assembly of park ornaments. This, a copy of the Theseion at Athens, has the distinction of being the first Greek Revival building ever erected. Other eyecatchers include, to the north on Wychbury Hill, an obelisk, a dilapidated rotunda, and a sham castle which Horace Walpole thought had 'the true rust of the Barons' Wars' – a judgement which says less about it than about him.

East of Hagley lie the **Clent Hills**, Adam's Hill and Walton Hill, over a thousand feet, now a National Trust preserve for good walking among the beech groves but, for some people's tastes, too enthusiastically galloped across by serious-looking equestriennes in cork helmets. Clent parish was one of several to retain the curious custom of 'crabbing the parson'. In this parish the custom of pelting the vicar with apples while still in the pulpit, observed annually on St Kenelm's day (28 July) originated when a clergyman took some dumplings to eat during the service and hid them in his surplice sleeves, whence they rolled on to the head of the clerk below. Having himself brought some crab-apples to munch, he promptly chucked them back at his Reverence.

It was not so in Shenstone's day. Here he set up in rivalry to Lord Lyttelton, who always tried to spite him by leading Hagley ramblers over the hill to whatever spots would show Shenstone's prospects at their silliest. The Leasowes, however, had its admirers. The eighteenth-century man of letters, Robert Dodsley, rounds off a delighted effusion with:

> *No more the swain,*
> *For lo, his Damon o'er the tufted lawn*
> *Advancing, leads him to the social dome.*

The social dome alas! was doomed by the poet's improvidence. Dr Johnson, no friend of his, says coldly: 'His house was mean and he did not improve it; his care was of his grounds . . . In time his expenses brought clamours about him that overpowered the lamb's bleat and the linnet's song; and his groves were haunted by beings very different from fauns and fairies.'

Though it is tempting to trace suggestions of it in the landscape, the Leasowes and its adornments have gone. Poor Shenstone! I choose to think that he was a bit like the shepherd in his *Pastoral Ode*:

> *Griev'd him to lurk the lakes beside,*
> *Where coots in rushy dingles hide,*
> *And moorcocks shun the day,*
> *While caitiff bitterns undismay'd*
> *Remark the swain's familiar shade,*
> *And scorn to quit their prey.*

In his day the Leasowes, in **Halesowen** parish, was part of Shropshire, so the adjective 'Salopian', so flexibly iambic, turns up frequently in poems addressed to him. Halesowen, like many of the surrounding villages, was a centre of nailmaking, a trade which declined during the nineteenth century through competition with better wages in other industries. There were nailshops between here and Bromsgrove since the early thirteenth century, but work was given a boost by the arrival of Huguenot nailers in the 1690s. One of their words, '*brisées*', survived as 'breezes', the broken coal chunks used to heat up the metal. Evangelical and pigeon-fancying in best Black Country tradition, the nailers lived in wretched one-up-one-down hovels, as many as five to a fifteen-by-nine room. Nailmaking itself is best described in a local rhyme:

Yow gets a piece o' wire, yow puts it in the fire,
Yow teks it out, yow gis it a clout,
Yow yods it and yow got a nail.

Keeping the town firmly on our left, we turn off the A456 towards **Romsley** and Frankley, passing the remains, now incorporated in farm buildings, of Halesowen Abbey, founded in 1214 for Premonstratensian canons by Peter de Roche, Bishop of Winchester. Romsley's church has an exceptional Perpendicular tower tacked on to a Norman chancel and nave with a tympanum showing Christ in glory. All the bounce and verve of late medieval art is reflected in the crockets, battlements and buttresses of this slender tower, stuck with gargoyles like sprigs of holly on a Christmas pudding. The church is dedicated to St Kenelm, eight-year-old martyr king of Mercia. In 819, according to chroniclers, his sister, Quendreda, ambitious for the throne, persuaded her lover, Ascobert, to kill Kenelm and bury him on a Clent hillside under a thorn tree. The body was miraculously discovered by the appearance of a dove to the Pope in Rome, bearing a scroll with the words 'In Clent cowpasture, King Kenelm lies headless beneath a thorn tree.' Messengers were forthwith sent to remove the body to Winchester, Quendreda dropped dead, and a spring with miraculous properties bubbled up in the undercroft of the church.

On the other side of the M5 at **Frankley**, once a seat of the Lytteltons, whose house was burnt by Prince Rupert to prevent it from falling to Parliament, is the tiniest of National Trust enclaves, Frankley Beeches, a hilltop clump with fine views towards the encroaching city. South of here, on the A38, is Rubery, and below this lie the **Lickey Hills**, mostly wooded (beech on sandstone again, and conifer plantations) with popular nature trails on the top, promising a sight of foxes and badgers, though what are most generally seen are grey squirrels. The obelisk east of Lickey church is by John Hanson, 1834, to Henry, sixth Earl of Plymouth.

Further east, Cofton Hall, at **Cofton Hackett**, has a medieval core, with one outstanding hammerbeam trussed roof. It belonged to the Joliffe family, one of whom, Thomas, attended King Charles to the scaffold. The parish church, rebuilt in 1861 by Henry Day though retaining its Tudor porch and bellcote, contains Joliffe memorials and an incised slab in the chancel to William Leicester, who died in 1508, and his two wives, Eleanor and Anne. All three are separately canopied, he in armour, his head upon a roebuck-crested tilting helm, the two women swinging pomanders from their girdles.

Almost on the edge of the county, **Wythall's** spectacular tower, ennobling an unremarkable church by Preedy, was designed by W. H. Bidlake in 1908 for the Misses Mynors of Weatheroak Hall in memory of their father. Patterned in alternating stone and black brick, with a corner stair turret, it is closely modelled on similar designs in Normandy. To the south lies **Beoley**, of which Habington says: '. . . the Churche mounted on a hyll in the myddest of a large parcke replenyshed with deere, inryched and grand with timber and woodes, and lastly the mannor attended with tenants wanting nothinge concurringe to greatnes.' The manor belonged to the Sheldons, a Warwickshire family who acquired it in 1544 and lived at Beoley Hall, a late Restoration house (the first was burnt down in the Civil War) to the east of the Ryknild Street just before it joins the A4023. At nearby Bordesley, William Sheldon set up the first English tapestry manufactory, which he had originally started at Barcheston, near Stratford, having sent Richard Hicks to learn Flanders arras-weaving. The firm's speciality seems to have been giant tapestry maps of Midland counties, several of which survive in the Victoria and Albert Museum, fascinating study in their topographical detail for any local historian. The Sheldons were recusant and royalist. Ralph Sheldon, compiler of the first English peerage and friend of seventeenth-century virtuosos like William Dugdale and Elias Ashmole, became a second Habington in antiquarian expertise.

The park above which the church stands is still there, though the deer are gone. Sheldons added the north chapel in the late sixteenth century to a building with a Norman chancel arch and a Perpendicular tower. An earlier Ralph and William, the tapestry king, lie under the arched canopies of elaborate Italianate monuments of Jacobean date. Royalist William, dying in 1659, is the subject of verses with a distinctly professional cadence:

> *Here entomb'd a Sheldon lyes*
> *Whom not envyes selfe denyes*
> *Nor suspicion ere could doubt*
> *Verteous, loyall, wise, devout.*
> *Hee in these oreturning times*
> *Owed his standing to noe crimes;*
> *Some by others falles are knowne*
> *Highe to rise, hee by his owne.*

Ipsley, once in Warwickshire, has associations with the boyhood of Walter Savage Landor, whose mother, Elizabeth Savage, was heiress to the manor. While actually there, he seems to have detested it: 'never was any habitation more thoroughly odious – red soil, mincepie woods and black and greasy needlemakers', though in later years, especially in the poem *Ipsley, when hurried by malignant fate,* he regarded the place with some nostalgia.

The needlemakers came from Redditch, where the industry still flourishes, together with the production of springs. Skirting the town, turn left at the crossroads with the A441, then right, and out into the thick scatter of woods around **Hewell Grange,** a heavy-featured, pseudo-Elizabethan pile by Bodley and Garner, built 1884–91 for Lord Plymouth. The Windsor family, later Earls of Plymouth, had come into Hewell by an exchange of property with Henry VIII. At an earlier house by Thomas Cundy, whose original Repton grounds remain, the Duchess of Kent, Princess Victoria and the inevitable Sir John Conroy visited in 1832. This one, in red sandstone with a colossal entrance hall and a wooden-ceiled chapel by the nowadays somewhat neglected late Victorian designer, Detmar Blow, is now a borstal.

Tardebigge sounds like some form of Chaucerian accoutrement, counterpart to the hamlet of Cakebole on the other side of Bromsgrove. Its appearance, however, is emphatically early industrial. Up-on a hill amid handsome Georgian farmhouses, its church, built in 1777 by Francis Hiorn (the chancel is a later addition by Henry Rowe) has a glorious soaring steeple, round-arched windows and a bright, well-kept interior. Chantrey's mourning Countess of Plymouth holding her dead husband's urn is all very well, but what are we to make of the barely-subdued eroticism implicit in the well-carved Restoration wall monument to Lady Mary Cookes? In a white marble confection of putti and weepers, with a skull for mortality's sake, Sir Thomas, in periwig and lace stock, holds his wife's hand, while she exposes, seemingly for his benefit, a frankly ripe-looking breast.

The old church was cut in two by a former county boundary, with nave in Worcestershire and chancel in Warwickshire, so that poor Habington could not cross into the latter at all, for fear of breaking his parole. In the churchyard lies Walburga, Lady Paget, the faithful 'Wally' of Queen Victoria's letters and lady-in-waiting to the hapless Empress Frederick. Below the sharply falling slope, the Worcester-shire and Birmingham canal runs north through the 580-yard

Tardebigge tunnel, and south to Stoke Prior in a phenomenal series of thirteen locks.

This is owing to the declivity of the plateau on which Birmingham and its suburbs lie. A similar problem had to be faced at **Bromsgrove** with the arrival of the railway in 1840. Brunel, thoroughly baffled, handed in his notice to the Gloucester and Birmingham directors and went to work for the Great Western, so it was Captain Moorsom who designed the one-in-thirty-seven Lickey Incline, rising to 400 feet over two miles. Bromsgrove itself has never been too self-conscious of its charms, but its setting, in a series of dips and ridges, is arresting, and there is a handful of good buildings, including the timber-framed Tudor House of 1572 in the High Street, reminding us that we are in Feckenham Forest. Bromsgrove was always a lively, bustling sort of a place, clanking with nailshops and ironworks. In 1651 Prince Charles, escaping after the Worcester fight, stopped here to have his horse shod and laboriously maligned himself to the Parliamentarian blacksmith. In 1852, when the town tradesmen shut up shop on the day of the Duke of Wellington's funeral, a Quaker named Dell refused, for which the schoolboys scragged him and tossed him in a blanket until he swooned for fright. In the same year, incidentally, a Bromsgrove lady, faced with a strange curate in her parish pulpit, irresistibly remarked: 'He is all very well for maid-servants, shopgirls and children, but to save the souls of the upper classes we must have the Vicar.'

St John the Baptist, the parish church (locked – key at the vicarage) is grand red sandstone Perpendicular, reached by steps up a hillside into a spacious churchyard. Well restored by Scott in 1858, it has all the best period features of crocketing and crenellation, with saints in niches high up the spire. In the shadow of the stolid roof and bold chancel arch, Sir Humphrey Stafford lies next to his wife, Elizabeth Maltravers. He was killed with his brother in 1450, fighting Jack Cade's rebels, whom Shakespeare makes him address, in *Henry VI part ii*, as 'Rebellious hinds, the filth and scum of Kent'. 'They fight: both the Staffords are slain', says a laconic stage direction. Stafford's manor of Grafton passed to the Talbots, and Sir John Talbot (d. 1501) between his two wives, Margaret and Elizabeth, has a meticulously detailed alabaster tomb.

The church roof is said to carry a sheet of lead inscribed: 'This sheet of lead was used as a pan under an ox which was roasted near the Market Hall in this place on the tenth day of June 1814 in commemoration of peace with America.' Down below in the churchyard on the north side are the famous rhyming epitaphs to two young railway engineers killed in 1840 by an exploding boiler, inscriptions too long, alas, to quote here. Various surrounding headstones commemorate former pupils of Bromsgrove school, re-established three times over from the original medieval foundation. Edward VI, or his sinister guardians, simply confiscated its lands and kept up the revenue from other sources, Philip and Mary gave it a charter, and Sir Thomas Cookes of Tardebigge reconstituted it, providing scholarships at his proposed Oxford foundation, later Worcester College. Famous pupils include A. E. Housman, the modern dramatist, David Rudkin, and the stupendously-named Sir Bickham Sweet-Escott, KCMG, High Commissioner of the Western Pacific.

Housman was born at **Fockbury Farm**, Dodford, just off the A448. It is not very difficult to transfer some of the hypothetical 'Shropshire' settings of his poetry to Worcestershire, or to feel that 'the land of lost content' is a good deal broader than what is contained in the boundaries of Salop. **Dodford** itself has an oddly rectangular layout, owing to Feargus O'Connor's Chartist Land Company establishing a settlement here in 1848, similar to that at Corse near Malvern. There are the usual rather pretty gabled bungalows and paddocks laid out on land once belonging to a Premonstratensian priory founded in 1148, one wall of which still stands to the right of the road leading to the church. This, by the way, is a jewel of Arts and Crafts Gothic, dating from 1907, by Arthur Bartlett, and it is impossible to name its counterpart in Worcestershire. Among other features Bartlett brought in an effective rose window and emphatically Art Nouveau glazing.

We are now in recusant country, and west from Bromsgrove, on a web of by-lanes, runs a network of Catholic refuges. **Grafton Manor,** for instance, belonged to the Talbots, and still does. Most of the house is early Tudor, but the Roman Doric porch carries Elizabeth's royal arms below a pedimented window. The Grafton Talbots, though continually fined for recusancy, wisely avoided the Gunpowder Plot. Here in 1660 Charles Talbot, Duke of Shrewsbury, was born, a Whig, a Protestant, and one of the most easily likeable of Augustan politicians, to whom Queen Anne on her deathbed gave the white staff of a chief minister, thereby ensuring Hanoverian succession.

The Talbots also owned **Badge Court**, to the west, which had belonged to the staunchly Catholic Wyntours. In the timber-framed house, with linenfold panels in hall and parlour, the Wyntour arms can be seen in the porch ceiling. Barely a stone's throw away is

Purshull Hall, warm Jacobean brick, with relics of a chapel in the kitchen roof. At **Rushock**, close by, lived Francis Finch, one of precious few loyal supporters remembered at the Restoration by Charles II, who made him Commissioner of Excise. Here in 1679, during Popish Plot fever, Father John Wall was arrested and taken away to trial and ultimate martyrdom in Worcester.

Back on the A 448, **Chaddesley Corbett** apparently takes its name from a royal forester, Corbett. Its village street is among the county's best, domestic Georgian blending with black-and-white cottages of an almost clichéd perfection. The dedication of its church is unique in England: St Cassian of Imola (whose cathedral holds his relics) was a harsh schoolmaster, martyred during the Decian persecutions by being stabbed to death with the styli of his long-suffering pupils. The earliest parts of the building are the heavy Norman nave arcades and the energetically worked late twelfth-century font, generally accepted as a piece of 'Herefordshire School' carving far from its native springs, the bowl carried on four leering dragons with twisting tails. We enter under a west tower modestly rebuilt in the eighteenth century. The Decorated chancel has several good monuments, some very recently refurbished by Clayton & Bell. There is a brass of 1511 to Thomas Forest, ranger of Dunclent Park, part of Feckenham, an unidentified effigy of a cross-legged knight, and a stately memorial in black and white marble to Humphrey Pakington of 1631.

The Catholic branch of the great Worcestershire family of Pakington lived at **Harvington Hall**, a late medieval moated manorhouse refaced with Elizabethan brick, now cared for by the Roman Catholic archdiocese of Birmingham. Perhaps deliberately, the house has not been restored to such a painstaking degree that its intensely-communicated atmosphere is lost. Nowhere else in this part of England imparts so strong a sense of sadness, of muted suffering and spiritual endurance. Sometimes the whole recusant experience of fire and torture, muddled loyalties, fines and penal laws, seems to be summed up here. In its various entrances, its big windows commanding the approaches, and, of course, in its amazing honeycomb of priestholes, the L-shaped mansion has a perpetual air of nervous readiness about it, as if a justice's posse were even now going to sweep in along the drive.

Much of the flooring and raftering of the Pakingtons' Elizabethan house remains as it was, and though the panelling was stripped for removal to Coughton, Warwickshire, in the last century, there is still a section of what must once have been a much larger scheme of

111

mural painting, showing helmeted figures in a distinctly Flemish style. Relics of Father Wall are preserved here, and a part of the library belonging to Charles Dodd, priest at Harvington from 1726 to 1743. Born in Lancashire and educated at Douai, Dodd, whose real name was Hugh Tootel, wrote a *Church History*, printed ostensibly in Brussels, but actually in Wolverhampton and paid for by the Duke of Norfolk.

Harvington's priestholes were mostly installed by Nicholas 'Little John' Owen, already met at Hindlip. Most ingenious of the various hides (which include a false floor in the chapel for stowing plate and vestments) are those behind a fake fireplace in one of the bedrooms and below a hinged tread on the staircase, which lifts to give access to a shaft below. Significantly, no notable arrest ever seems to have taken place at Harvington.

CHAPTER EIGHT

Bewdley to Worcester

❧

In the farthest north-western corner of the county, and spilling over into Staffordshire and Salop, spreads the **Wyre Forest**, whose official limits may once have been the gates of Worcester – 'Wyreceastre'? – itself. The woodlands, slowly eaten into by farmers and squatters, gave life to the local industries of tanning, charcoal-burning and boat-building, and the making of baskets and brushes. With the disappearance of these, the forest has assumed in many places the characteristically dour look given to English woods since the war by the Forestry Commission's dreary plantations of dark, life-extinguishing conifers. Some good deciduous growths remain along the brook which shares its name with **Dowles**, whose old manorhouse, on terraces above the valley, was built of stone and forest timber in about 1560. The gardens here are occasionally open to the public, and four rooms in the house have gaily primitive Elizabethan mural decoration.

Bewdley, between the forest and the Severn, rivals Upton and Pershore as a Georgian beauty among Worcestershire towns, but it was already charming visitors when Leland wrote of it in 1539: 'soe comely, a man cannot wish to see a Towne better. It riseth from Severne banke . . . soe that a man standing upon a Hill trans pontem may discerne almost every house in the towne, and at the rising of the Sunne from East the whole Towne glittereth (being all of newe Building) as it were of gould.' Its prosperity depended upon the 'carrying-trade' of the Severn barges, and the seventeenth century saw it a flourishing centre of cap-making, weaving and the manufacture of saltpetre, as well as a lively market for articles in brass, pewter, horn and leather. It was the son of a prosperous Bewdley tanner who, after education at the local grammar school and Wadham, Oxford, rose as a Whig career clergyman to become Bishop Richard Willis (1664–1734) successively of Gloucester, Salisbury and Winchester.

All this, however, decayed rapidly after the corporation's shortsighted refusal to let Bewdley become the junction of Brindley's

113

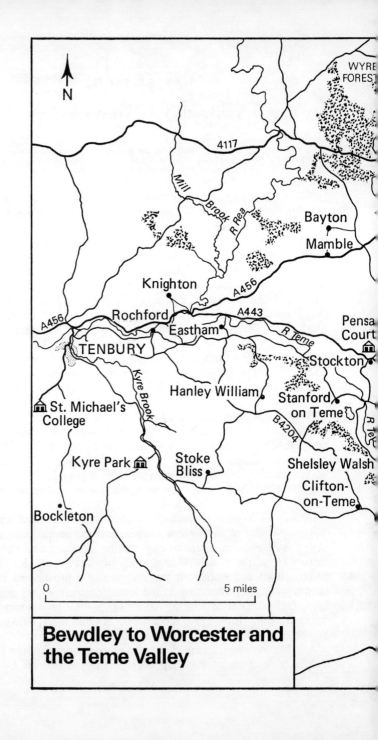

Bewdley to Worcester and the Teme Valley

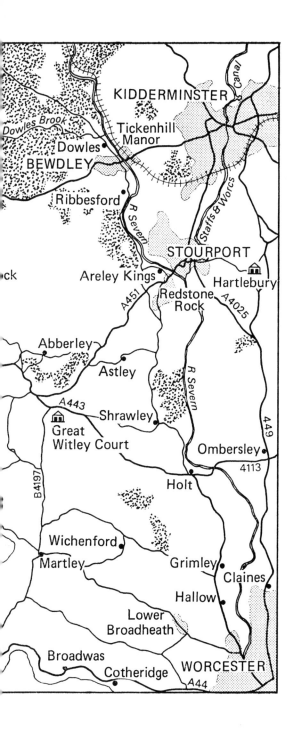

Worcestershire–Staffordshire Canal, though the story that they scoffed at it as 'a stinking ditch', told in every guidebook, is quite unsubstantiated. So the town declined, rather like Pershore turning up its nose at the railway, into a genteel backwater, still keeping many of the pubs and pothouses which had served the twenty-man teams used for bowhauling Severn barges. The western shore had most of these, including the Labour in Vain, the Bug & Blanket and the Sow-Cutter's Arms: Wribbenhall, on the eastern side, having fewer, became known as the Christian shore.

The bridge across the Severn is Telford's design, completed in 1801 (he called it 'no contemptible work for your humble servant') built by a Shrewsbury mason, John Simpson, for £9264. To the left, once into the town, runs a handsome riverside walk of seventeenth- and eighteenth-century houses, recalling those on the Frome at Bridgwater, or beside the Ouse at Wisbech. From the bridge Load Street fans out broadly, amid a medley of good Georgian and local timber-framing (it is nice to see a periwigged George I on an inn sign here) to hold St Anne's church, its tower built in 1695 by Salwey Winnington, MP, and the body of it, with Tuscan columns and round-arched windows, in 1745–8 by Thomas Woodward, who had worked on St Swithun's, Worcester. Load Street also has one of the county's best small museums, with absorbing displays devoted to local crafts such as ropemaking and charcoal burning.

To the east, the High Street's Roman Catholic church of the Holy Family was formerly a Presbyterian chapel, built in 1680 for Henry Oasland, described by Baxter as 'the most lively, fervent, moving preacher in all the county'. Further along, the Methodist Chapel of 1795 replaces one at which Wesley preached in 1774. There is more good Georgian work in Lower Park Street, especially at number 15 on the corner of Lax Lane (*Lax* is a Norse word for salmon) where Stanley Baldwin was born on 3 August 1867. According to the good Worcestershire custom, his nurse carried the newborn child to the top of the house, stood on a chair and held him over her head, so that he would rise high in the world. With three premierships to his credit he seems not to have done too badly.

The top of Load Street may have provided the setting for one of Bewdley's magnificently splashy bursts of civic hospitality when, in 1593, the Bishops of Hereford and Worcester were treated to stirrup-cups of wine and sugar, beer and metheglin. Five years later the bells were rung for Mary Sidney, Countess of Pembroke, who got a sugarloaf, two boxes of comfits and four of marmalade. At Prince Rupert's visit in 1643 a hogshead of claret was broached.

All this may have had to do with the importance of **Tickenhill Manor**, in Park Lane, whose plain brickwork conceals the roof timbers of a late medieval hall. Tickenhill, formerly belonging to the ubiquitous Mortimers, passed to Richard, Duke of York, whose refurbishment of it as a palace kept Bewdley firmly Yorkist in its allegiance, finally conferring borough status in 1472 for good service at Tewkesbury. Henry VII assigned Tickenhill to the Council of the Marches, and here on 19 May 1499 the proxy marriage took place between Prince Arthur and Katharine of Aragon, the Prince holding the hand of Katharine's proctor, Gonzalvez de Puebla, a deed having been read that she had signed. After some early Civil War damage the palace was left to decay until its Georgian rebuilding.

The Herbert family had long connections with the government of the Marches, and Sir Henry Herbert, King Charles I's master of the revels, lived at **Ribbesford** on the road down the right bank of the Severn towards Worcester. He bought the turreted mansion in 1627, though old Sir Edward Blount of Kinlet told him it was 'pleasant for the somer, but not healthfull for the winter'. His efficiency, as censor of Caroline dramatists and supervisor of theatres, was almost obsessive, and he was naturally given his old job back at the Restoration. In one of the turrets of the manorhouse, his grandson, Henry, a feckless ne'er-do-well, hanged himself in 1738.

Herbert's brother was the immortal George, and a local legend has him preaching a sermon in the church while Henry Vaughan reads the lesson and Milton plays the organ. Well, not wholly impossible, I suppose. Herbert probably restored the north porch in 1633, under which a Norman tympanum shows a scene based, apparently, on a real-life incident, when a forest archer, aiming at a stag, transfixed a leaping salmon with his arrow instead. Inside, the south arcade is a remarkable piece of medieval timbering, but the rest was rebuilt in 1877 after the church had been struck by lightning. The west window, by Burne-Jones, made in 1875 by Morris & Co., commemorates his mother-in-law, Hannah Macdonald, who scored a neat double in being grandmother to Rudyard Kipling and Stanley Baldwin.

Stourport is really better explored than described. This unique phenomenon, one of the Industrial Revolution's oldest and prettiest children, grew up through the creation by James Brindley of the Staffordshire and Worcestershire Canal between 1766 and 1771. Bewdley having suicidally rejected the canal outlet, Stourport was soon fashioned in rows of neat cottages round the central basin, with

117

its nowadays rather dilapidated Tontine Inn of 1788 (a Tontine is based on a scheme by the French banker, Henri de Tonti, whereby heirs or investors grow richer as each dies, the last one taking all). The canal is still working today, and barges and narrowboats ply between here and Wolverhampton, along with every sort of pleasure-craft.

Areley Kings, further along the road, has become a transpontine extension of Stourport, though it, too, preserves literary associations. Its church, 1880s undistinguished, by F. Preedy, has a Norman font marked on the base '*Tempore La.amanni santi*'. Layamon, who may have been banished to the nearby hermitage at Redstone Rock from Worcester Priory to curb his vainglory, was a twelfth-century priest at Areley and author of *Brut*, a narrative verse history, in early Middle English, of ancient Britain, based on French sources. A monumental slab in the chancel floor is inscribed: 'Here lieth ye body of Walter Walsh who departed this life 3rd day of November, being aged 83 years, 1702, Son of Michael Walsh of Great Shelsley, who left him a fine estate in Shelsley, Hartlebury and Areley, who was ruinated by 3 Quackers, 2 Lawyers, and a fanatick to help them.'

On the western edge of the churchyard is Areley's major curiosity, the four-foot-six-inch stone block bearing the words: '*Lithologema Quare: Reponitur Sir Harry*' and known as the Coningsby Wall. Sir Harry Coningsby, from a family settled confusingly in Hertfordshire and Herefordshire, retired to brood in a remote farmhouse here after having accidentally dropped his small son Thomas in the moat of his Hertfordshire manorhouse. When he died in 1701 'being very ancient', it was said that he had left a clause in his will asking parish boys to crack walnuts on his tomb on a certain day in the year. Though walnuts certainly grew close by, his will contained no such entry, and the '*lithologema*', unless the final quirk of a grief-crazed parent, remains a mystery.

More positive parochial activities seem to have abounded in Areley, where charitable bequests provided bread and flannel for the poor, for keeping the churchyard tidy and relieving impoverished members of the choir. The living, too, was enhanced by a fine rectory, mingling Georgian and Jacobean, and with the added luxury of a garden house built in 1728 by an incumbent who wrote over the door: '*Ricardi Vernon A.M. a domesticis rebus recessus*'. Not far away from Vernon's retreat from '*domesticis rebus*' is his predecessor Layamon's refuge from '*monasticis rebus*' at Redstone Rock, overlooking the river. Here in the terracotta-coloured bluff is a network of caves, inhabited until the nineteenth century. Writing to Thomas

Cromwell, Bishop Latimer speaks of 'an hermitage in a rock by the Severn, able to lodge 500 men, and as ready for thieves and traitors as true men'. From a hermitage it was later turned into an alehouse and a school.

Minor roads to the right lead westwards to Astley, at whose Jacobean hall Baldwin, as Earl Baldwin of Bewdley, died in 1947. St Peter's church incorporates much Norman work (the sturdy chancel arch is particularly good) and has a pinnacled Perpendicular west tower, and a font of roughly similar date. In the chancel is a fine pair of Elizabethan table tombs, with the traditional heraldry and recumbent effigies. To the south lie Sir Walter Blount with his wife Isabel, his feet resting on a lion, to the north his brother Robert and his wife, both by the Hereford sculptor, John Gildon (or Guldo), made in 1577 and carrying traces of their once garish painting. Look, too, at the pretty memorial to Sarah Winford by John Bacon, 1793, almost an allegory of some Drury Lane tear-jerker by Cumberland or Mrs Inchbald, with its figures of Benevolence with a pelican and Sensibility with flowers.

Outside in the churchyard, yet more of Worcestershire's endless minor writers – one, it often seems, in every village. On the west side lies the Reverend W. H. Havergal, vicar from 1829, recalled in Astley as much for having given the church a north aisle and its excellent clock as for writing widely-used hymn tunes and psalm chants. His daughter Frances (1836–79) was that fatally Victorian figure, the consumptive prodigy, Bible-reading at the age of four, following her father as a church composer, and finally turning away to produce a wealth of religious poetry (at least three 'Hymns Ancient & Modern' are hers) which perfectly captured the popular mood in its vein of not altogether artless simplicity. Her father, a splendid Grantleyesque parson, was a true-blue hang'em-and-flog'em old bigot in his rooted opposition to Catholicism.

He would scarcely have approved of the Anglican foundation created in the stabling of the vanished Glasshampton Manor east of the church. This began as the monastic retreat of William Sirr, a Christian Socialist better known as Father William of the Society of the Divine Compassion, and was taken over in 1947 by the Society of St Francis as a centre for novices.

The name of nearby Yarhampton calls to mind a local man of as much vision and vigour as either Havergal or Fr William, a figure to rank with the county's greatest – the inventor, Andrew Yarranton. Born at Astley in 1616, he was one of those solitary geniuses decades ahead of their time, whose brilliant foreshadowing of later men's ideas evokes a rueful 'If only . . .'. After apprenticeship to a Worcester linendraper and a captaincy in the Parliament army (how the Victorians loved the details of his 'Protestant work ethic' success story) he devoted the rest of his life to technological studies whose boundlessly imaginative variety is unique to its period. In the west Midlands he introduced clover and sainfoin, supplying seed to pioneer landowners, he tried to join Droitwich to Worcester by navigation work on the little river Salwarpe, and did the same on the Stour between Stourbridge and Kidderminster, he went to Saxony to learn the secrets of tinplating, returning to find his scheme for a comparable English industry thwarted by an inept rival obtaining the patent. In 1677 he produced his masterly survey of the industrial state of England, whose title page says everything about its author: *England's Improvement by Sea and Land, to Out-do the Dutch without Fighting, to Pay Debts without Moneys, to set at Work all the Poor of England with the Growth of our own Lands, to prevent unnecessary Suits in law*, etcetera etcetera.

On the south side of the path from the bridge to the river, by the Dick Brook, is the site of one of Yarranton's furnaces, recently excavated to reveal big lumps of slag. The wheelpit and the opening of the leat which powered the wheel with water from the brook are both clearly visible.

'A lanterne of the shyre' Habington called St Mary's, **Shrawley**, a Norman building with a seventeenth-century tower, which retains good roof timbers in the nave, and has kept its gallery, box pews and a set of Rudhall bells. The road joins the A4113 at Holt Heath, where a stretch of river near Telford's elegant single-arched iron bridge of 1828 is popular with yachtsmen. **Holt** itself, though, is no more than a church and fortified manorhouse reached down a dead-end lane left of the A443. The 'castle' (on which see Pevsner's imperishable footnote) is a fifteenth-century hall and solar tacked on to an earlier tower built by John, Lord Beauchamp of Kidderminster, executed for treason in 1388, accused of having encouraged the young Richard II to form a corrupt court. The church opposite provides a worthy Norman counterpart, with its exuberant south porch decoration (I particularly like the man spewing leaves) and the story of the fox and the crane on the north doorway. There is a superb chancel arch of the same period with a massive animal head for its keystone, and the font, too, features wild monster masks around the bowl. Clearly this inspired an anonymous Victorian lady to design a pulpit and lectern in similar style. Was it she who added the mosaic over the chancel arch, and did the rather tasteless repainting of the recumbent medieval lady on the south side? Mercy Bromley, who died in 1704, has a robust baroque memorial flourish on the wall above.

Grimley, to Worcestershire, means gravel pits, but before these were worked it was a manor of the Dean and Chapter of Worcester and its cornfields supplied 'the chief upholding of the Bishop's hospitality'. Once again the church is down a riverside lane. It has a Norman south porch and a fifteenth-century tower and east window. Fragments of old glass at either side of the church show the Annunciation, God blessing, and a saint holding a paten. In the churchyard lies Sir Samuel Baker (1821–93) discoverer of Lake Albert Nyanza and the Murchison Falls. By far the most congenial of East African explorers, with neither Livingstone's evangelical drabness nor Speke's neurotic obsessions, he was the perfect Victorian globetrotter, starting from Ceylon and Mauritius, building a railway from the Danube to the Black Sea, and governing Equatorial Africa for the Khedive Ismail, as well as deer-stalking in Japan and bear-shooting in the Rockies. Lying here in Severn Vale, he must get a little restless. Does anyone in Grimley see his ghost?

Set back to the right of the main road is neo-classical Thorngrove, in faintly Reptonish grounds, where, during exile ordained by his jealous brother, who had tried to stop his marriage to Mme Jouberthon, ex-wife of a Santo Domingo planter, Lucien Bonaparte chose to live. After a spell at Ludlow as guest of Lord Powis, he bought Thorngrove for £9000 from an émigré, M. Lamotte, and settled down to write his twenty-four-book epic *Charlemagne*, 'one of the most pre-eminently tedious and monotonous productions in the shape of an epic poem extant', and a tragedy, *Clotaire*. His wife clearly shared a predilection for Merovingians, and wrote her poems, *Bathilde, reine des Francs*, in pentameters – singularly inappropriate, given that her name was Alexandrine.

At **Hallow**, with one of the most characterful Victorian church spires in the west Midlands (by W. J. Hopkins, 1867–9) we are almost in Worcester, and although Hallow Park is now a dingy council estate, I cannot resist quoting Habington, to whose family it belonged, on Queen Elizabeth's visit there, when a nifty pair of shots from the royal bow felled a brace of buck. Hallow's 'higher ground aboundinge in mynte yeeldeth a sweet savor . . . in so much as Queene Elizabethe hunting theare (whylest the abundance of hartes beatinge the mynt dyd bruse but a naturall perfume) gave it an extraordinary commendation, a deynty situation scarce second to any in England.' Mint still grows here, but the fishponds of this former monks' retreat of Worcester Priory are wooded dingles.

Working northwards out of Worcester on the east bank of the river, we reach **Claines**, one of those suburban villages whose self-possessed Georgian houses in large gardens reflect the spread of well-to-do Worcester in the days of Dr Wall and Bishop Hurd. Its church of St John the Baptist is late Perpendicular with ogee-headed windows and a spiky south chapel. The north porch, 1886–7, by Aston Webb, has Malvern tiles on the floor. Inside, John Porter 'which was a lawyer' lies on a tombchest whose inscription includes the jingling Latin elegiacs:

Omnia transibunt, nos ibitis, ibimus, ibunt
Ignari, gnari, conditione pari.

Smartest of Claines's mansions is Bevere House, on the road down to Bevere Island, whither Wigornians fled from Danes and the plague. Anthony Keck made the graceful design in 1750, and Dr Nash, author of an immensely dull and worthy county history, lived here. 'Bevere' is 'beaver island', as nearby Barbourne is 'beaver stream'. A pity that no one has thought of reintroducing these animals to Worcestershire, where they must have died out before the Norman Conquest. Giraldus Cambrensis reports seeing them on the Teifi in 1188 and quotes Juvenal and Cicero in support of the bizarre story that they bit off their testicles to distract pursuing hounds.

North of Claines we cross the Salwarpe and keep on across the well-watered plain towards **Ombersley**, where Charles II is said to have paused at the King's Arms in his flight from the battle of Worcester. This is commemorated by the royal arms on the ceiling of the northerly ground-floor room, which also shows a mermaid, like the one in the song, 'with a comb and a glass in her hand'. The local great family of Sandys, migrants from Yorkshire, sported the customary Royalist-Parliament divisions. Bishop Sandys had bought Ombersley in 1559, and his second son, Sir Edwin, was one of the charterers of the *Mayflower*. Another son, George, drew up the New England constitution. In 1815 Lord Arthur Hill, a member of the family, was forbidden by his anxious mother to join Wellington's forces departing for the Waterloo campaign. Missing the transports, he nevertheless managed to ride to the coast and persuade a local boatman to row him over the Channel, after which it need hardly be added that he outdid himself in glory on the battlefield.

Sandyses still live at Ombersley Court, glimpsed from the road that skirts its parkland. What we see is a Regency refacing by James Webb (designs by Nash were rejected, presumably as being too expensive) of the original building (1723–6) by Francis Smith of Warwick. Ombersley village, full though it is of the best kind of liquorice-allsort timber-framing, is now perhaps irrevocably wrecked by the A49 bundling heavy lorries through to Kidderminster. St Andrew's church is worth a visit from anyone fond of the work of that Gothic Revival apostle, Thomas Rickman. Built in 1825–9, it has an almost dandified elegance, as though a valet de chambre had been at work brushing up the pinnacles and flying buttresses on the tower, and its interior, in pale blue and white plaster with plain stained glass, gives out a sprightly harmony which the gaslit pedantry of Worcestershire's other nineteenth-century churches seems to lack. On the south side the chancel of the old church, turned into a Sandys mausoleum, contains a bust of Edwin, Lord Sandys, by Nollekens.

The country to the north is some of the dullest in the county – by Worcestershire standards at any rate – and it is a relief to be able to turn off to the left on the A4205 and thence down minor roads to Hartlebury. King Burhred of Mercia gave the manor to Worcester diocese in 850, and the place has been a residence for every bishop since St Oswald, Worcester being nowadays, as far as I know, unique among dioceses in the province of Canterbury in keeping a moated country castle for its 'right reverend father in God'.

Most of the present crenellation is of eighteenth-century date and little survives save the moat of the original defensive works begun by Walter de Cantelupe in 1255. Cantelupe, uncle of St Thomas of Hereford, was a stern, highly-principled, strong-willed politician, whose enduring loyalty to Simon de Montfort (whom he feasted at Kempsey the night before Evesham fight) must have increased his need for an embattled refuge here. Completed by his successor, Giffard, it was visited by Edward I on his way to Wales, though the most strongly-felt royal presence was Queen Elizabeth's, the truly horrendous expenses of whose visit to Bishop Bullingham the diocese spent years trying to recoup.

George III and Queen Charlotte came to Hartlebury on 2 August 1788, and as Bishop Hurd says, 'took several turns on the Terrases, especially the Green Terras in the Chapel Garden. Here they shewed themselves to an immense crowd of people, who flocked in from the neighbourhood, and standing on the rising grounds in the Park, saw and were seen to great advantage. The day being extremely bright, the shew was agreeable and striking. About two o'clock, their Majesties etc. returned to Cheltenham.' Altogether 'their Majesties etc.' seem to have liked it so much that the palace was later earmarked for a royal bolt-hole in case of Napoleonic invasion. Hurd, handsome, talented, charming and successful, was the last of a series of eighteenth-century bishops who, though Worcester was defined as 'a diocese for men of ease and fashion', effectively give the lie to the notion of Georgian Anglicanism as a hive of port-swigging drones. An author in his own right as a critical precursor of the Romantics, he began the first-floor Library here in 1782, to designs by James Smith of Shifnal (his only known work) a dignified case for the books he had amassed from the collections of Pope and Warburton.

No wonder he loved Hartlebury enough to reject the King's offer of Canterbury. Bishop Fleetwood, formerly Provost of King's, Cambridge, and a devoted royalist, began repairing Civil War damage to the palace in the 1670s: his arms are over the porch. Octogenarian Dr Hough filled in part of the moat as a garden: 'old as I am, I cannot forbear, after the winter's confinement, to peep out, as insects do, and see how the little improvements are carried on about me.' Bishop Maddox planted mulberries and cedars and refurbished the chapel. Its fan vault and windows are by Henry Keene, 1726–76, an early Gothicizer, who did the Vandalian tower at Uppark, High Wycombe church, and the Radcliffe Observatory, Oxford. Bishop Johnson, in a burst of activity in 1759, restocked the deerpark, walled the gardens, put in greenhouses, a carriage sweep and new gates on the bowling green, though his most enduring memorial is the fancy rococo saloon on the ground floor.

One wing of the palace is given over to the **Worcestershire County Museum**, an immense collection, staggering in its detail and diversity and more or less resistant to any adequate description. It is enough to say that the rooms contain a series of displays dedicated to practically every aspect of Worcestershire life, from the Black Country industries to rural crafts, farming, fishing and hunting, as well as a large number of exhibits included for their period interest from the Parker collection formerly at Tickenhill.

Hartlebury parish church, like Ombersley's, was rebuilt by Rickman in 1836. The tower is Elizabethan, 1587 for Bishop Sandys, the chancel north chapel of *c.* 1300, and the chancel itself Rickman's own, with very slim columns and a small rose window. A former rector was Dr Kilvert, the funeral of whose widow, Maria, at Worcester makes one of the most striking episodes in her great-nephew's famous diary. Even more famous was Richard Bentley, vicar from 1690 to 1696, and later Master of Trinity, Cambridge, 'improver' of Milton and the greatest of English classicists. He was chaplain to Bishop Stillingfleet, who was much amused by his vanity. One evening at a Hartlebury dinner, a guest sitting next to Bentley turned to the Bishop remarking: 'My lord, that chaplain of yours is certainly a most extraordinary man.' 'Yes,' said Stillingfleet, 'had he but the gift of humility, he would be the most extraordinary man in Europe.' When Bentley was called to Cambridge, the Bishop said that there was surely no better man to keep quiet the unruly fellows, 'for since he has lived in my household he has completely ruled us.'

CHAPTER NINE

The Teme Valley

❦

I caught my first fish – a fat chub – in the Teme and have loved the river ever since. Of all west-Midland waters, Avon not excepted, it has the most continuously lovely course, from its source in the Kerry Hills of Radnorshire to its confluence with the Severn east of Powick. Strange that no poet, barring the inevitable Drayton, has celebrated it – still more odd that eighteenth-century landscape enthusiasts left it untouched, since so many of the prospects to which it forms the centre recall the softened Romanticism of Richard Wilson or Paul Sandby. Aesthetically it provides the perfect articulation between the three English counties it crosses: in Worcestershire it prepares us for the wooded, blossoming surprise of a rolling Herefordian remoteness: in Herefordshire it snakes, glassily sinuous, up across the Shropshire border to wind round Ludlow Castle's craggy feet over scattered rocks already Welsh-looking.

Taking the A44 out of Worcester towards Leominster we pass **Cotheridge**, whose church and court lie down little dead-end lanes close to the river. The whitewashed St Leonard's church, with a timber tower, is solidly Norman, with a single fifteenth-century south window, and a Jacobean or Caroline north chapel. On the chancel floor are a few medieval tiles and the nave retains box pews which agreeably complement a Georgian altar rail and a seventeenth-century pulpit sporting its sounding board which, in 1710, deflected the High Tory tones of none other than Dr Henry Sacheverell.

Sacheverell would doubtless have stayed with the Berkeleys of Cotheridge Court, one of whom, Thomas, dying in Greece in 1669 on his way to Turkey as Charles II's ambassador to Sultan Mehmet, is commemorated by a marble urn in the chancel. His family were relatives of the Spetchley Berkeleys and so, apparently, staunch royalists, but it was against his will that, in 1651, squire Rowland Berkeley rode to Worcester to fight for the king. Both his horses were piebald, and after the battle he dodged suspicious Parliamentarians by stabling his spent mount with a neighbour and showing his pursuers the fresh one. Some of his house can be seen to the right of the church, though its front was tacked on in 1770.

North of Cotheridge, at **Lower Broadheath**, is the Elgar Birthplace cottage, where the composer was born on 2 June 1857. In essence it is no more than the simplest labourer's cottage, of brick, with tiny rooms, a narrow staircase and an orchard garden, and can have been only just adequate to the needs of the Elgar family, who soon afterwards moved to Worcester to live over the music shop. Perhaps more significant than the house itself are the views of the surrounding Worcestershire countryside, with the dim Malvern shapes in the distance, seeming as they do to explain the supple-sinewed, elegiac romanticism of Elgar's music, much of which is preserved here in original manuscript, with an amazing variety of other relics, scores and photographs.

The river loops and folds back and loops again – Teme has none of Severn's monotonous straights – and we are at **Broadwas**, with handsome houses along the road betokening a self-conscious nearness to Worcester. Like Cotheridge's, the tower of St Mary Magdalene, riverside again, is of timber and has at least one ancient bell, of 1346, inscribed '*Iohannis: Prece: Dulce: Sonet: et: Amene*'. Architecturally the building shows an admirable interplay of medieval styles, between the freshness of Early English in the nave windows and the Decorated arches of the south chantry chapel. The Caroline pulpit's curlicued panels are of 1632.

The land soon rises into the beginning of that long ridgeback upland running all the way to the Shropshire border and which, for all its continuing astonishments, quite as many as are offered by the Malverns, has remained just an intriguing jumble of hilltops. Ankerdine Hill marks the range's southern spur: next to it is Berrow, topped by an Iron Age camp, and to the east the straight road leads down to **Martley**, by the Laughern Brook. The big, rust-coloured church, with its trim graveyard, stands on a bank above the lane. Nave, chancel and north porch all date from the twelfth century, but the impressive roof timbers are of two hundred years later. On the north nave wall are traces of fifteenth-century painting: an *Annunciation*, an *Adoration of the Magi*, and *St Martin and the Beggar*. The unnamed knight on the tombchest of the same period is perhaps Sir Hugh Mortimer of Martley and Kyre, sporting, like any good Mortimer, his Yorkist badge of suns and roses.

At the fine old rectory nearby, that most charming of Victorian minor muses, C. S. Calverley, was born in 1831. At Harrow and Cambridge he was a Latinist of indolent brilliance, but an intended legal career was cut short by a skating accident in 1866, which brought about a slow relapse ending in his death eighteen years later. His fame endures alike in the wistful delicacy of serious lyrics and in his vigorous parodies of popular Victorian poets like Jean Ingelow and William Morris. As vicar of Martley, his father was succeeded by the Reverend James Hastings, who died, still in canonical harness, aged a hundred in 1856. Hastings's son, Charles, a leading Worcester GP, founded the British Medical Association in 1832 'with a view to raising the tone of provincial medical practice'.

Rising near Little Witley, the Laughern joins the Fitcher at Kenswick and forms a mesopotamia for the western skirts of Worcester in its parallel course with the Severn before striking the Teme at Powick. We cross it to get to **Wichenford**, whose church (key at vicarage) is worth visiting for a contrasting pair of monuments to Jacobean and Caroline members of the Washbourne family. The two kneeling women are Mary Savage of Elmley and Eleanor Lygon of Madresfield, and the lower figure is their father-in-law, Anthony Washbourne. Pevsner's indignant outburst at the primitive workmanship here is probably answered by the fact that the Washbournes, like several of the smaller county gentry in early seventeenth-century Worcestershire, were falling on evil days. They lived at Wichenford Court, now a decent rectangular Restoration box, but once a fully-moated medieval mansion, in which, it was said, an earlier Lady Washbourne murdered a French prince confined there during Glendower's rebellion in 1402. For this her ghost is held to walk here, wielding a bloody dagger, while that of yet another Washbourne dame paddles about in the moat playing the harp, in a silver boat drawn by white swans. The fine Elizabethan dovecote nearby is managed by the National Trust.

Back on the ridge the B4197 skirts the edge of woodland slopes falling to the meandering river. On our left, beyond the Shelsley Beauchamp turn, the sizeable ramparts of Woodbury Hill were put to good use by Owen Glendower's Franco-Welsh army, which had marched on Worcester and thence veered back to confront Henry IV's troops based at Abberley, but beyond a little desultory skirmishing and several single combats between selected champions in the valley, the two sides never gave each other battle.

We join the main road to Worcester to visit one of the wonders of the county, a work more beautiful in dereliction than perhaps it ever was when inhabited, a ruin whose hulking, rawboned grandeur, frowning at the traveller from the hillside, draws an inevitable 'Ah!'

of surprise – **Great Witley Court.** Witley belonged to the Foley family, who had made their fortune in iron during the Civil War, and lived in high style until the rakehellish second Viscount ran them into irredeemable debt before his death in 1793. Hamstrung by his grandfather's extravagance, the fourth Viscount sold the property to Lord Ware for £900,000 in 1837, and the reign of the Dudleys in Worcestershire began. Or very soon afterwards, for Queen Adelaide, widow of William IV, lived here from 1843 until her death. Enquiring after a piano tuner, she was recommended a young Mr Elgar from the firm of Coventry & Hollier in Dean Street.

The house the Queen knew was a Jacobean mansion with Georgian additions, and some of this is laid bare in the ruins. In the 1860s, however, Samuel Dawkes, who had designed Abberley Hall in 1846, began work on alterations, Italianate in their massive restraint, a soberly elegant spread of Ionic columns and round-headed arches, curving, on the garden side, into a grand pavilion. The gardens themselves were laid out by W. H. Nesfield, landscape painter turned garden architect. To stray across the forlorn parterres and overgrown terraces conveys all the 'ubi sunt?' melancholy of an archaeological site. The twenty-six-foot-high Perseus Fountain, by the way, is the work of James Forsyth, designer of the Wellington Fountain in Bombay.

Though the court was a destined victim of fire on 7 September 1937, the **church of St Michael** next to it was miraculously spared. Visual stunner as this is, it has always seemed to me rather an impostor, since, bar the monuments, none of its furnishings belongs to it, the whole decorative scheme having been bought up lock, stock and barrel by the Foleys from the Duke of Chandos's dismembered estate at Canons Park in 1735, and specially fitted inside the building by James Gibbs. Nevertheless, the rococo interior (at present needing a clean) seldom fails to amaze, as though something from a Bavarian monastery had come precipitately to earth among the unassuming homespun of Teme valley parishes.

The ceiling mouldings in gold and white are copies (using the newly-invented papiermâché process) of the Canons stucco decoration by Pietro Martire Bagutti, and these surround twenty-three ceiling paintings by Antonio Bellucci (1654–1726), a Trevisan who worked in Venice and Vienna before coming to London in 1716, and whose style tellingly mingles shadowy baroque with airy rococo. Handel is, of course, said to have played the organ: he certainly knew the case, since it came from the chapel for which his Chandos

Anthems were written, and the cheerful radiance of the painted glass on either side of the nave, designed by Francesco Sleter and executed by Joshua Price, always reminds me of the lovely duet in his *Il Moderato, As steals the morn upon the night*, with its line about Reason restoring 'intellectual day'. The fittings of the chancel include a disgusting piece of well-meant Victorian mosaic, which nearly destroys the sprightliness of everything else, but yet more repellent is Rysbrack's gigantic monument to the first Lord Foley. Contemporary admonitions about storeyed urns and animated busts were seldom better justified than by this groaning pomp.

Samuel Dawkes's work was similarly successful at **Abberley**, where he built an Italianate hall, with tower and verandah, for Joseph Louis Moillet of Geneva. A little way away, in 1883, J. P. St Aubyn added the huge red campanile, with its twenty-bell carillon playing forty-two tunes, lording it splendidly over the surrounding country – and this, as we move on towards Stockton and Pensax, becomes frankly stupendous, a landscape of hopyards and cherry orchards, whose subtleties challenge anything in Sussex, Devon or the Cotswolds, a place of remote, unyielding beauty.

Stockton's church of St Andrew preserves the Norman work so typical of the area. Some sculpture of the period also survives in the chancel arch, showing a lamb with a cross and a lion, presumably survivors from a set of Evangelistic symbols. An ornate wooden tomb of Thomas Walsh (1593) bears the glum inscription:

> *Such as you are such were we.*
> *But such as we are now such shall you be.*

More immediately appealing is the little brass in the floor of the nave east end, which enjoins us: 'Of your cheryte pray for the sowllis of Wyllyam Parker Sebyll and Elizabeth hys wyfys'.

Tips and abandoned workings hereabouts tell of open-cast coal mining formerly carried on. The top layer of the seam, running between Bayton and Pensax, was a sulphur coal, used in hop-drying and said to give the hops a better flavour, and underneath ran a layer of sweet coal mined for household fuel. At **Pensax Court**, across the road from St James's church (very correct 1832 Gothic, by Thomas Jones) lived the Brocks, later the Clutton-Brocks. The present house is handsome early Victorian, but to the gardens of the old court came Charles James Fox, staying over at Stanford with the Winningtons, to look at the huge ilex tree, some twelve feet in girth.

North of Pensax, **Rock**, once a planted borough of the Mortimers, has a veritable cathedral among Norman churches, and the surface detail of its exterior has survived very well. Opinions differ as to dates and hands involved, though the chancel arch and north porch are apparently by different architects: the first is flamboyant and consequential, the second, with serpentine patterned capitals and ornate abaci, an overpowering statement. The roof, too, fourteenth-century collars and windbraces, is worth craning a neck at, and the Perpendicular west tower and south chapel were built by Judge Humphrey Conyngsby in 1510, as we know from a former inscription on his father's tomb in the chancel. The Conyngsbys lived at moated Bowercourt Farm, to the right off the road to Bliss Gate and Heightington: recalcitrant ex-pupils of Sir Humphrey's free grammar school here no doubt found their way into the stocks and whipping-post outside the churchyard's north wall.

Over Clow's Top, **Bayton** and **Mamble** have the solitariness of the frontier posts they may first have been. The same carver of the Norman font at Rock may have given Bayton its scrolly tub. The Regency tower (1817) once sheltered a barrel organ, which had a dual function at services and dances: one morning, after a Saturday night hop, the sleepy clerk forgot to change the barrel and the startled parishioners heard *The Keel Row* cranked out for a hymn.

Mamble – its lazy-sounding name simply means 'Momela's folk' – gct a poem to itself from John Drinkwater, best Georgian ale-mug whimsy, which ends:

> *So leave the road to Mamble*
> *And take another road*
> *To as good a place as Mamble,*
> *Be it lazy as a toad;*
> *Who travels Worcester county*
> *Takes any place that comes,*
> *When April tosses bounty*
> *To the cherries and the plums.*

The church is a good-looking mixture of Early English stone, timber bell-turret (note the supporting braces) and an Elizabethan brick chapel to the Blount family. The upper Teme is in fact Blount territory (Pope's Martha was the most distant of relatives) and it is worth comparing Thomas Blount's monument (1561) lying near some huge brasses to his grandparents, with the Blount tombs at Kinlet in Shropshire: both feature, vividly gruesome, the stretched-out cadaver, though at Mamble this actually replaces an effigy altogether.

The A456 takes us down to the confluence of Rea and Teme, above which stands **Knighton** (not, incidentally, the Temeside Knighton where Housman's 'lads knew trouble' – that is in Radnorshire). Here the fine fifteenth-century church roof, with its moulded tie-beams, suggests a pun on 'Knight-tun' in the crowned barrels and roses on the reversed shields nailed to the jacklegs. The building is Norman, with that blank arcading over the south doorway found elsewhere in this part of Worcestershire.

Hugging the river and the course of the old Kidderminster branch line, we come down at last into the valley, to the border town of **Tenbury**. Tenbury was made a borough in 1248, though its church and manor belonged to the Norman abbey of Lire. St Mary's church, considerably restored in 1865 by Henry Woodyer, retains a twelfth-century tower and a medieval chancel, whose Easter Sepulchre holds a little cross-legged figure rescued from a rubbish-heap, a knight holding his heart. Joyce Lucy, wife of Shakespeare's Justice Shallow Sir Thomas, put up the rich tomb to her parents, Thomas and Mary Acton, with excellent alabaster effigies, in 1581.

Tenbury's moment came in 1839, when a search for domestic water supplies revealed saline springs, and a possible rival to Malvern and Droitwich was expected. *Inland Watering Places* (1891) describes the waters as 'wonderfully efficacious in cases of scrofula, enlargement of the glands, scurvy, liver complaints, gout, rheumatism, gravel etc.', suggesting a wineglassful three or four times daily. The inimitable Dr Augustus Bozzi Granville says: 'Immediately upon swallowing half a tumbler of the Tenbury water, a disturbance, or rather commotion, is set up in the abdomen, which, upon repetition of the same quantity of the fluid, after a proper interval, will be found, in most cases, to end in a way desirable under such circumstances.' The sole relic of what was never a flourishing spa is the funny hat-shaped thing built as a miniature Kursaal in 1862 in gardens behind the Crow Hotel. Teme Valley denizens can never, in any case, have much needed the waters, longevity in these parts being phenomenal. There was Betty Palmer of Rock, who died aged 113 in 1782, Jane Corkin at Mawley, 126 in 1710, Mrs Perkins of Tenbury, who lived to 105, and old Sarah Davis, 103, who 'had been a spinster all her life, and had a strong aversion to the male sex'.

Were their memories as phenomenal, I wonder, as that of Lizzie the Wombwell circus elephant? On her visit to Tenbury in 1874 she was treated for toothache by the local chemist, Mr Turley. A year later, as he stood in his shop door, watching the menagerie return, he found himself encircled by a grey trunk and gently lifted on to the back of the grateful Lizzie.

It is worth leaving Tenbury by the Leominster road to visit **St Michael's College**, where Woodyer was architect rather than restorer, offering a tall apsidal church of true Puseyite splendour, as adjunct to a college founded in 1856 by Sir Frederick Gore Ouseley to give 'a liberal and classical education to the sons of clergymen and other gentlemen'. The famous musical traditions of St Michael's are supported by a library of 8000 manuscripts, including Handel's conducting score of *Messiah*, early part-books for the Tallis forty-part motet *Spem in Alium* and works by Byrd and Purcell. Ouseley (1825–89) was a child prodigy. At eight years old he composed an opera on Metastasio's *L'Isola Disabitata*, and went on to become Mus.Doc. at Oxford and precentor of Hereford Cathedral. For the last twenty-five years of his life he wrote a daily canon as a contrapuntal exercise, but the frigid classicism of such works as *The Martyrdom of St Polycarp* has left most of his oeuvre to gather dust.

Out of Tenbury we can either follow the quieter road along the southern riverbank, or keep to the hilltops on the B4204. The former leads to **Rochford**, divided into Upper and Lower, with a riverside church. Here the Norman carving is rudely muscular, especially in the Tree of Life motif on the tympanum of the north porch. There is an eighteenth-century organ, and the east window, in cool, limpid colours, is by William Morris. **Eastham** is another riverside village, adding to its building materials of brick and timber the local tufa used in the construction of the church. To the right of the south doorway, with its regulation valley blank arcading, look for the small panels showing Sagittarius and a crouching lion; the nave has a similar pair, of a monster and the Agnus Dei. There is a boldly simple west tower of 1825, with deep-set lancets, starkly Gothic. Inside, an eighteenth-century brass to a dead baby is inscribed: 'The little stranger began to sip the Cup of Life, but, perceiving the bitterness, turned away his head and refused the draught.'

Habington says of the much-contested manorial rights of **Hanley William**, south of Eastham: 'Hanley it sealfe hathe byn tossed in controversies through all the Courtes of Westminster hall, in which cause, as I have often byn a wytness, so shall I neaver be a judge'. Very tactful. After such turmoil the place thankfully settled down to enjoy the same delicious solitude as **Stoke Bliss**, lying in shy retirement up winding lanes, a scattered hamlet less Worcestershire than Herefordshire in character. 'Bliss', prosaically enough, comes from William de Bledis, who held the manor in 1212. The church has a good Perpendicular screen and a pulpit and reading desk of the

1630s, the latter featuring robust little carvings.

On the other side of the Bromyard road is Perry Farm, home of the Pytts family before they moved to **Kyre Park**. Sir Edward Pytts bought the medieval stone hall from the Comptons in 1575 and rebuilt it from 1586 to 1611. His diary, published in 1890, makes extraordinary reading. Every expense is recorded, from charges for quarrying at Kyre and carriage of Shropshire stone from Bewdley (with the modest addition 'and I myself carried 9 tonne') to the payment of handymen called Roo and Lem, 'drunken Reve', 'boy Jack', and the eminently Shakespearean 'Thomas his unthrifty son'. We learn the exact number of bricks, their styles and making, and the cost of 'Tymber Bourde Waynscott and sawynge'.

Designs were submitted by John Bentley, builder of part of Sir Thomas Bodley's library at Oxford, and there were to be two chimneypieces by a Dutch carver whom Sir Edward calls 'Garrett Hollyman', representing Susanna, and Mars and Venus. Round the house, as at Castle Ashby in Northamptonshire, ran carved inscriptions:

> *Well gotten am I sure, so spent I hope,*
> *Lett God have the praise, and Momus a rope,*
> *More foole, but his owne, all follishe dothe deeme.*
> *Man absolute wise was never yett seene,*

and

> *Feare God: lyve well: regarde his lawes,*
> *Be firme: please not popular Dawes.*

Most of this has, alas, disappeared; though the shell remains, with substantial additions made by the Warwick architect, William Hiorn, in 1754, when the grounds (often said to be by Brown) were laid out around a series of lakes. A gabled brick barn and a medieval dovecote survive from Sir Edward's time: the house itself is now a local authority reception centre.

Near St Mary's church, which has a bier of Charles II's time, some smart Georgian woodwork, and an exquisite painting of the Virgin to the right of a south chapel window, Anne Pytts founded Pytts Hospital in 1715, old-fashioned-looking almshouses for eight aged widows. Doubtless the celebrated Teme Valley longevity needed catering for, and Mrs Pytts may well have taken note of the fact that Kyre's last incumbent, Hugo Thomas, having held the living for sixty years, had died in 1693 at the age of 107.

Keeping Iron Age Garmsley camp on our left, we reach **Bockleton**, perched on the very edge of the county. The church has two good monuments, the first a sandstone effigy tomb of 1594 to Richard Barneby and Mary Habington. Barneby wears armour and his lady a fur cloak, while their children kneel by a tombchest sporting caryatids. Above, on the pediment, Father Time and a bubble-blowing boy admonish us of transitory life. The other is Thomas Woolner's white marble figure (1867) of William Wolstenholme Prescott, shown in relief holding the hand of the gamekeeper whom he died tending.

The roads here are, to say the least, vestigial, and it is best to return in the direction of Kyre and Hanley William before striking off to the river and **Stanford on Teme**. This is Winnington territory – they lived at Stanford Court, and of all the valley squires they have held out the best. Stanford church, on the hillside by the road, is, rarely for Worcestershire, eighteenth-century Gothic, grey ashlar with crenellations, 1768–9, by James Rose, and incorporates from an older building the alabaster effigies of Sir Humphrey Salwey and his wife, Joyce, his feet on a lion, hers on two dogs, the whole composition dating from 1493. The tower has late-medieval bells, of about 1450. Mrs Sherwood, authoress of *The Fairchild Family* (see ch. 5) was born at the rectory.

Between Stanford and **Shelsley Walsh** is Southstone Rock, the largest piece of travertine in England, which used to support a hermitage, the remains of whose chapel of St John can still be seen. Until 1600 a 'pedling faire' was held here on the saint's day. The Walshes of Shelsley hung on until the death of Sir Richard, a zealous county sheriff who had helped to round up the Gunpowder Plotters at Holbeach House. His kinsman, Francis, who died in 1596, is commemorated in the church with a wooden tombchest below panels containing shields. The roof has wonderfully stolid timbering, but the best thing here is the finely-wrought fifteenth-century oak parclose screen.

Abberley used also to belong to the Walshes, and it was here, in August 1707, that the young Alexander Pope came on a visit to the last and most famous of the line, the poet William Walsh (1663–1708). Besides representing the county in Parliament, Walsh found time to collaborate with Congreve and Vanbrugh in *Squire Trelooby*, an adaptation of Molière's *Monsieur de Pourceaugnac*, and as correspondent and discerning critic of the young Pope, earned praise in the *Essay on Criticism* and the *Epistle to Dr Arbuthnot*. Dr Johnson, however, had better be given the last word on Walsh's verses: 'He has more elegance than vigour, and seldom rises higher than to be pretty.'

Walshes and Winningtons married into the Jeffreys family, who lived down at Ham Castle (now a farm) on a loop of the river below Shelsley, and Jane Winnington, who married Henry Jeffreys, commissioned monuments for them both from Grinling Gibbons in 1688. Gibbons obliged with the plain tablets now to be seen in St Kenelm's, **Clifton-on-Teme**, which, as its name implies, is impressively high up on a bluff above the stream. The cross-legged knight in the church is said to be Sir Ralph Wisham, who died while walking with a faithful hound, shown on the tomb. Clifton had a brief florescence as a borough, with a weekly market and four-day fair, created in 1270 by Henry III. It also had its own bard: though no Walsh, yet perhaps a local McGonagall, Richard Gardner was a self-educated labourer:

> *I defy any person to say*
> *I had instructions poetical,*
> *Or any learning any way*
> *Or ever taught grammatical.*

His poetry was published in 1825, together with *Bonaparte, a Tragedy in 4 Acts*, rather as a joke, we must assume. He certainly had clear-cut notions on the subject:

> *If I could put a fine polish on my words,*
> *My poetry would far excel the Bard's;*
> *A deal of the Muses I have quite forgot,*
> *I am outshone by one Sir Walter Scott,*
> *Sometimes I come in when it is my turn,*
> *And sometimes beat by Mr Robert Burns;*
> *And when I write with black and white before,*
> *Then I am beat by Mr Poet Moore.*

CHAPTER TEN

The Malvern Country

.ᡐ

The Malvern country is in every respect the most richly rewarding to the traveller. Because it was never intensively cultivated, the landscape today, still with a goodly number of forest trees and an attractive mélange of orchards, dairy pastures and a sprinkling of hopyards spilt over from Herefordshire, possesses tremendous visual allure. Out of Worcester on the A449 and crossing the Teme by a graceful iron bridge of 1837 (the old stone one to the west was the scene of an early Civil War skirmish), we come to **Powick**, a village scattered among woods along a tall bluff. Though the manorhouse has fallen a victim to bungalows, there are some prosperous-looking Georgian houses in stucco and brick, and the village shops have a certain old-fashioned smartness. Remarkable, too, is a big brick and timber house behind high walls, now literally islanded like some immense beached vessel, by the two lanes of the main road curving round it. Powick parish church, as is clear from Norman work in the transepts, is a thirteenth-century rebuilding with Perpendicular additions in the tower and nave arcades. There is one outstanding monument, to Mrs Russell by Thomas Scheemakers, 1786, a neo-classical elegy of downcast eyes, drooping wrists and limp draperies above a relief panel representing the dead woman's fondness for music, with almost a small chamber orchestra of instruments.

Further along to our left, as the Malverns surge grandly into view, is Powick Hospital, a mental asylum at which Elgar used to conduct the inmates' band. Down the hill both left and right turns lead along interesting by-ways. To the south are the precincts of **Stanbrook Abbey**, built in 1878, around an earlier Georgian house, by E. W. Pugin, with a tall candy-striped Italianate tower. This was the final home of the English Benedictine nuns moved from Cambrai after the French Revolution and settled for twenty years at Salford Priors, Warwickshire. Past Callow End village lies **Old Hills**, a romantic stretch of rough common, excellent for winter walks.

North-west of the Worcester road, the turn leads out to Bransford and Leigh. The church at **Bransford** has a timber bell-turret, a

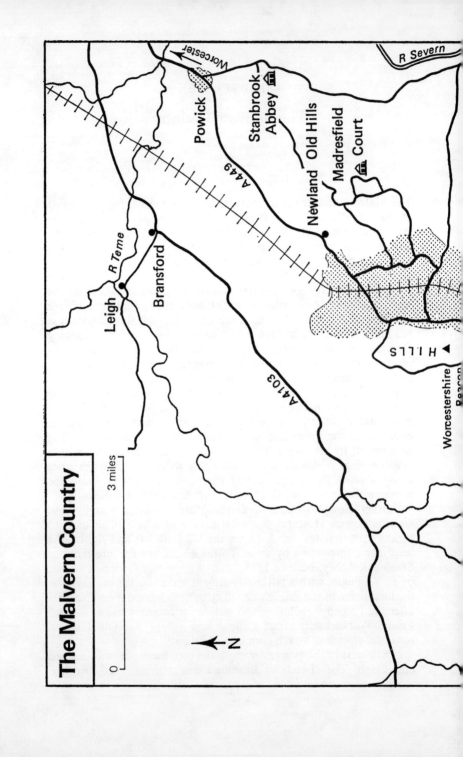

The Malvern Country

0 _____ 3 miles

N

R Severn

Worcester

Powick

Stanbrook Abbey

Newland   Old Hills

Madresfield

Court

A449

R Teme

Leigh

Bransford

A4103

HILLS

Worcestershire

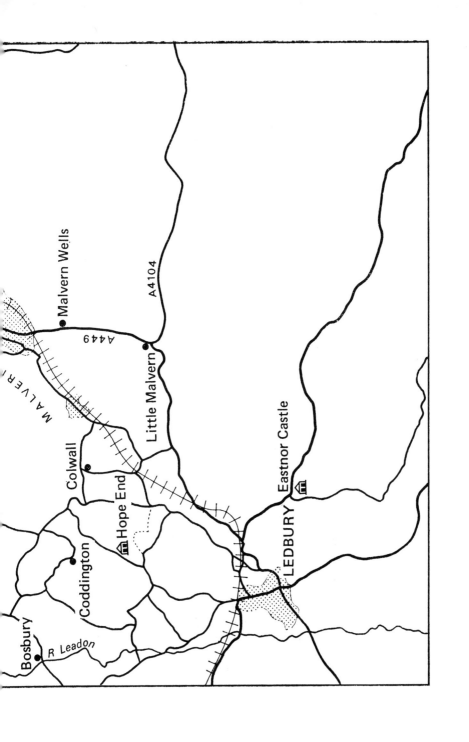

sturdy wagon-roof and a Jacobean communion rail. **Leigh** (pronounced Lye) has what, Morris and Great Coxwell notwithstanding, ought really to be considered a cathedral among English farmbuildings, especially here where there is so much to enjoy in the way of farmhouses and cottages. This is the great medieval barn at Leigh Court, next to the church, the biggest cruck construction in England and, at 150 feet by 34, the longest barn, a nave of huge trusses with crucked wagon porches. We can safely assume that it belongs to the early 1300s.

Dedicated to Pershore's saintly abbess, Eadburh, the big church has a Norman nave and chancel in pinkish sandstone, with later medieval windows here and there, and a Perpendicular screen in the south aisle. Over the north doorway is a superb hollow-eyed standing figure of Christ blessing, taken from an Early English coffin lid. The chancel has a Jacobean monument to Edmund Colles, whose local reputation for crooked dealings survived in the legend of Wicked Old Coles, whose ghost 'drove a coach-and-four at dead of night with *vis insana* over the barn at Leigh Court, thence to cool the fiery nostrils of his steeds in the waters of Teme'. The spirit was finally laid, like those of several other local nightwalkers, by twelve parsons reading their Bibles by an inch of candle. Among Leigh church's various Stuart kneelers and recumbents of the Colles and Devereux families is poor Essex Devereux, who, with George Freke commemorated in the nave, was drowned while crossing the Teme in 1639.

The Worcester road strikes the outskirts of Malvern amid typical stretches of common, survivors of clearings in old Malvern Chase. Just past the Swan Inn are the church and almshouses of **Newland**, built in a style most obviously recalling Keble College, Oxford, by P. C. Hardwick in 1860–4. The whole composition is markedly Frenchified, especially the pitched roof of the gateway, though several later additions have rather blurred Hardwick's original effect. He was also the architect of **Madresfield Court**, entrances to which lie round the corner from the church. Though only the gardens, with their poplar walks and maze, are open to the public, on August Bank Holiday with a rollicking cattle show going on in the adjacent meadows we can still appreciate the stress on surprise and variety in the design, carried out between 1863 and 1885, on medieval and Elizabethan foundations, for the Lygon family, Earls Beauchamp. The chapel is a stunning example of Birmingham Arts & Crafts, with a Morris-influenced triptych by Charles March Gere and murals by Henry Payne. It was a wedding gift, in 1902, from

Lady Lettice Grosvenor to her husband, the seventh Earl. Victorian and Edwardian Lygons were unusually artistic – Lady Mary, for instance, is recalled as a friend of Elgar – so it comes as no surprise to find two park lodges and a dovecote by Norman Shaw, and cottages of 1901 by Voysey. Madresfield, often visited by Evelyn Waugh, is held to be the original of his revisited Brideshead.

In the past twenty years, **Malvern** has changed very much for the worse, yet still has an imperishable singularity. In my childhood it always seemed full of old ladies and schoolgirls: the former have, alas, broken ranks, but the latter remain in force – four girls' boarding schools, the famous Malvern College for boys, and six prep schools. Malvern's newer downward growths across foothills and fields has made settlement layers as clear as tree rings. On the outer edges are careless ribbons of new housing, checked here and there by broad spreads of common. Then come stolid, portly villas built while the water-cure flourished, in brick and knobbly lumps of hill granite, with its pinkish tinge. After an inner layer of big mid-Victorian mansions in every style from Fiesole *villino* to mock-Tudor and Scotch baronial, Malvern's core is reached in the pretty little lodges and cottages *ornées* of the spa's earliest days.

The reason for everything at Malvern lies, ultimately, in the hills, triumphant in their suddenness, commanding such a sweep across all our region as to form its logical pivot. Weather conditions and changing seasons guarantee romance: a snow-covered Worcestershire Beacon can look like a Japanese volcano, mist over the British Camp shrouds the ghosts of Celtic warriors, and a summer bracken fire can make a Vesuvius of the North Hill. On a bright spring day, however, when the coloured clothes and kit of hilltop walkers are clearly seen, you realize that these old, hard pre-Cambrian rocks – hornblende, gabbro, diorite and granite – so old, indeed, as to be fossil-free, are not 'the English Alps' spoken of so admiringly by John Evelyn and Celia Fiennes, riding up their stony passes in the seventeenth century, but a brilliant landscape illusion.

Views, whether towards the Vale and the Cotswolds, down to the Severn estuary, or over the Herefordshire cornfields to the Black Mountain bluffs, are inevitably rewarding. Poets from Auden and Masefield to the rather more pedestrian muse of Southey's friend, Joseph Cottle, have been stirred simply by the experience of standing and looking. Ruskin sketched here, and Elgar, as everyone is nowadays ready to tell you, was inspired to his most heartfelt composition, the *Introduction and Allegro for String Orchestra*, by hearing snatches of Welsh song on the hills.

The southern end of the range is really the more interesting. Wilder and less easily accessible, it provides a stupendously mixed and exhilarating walk. Starting from Wynds Point, a laurel-embowered house once belonging to the diva, Jenny Lind (of whom more later), we cross the main Hereford road to climb the massive concentric earthworks of the British Camp. This was an early Iron-Age fort, strengthened with additional rings in about 50 BC against Belgic tribal invasion, though there is no evidence to suggest that it was ever attacked. Local tradition, eagerly seized on by Elgar and his appalling librettist, Acworth, in their cantata, *Caractacus*, makes it the scene of the old warrior's last stand, which it wasn't.

Keeping to the west of the reservoir, opened by Princess May of Teck, later Queen Mary, we come down over a ridge past the small, man-made Clutters Cave (origins unknown – not Celtic) and along the top of Hangman's Hill. From here we can either descend to Castlemorton Common or go on towards Midsummer Hill, which itself has a prehistoric double-ditched camp, dating probably from the second century BC. The tall obelisk here was erected in 1812 by Lord Somers to commemorate a relative, Major Cocks, killed at the siege of Burgos. As the town fades away behind to the east, and with the woods of Eastnor Park falling into gentle valleys on the Hereford side, the landscape assumes an immoderate beauty. In summer the hillsides are sprinkled with gorse, bracken and harebells, there is the occasional quiver of a grass-snake or an adder among the ferns, hawks tower over the green slopes, and the two most southerly hills, Raggedstone and Chase End, distilling essential solitude, are loud with larks and the bleating of sheep.

Between Midsummer and Raggedstone, clearly visible by the roadside, is a deep trench, all that remains of the great 'Red Earl's Dyke' dug by Gilbert de Clare, Earl of Gloucester, in 1287 after boundary disputes with the Bishops of Worcester and Hereford. This was a ha-ha of sorts, to prevent the deer from his Malvern Chase jumping on to episcopal preserves, and cunningly sited so that the bishops' bucks and does could not, once over, leap back again. The thickly-wooded chase, not disafforested until 1632, may have offered shelter from marauding Danes to Malvern's earliest monastic community, though the story of its foundation by the 'martyr' abbot Werstan of Deerhurst is probably a fifteenth-century taradiddle. The monastery was most likely begun as a small hermit-age during the 1100s.

Finally established in 1085 by Aldwin, a monk of Worcester, and endowed with lands by Urse d'Abitot, it became a dependent priory of Westminster, whose continued strife with Worcester over jurisdiction came to a head in 1282 when Bishop Giffard heard accusations of mismanagement against the prior, including charges of adultery with twenty-two women! After the dispute had become a *cause célèbre*, with appeals to the king, the archbishops and even the Pope, Westminster carried the day. The priory, with buildings scattered over the central Malvern area now occupied by the Abbey Hotel and the Priory Park, stayed in being until 1539 when Richard Whitbourne surrendered it to King Henry VIII's commissioners. Nearly all the conventual buildings were dismantled, and it was only through the good offices of monastic bailiff John Pope that the church, whose cloisters and Lady Chapel had already gone, was saved by a parochial contribution of £20.

What Pope saved, as **Malvern Priory Church**, is externally an outstanding Perpendicular piece, with characteristic open battlements above the nave, very big end windows, and a thrusting central tower with square pinnacles, panelling and tall ogival bell-openings. Inside, the six-bay Norman nave belongs to *c*. 1120, though the chancel is of the same period as its exterior case. Victorian and later restorations have been careful, and the result is an agreeably bright, broad interior, full of good vantage points for admiring the Priory's superb remnants of late medieval glass. Two of the windows, in the north transept and the chancel east lights, are sadly scrambled. The former, given in 1501 by Henry VII after a visit the previous year, shows the eleven joys of Mary, surrounded by saints and angels, with members of the royal family below, rich blues and yellows predominating. The east window, once no doubt easily comparable with York Minster, has a layer of benefactors and a gallimaufry of scenes and figures, some of them from Christ's Passion, but now defying reassembly. The west window, dated between 1461 and 1483, has the finest range of colours as well as the boldest figures, saints and bishops beside three different representations of the Virgin. In the chancel clerestories are scenes (north side) from the life of the Virgin and the legend of St Werstan, and (south side) a group of saints and angels.

Behind the high altar, above its flanking rows of twelve misericord stalls, runs an ambulatory, with part of the screen wall tiled in a way utterly reminiscent of Islamic Spain and Portugal. This is the only medieval glazed tile walling in England, and we know that these brown and yellow squares (in nearly a hundred patterns here) were the priory's special manufacture. We also know that Malvern's Prior Walcher of Lorraine introduced Arabic numerals into England through his translation of a Moorish astronomical work. He may have returned from one of his Spanish journeys with more than manuscripts. A conjecture, but a fascinating one.

The Priory, and its surviving gateway by the Abbey Hotel, are older by three centuries than anything else in Malvern, whose history really begins again, and in earnest, with the famous water cure.

> Malvern water, said Doctor Wall,
> Is famed for containing nothing at all.

We have already met Dr Wall at Worcester, and although the pure H_2O, later bottled by Schweppes and drunk by the highest in the land, had been scooped up in handfuls and cupfuls from hillside springs since the Middle Ages, it was the doctor who gave Malvern its opening boost with his *Experiments and Observations on the Malvern Waters* in 1757.

Like all spas, the town grew fastest in post-Napoleonic decades. In the long twilight of Romanticism, its natural beauty of setting was a real advantage. The hills reminded restless Fanny Kemble of the Alban hills overlooking the Roman Campagna, and Tennyson, visiting Cintra in Portugal, one of Europe's most enchanting spots, deemed it 'merely a sort of Cockney Malvern'. The air, too, was enough to knock any invalid back into shape: the formidable Benjamin Jowett, finishing his version of Thucydides here in 1875, said that the breeze had 'the property of Falstaff's sherris sack'. Royalty gave the odd fillip when the Duchess of Kent and Princess Victoria stayed at Holly Mount on the Worcester Road, and Queen Adelaide trotted about the hill paths on a donkey named Moses.

Most of the nineteenth-century notables came here for health, relaxation or amusement, though Malvern was always quietly respectable. Wordsworth, Darwin and Florence Nightingale all took the cure, Balfour, Baldwin and Campbell-Bannerman shook off cares of state in West Malvern, Henry James sought relief from constipation, Dickens made Malvern the scene of a one-act farce, and Trollope created a piquant contrast between Griselda Grantley's honeymoon in Rome with Lord Dumbello and Olivia Proudie's rather humbler wedding trip to Malvern with Mr Tinkler. Jane Welsh Carlyle, however, was unimpressed: 'beautiful Nature, which

---

The Malvern hills from the western (Herefordshire) side
Stoke Bliss: carved panel on the church reading desk, *c.* 1630

you look out upon from pea-green arbours, which you dawdle about in on the backs of donkeys, and where you are haunted with an everlasting smell of roast meat – all that I do declare to be the greatest of bores.'

The cure was based on successful attempts by two doctors to promote the hydropathic treatment popularized by Vincenz Priessnitz at Graefenburg in Silesia. James Wilson and James Gully became partners here in 1842, initiating their treatment centres with spectacular cures. Gully was later to set up independently, and to be professionally compromised in the notorious murder case involving the suspected poisoning by his mistress, Florence Ricardo, of her husband, Charles Bravo. Malvern patients, on a very strict regime of diets and early bed, were brought back to health through the shock to the jaded system created by cold water douches, wet packs, hill walking and copious draughts from the Malvern spring.

Malvern is really a cluster of forest villages, and Malvernians still use their names, 'Barnards Green', 'West Malvern' or 'Lower Howsell' familiarly. Most of the water-cure installations have gone, but a walk through the centre of the town is rewarding. We can start high up at **St Anne's Well**, most obvious and, indeed, almost sole relic of early spa days. Like so many English springs dedicated to Anne or Agnes, it is named from Anu, a Celtic water goddess, but mortal bounty gave it its dolphin-head basin, the gift of Emily, Viscountess Foley, Victorian Malvern's lady of the manor. In her yellow carriage drawn by matched greys, she was an uncrowned though by no means unacknowledged doyenne, and her impress on the town, as imaginative as it was firm, is still clearly sensed.

The well-house remains, though the German band and the donkeys have gone. On the drive at the foot of the hill we can either turn left past the Italianate belvedere of Aldwin Tower and down among the pretty cottages of Red Lion Bank to the Unicorn, Malvern's old posting inn, or right past Bello Sguardo (1836 – no prizes for spotting the inspiration) and down the ninety-nine steps on to **Bellevue Terrace**. Notice, beside the Priory Gateway, the handsome late Regency Gothic butcher's shop. The terrace itself still has a certain rather vulgarized grandeur, stretching from the Mount Pleasant hotel (1817) to the eye-catching bow front of Barclay's Bank, originally the Royal Library, begun by the local architect, John Deykes, in 1819. His father, Samuel, had built the

Deerhurst church: a view towards the Saxon west end

Foley Arms Hotel, the town's best Regency piece, a little to the north in Worcester Road, and was to supervise the creation of a Pump Room and Baths in the buildings next door to the Library, reflecting a late Greek Revival style seen also in several of his son's larger villas further up the road.

At the foot of Church Street (on the right, below the Priory, Cecilia Hall, behind a former music shop, preserves the Victorian concert room where Jenny Lind gave her last recital) Grange Road has the **Malvern Festival Theatre**, scene of the drama festival which enlivened the town between the wars. Its guiding spirit was Barry Jackson, who intended Malvern as 'an English Bayreuth of the drama' and its fame was ensured with several late Shaw premières, including *The Apple Cart*, with Cedric Hardwicke and Edith Evans.

Graham Road, in the other direction, is the essential Malvern experience, a beautifully complete statement of Victorian town planning. Lady Foley was once again the guiding spirit: every house was to be in a different style, garden plots were to be at least an acre broad and planted with suitable trees. Though most of the finer growths have now gone, the ample mid-nineteenth-century houses remain, creating, behind their trim hedges, an effect of pre-eminently dignified repose.

Finally, for train travellers, the surprise of Great Malvern **railway station**, designed by E. W. Elmslie, with a connecting tunnel to the Frenchified magnificence of the Imperial Hotel (now Malvern Girls' College) and adorned on its cast-iron columns with sprays of flowers and foliage. The waiting room on the up-platform was specially built for Lady Foley, who refused to travel through the Colwall tunnel and came to Malvern by carriage from Stoke Edith to begin her Paddington journeys. North-east of the station, behind Christ Church, Wilton Road cemetery contains (east side) the **grave of Jenny Lind**, a modest enough memorial to one of the greatest sopranos of her day. 'She was a woman who would have been adored if she had had the voice of a crow,' said her sardonic American promoter, P. T. Barnum, as the dollars kept on coming and the police had to turn firehoses on the crowd who watched her land at New York. A favourite with the Queen and Prince Albert, adored by the aged Wellington, she was a fine Norma and Amina, and created the roles of Vielka in Meyerbeer's *L'Étoile du Nord* and Amalia in Verdi's *I Masnadieri*.

Malvern's other musical memorial is reached along Wells Road, the continuation of Worcester Road into Malvern Wells. On the left just before the turn up to the British Camp is **St Wulstan's** Roman

Catholic church, where in 1934 Sir Edward Elgar was laid beside his wife, Caroline Alice, in the churchyard. This was a fitting close to a lifelong association, despite periods of residence in London, Sussex, Hereford and Worcester, with a place whose colours, lights and vistas still seem the perfect reflection of his lonely, introspective genius.

Not a stone's throw from St Wulstan's is **Little Malvern Priory**, the tower and choir of a former Benedictine cell of Worcester, dissolved in 1534. Recent restoration has enhanced the good clean Perpendicular lines of Bishop Alcock's 1480 rebuilding, which instantly followed his discovery that the undisciplined monks, who had to be sent to Gloucester Abbey for a period of correction, had allowed their church to fall into ruin. Dating from this period are most of the windows, some of them retaining original glass fragments (the east window has portrait figures of the family of Edward IV) and the misericord seats, supposedly mutilated during the Civil War. The tiles on the sanctuary floor are, of course, local work from Malvern Priory, and there is a finely carved vine-trail-decorated rood beam over the late fourteenth-century screen.

Next to the church, **Little Malvern Court** has as its nucleus the half-timbered Prior's Hall. The house has belonged to the recusant Berington family since the seventeenth century, and formed the original of the manor described in the opening chapter of J. H. Shorthouse's *John Inglesant*.

The Herefordshire side of the hills, which always seems a real countryside in contrast to the tamer landscapes of Worcestershire, has a cluster of worthwhile villages along narrow winding lanes. **Colwall**, close under the hills below the Wyche Cutting, is held to have been the place where William Langland, asleep on 'Malverne hulles', saw his 'faire field full of folk' at the beginning of *Piers Plowman*. The old village is half a mile from the newer and bigger settlement, a sort of Palm Beach for wealthier elderly Malvernians, and consists of Park Farm, its medieval timber-framed gables possibly those of a hunting lodge of the Bishops of Hereford, and a modest little priest's house beside the church. The masonry at the foot of the tower is newer than it looks – a fourteenth-century base carrying Perpendicular upper stages. The solidly-roofed nave has a Jacobean pulpit with its tester, and a brass in the south chapel commemorates Elizabeth Harford (1590) with her husband, Anthony, and their six sons and four daughters. Among houses in the newer village, Perrycroft stands out, 1893 by Voysey, with many of its original fittings, including Morris wallpapers.

West of old Colwall turns lead to Bosbury and Coddington, through country as tranquil as any 'Clunton, Clunbury, Clungunford and Clun', and wonderful for adventurous cyclists, not afraid to push hard up to Wellington Heath and come hurtling breakneck down on the other side. **Bosbury**, an ugly, draggletail place, is still rather special. Like much else hereabouts it belonged to Hereford diocese, whose bishops were either forced, or chose, to travel extensively and kept a country house here. Old Court Farm, behind the church, still has the stately Decorated gateway to the old palace where St Thomas Cantelupe stayed and Bishop Swinfield, fascinating accounts of whose diocesan tours survive, died in 1316. Temple Court, to the west, was a Templar preceptory. In the Crown Inn an Elizabethan oak parlour, with shields of arms and the initials of Richard and Martha Harford, suggests that this was once their house. They themselves lie in the church, beneath one of a companion pair of tombs in the chancel. The earlier of the two, to John Harford (1573) is signed and dated by John Gildon, or 'Guldo', of Hereford, a sophisticated Renaissance hand reminiscent of his Italianate architect contemporary, Robert Smythson. Five years later Richard and Martha's monument was built to correspond, not by Gildon, but far rougher and much more interesting in its farouche Celtic feel.

The big church, with its detached, defensive-looking bell-tower, has splendid Perpendicular features: the chancel east window, the screen with its ribbed and panelled fan-vaulting, and the Morton Chapel, built between 1503 and 1511 for Thomas Morton, relative of Henry VII's cardinal archbishop, whose rebus of M and a tun appears in a vault.

Between Colwall and **Coddington**, with the lovely view into pastoral Herefordshire from its churchyard, is **Hope End**, site of the house lived in by Elizabeth Barrett, whose momentous fall from her pony and consequent back injury brought her at length into the arms of Robert Browning. The Barretts' Hope End was a sort of Brighton Pavilion cum Sezincote, built with West India plantation money by Edward Moulton Barrett, a legendary tyrant but actually a loving and liberal father during the childhood of the precocious 'Ba'. Here, besides reading Homer at eight years old and writing, at eleven, her four-book epic, *Marathon*, she learned to love these western slopes and celebrated them touchingly in the unfairly-neglected verse novel, *Aurora Leigh*.

Between the main Malvern–Ledbury road and the hills is **Eastnor Castle**, standing in carefully-tended woodlands and best seen among them from the side of Raggedstone. I often wonder if the young

Smirke did not climb to this vantage point with his overall design for the Norman Revival castle (1812–15) still in his head, envisaging it rising in dandified romanticism over the bushy treetops. Romantic it remains, in every connotation of the term, but somehow far more Tennysonian or Disraelian, within and without its 'four grey walls and four grey towers', than a place for Keats or Coleridge to linger in. A shrubby, hauntingly sombre 'high hall garden' flanks the drive, and the south front opens on to a terrace above a lily-flecked lake. Within are a number of big staterooms opening off the massive galleried shaft of the central hall. The two libraries display Italian woodwork from various sources: in the smaller, the walnut panelling was originally designed in 1646 for the Accademia degli Intronati at Siena. Best of all is the Pugin Drawing Room, given its present form by the great Gothic apostle in 1851. Fan vaults in wood and plaster spring to an opulently bossed ceiling. The chandelier, shown at the Great Exhibition, is by G. E. Fox, decorator of the Italian Romanesque church at Hoarwithy.

The Somers family, owners of the castle until it passed to its present châtelaine, had connections with Virginia Woolf through the marriage at Pondicherry of her great-aunt, Virginia Pattle, to the third Earl Somers. His daughter, Lady Henry Somerset, hounded from society for divorcing her husband, turned to good works at **Ledbury**, carrying soup and tracts to the poor and becoming a militant temperance campaigner. Ledbury has done rather well out of good works. In Edward II's reign, Katharine Audley, in search of a hermitage 'where the bells would ring of themselves', heard them do so as she and her maid, Mabel, stumbled wearily into Ledbury. She settled in a rude shelter near the church, living on herbs and milk and an annuity of £30 granted by the king. A St Katharine's Hospital had already been founded here in 1232 by Bishop Foliot, but as the county's oldest charitable foundation it has ever since been associated with the saintly recluse. Queen Elizabeth refounded it in 1580 for seven poor men and three women.

What everyone at once notices on arrival in Ledbury is the excellent composition of the broad main street, with its slight central dip, the market house and the enormous parish church behind. There is much to admire in the characteristic arrangement of stuccoed shop fronts, many of them concealing earlier timber structures, alternating with flamboyant black and white, such as the grandiose Elizabethan Feathers Hotel, the Talbot in New Street and, at the junction with the Southend (to the north the street becomes the Homend), **Ledbury Park**, a massive house begun in *c.* 1600 by the Hall family. The fabric has been so well cared for over the centuries that it is often hard to believe that everything here, apart from the Georgian stables, is authentic late Elizabethan and Jacobean.

The pretty market hall, on its sixteen pillars of Spanish chestnut, was built in 1633, evidently by the same master (not John Abel) as that at Newent, some ten miles away. Opposite is St Katherine's Hospital, with an early fourteenth-century hall, splendidly raftered, and chapel with medieval glass fragments. Part of the actual hospital premises is by Smirke (1822) and there is a long seventeenth-century brick barn behind. Next door is the Barrett Browning Memorial Institute and clocktower, 1892, by Brightwen Binyon, rightly censured by every architectural commentator on Ledbury, and probably the county's most successfully hideous building, almost obscene in its misused shapes and colours.

Up from the market hall runs the supremely photogenic Church Lane, with the derelict fifteenth-century Grammar School where the poet, Thomas Traherne, was educated, debouching amid some very handsome houses which form a little close around the great church of **St Michael and All Angels**. Resting on a probable Saxon foundation, its earliest parts are Norman, including the chancel and west doorway flanked by turrets with clustered shafts and pyramid roofs, reminiscent of Tewkesbury and Bishop's Cleeve. The most exceptional later medieval piece is the north chapel, an outstanding thirteenth-century example, with a richly-moulded two-centred head of quatrefoiled tracery in the window and an extension added perhaps by masons who had worked at Leominster Priory. Some mixed glass here includes a contemporary *Flight into Egypt* and *Massacre of the Innocents*.

Here also are some of the church's rich collection of monuments. An unnamed lady of the Pauncefote family lies on a tomb decorated with a perfect armoury of shields, in a pose familiar all over the region, the hem of her skirt lapping slightly over the tombchest. Edward Moulton Barrett has an expressive memorial by J. G. Lough, showing a mourning woman at the foot of a couch, with an angel hovering at the door.

In the chancel, under one of the admirable sections of medieval roofing for which the church is noted, is a Caroline monumental cluster – a pair of clerical demi-figures and a husband and wife above the usual bunch of children. The Victorian memorial to little John Hamilton, by Mr and Mrs Thorneycroft (can there have been that many sculpturing couples?) was shown at the Great Exhibition. In the south arcade, Captain Samuel Skynner's cheerful bust, with a naval trophy, is of 1725, by Thomas White. Tucked away in awful railed-off gloom at this end of the church are the effetely disdainful figures of Anthony Biddulph and Constance Hall, reclining foot to foot, Augustan to the fingertips. It was this marriage which brought Ledbury Park to the Biddulphs, who still have connections with the town.

The tall, detached thirteenth-century tower was given its 127-foot spire by Nathaniel Wilkinson in 1727. Its seventeenth-century peal of Rudhall bells gave a lasting childhood memory to John Masefield, who gave the profits of various books towards restoring them. Not a great poet, though sometimes a good one, and a highly individual novelist besides, he grew up in Ledbury and wrote about it with an eloquent plainness in his autobiographical sketch, *Grace Before Ploughing*. Is it too chauvinistic of me to urge a Masefield revival?

Up behind the churchyard lay the vineyards of the Bishop of Hereford's manor. When Mr George Skipp owned the estate in the 1680s, he made red and white wine, pressing the grapes in a screw, mixing them with raisins, plums and elderberries, then leaving them to work for five days. His garden grew excellent fruit (the ground still does) – among others 'the Argier Apricocke, the Virgillo pear, the rombullion peache and the Persian nectorine'.

CHAPTER ELEVEN

South-West Worcestershire

❦

South of Worcester the Tewkesbury road hugs the east bank of the Severn closely for most of its length. The curious can turn off to the left, just before Timberdine Farm, and follow on foot the course of an unnamed Roman road which presumably led down to the camp at Kempsey. **Kempsey** itself straggles beside the main road for too long to be enjoyable as a village, though it has a number of handsome houses in various styles, and a parish church whose east window is an imposing cluster of five long lancets. Against the north chancel wall is the tomb of Sir Edmund Wylde (1620), with kneeling effigies of his sons, Edmund and Walter, guarding his own recumbent image. A horse chestnut tree used at one time to grow right out of the tomb.

Beyond Kempsey, pitched on the same low-lying hams, with magnificent views of the long folds of Malvern hills, is **Severn Stoke**, which had its moments of drama in the seventeenth century. During the Civil War its minister, Mr Weyborough, was shot at in his own pulpit by the Parliamentarian lawyer, John Somers, father of the famous Whig Lord Chancellor Somers, and in 1671 it was the headquarters of 'a sort of rude and dissolute people called Levellers, the principal being one Nich. Fowler' who, at the head of his gang, all with Robin Hood nicknames, stole geese, hens and ducks, shore off horses' tails, burnt down farms, 'carried muck and dung out of men's foldyards' and were only suppressed by a volunteer force raised among the local gentry.

Up the hill past the Kinnersley turn, the surprising glimpse of a domed eyecatcher, commanding a splendid prospect across the Avon vale to Bredon, tells us that we are on the old **Croome** estate of the Earls of Coventry. This park ornament, known as the Panorama and designed by James Wyatt, is one of several, for which a possible allegorical layout has been suggested. They dot the great park laid out by Capability Brown for the sixth Lord Coventry in 1751, and though the estate is now administered from an office in Worcester and the motorway jangles savagely through Brown's landscape harmonies, there is still enough here to feast the eye.

The house itself, probably by Sanderson Miller, who was to design Hagley for Lord Lyttelton, is best seen in summer across the cornfield south of the road past High Green. Precise without stiffness, its flanking towers with pitched roofs are a legacy of Jones and Kent, and the drive makes a beautifully sudden swoop down the slope to fetch up beneath the butterscotch Bath-stone north front with stairs to a mezzanine porch. Much of the interior (some of it by Adam) is gone – the house is now a Catholic school – though you can see the library bookcases in the V. & A. and a whole room in the Metropolitan Museum, while the grounds have been farmed over and some of the park ornaments allowed to decay. A far cry, this, from the days when William Dean, gardener to the seventh Earl, could publish his *Hortus Croomensis* (1824) which, with its obsequious preface and its choicely engraved views, is the best guide to Croome in its great days.

Dean is pardonably ecstatic throughout, full of praise for the elegant, the picturesque, the pleasing, the enchanting, determined that we should be breathlessly thrilled by everything from the Claudes in the drawing room to the moral beauty of the late Countess (she was one of the stunning Miss Gunnings, so attractive that George II gave them a guard of twelve soldiers to keep off the gawping crowds). We move through the Home Shrubbery with 'some of the finest magnolia grandifloras ever known' and the Dairy, with its marble milk-troughs, Dutch tiles and Wedgwood churns, to the artificial river and lake and the urn commemorating Brown himself, who had turned a morass into Arcadia. I cherish Dean's two-line entry on the Library: 'this room is plainly, but appropriately furnished. It contains a collection of books, not large, but choice.' Enough said.

The estate church, on the hillside east of the house, is reached by scrambling over a fence among feggy grass and nettles, and is always locked (key at the house). The greater pity, since the design is by Brown and Adam, and at least one of the monuments, perhaps by Nicholas Stone, to Thomas Coventry, Charles I's Lord Keeper, is among the best of its period, characteristically contrasting black and white marbles with Flemish-looking allegories. His great-grandson, John (unmarried – *castitas heu! nimium severa*, says the inscription), has a tomb by Grinling Gibbons, patently more interested in the carved surrounds than the effigy.

Lacking a key you can, as I first did, scramble up on to the stone ledges and peer through the plain-glazed windows at a perfect

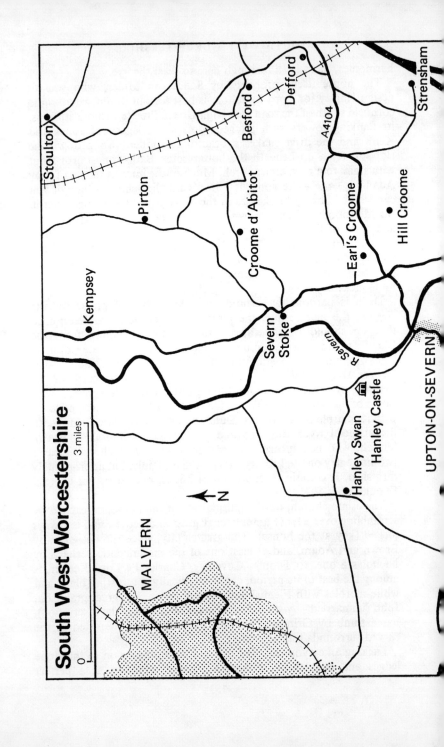

South West Worcestershire

0 ___ 3 miles

N

MALVERN

Kempsey

Stoulton

Pirton

Croome d'Abitot

Besford

Defford

A4104

Strensham

Earl's Croome

Hill Croome

Severn Stoke

R Severn

Hanley Castle

Hanley Swan

UPTON-ON-SEVERN

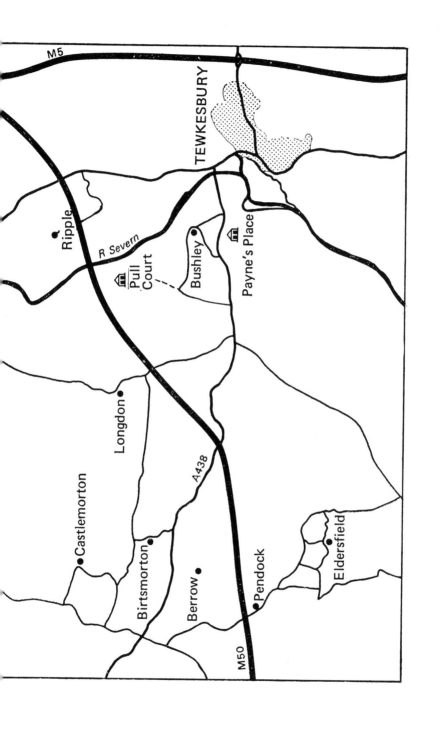

Georgian Gothic interior – fanciful pulpit, slender giraffe-leg pillars, and a clutter of Coventrys in the chancel.

This is the manor of Croome D'Abitot: **Earl's Croome**, to the south (the earls were of medieval Warwick), has an exceptionally fine Elizabethan manorhouse fronting the road through an avenue of young limes, a church with good Norman features, and yet another of the Croome eyecatchers, Miller's shameless Gothic ruin known as Dunstall Castle, in a field beyond the motorway. **Hill Croome**, off the Pershore road to the right, is little more than a church and a farm on a ridge. The former has a splendid roughness about it, with its sharp tower roof and furnishings rustic Jacobean.

Typical, this, of the lonely, windswept upland between Pershore and Upton, where signposts may point the wrong way and some roads have none at all. The surprise of it is oddly enhanced by the M 5, slicing through like a giant ha-ha. From Croome D'Abitot, the B-road runs due north to **Pirton**, whose manor was held of Queen Elizabeth for rent of a pair of penny gloves and a pound of cumin: the gloves must have come from Worcester, but where did the cumin grow? Perhaps in the gardens of Pirton Court, a half-timbered house, somewhat over-restored, whence we go right and then left to St Peter's church. Couched in the waving grass, reddish pink like some beautiful shorthorn heifer, it has an excellent timber tower, into whose lower storey you can climb by a north door to examine the fourteenth-century cruck beams. The rest of the fabric is basically Norman, with round-headed doorways and windows, and traces, in the jumbled masonry at the east end of the nave, of an earlier tower. Notice the early medieval door-hinges.

North of the church, a right turn takes us over the railway line to Wadborough and up to **Stoulton**. Though the tower of St Edmund's was rebuilt in 1936, the nave and chancel are Norman work once more, with projecting doorways, one of which, on the south, has blank arcades more reminiscent of the Teme valley than Pershore vale. Besides a solid Norman font and some seventeenth-century altar rails, the church boasts a late medieval sword and helmet, whose crest of a bleeding boar's head pierced by a sword belongs to the Acton family (no relation to the historian or the aesthete). Their estate, acquired in 1585, is at Lower Wolverton, where they rebuilt the house in brick in the early eighteenth century.

George Allen, Stoulton's curate, built a wooden bridge and 'causey' over the stream at Hawbridge in 1625 for £5 5s 4d. The A 44 here leads down to Pershore, but just before entering the town we can turn off to the right, crossing the Bow Brook and following the lanes to end up at **Besford**, with one of the loveliest and remotest churches hereabouts. It lies almost in the gateway of a farm (where the key is to be found – but ring hard!) and as a proper forest church it has a complete medieval timber-framed nave and porch, and a rood-loft with embattled beam and carved roses, while round the walls runs Jacobean panelling. So much timber gives the church a warm, scented darkness on hot summer days.

In Elizabeth's time the great Besford family was that of Harewell, two of whom are commemorated in bizarre effigies in the chancel. At the south-west end of the church is a unique delight, a painted triptych, its wings folding and latching like a cupboard. This is for Richard Harewell, dead at fifteen in 1576, and the whole sadly damaged composition is an anthology of sublime Renaissance clichés on mortality. Death and Time appear, cupids with a flower and bubbles, Christ on a rainbow, Richard playing, praying, dying, and an inscription of chilling bleakness:

> An Impe entombed heere dothe lie
> In tender years berefte of breath;
> Whose hope of future virtuous lyfe
> Was plaine forshewed by lyfe and death.
> A Childe he seemed of graver years,
> And childishe toies did quyte dispise:
> He sought by yealdinge parents due,
> And serving God to clime the skies.

The Harewells lived at Besford Court, up the lane to the left, a fine early Tudor house with some more-than-competent additions by Randall Wells in 1912. Working in the best eclectic Edwardian traditions, Wells provided a mock-Tudor south front whose language is articulate, intelligent and humorous. Within, he built a chapel, cloister and plain stone staircase, and while working on these, he fell in love with the owner's wife, with whom his elopement is said to have given Galsworthy the idea for Irene and Bosinney in *The Forsyte Saga*.

South of Besford lies **Defford**, its village street, with a handful of good houses, curving off the A 4104 to the timber tower of St James's church, one of a few in Worcestershire retaining their Georgian west galleries. The sudden and startling bareness of Defford Common, with its disused airfield, reminds us that we are in the southern reaches of the ancient Horewell Forest, running originally from

Strensham to the Worcester suburb of Battenhall. Disafforested in 1229, Horewell clung hardily on until the 1770s, and it is hard not to think of the numerous small woods and copses around here as being its last fragments.

The motorway cuts **Strensham** decisively in half. Lower or Nether Strensham is the older of the two ends, with scant traces of the castle licensed for crenellation to Sir John Russell in 1388, and a church lying away from the village across fields, on a wooded cliff overlooking the Avon. St Philip and St James is a forlorn treasure-house, crumbling and neglected, its wagon-roof (the angel shield-bearer on the tie-beam sports Russell arms quartering Lytton) topped by makeshift asbestos sheets replacing stolen lead. The west gallery has the original chancel-screen panels, resting on crocketed and finialled canopies. More Norfolk than Worcestershire (it recalls Ranworth), this set of twenty-three paintings is extraordinary: we start with Sts Antony, Stephen and Lawrence, then come a king and a bishop, the twelve Apostles, St Paul, Christ, St Edmund and John the Baptist alternating with archbishops.

More fine woodwork lines the nave (there are still some old hatpegs) and the Russell pew is stolidly Jacobean. The floor is of medieval tiles from Malvern priory. In the chancel, half smothered in darkness, are glorious monuments, but first of all look down at the angular brasses to Russells from 1490–1562. Stiffly recumbent above lie the Caroline Sir Thomas and his wife, Elizabeth Spencer, on a tomb-table over a scroll-footed urn and a columned canopy over heraldic pomps and admonitory skulls. Next to these is my favourite Worcestershire tomb, a great piece of English art, full of unrivalled zest and excitement. Edward Stanton's superb fantasia on the death of Sir Francis Russell in 1705 is as much Gothic as baroque in its marble *schadenfreude*. His face (a portrait surely) a wrenched simian mask, he is shown half-lying as his kneeling wife beckons him towards a heaven blobbed with clouds and putti whirling a coronet.

Lady Russell was Anne Lytton of Knebworth, and Sir Francis was the last of a family which had held Strensham for four centuries. He it was who, in 1697, built the Upper Strensham almshouses, now tumbledown brick ruins with Russell and Lytton arms above the door. Strensham Court, built by George Maddox, Decimus Burton's drawing-master, has recently been demolished, though it is still possible to walk into the grounds.

In a county rich in minor writers, Strensham has its own worthy, and a very good minor writer he is. Somewhere in the parish, in a house called 'Butler's Tenements', the one and only Samuel 'Hudibras' Butler was born in 1612. Educated at Worcester under the great schoolmaster, Henry Bright, he was too poor to attend university, but as a page to the Countess of Kent and a justice-clerk to Puritan JPs, he must have had ample opportunity to gather material for that astonishing one-off, 'a witty poeme called *Hudibras,* which tooke extremely'. *Hudibras,* if read at all now, is recalled for such wildly audacious rhyming as:

The pulpit – drum ecclesiastick –
Was hit with fist instead of a stick.

A pity, since its irrepressible high spirits made it a bestseller for decades after Butler's death, in disappointed poverty, in 1680. He had been promised a pension by that notorious promiser, Charles II, whose favourite poet he was. Aubrey, a pall-bearer at his Covent Garden funeral, says of him: 'Satyricall Witts disoblige whom they converse with; and consequently make to themselves many Enemies and few Friends; and this was his manner and case.'

From Upper Strensham we can come back through Hill Croome and Naunton and across the A 38 to **Ripple**, enchantingly sequestered where the vale edge meets the Severn. Here the cottages are grouped around a little piazza with a cross at the centre, but the church of St Mary stands a little way back from them, up a lane past the Old Rectory, a tall house of russet brick with ornamented keystones, built for rector John Holt in 1726. Under his predecessor, Lloyd, the crossing tower was raised fifteen feet, after standing for over a hundred years in a pile of debris from its lightning-struck steeple. Its flat top was elegantly pinnacled and balustraded in 1797, when also an upper storey was given to the west porch. This porch is one of several doorways added to the nave in the early thirteenth century, and passing under its inner arch we come into a long, shadowed nave of six-bay arcades lit by little clerestory lancets. The building's sheer size is explained by three factors: the possible presence of a Saxon monastery, the maintenance, from 1320, of chantries in the transepts, and the broad extent of Ripple manor, formerly taking in Croome and other riverine parishes to north and west.

In the transepts, note the round-headed altar recesses, before which Augustinian canons said masses for the soul of John Salemon, aided by twelve shillings a year and sixty-four acres of land. The chancel, added or rebuilt in the thirteenth century, has a Perpendicular east window, and features a tablet to Dr Holt, builder of the rectory, by Thomas White of Worcester, with typically delicate pear-blossom sprays, as well as brass plates to members of the Woodward family (one of them a yeoman of the guard to Bloody Mary's King Philip), wardens of Malvern Chase, whose foresters' arms show stags' heads bordered with oak leaves.

What makes Ripple outstanding among Worcestershire churches is the set of fifteenth-century misericord stalls lining the chancel. Twelve of these show the seasonal labours of the village year – January wooding, February hedging and ditching, March sowing, April bird-scaring and May blessing Rogationtide crops, with a pagan Madonna of flowers ready to be carried round the fields. June brings the hawking season, while July shows a Lammas watch over the manorial bakery, August takes us among the reapers, September to the corn hopper. The October acorn crop fattens the swine for November killing, and the year ends in huddled cosiness by a December fireside. Throughout, the carvings are gloriously exuberant, full of a real feeling for the life they depict: the bird-scarers, for example, run at us, arms flailing, out of the ploughland, the November hog squeals in vain reluctance, and the cat purrs beside the spinning goodwife beside the winter fire.

In the lanes and fields north of the village, on 13 April 1643, the Royalist army achieved its last decisive victory in the west Midlands, when Prince Maurice routed the dragoons and musketeers of the Parliamentary force under Sir William Waller. Royalist tactics were typically impetuous – a headlong charge, which Haselrigg and Massey's troops met with tough resistance before making off, without Royalist pursuit, to Tewkesbury. Some of the local field names, such as Deadland and Scarlet Close, commemorate the engagement, while Old Nan's Hill is, of course, Ordnance Hill, from which the artillery discharged their field-pieces.

Ripple lies close to the town of **Upton-on-Severn**, whose leading families, the Bromleys and the Lechmeres, were staunchly Parliamentarian. Its position at the western end of the only bridge between Worcester and Tewkesbury made it a continual stamping-ground for both armies, though the bridge was finally broken by Massey marching, a renegade to the Royalists, towards Worcester in 1651. A single plank, however, negligently left in place, allowed the Ironsides to horse it across 'as though it were their wooden Pegasus', and seize the church while the cavalry forded the river, and Massey's men were driven through the streets, abandoning their baggage wagons.

Forest of Dean: Newland village

In the evening Cromwell himself arrived, and tradition says that while reviewing his soldiers (in the open space between the old church and the Malvern turn) he looked up and saw a beautiful girl at a window. On being told that she was Miss Morris he forthwith pardoned a brother of hers he had that day condemned to be shot.

Civil War Upton survives in the layout of main street and by-streets which, rather wonderfully, fall plump into the fields, so that any approach to the town (the best is from Malvern, a prospect as charming as anything in Emilia or the Veneto) is invariably a delight. There are several good timber-framed houses in the High Street, most notably the Anchor Inn of 1604, one of Upton's plethora of pothouses. When Mrs Lawson wrote her parish history in 1884, there were nineteen of these, but it always seemed to me as a child that every other house was a pub. The White Lion, its stuccoed front, with a lion holding a ball under his paw, recently repaired, has achieved twofold literary fame. It provided the scene for the up-roarious 'Inn at Upton' episode in Fielding's *Tom Jones*, and one of its landlords was immortalized in the cynical epitaph:

> *Here lies the landlord of the Lion,*
> *Who died in lively hopes of Zion;*
> *His son keeps on the business still,*
> *Resign'd unto the heavenly will.*

It may also have seen an early performance by young Miss Kemble, member of her father's travelling company, and much better known as Sarah Siddons.

In the old church, Philip Doddridge, the eighteenth-century preacher and hymnodist, was married, though surely more remark-able was a wedding on 13 June 1716, at which the groom was a Mr Lyes, whose Christian name was Tell-no. The building was demolished in 1937, all except the medieval tower topped by a jolly green and white cupola and lantern given in 1769 for £275 by Anthony Keck. From here we can walk along the waterside, facing a discreetly concealed yacht marina, to admire a pair of tall hand-some houses built at the height of Georgian Upton's prosperity as a river port. Nowadays its boats are all pleasure craft – perhaps too many of them.

Leaving the town along Old Street on the A4104, we pass the

Severn Estuary: abandoned boat at Purton
Tewkesbury Abbey

Town Hall, best pseudo-Smirke Greek Doric of 1832, and a demure little Baptist Chapel of a hundred years earlier, retired down a courtyard. The new parish church of Sts Peter and Paul, built for an increased population in 1879, is Blomfield and boring, but its slim beige spire acts as a perfect waymark to the departing traveller.

Up the hill across the track of the old railway line from Malvern to Tewkesbury (a good day's walking for those game enough) we strike the rolling, hedgy borderlands of the Worcestershire-Gloucestershire boundary. A rum sort of frontier it is, too, zigzagging about Forthampton north of the Severn, looping down to take in Eldersfield, just missing Staunton and hurtling up to Herefordshire at Chase End. This is immemorial forest country, full of patchy woodlands, little farms, lanes ending in a muckyard, and places with names like Drugger's End, Drinker's End, Snig's End, and a wealth of 'greens' that betokens assarting in the clearings of Malvern Chase.

Left at the top of the hill out of Upton takes us down a leafy stretch to Longdon Marsh, boggy fields full of absorbing plant-life and formerly visited by sea-birds as if in memory of the fact that aeons ago it was under the waves lapping the Malvern hills. Elgar used to enjoy bicycling here, to muse on composition of *The Apostles*. Not long before he was born, a gruesomely Hardyesque episode took place here. A young labourer who had quarrelled with his sweetheart decided to kill them both and poisoned two mugs of beer. One of his fellows saw him, and poured the girl's draught away on the sly, refilling the mug afterwards. The labourer knocked back his brew, and set off to his cottage, where the poison started taking effect. Hearing his groans, a frightened passer-by ran down to fetch the servants from a nearby house, who told him as he died that the girl was still alive.

Longdon itself has an intriguingly mixed parish church: the tower is finest early fourteenth-century Decorated Gothic, but the nave whisks us suddenly into a reasoned late Georgian harmony of round-arched windows, a handsome brass chandelier, and a decent, gentlemanlike pulpit. The chancel, a surprise but not a shock, is apsidal neo-Norman, designed in 1868 by the vicar, C. F. Secretan. In his time Longdon's children sang (do they still?) an old New Year carol:

> *Bud well, bear well,*
> *God send you fare well,*
> *Every sprig and every spray*
> *A bushel of apples next New Year's day.*

Morning, master and mistress,
A happy New Year,
A pocket full of money,
A cellar full of beer.

Across the motorway, Bredon School now occupies **Pull Court**, designed in 1836 by Edward Blore as a grand, though never pompous, Jacobean house, and standing in grounds attributed to Brown. Blore is often given St Peter's, **Bushley**, as well, but it seems likely that Scott did it all: both church and manor have long connections with the Dowdeswell family, distinguished by William Dowdeswell (1721–75), Lord Rockingham's chancellor of the exchequer. Burke, in a monumental eulogy here, describes him as 'a senator for twenty years, a minister for one, a virtuous citizen for his whole life'. Others were not so sure, including Horace Walpole, who called him 'a butt for ridicule, unused in every graceful art and a stranger to men and courts', and Bishop Warburton, who described him and his ministerial predecessor, Lyttelton, thus: 'the one just turned out never in his life could learn that two and two made four; the other knew nothing else.'

His son, William, was altogether more dashing as governor of the Bahamas and commander at the battle of Bhurtpore in 1805, retiring to Pull Court to assemble a noted print collection. Bushley granted shelter to a less fortunate refugee in 1471 when, after 'the aventure of the battayle' of Tewkesbury, Queen Margaret fled to **Payne's Place**, the timber-framed house past the crossroads to the south.

Eldersfield's recessed spire beckons to a church of interesting patchwork: Norman south door and chancel arch, thirteenth-century chancel, and a Perpendicular transept. The font shows local family arms, Beauchamp, Despenser, Berkeley and Whittington. A monument recalls Henry Savage, master of Balliol College, Oxford, from 1650 to 1672, whose *Balliofergus* was the first college history based on authentic records.

Keeping the hill fort of Gadbury on our left, we reach **Pendock**, whose Norman church has Jacobean altar rails and some Tudor bench-ends. Vicar here in 1845 was W. S. Symonds, one of the most notable of Victorian natural historians, founder of the Malvern Naturalists' Field Club, and father-in-law of Joseph Hooker of Kew. There is a tablet to him in the church. **Berrow**, to the north, is one of those 'because it's there' places that have to be visited for their sheer solitude – a church (St Faith's, with a Norman font and an artless Jacobean pulpit) a vicarage (where the key is kept), a farm, all among fields and hedgerows – nothing more.

A right turn from the church leads back across the main Tewkesbury to Hereford road, and lands us in **Birtsmorton**, at the entrance gates to one of the loveliest manorhouses in Worcestershire. Shakespeare never visited here, but I like to think of this as the perfect moated grange for his lonely Mariana of *Measure for Measure*. Entered through an embattled medieval archway of pink sandstone, the little courtyard is surrounded by fifteenth- and sixteenth-century ranges, the east wing with a high galleried hall, and on the south an even bigger hall forming the main entrance. On the west side, immediately overlooking the moat, is a magnificent panelled parlour, of about 1570, with coats-of-arms of members of the Council of the Welsh Marches in the frieze. The wide moat itself runs right round the house under grassy banks, and further to the west, from a walled garden and a small avenue beyond, there is a soaring view of the steep Malvern flanks.

Once this belonged to the Hakluyts of Herefordshire, but in Henry VI's reign it was given to Sir John Nanfan, whose son, Sir Richard, was the protector of the young Thomas Wolsey (he may have served as chaplain here). Last of the Nanfans was Catherine, who had four husbands: the first, Lord Bellomont, died in New York, as Governor of New England, in 1701, the third was Edmund Pytts of Kyre, and the last was Sir William Bridgen, Lord Mayor of London. It was the second, Admiral Caldwell, however, who died at Birtsmorton in 1718, and is buried in the church next door to the court.

Caldwell's tomb, on the chancel north side, is a beauty, complete with semi-recumbent admiral, trophies of war, a flagship, and a remarkable carved clutter of nautical paraphernalia. In any case, husband-hunting among the Nanfans was not confined to Catherine: her ancestress, Jane, had three, and may lie in the nave in an unnamed Tudor tombchest decorated with kneelers, but now covered with an unsightly protective box. The church has no memorial to Birtsmorton's most famous son, William Huskisson, MP (1770–1830), whose father rented the house from Lord Bellomont. Described by Greville as 'tall, slouching and ignoble-looking', he succeeded Canning as MP for Liverpool, and fell the earliest casualty to a railway engine, when he was crushed to death by the Dart engine at Parkside station on his way to Manchester.

Castlemorton has the most romantic of all the stretches of common around the lower slopes of the Malverns, a broad sweep of heath, with furze, bracken and small ponds, and shaggy cows and sheep grazing it. The B4208 from above Castlemorton runs through Welland and Hanley Swan to Hanley Castle. The first is unremarkable, incongruous suburbia; at **Hanley Swan** St Gabriel's church has a Clayton & Bell reredos, but far worthier of a visit is the Catholic church of Our Lady and St Alphonsus along the Guarlford road. This is an unrestrainedly opulent piece, designed (1846) by Charles Hanson, with furnishings by Pugin, and the reredos makes a particularly interesting comparison with similar work in Anglican churches of the period.

Hanley Castle, to the south-east, is really two things: a scattered village, mainly of timber-framed forest cottages converging on the little square in front of the Three Kings inn; and Severn End, the riverside manorhouse belonging to the Lechmere family. The Lechmeres are perhaps the *premier gratin* of Worcestershire, having been at Hanley practically since the Domesday Book. In the Civil War they were doughty Parliament men, and as Whig lawyers reaped appropriate rewards after the 1688 Revolution, including the family baronetcy. Though Nicholas Lechmere, violent and overbearing, died of apoplexy in 1727 and his brother, Edmund, had perished fourteen years earlier of wounds while directing an attack on a French privateer, a Wordsworthian longevity seems to have marked several of their descendants – Anthony, for instance, living from 1766 to 1849.

They did much for both village and estate. Though Severn End was severely damaged by fire in 1896, there is enough evidence, in barn, dovecote, summerhouse and brick wings, of the first Nicholas's keenness to rebuild after the Civil War. He it was who added the glowing brick chancel and tower to the church, blending them conservatively with the Gothic nave. Inside, the Victorian glass is at any rate eloquent, if a trifle florid in places. Opposite the church is Hanley Castle Grammar School, established by the Lechmeres in 1544 and thus among the earliest foundations of its kind in the county.

CHAPTER TWELVE

The Vale of Tewkesbury

❧

The Vale of Tewkesbury was for centuries perhaps one of the least prosperous parts of Gloucestershire, offering a powerful contrast to the sheep-rich Cotswolds and the industrial Forest of Dean. In Elizabethan and Jacobean times its impoverished husbandry led to several pioneer improvement schemes, among which was the planting of tobacco, and to the recruitment of volunteer labour for the American plantations. None of the villages, therefore, is especially big or opulent – match them, for example, with their Bredon neighbours – but few are without individual interest.

We enter the county from Worcestershire through a curious territorial lump sticking out of the boundary line and enclosing the junction of the Ross Spur (M 50) with the A 38 at a place called The Twittocks, which sounds like some agricultural disease. Puckrup Hall, the imposing white neo-classical frontage on the right opposite the Twyning turn, is an old people's home. Twyning itself (pronounced Twinning) is an enjoyable scatter of cottages in every style, along a T of roads towards the Avon. The church, though rebuilt in 1868, has some interesting traces of Norman masonry in the big stones of the lower courses of the wall, and in the reworked doorway. Under the tower, with its fifteenth-century bell frame, is a jolly wall monument of 1676, showing William Hancock and his three sons (note the punning coat-of-arms, a hand and three cocks). He was a Bristol merchant, which explains the painted frieze of fully-rigged ships. Sybil Clare, on the other hand, has a very solemn alabaster effigy to herself and her baby, who died in 1575. Particularly refined is the detailing of her puffed sleeves.

The main road crosses a big stretch of common and rises up the Mythe Tute, which is really two words meaning a hill, Welsh 'mynydd' and English 'toot'. George III and Queen Charlotte once scrambled up here on their hands and knees to get a good view of the vale, and the prospect of Tewkesbury is still spectacular. The rather battered stone house on the right, known as King John's Castle, was begun in the fifteenth century, perhaps as an abbey infirmary. Below us stretches the broad town meadow of Tewkesbury, immemorial scene of fairs and horse-races, with the Avon to the east, bridged by medieval arches whose foundations date from the thirteenth century. To the west, out of sight, flows the Severn, crossed on the main Ledbury road by Telford's cast-iron bridge of 1823-6, complete with its toll house.

Tewkesbury is the most purely English town in the Midlands. By this I mean that it not only looks English, but that its feeling and experience are more inalienably English than even such superficially interesting spots as Stratford and Warwick. Its setting, in the convergence of Severn and Avon with the little rivers Swilgate and Carrant, is matchless, always dominated by the beautiful, solemn heaviness of the Norman abbey tower. So many streams coming together here account for the close packing of houses along three main streets, and for that strongly marked Tewkesbury feature of rows of little cottages down the courts extending behind the larger buildings fronting the roadway.

In the Middle Ages it was a place of much importance. King John kept Christmas here in 1204, Henry III made a truce with the Welsh in 1236 and King Alexander of Scotland came to do homage to Edward I. In 1471 the great battle took place at the southern end of the town between Queen Margaret's Lancastrian force and the Yorkists led by Edward IV. It was a total rout for the Red Rose, and in the dreadful slaughter which followed, Margaret's son, the young Prince of Wales, was killed near the abbey, having been felled by a blow from King Edward's gauntleted fist.

Shakespeare brings the battle on to the stage in *Henry VI pt ii* and also mentions the famous Tewkesbury mustard, sold in oval balls and used for a medicine as well as a condiment. Many of the statelier timber houses in which the town is, or was, so rich were built on money earned from the clothing trade and brisk river traffic in corn to Bristol, Wales and Ireland, reaching its peak in the early eighteenth century, when Defoe reported 'a quiet, trading, drunken town, a Whig baily and all well'. Though prosperity fell off during the Industrial Revolution, and the town, frequently menaced by floods, was dealt a further blow by the decision to carry the Gloucester–Birmingham railway past it to Ashchurch, it has recovered in recent decades. Some would say that the developments have not all been for the best. The violent scarlet shopping centre on the left as we turn from the bridge is frankly hideous, but there is much else to please, and its effect soon dissolves as we begin to acquire Tewkesbury's singular language of sedate Georgian and

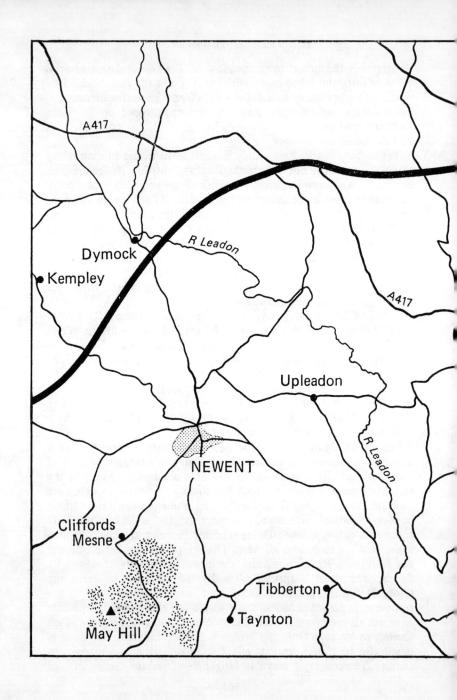

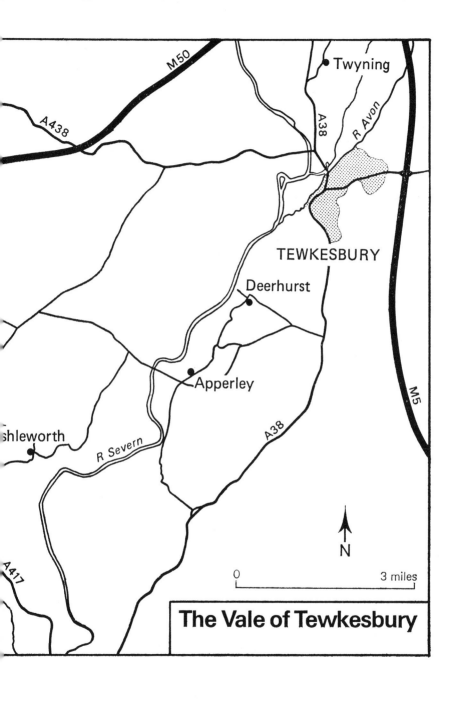

The Vale of Tewkesbury

rather pompous Tudor and Jacobean.

'Drunken' indeed it has always been, like its neighbour, Upton. The corn trade was ever a thirsty business, and there is a plethora of pubs and inns, many of them, like the Bell, with its seventeenth-century wall painting, the late medieval Black Bear, the Berkeley Arms and the Hop Pole, proud of its mention in *The Pickwick Papers*, well pickled in years. The farming connection is perpetuated also in the handsome Town Hall, half-way along the High Street to the right, built by Sir Christopher Codrington in 1788, and most sensitively altered in 1891 by Medland & Son. James Medland had designed the Gloucester Eastgate Market, and provided the same cosily satisfying classical solution here, with sculptured figures and wheatsheaves on the keystones.

The High Street soon becomes Church Street, and takes us to two worthwhile buildings in the shadow of the abbey. On the left is a row of cottages, recently restored according to traditional techniques as a reconstruction of those built by the monks in the early fifteenth century for town tenants. Their rebuilding was dedicated to the memory of John Moore, son of a local auctioneer and the best modern writer on the English countryside, in the Edward Thomas-Richard Jefferies vein. His *Brensham Trilogy* is a superb conspectus of life, faintly fictionalized, in Tewkesbury ('Elmbury') and the Bredon villages between the wars. Opposite, next to a very good tea-shop, is Old Baptist Chapel Court. The town's strong dissenting tradition is reflected in this moving survivor from the early non-conformist days, a mid-seventeenth-century conflation of three cottages into a chapel (now being restored), complete with its gallery, plain benches, pulpit and brass chandelier.

At the back, a melancholy little graveyard peers over the wall on to the Avon, and the big early nineteenth-century corn mill, which is always identified as 'Abel Fletcher's Mill' in Mrs Craik's classic of self-help, *John Halifax, Gentleman*. I find the novel stilted and maudlin – the author could have learned something about narrative from her contemporary Worcester penpusher, Mrs Henry Wood – but its popularity is undimmed, and its sketch of life in 'Nortonbury' has a certain faded charm.

Tewkesbury's most enduring fact is the **Abbey of St Mary**, founded here by Robert Fitz Hamon at some time before his death in 1107, and consecrated in 1121. There was a church here before the Conquest, though a suggested foundation by two earls named Odo and Dodo sounds merely like a monkish joke. The nave was built first, then came the tower, probably raised for Henry I's bastard son,

Robert Fitz Roy, Earl of Gloucester, from whom Tewkesbury passed to the De Clares. Hugh Le Despenser, whose wife was a De Clare, ringed the ambulatory with a chevet of chapels during the early fourteenth century, and the building was saved from demolition by Henry VIII's commissioners through the payment of £483 by the bailiffs and burgesses.

Four external features are noteworthy, as we enter the churchyard through the wrought-iron gates designed by William Edney in 1734 for the borough MP, Lord Gage, whose arms surmount them. To the west are all that remain of the monastic buildings, the tall stone 'Abbey House', perhaps a wing of the Abbot's Lodging, the fifteenth-century gatehouse beyond, and traces of a cloister between these and the south side of the church. Then the big west window, actually a rather successful piece of Gothic survival, built in 1686 after twenty-five years' levying for repairs by churchwardens. Above, and, indeed, it seems, everywhere, the finest Norman tower in England, built in Caen stone and enriched with bands of chevroned and interlaced arches. From the top of this, among the pinnacles and battlements added in 1600, there is a telling view of Tewkesbury's medieval and Jacobean town layout. At the east end, the beauty of the chevet, six polygonal chapels growing out of the church like toadstools from a tree trunk. The central Lady Chapel went, alas, at the Dissolution.

The nave is grandly Norman, with fourteenth-century clerestories and vaulting. There is a useful mobile mirror for viewing the central bosses, with scenes from the Life of Christ, those at the sides featuring angel musicians. Under the tower the lierne vault is decorated with bosses carrying the arms of Sir Guy de Bryan, Edward III's standard-bearer at Crécy, who died in 1390 and is buried in a canopied tomb on the north side of the ambulatory. In the floor here below, Edward, Prince of Wales, was buried after Tewkesbury fight.

The choir, with its magnificent fourteenth-century vaulting, contains what, for many, is the building's prime treasure, the almost intact complement of medieval glass, probably presented by Eleanor de Clare in 1340–4. Besides scenes of the Last Judgement and the Coronation of the Virgin, there are series of prophets, patriarchs, kings and noble benefactors, all of them distinguished by their vigorous lines and the dominant brilliance of red, green and yellow. The De Clares and Despensers did well for their abbey, taking care, however, that the chapels they provided should have strong family links. The first of these, to the north, is dedicated to their relative,

St Margaret of Scotland. In St Edmund's Chapel, with an altar to St Dunstan as well, look up at the vivid portrayal, in the bosses showing St Edmund's martyrdom: here he is shown pierced with arrows 'just like a hedgehog' as his Saxon biographer puts it, and there guarded in death by a wolf.

Outside this is the grim fifteenth-century memorial to an abbot, his effigy shown as a grisly cadaver, crawled over by a snake, a worm and a spider, a wonderful piece of late medieval moral horror. Opposite is the floor grating over the vault containing the bones of the Duke of Clarence, brother of Edward IV and Richard III. During my childhood these bones were exhibited in a glass case on the vault wall, and it was my fancy, knowing the story of his death in a malmsey butt, that the wine had somehow given them their reddish tinge. On the south-east side St Catherine's Chapel has become a sort of *Opera del Duomo* with carved fragments from various parts of the abbey. Next to it, the vestry door is lined with metal plates, supposedly fashioned from armour picked up on the battlefield.

The inner side of the choir is mostly devoted to the Despenser family and their siblings, in a series of very pretty little chantries, all of them built between 1370 and 1430 in a more or less homogeneous style. Sole exception is one which does not in any case jar too much, the richly adorned tomb of Hugh, Lord Despenser, and his wife, Elizabeth Montacute, belonging to the mid-fourteenth century. Otherwise the prevailing form is the same in (from the north-west) Fitz Hamon's Chapel (1395), the Beauchamp Chapel (1430) and the Trinity Chapel (1375): the compositions take in stone screens, fan vaulting and other features of Perpendicular at its freshest. The Beauchamp Chapel, built by Isabella Despenser, Countess of Warwick, for the soul of her husband, Richard, is a veritable pavilion, its two storeys encrusted with decoration. On the roof of the Trinity Chapel is the almost life-size figure of Lord Edward Despenser, armoured and at prayer under a vaulted canopy. In his own time he was a pattern of chivalry, and besides receiving an approving notice from Froissart, he figures in a fresco by Andrea da Firenze in the Spanish Cloister of Santa Maria Novella, Florence.

The abbey organ has an interesting history. It was bought in 1737 from Magdalen College, Oxford, for which Thomas Dallam had made it in the late sixteenth century. In 1654 it had been presented to Oliver Cromwell, and Milton is said to have played on it at Hampton Court. Given back to the college at the Restoration, it was rebuilt in 1690 by the great Renatus Harris, and much of its original pipe and case work survives.

There can be fewer more consistently enjoyable drives than those westwards from Tewkesbury through the lanes of the well-watered vale between the Severn, the Leadon and the purlieus of the Forest. An excursion which samples this countryside – motorists and cyclists must face the likelihood of meeting impassable tractors or herds of cows on these narrow roads – and leads on to Newent, Dymock and Ledbury, can also take in a trio of interesting villages.

Further along the A 38 towards Gloucester is the turn to **Deerhurst**, where in 1016 King Edmund Ironside met to make an abortive peace with the Danes under Canute. Its importance in Saxon times owed much to the existence of a priory, which declined after the Conquest, leaving a single, highly significant relic in the form of its church, adapted for parochial use. The exterior at once suggests Saxon origins in its herringbone masonry, and the nave probably belongs to the earliest building, dating from c. AD 800. So, too, must the two steeply pointed arches opening high up on the inside west wall. Lying so close to the river the church would fall an easy prey to Viking raiders, and there is evidence that it was substantially rebuilt in the tenth century, when the elaborate chancel arch and other round-arched doors and windows were added, which survive at various points throughout the building, subsumed into later medieval reconstruction apparent in the fluent Early English of the nave arcades and some uninteresting Perpendicular windows.

The font is a spiral-decorated bowl of the late ninth century, strongly linked with the sort of patterns found in the Hereford Gospels, and rediscovered at Longdon church after its stem, by a miraculous chance, had been dug up at the nearby village of Apperley. The two were reunited in 1870. Other furnishings include a fine three-foot brass in the north aisle to Sir John Cassy, Chief Baron of the Exchequer (d. 1400) and his wife, Alicia. Her feet rest upon her little dog, whose name, as the inscription tells us, was Tirri. He is one of only two dogs named on memorial brasses, the other being Jakke, Lady Cecilia de Stapleton's dog at Ingham, Kent.

South-west along the lane from the church stands Odda's Chapel, a truly amazing survival of a Saxon chapel through vicissitudes as a house, only rediscovered in 1885 and linked with the stone, now at Oxford, on which is inscribed 'Earl Odda has built and dedicated this royal hall in honour of the Holy Trinity'. We can now see it as the rough-hewn nave and chancel consecrated to the memory of Odda's brother, Aelfric, who died at Deerhurst in 1053, and dedicated on 12 April 1056.

We cross the river at Apperley, turn left at the Tirley crossroads and go south towards **Ashleworth**. This was once a grange of St Augustine's Abbey, Bristol, and two big medieval houses here are possible candidates for the abbot's summer residence. One is Ashleworth Manor, the timber-framed vicarage with its doorway crowned by sharp leaf-spandrels, and the other is the Court, built in the mid-fifteenth century, and retaining its L-shaped pattern, all of stone, with pointed windows and a contemporary stone staircase. In the same friable, greyish-yellow limestone is the twin-porched Tithe Barn next to it, with stout roof trusses, probably built at the turn of the fifteenth and sixteenth centuries, and still in use as a farm building.

Beyond this is the parish church. The herringbone work here is deceptive: it may belong to a decade well after the Conquest. The south aisle lends some architectural distinction with its Perpendicular windows, complemented in a rood screen and loft of the same period. At the west end of the aisle, painted on boards over a blocked medieval arch, hang the royal arms of Queen Elizabeth I. Ashleworth, as can be seen by memorial tablets under the tower, has a strong bell-ringing tradition. In 1977, in two hours fifty-three minutes, we are told, 5040 'Ashleworth Surprise Minor' were rung. Belfry rules here include 'no drinking, smoking, loud and boisterous talking or jesting, and above all no spitting'.

West through Corse, with an attractive set of Charterville cottages, we reach lonely **Upleadon**, beside its court farm. The church stands on a mound which may well occupy a pagan religious site. Its Norman nave is entered under an Agnus Dei tympanum, and inside the sanctuary, on the chancel arch, is a single carved pig's head, perhaps a re-used Norman corbel. Recently given a complete restoration, the church retains its Restoration pulpit and 1611 Black-Letter Bible, but the real delight of Upleadon is in its remarkable Tudor tower. This, close-studded and capped with a conical roof, is timber-framed up all its four storeys, poised on arched cross-braces and pinned together with iron bolting here and there to resist inevitable subsidence from the clay mound beneath. It is a great treat of the Vale, and makes a potent contrast with the tower of Tewkesbury Abbey.

Hence to **Newent**, a little market town which grew up on an old drove-road into Wales. Its market house, at the convergence of the main streets, closely resembles Ledbury's, a timber upper storey on wooden posts, and may have been its original. Unlike Ledbury and Ross, however, Newent has never sufficiently prospered for its town houses and shops to achieve real grandeur and consequence, and there is always a slightly draggletail look about the place among its great red clay banks.

Natural disaster struck the parish church in 1674, when the nave roof collapsed under a weight of snow. Reconstruction, patronized by the King and the Archbishop of Canterbury, was supervised by Edward Taylor, a Newent carpenter who had worked under Wren. Completed in 1679, his nave is an amazing synthesis of medieval plain lines with massive baroque elements in the broad windows and huge supporting pilasters, the central column creating a double chancel. The whole design, a great square of thrusting verticals, has obvious affinities with the layout of Nonconformist chapels.

Under the west window, in a glass case, is the Newent Stone, carved with a Crucifixion and the figure of a priest, with the name 'Edred' above. This, it has been suggested, was Edred's portable altar, dating perhaps from the eleventh century, and later used as a pillow stone for a burial, excavated in 1912. In the chancel lie a knight of Edward III's reign and his lady, traditionally Sir Thomas and Margaret Grandison, of the nearby Herefordshire clan. The excellent old organ belongs to the eighteenth century and is presumably contemporary with its pompous finialled case.

We are on the fringes, at Newent, of the Forest of Dean and not very far from the Severn Estuary. The best way to understand this unique Gloucestershire mingling is to take the southward-leading roads to **May Hill**, a broad, high forest outlier, wooded on one side with a most sinister fir plantation, but for the most part open, with gorse and bracken, and a clump of trees at the summit, from which we can look over to the Malverns, far away to Bredon or the Cotswolds, or down to the silver loop of the widening Severn. Between here and Newent, at **Cliffords Mesne**, is the Falconry Centre established by the Glasier family in 1967. This is one of the world's biggest collections of birds of prey, hawks, owls, kites and eagles, and its exhibitions and demonstrations are devoted as much to showing the natural skill and accuracy of the raptors, hovering on thermals and plunging swiftly to the lure, as to the immense variety among the birds, ranging from vultures to the tiny falconet. The whole venture, which also involves the breeding of different species, well merits its obvious success.

South of here, Taynton and Tibberton are an attractively sheltered pair of villages. **Taynton** church was built in 1647 by order of Parliament, after the earlier building was destroyed. Most of the furnishings, pulpit, altar and font, are contemporary, and the west doorway, with fluted Corinthian pilasters, is especially sumptuous. The parish orchards are a pale shadow of their originals, which produced the Taynton Squash perry pear. Many of them belonged to John Holder, whose initials and the date 1695 are carved on the brick barn of Taynton House, to which he added a cider mill and walled gardens. A highly acquisitive squire, he often breaks into gleeful verse in his diary:

> *The course I took to make this purchase here*
> *Was treating of the Owner with strong Beare.*
> *That fail'd, tho' what I often heard him speake*
> *Declar'd the sinews of his Pocketts weake.*
> *Another time, to favour my designe,*
> *I sett him first, then call'd and drank Port Wine*
> *Where I had fix'd myself designedly*
> *To face and then salute him passing by.*

Tibberton has an extremely elegant great house, altered by the noteworthy local hand of James Medland in 1852, who developed its Georgian classicism with a verandah and balcony, and added a tall Italian belvedere tower. The church is an interesting synthesis of Norman work (nave and chancel arch) with Decorated windows, and the chancel inscriptions make touching reading.

This north-western part of Gloucestershire is often called 'the Daffodil Country', and with good reason. The flowers grow here as nowhere else, it seems, and **Dymock** has given its name to the popular Little Dymock strain. The village stands on a ridge, and the church comprises early and later Norman features in its blank chancel arcading and south doorway, highly ornate with its Tree of Life tympanum. The chancel itself is a rebuilding and the tower was added in the fifteenth century. Preserved in the church are the last Dymock Station railway ticket, issued on 11 September 1959, and the last letter from the village franking office, dated 31 March 1962.

Dymock has two famous associations. The first is with the Dymock family, who acquired the office of King's Champion in 1377 through a marriage to the great-granddaughter of Sir Philip Le Marmion, hereditary champion of England. The duty, as is well known, involves challenging claimants three times at the Coronation. The second touch of celebrity was given by the Dymock Poets, a group of writers who sought the seclusion of the daffodil country in the years immediately preceding World War I. In the surrounding hamlets of Ryton, Greenway and Leadington lived Lascelles Abercrombie, Wilfred Wilson Gibson and Robert Frost. Rupert Brooke and John Drinkwater also came here, and it was while walking across moonlit fields near Dymock that Edward Thomas meditated writing poetry for the first time.

None of them forgot the calm of the place, so keenly hankered after amid the gloom of the trenches, and Frost himself came back here in 1957. Their poetry, however scorned nowadays, seems to have taken a certain freshness of inspiration from this countryside. But then there have always been bards at Dymock. Somewhere in the churchyard, it is said, is a stone with the following epitaph:

> *Too sweeter babes youm nare did see*
> *Than God amity give to wee,*
> *But they were ortaken wee ague fits,*
> *And yur they lies as dead as nits.*

At last to **Kempley**, amid the delectably watery meadows. The newer of its two churches is St Edward the Confessor, by Randall Wells, a tremendous morsel of 1903 Arts and Crafts, using local materials and ironwork by the village blacksmith. The variety of its exterior shapes is not unpleasing – the steep pitch of the west gable, for instance, countered by the saddleback tower, with its amusing compendium of round and pointed windows. Among the interior furnishings are several pieces of woodwork from the doyen of the entire movement, Ernest Gimson.

The older church stands away from the village opposite the court and vicarage. Its Norman fabric is a box for the unique cycle of Romanesque frescoes dating from 1130 to 1140 and uncovered in 1872. These astonishing survivors are all carefully adapted to the shape of the apsidal chancel, and focused on the seated figure of Christ, on the ceiling, surrounded by sun, moon and stars and the evangelistic symbols. The Twelve Apostles line the side walls, whose windows are topped by towered buildings, and between these windows and the altar are figures of the donors, who seem to have been pilgrims to Santiago de Compostela. To what extent a foreign influence was absorbed here or who the artist was it is impossible to say. In their bold, somewhat crude way, the Kempley frescoes hold an unforgettable force, all the more vivid in the context of the soft countryside where they lay hidden for so long after the Reformation.

CHAPTER THIRTEEN

The City of Gloucester

❧

At first glance, Gloucester seems nothing but the worst sort of urban provincial mess, yards of Tesco, Manfield, Dewhurst and British Home Stores. Apart from its brief spell as a spa in the early nineteenth century, it has never indeed pretended to be anything but a working city, with heavily industrial fringes centring on a commercial port. In fact, however, it has resolved its problems far more successfully than most west Midland towns (Hereford excepted) and stands as an enduring reproach to poor old motorist-gagged Worcester. There is much to see and to enjoy in Gloucester, and the work of the Gloucester Civic Trust in providing maps and conducted tours has made it all very easy.

The city's history begins with Ostorius Scapula's Roman military base in the northern suburb of Kingsholm during the first century AD. When the Second Legion moved westwards to Caerleon, the government established, closer to the river, a colony for retired veterans, given its charter during the reign of the Emperor Nerva in AD 96 and called Colonia Nervia Glevensia (Glevum for short). The Severn estuary and the Cotswold slopes and plateaux made Roman Gloucestershire, honeycombed with villas, a playground for the rich, though the growth of Corinium (Cirencester) was perhaps Gloucester's economic undoing.

In Saxon times the invading Danes pitched camp in the imposing ruins, of which there must have been enough left to inspire the redoubtable Aethelflaed, Lady of the Mercians, to rebuild the city within the former Roman walls. The ground plan of this Saxon rebuilding can be traced in the modern street layout, and only Northgate and Southgate can be determined with any certainty as an original section of the Roman grid. There was already a Mercian palace at Kingsholm and with the re-establishment of the monastic foundation which later became St Peter's abbey (the modern cathedral) Gloucester's urban growth began.

Though it was never among the first of medieval towns, its prosperity seems to have been assured, and during the Civil War, when it was a cathedral city with suburbs spreading well beyond the walls, it was one of Parliament's major western strongholds, commanding a key route across the Severn and into Wales. In 1643, with all going well for the Royalists, so well indeed that scarcely any substantial Parliament resistance remained in southern England, King Charles drew up eight thousand infantry against the none too stout old walls. The city's governor, Colonel Massey, held firm for nearly a month, as supplies dwindled and Prince Rupert's cavalry patrolled the approach roads. Then, on 5 September, with only three barrels of gunpowder left in the magazine, the defenders saw on the hills the camp fires of a relief force of London trained-bands, whose appearance was enough to scatter the Royalist army in one of its more typically self-destructive moments. The heroic walls, save a few fragments, have long since gone, though my brother and I as boys used to visit a junk shop in the Westgate whose owner sold spurs, bullets and basket-hilted swords which he guaranteed as relics of the siege.

Pride of place in Gloucester's skyline, then as now, went to the soaring Perpendicular tower of **St Peter's Cathedral**. There was certainly an abbey here by 940, when Athelstan, dubbing himself with Byzantine sophistication and some truth 'Basileus Totius Britanniae', died in the city: Cyneburh, sister of its founder, Osric, was the first abbess, over a joint community of monks and nuns. In 1058 the church of a refounded Benedictine house was burnt down and rebuilt, but it was in 1089 that the earliest portions of what survives today were begun by the Norman Abbot Serlo and completed in 1160. Gloucester's is still substantially a Norman cathedral, in many places altered rather than totally rebuilt by subsequent medieval generations – this can be felt most obviously in the choir aisles and transepts, though the plainest Norman statement is, of course, in the huge cylindrical columns of the nave.

These tall pillars, thirty feet seven inches high, are in fact rubble-filled shells, and carry a strangely low triforium, explained by the addition of an Early English rib vault in 1242. This, while in itself graceful, particularly in its Purbeck shafts, stiff leaves and grimacing corbel heads, sadly diminishes the dramatic thrust of Norman arcades. On either side the nave is full of good eighteenth-century monuments and inscriptions. In the north aisle there is an outstanding early Flaxman group (1784) showing Mrs Sarah Morley, dead in childbirth at sea, rising heavenwards, clutching her baby and tended by angels: in the south aisle, note Mrs Mary Strachan, with fashionable powdered and piled hair, on a medallion, with a weeping

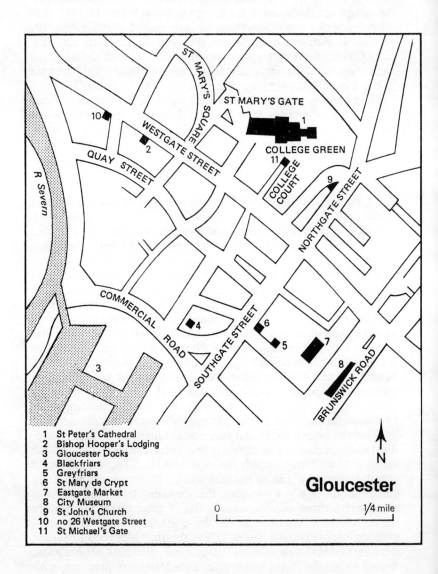

1 St Peter's Cathedral
2 Bishop Hooper's Lodging
3 Gloucester Docks
4 Blackfriars
5 Greyfriars
6 St Mary de Crypt
7 Eastgate Market
8 City Museum
9 St John's Church
10 no 26 Westgate Street
11 St Michael's Gate

Gloucester

0   1/4 mile

cherub and a nice cartouche of arms. This is 1770, by Ricketts of Gloucester. The monument to Sir George Onesiphorus Paul nearby justly commemorates his links with prison reform. As high sheriff of Gloucester in 1780 and member of a leading family of clothiers, he was admirably placed to put his model prison system into practice, with five new county gaols built on principles suggested by John Howard, of which two in our area survive, at Little Dean and here at Gloucester.

The north and south **transepts** are both fundamentally Norman, overlaid with Perpendicular during the fourteenth century. This overlay marks a historic development in English architecture, for Gloucester was, as far as can be established, the first building in which the style was used. Thus the tracery of the south transept south window, dating from *c.* 1330, has unique importance, though historians suggest that Gloucester Perpendicular is an independent interpretation of an already existing court style in London. As the cathedral south side was in danger of collapse, there was a need for buttresses, and the effect of this shoring-up can be seen in the transept. Notice here, incidentally, the fine fifteenth-century parclose screen at the north-east corner, and the exceptionally good tomb of Alderman Blackleech and his wife, Gertrude, 1639, anonymous, but highly reminiscent, in the expressive splay of his hands and the floss of hair under her hood, of similar monuments in Herefordshire.

The north transept features a distinct oddity in the painted stone tomb of Alderman Bower and his wife, Joan, with their nine sons and seven daughters. The enriched Early English screen probably comes from a former Lady Chapel. Through this an entrance has recently been pierced to the big Norman locutorium, where monks from the cloister, where silence was enjoined, could come and talk. This has now been made into a Treasury, with an exhibition of communion plate from Gloucestershire churches. On the western corner of the transept, where it joins the nave aisle, is a memorial to John Stafford Smith, composer of the tune of *The Star-Spangled Banner* (appropriately floating above).

We enter the choir through pretty little doorways with moulded lintels over the ambulatory steps. The ambulatory itself is an excellent vantage point for seeing how the mid-fourteenth-century builders, when raising the choir ceiling, coped with the crossing vault under the tower. They solved the problem by floating ribs across the north and south arches, with verticals rising from them to take the strain. With its high clerestory and deep galleries and a fretting of lierne and tierceron over all, it is very much a synthesis of Norman and early Perpendicular ideas. The organ, in its proper place above the screen, dates from 1666 and the painting on its display pipes, showing royal, noble and prebendal coats-of-arms, is of the same period, by the local painter, John Campion. Before the altar steps, on a late medieval tombchest, lies the thirteenth-century wooden figure of Robert, Duke of Normandy, as a cross-legged knight. Eldest son of William the Conqueror, he lost the battle of Tenchebrai against his brother, Henry, in 1106, and died a prisoner at Cardiff twenty years later, an old man of eighty.

As we look upwards again, the magnificent roof bosses, especially those towards the east end with musical angels hovering towards the figure of Christ, make an airy preparation for the glory of Gloucester, the stunning seventy-eight-foot-high **east window**. This was installed in 1349–50 as a kind of memorial to knights of the Hundred Years War, and may well be the largest single window in the world. Its theme is the glorification following the crowning of the Blessed Virgin, who is shown in a central group with Christ and the Apostles. Below are martyrs (St Catherine without her wheel) and saints, and below these and a row of royal and ecclesiastical dignitaries are the shields of the paladins of Crécy and Calais. The prevailing colours across the thirty-eight-foot span (a bay with two inward-turning sides) are red, blue, yellow and a very clear white.

On the ambulatory north side, in a little case, is the stone cross carved in a North Korean prison camp by Colonel J. P. Carne, VC, after the Gloucester Regiment's heroic stand at the Imjin River in 1951. Near this is the clumsily executed figure of Osric, sub-regulus of the Mercian Hwicce tribe and honoured as the abbey's founder. Next along, and in altogether superior style, is the tomb which in a sense was the medieval abbey's making. Edward II's body was received here for burial in 1327 by Abbot Thokey after the King's murder at Berkeley. Such a move combined devotion with political foresight for, with Mortimer executed and Isabella under house-arrest at Castle Rising, Edward III was free to encourage the sort of reverence his father had seldom been given in his lifetime, and showered privileges on the abbey, where the tomb had become a pilgrimage object. Perhaps it was he who paid for the wonderful filigree crocketing of the canopy, like a growth of coral, restored during the eighteenth century by Oriel College, Oxford, Edward's foundation, and for the alabaster effigy, whose curled and bearded head is surely a portrait.

Behind the choir is the **Lady Chapel**, very bright and pure Cotswold wool-church Perpendicular, built between 1470 and 1483, with similar vaulting to the choir's, though the east window glass, knocked out in the Interregnum and re-set, can only just be pieced together as a composition showing scenes and figures connected with the Virgin. Details of this jumble are tantalizingly good: the work is probably by Barnard Flower, the royal glazier, and was the gift of Edmund Compton, ancestor of the Marquises of Northampton. The whole chapel, with its singing galleries and chantries, is like a palace with little pavilions. Best of its monuments is by Thomas Green of Camberwell to John Powell, a judge of the Queen's Bench who died in 1713 – a vigorous marble full-length in judicial robes, flanked by eloquently weeping putti.

St Peter's abbey became the cathedral of the Holy and Indivisible Trinity in 1541. The extensive later medieval rebuilding had girdled the church with a whole range of conventual buildings and many of these, or fragments of them, were absorbed into the cathedral clergy houses. Gloucester's most substantial relic of monastic life is one of the major statements of English Gothic – the **cloisters**. These form the earliest known example of fan-vaulting (the east side is of 1350–77, the others of 1381–1412) and offer the most vivid expression of the progressive spirit which prompted the various phases of the late fourteenth-century rebuilding. The north walk contains a washing trough or lavatorium, where monkish hands were cleaned before meals, and opposite this is an almery (from the same Arabic word for cupboard as the French armoire) where towels were kept. Refectory and kitchens, however, have long since gone. In the east walk is the late Norman chapter-house, where the Domesday Book was completed in 1086 by five justices. Buried here are several of the toughest of the Conqueror's strong-arm men, including Bernard de Newmarch, Walter de Lacy, and Richard de Clare, better known as Strongbow.

College Green, the cathedral close, is too full of parked cars for many of its best houses to be adequately appreciated. Nicest of these is the small group in the south-west corner, mostly of brick with stone facings and string-courses and ideally discreet behind a screen of trees. To the north-west is Miller's Green, under a medieval arch, with, on the right, the house in which S. S. Wesley lived as organist until his death in 1876. Oldest of the gateways is the St Mary's Gate in the western precinct wall, half-timbering over a Norman vault, and from here we can begin a tour of the city.

Opposite us on the lawns of St Mary's Square, a new estate, is Edward Thornhill's dignified 1862 commemoration of the Protestant martyr, **Bishop Hooper**. A doughty iconoclast but a good pastor,

Hooper was executed here in 1554 after trial in London. After praying aloud for half an hour, he was given a box containing Queen Mary's pardon, conditional upon his recantation of heresy. 'If you love my soul, away with it!' he cried, whereupon he was stripped to his shirt, the guard fixed bladders of gunpowder to his armpits and groin, and Hooper himself gave directions as to the stacking of faggots for his own fire. However, as the wind was in the wrong quarter and the timber was green, the fire would not kindle and the bishop cried out: 'Good people, if you love me, let me have more fire.' At length, before a huge crowd, many of them in tears, he gave up the ghost with the words 'Lord Jesus receive my spirit.'

Just before leaving the square, notice, at the end of the terrace on the right, a worn stone figure of King Charles II. This was carved by Stephen Baldwyin in 1662 for the Wheat Market in Southgate and rediscovered thirty years ago in a garden at Westbury-on-Severn. In Westgate Street, the redundant church of St Nicholas is on our right. Basically Norman and Perpendicular, it carries an oddly truncated spire, the result of renovation in 1783. Immediately opposite stands **Bishop Hooper's Lodging**, the martyr's last stopping place, a tall, three-bay, early Tudor house, of which Gloucester only a few decades ago contained many more. It is now an excellent folk museum, with an annexe devoted to the Gloucester Regiment. The ground floor displays stuffed figures of the county's native animal breeds, the Gloucester cow, her coat a dark chocolate fading to ochre and white, almost extinct on farms, the Gloucester Spot pig and the local sheep. Upstairs is a floor devoted to Severn fishing, another to a wheelwright's shop, and a set of gawkily primitive portraits of the city's Elizabethan benefactors hangs above objects connected with her famous sons, Hooper, 'Vaccination' Jenner, preacher George Whitefield and Robert Raikes, the journalist founder of Sunday schools. Other exhibits include the Dymock Curse, invoking the aid of demons against a certain Sarah Ellis – upon whom, apparently, it worked.

Turning left into Quay Street, and then right, we follow the Quay towards **Gloucester Docks**. Gloucester was a Roman port, but during the Middle Ages it was substantially overtaken by Bristol. Commercial revival came in 1793 with the start of work on the Gloucester and Berkeley canal, and during the nineteenth century the city prospered as a centre of the timber trade – Moreland's 'England's Glory' matches, with their red, white and blue dreadnought boxes, made here, are as quintessentially west-Midland as Weston's cider or Banks's beer.

The working port belongs to British Waterways, but enough can be seen from Commercial Road and Southgate Street to appreciate the stark, Doré-like grandeur of tall warehouses, mill cranes, winches and derricks. From Severn Road we can see the central dock basin of 1810, out of which the canal flows down to Sharpness, and on its further side a row of mid-nineteenth-century warehouses. Behind these, in the Victoria Dock of 1847, salt brought down from the Worcestershire works around Droitwich was loaded for transport to the Continent. Oldest of the warehouses, a nobly derelict industrial relic, its upper windows bleared with moss, is the North Warehouse on Commercial Road, built in 1826. Beyond this is the splendid bulk of Priday Metford's City Flour Mills, dating from 1850 and still throbbing with dusty life.

Like other medieval cities Gloucester had its Dominican and Franciscan houses, surprisingly close to one another. **Blackfriars, at** the turn of Commercial Road into Southgate Street (but best seen from its own lane) was established in 1239, and significant remains of both church and cloister are preserved, their overgrown masonry, principally of the thirteenth century, now being subjected to some rather belated restoration. Before Greyfriars, reached down a pedestrian precinct past a pretty Friends' Meeting House, we can visit **St Mary de Crypt**, one of the only three good city parish churches. Mainly Perpendicular, it has one of those tall naves on slender columns, very much of a Cotswold type, a broad crossing under a lierne-vaulted tower, and a lofty chancel, its lower walls pierced with sedilia and piscinae, its upper stages carrying traces of wall-paintings and a clerestory. The roof bosses show angel musicians. All this Perpendicular work was projected by Henry Dene, Prior of Llanthony (not the Welsh priory, but its successor refounded at Gloucester) who died in 1501. In the south chapel is a memorial to Robert Raikes, and in the north transept are three-foot brasses of John and Joan Cooke (1544), founders of the Crypt Grammar School, whose old schoolroom can be seen through the door in the north-west corner of the church. George Whitefield was christened in the font and preached his first sermon in the seventeenth-century pulpit.

Beyond the churchyard stands a tall Regency house, built as a frontage to the gaunt ruins of the early sixteenth-century **Greyfriars**, whose nave and north aisle survive. The two shields of arms on the south side, of Chandos and Clifford, probably come from a tomb in the church. Green lawns of the former burial ground divide the ruins from one of Gloucester's two successful modern buildings (the other is the residential 'Dukeries' by the river), the **Eastgate Market** of 1973, a spacious covered shopping precinct with a wonderful neo-Palladian north portico from the Victorian market here celebrating the fruits of Gloucestershire earth. East of the market, in Brunswick Road, the **City Museum** has a small display of Roman and Celtic finds, among them an arresting series of goggle-eyed heads from what is thought to have been a Celtic temple.

Don't miss, just into Southgate Street from the Cross, the Edwardian clock chimes on the front of Baker the watchmaker's. The quarters are struck by Father Time, an Irishwoman, a Welshwoman, a Scot and John Bull, big brilliantly painted figures. **St John's Church**, Northgate Street, a Georgian body tacked on to a Perpendicular tower, is very obviously the work of the Woodwards of Chipping Campden, built in 1732 and strongly akin to their St Swithun's, Worcester, in its Venetian window with Ionic pilasters. The furnishings are nearly all contemporary, complete with mayoral mace rests and a pulpit once preached in by Wesley and George Whitefield, who was born at the Bell Inn, Southgate Street.

Westgate brings us back towards the cathedral past several of the older city pubs, such as the Fleece, which probably began as a medieval pilgrims' hostel and has an attractive inn yard, and the Fountain, with its medallion of an equestrian William III on an inner façade. Gloucester in his day was the scene of near-anarchy when Captain Pyrke of Little Dean, with forty followers, rescued the Whig Lord Lovelace from the gaol and beat up the Jacobite mayor and corporation.

Best of Gloucester's timberframes is **no. 26 Westgate Street**, a garden shop with a Georgian façade. Behind are the massive posts and beams of what was once the town house of the Guise family of nearby Elmore; later it was to provide a lodging for Colonel Massey during his governorship of the beleaguered city. Some neck-craning is necessary here, since the lane down the east side of the house is a very narrow medieval grope.

Returning through College Court, just before entering the Perpendicular **St Michael's Gate**, originally giving on to the lay cemetery in the abbey precincts, we pass an antique shop, whose associations make as good a farewell to the city as any, for here lived Beatrix Potter's *Tailor of Gloucester*.

CHAPTER FOURTEEN

The Vale of Berkeley

.𝅘

The Vale of Berkeley often seems to defy characterization in the way
it fuses all the better known elements of the Gloucestershire landscape. There is, for example, a good deal of dry-stone walling which
has dribbled down off the Cotswolds, a surprising amount of good
trees which look as if part of the Forest of Dean had detached itself
from across the river, and of course there is the estuary, much better
understood on this side as a component of the scene than on its
western shore. The building styles, however, belong distinctly to the
region – or perhaps one should say the building colours, since the
enduring impression is of that particular plum-coloured brick over
which something in the damp estuary air encourages a delicate
bloom of lichen, so that cottages, farmhouses and parsonages
appear almost as if built out of alabaster. This, what is more, is the
country of rich dairy pastures, producing the famous Double
Gloucester cheese.

Leaving Gloucester at the junction of the A 430 with the A 38 we
reach the turn to **Elmore**, crossing the Gloucester and Berkeley canal
and skirting the river before it reaches the village, a typical riverine
settlement of houses running higgledy-piggledy down to the shore.
Elmore Court, a large Elizabethan house begun in 1564 using stone
from a medieval castle, has many of its original Renaissance furnishings, including a huge Elizabethan staircase and the panelling of
the drawing room, grandly Jacobean with its strapwork above the
fireplace. The best thing at Elmore is not in the house but at its
approach, the florid filigree beauty of baroque wrought iron in the
entrance gates by William Edney of Bristol, originally made for
Rendcomb in the Cotswolds in 1712. Elmore has belonged to the
Guise family since Henry III's reign, when it was given to Sir Anselm
de Gyse of Apsley Guise, Bedfordshire, and their crest of a swan
surmounts the gates.

On the other side of the canal is **Hardwicke**, whose parish church
is primarily thirteenth-century, with an elegantly transomed Perpendicular west window and gargoyles on the tower. The estate

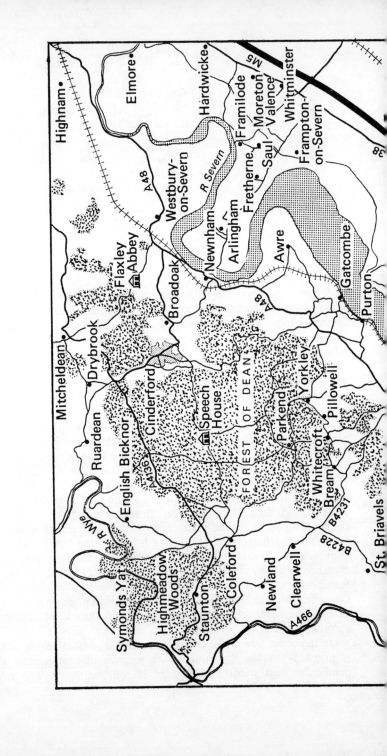

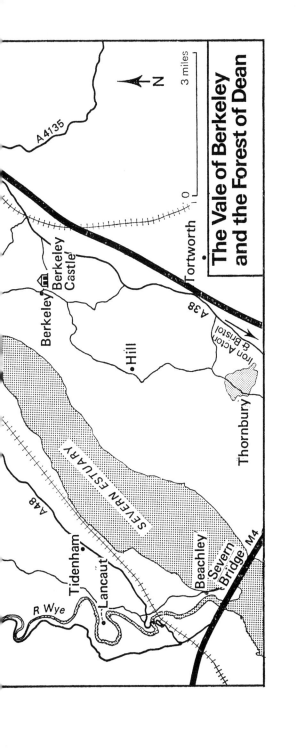

The Vale of Berkeley and the Forest of Dean

N

0   3 miles

originally belonged to the Trye family, several of whom are remembered here, among them, recumbent in full armour, John and his son, Peregrine, late Elizabethans. In 1720 Hardwicke was bought by Philip Yorke, one of England's greatest Lord Chancellors, 'architect of equity' and a pillar of the Whig establishment, who took his title from the village when he was raised to a viscountcy in 1733. Hardwicke Court, however, was built for Thomas Lloyd Baker in 1818 by Smirke, who provided a very simple, spare, Smirke-ish design, in harmony, perhaps, with the character of the owner, a pioneer philanthropist who set up in the grounds the first reformatory for delinquent boys.

Moreton Valence, to the south, has a scatter of consequential-looking houses along the lane going down to the church. This joins a typically rich Gloucestershire Perpendicular south aisle and gargoyled tower to a Norman chancel with a moulded arch and a short Norman nave. Of the same period, under the half-timbered north doorway, is the spectacular tympanum, showing St Michael tilting with a dragon. The carving here, though of comparable vigour with Herefordshire School examples such as those at Ruardean and Brinsop, lacks their fluidity and is altogether more angular in style.

We have to go back on to the main road and down to **Whitminster** to reach the turn on to the Arlingham peninsula. Past the village itself, the church and great house stand side by side, facing the parallel passage of the River Frome and the Stroudwater canal. The church has a Jacobean pulpit, a porch with such worthwhile medieval features as a wagon roof and original iron studding on the door, and a pretty little early-Caroline figure of Rebecca Lloyd at prayer. Whitminster House was begun in Elizabeth's reign, given Jacobean additions, and substantially rebuilt during the 1730s, both within and without.

The Arlingham peninsula is delectably remote, a romantic world's-end among silent fields, though there is evidence for settlement here since prehistoric times. **Saul** is chiefly notable for its clusters of nineteenth-century bargemen's and lock-keepers' cottages, while **Fretherne** has one of the district's best Victorian pieces, St Mary's church, built of brown sandstone with Bath dressings in 1846–7 by Francis Niblett. The stained glass by George Rogers of Worcester and the crocketed spire and flying buttresses contribute a bouncing exuberance which seems to have found its way into the dedication ceremony as reported in the *Illustrated London News*: 'At the conclusion of the ceremony, the Bishop and a numerous party partook of the kind hospitalities at the Rectory, which extended to the poor of the parish and the children of the school, who were regaled in the School-house (also newly erected by their esteemed incumbent) upon roast beef and plum-pudding, and other elements of good old English fare.' Later, Niblett built the church at **Framilode** (1854), with Rogers windows again.

I first visited **Arlingham** on a warm, moist autumn evening, when the place seemed almost haunted by its own stillness. The church (key from the farm on the south side) was begun in 1372, and the contract for the tower, built by Nicholas Wyshingre, 'cementarius' of Gloucester, is one of comparatively few to survive from medieval times. The north windows preserve some contemporary glass, showing the Virgin and St John, St Catherine and St Margaret (with a dragon). The glazing of the south-west window dates from a century later, and has fragments of what was probably a whole set of the Twelve Apostles.

Arlingham is rich in neo-classical memorials, mostly to the Hodgeses and Yates. Mary Yate's monument by Nollekens has the mourning figure of Piety. Of Priscilla Bromwich, who died in 1805, we are told 'Her person was graced by the correct manners of the old school', while Anna Maria Estcourt (d. 1783) is, with an inspired ineptitude, compared to an aged – masculine – oak tree:

Firmly he rears his branches to the Sky,
While most around at different periods die;
Till his deep roots, sap'd by impetuous Tides,
Feel no support surround their naked sides.
Their honour'd weight, unable to sustain,
He sinks lamented on the desert 'plain.

The churchyard complements all this with a lovely clutter of lurching tombstones.

South of the peninsula is **Frampton-on-Severn**, the Vale's most eyecatching village. Spread out for almost half a mile along either side of the road, the houses front a long, broad expanse of village green, with Frampton Court at one end and the parish church at the other. The size of the place is partly explained by its having belonged to the powerful Clifford family (though attempts to link it with Fair Rosamund are unconvincing) who established a market and fair here in the Middle Ages. Many of the houses do indeed date from this period, with several fifteenth-century cruck constructions and, most outstanding, Manor Farm, timber on top of stone like its neighbouring barn. Others are exceedingly handsome Georgian, built to match the animating mood in the design of **Frampton Court**. This is either by Sir Edward Southwell of King's Weston, or by John Strahan of Bristol. Whichever he was, the architect made strong and not altogether successful allusions to Vanbrugh. The collective result is undeniably 'a something', but the whole, in its yellow Bath stone, built between 1731 and 1733 for Richard Clutterbuck, a local clothier, should not be too closely examined by the aesthetically choosy. Forgive, for instance, those weird arched chimneystacks, a long way after Vanbrugh, and the cramped look of the door and windows between the pilasters of the main front. Inside is far more rewarding, particularly in the marvellous grained woodwork throughout the rooms, the staircase seen through the broad segmental arch across the hall, and the ingenious folding dog-gate out of a marquetry panel at the stair foot. Outside, at the end of a romantic canal, is a Gothic garden house attributed to William Halfpenny. The dovecote belongs to the same period.

Frampton Church is much-restored Perpendicular, its tower rebuilt in 1734. There is one of the six Gloucestershire lead fonts all cast from the same Norman mould (see Tidenham, ch. 15), a Jacobean pulpit of 1622, and one of those gorgeous brass chandeliers, made in Bristol during the mid-eighteenth century, which decorate so many of the Vale churches. In the Clifford Chapel in the north aisle are fragments of early glass from a window representing the Seven Sacraments, given, as the shield-bearing angel suggests, by a descendant of the effigy figures below, all of them belonging to the early decades of the fourteenth century, and all probably Cliffords.

At Splatt Bridge, immediately beyond the church, is one of the various lock-keepers' cottages installed during the building of the Gloucester & Berkeley canal in 1827 by Robert Mylne. Their designs are of a piece: severe neo-classical, with white Doric porticoes with columns in antis. The canal itself, still operative, can be followed along the towpath past the 'New Grounds', Jacobean reclamation from estuary mudflats, and the Severn Wild Fowl Trust, a sanctuary for aquatic birds, as far as **Purton**, where the Berkeley Arms Inn has local draught cider. From here there is a really worthwhile walk between the canal and the river, down to the great Victorian dock installations of **Sharpness**. All along this stretch is an astonishing, indeed unique prospect of beached boats. There are scores of them, blackened hulks, skeletons of old barges, scows, lighters and wherries, brought up the Severn to die here, as it were, many of them vanishing into the bank turf, some tilted upwards in stark, rotting pride, others keeled over to show the caulking of their timbers. This is one of the most haunting and eerie sights I know.

On the other side of the M5 and A38, **Frocester** ought not, perhaps, to lie within the scope of this guide, but since its manor belonged to the Gloucester monks and the ensemble of Frocester Court (basically a medieval grange altered in the sixteenth century) and the great Tithe Barn is so much that of a Vale farmstead, it merits inclusion here. The latter is of exceptional interest. Without the grandeur of Worcestershire's monastic barns, it is nevertheless very well preserved, especially in the collars, trusses and windbraces of the roof, covering a 186-foot length of oolite walls, buttressed, with wagon porches to the north-west. A Gloucestershire day might well involve an effective medieval contrast between the big fifteenth-century barn at Ashleworth and this longer and lower one of Frocester, built two hundred years earlier, during the abbacy of John de Gamages (1284–1306).

Back on the main roads, we turn off right to **Berkeley**, capital of the Vale, and now very much a dominant presence with its huge power station down by the river. The town itself, rather like Thornbury to the south, has perhaps lost some of its importance through Bristol's encroachments, and always seems somewhat forlornly respectable in its predominantly Georgian frontages. The Town Hall, Regency but old-fashioned in its language, is the grandest building, rivalled in consequence by the tall Berkeley Arms Hotel, of some fifty years earlier. It is all very obviously an estate town, firmly under the thumb of the great house, in this case one of the grandest in the whole county.

The Berkeleys, who can trace their line back to Edward the Confessor's horse-thegn Eadnoth the Staller, have been here since Henry II granted the estate to Eadnoth's descendant, Robert Fitz Harding. Heavy political involvement throughout the Middle Ages culminated in the battle of Nibley Green in 1470, a private quarrel between Lord Lisle and the sixth Lord Berkeley over possession of the manor of Wootton-under-Edge, in which the high-stomached noblemen led their private armies to war, and Lisle got the worst of it, killed by a Dean archer as he raised his visor. Beyond a brief participation in the Civil War and distinction in the Restoration naval conflict with the Dutch, the Berkeleys kept aloof from public life and contributed little to country or county save scandal and bad debts. The former broke in 1811, when the fifth Earl sought to legitimize his children by Mary Cole, a local bourgeoise (they received the castle and became Barons Fitz Hardinge) and the latter were quitted with the sale of the Mayfair estate surrounding Berkeley Square. Finally Berkeley, after a series of collateral zigzags, passed to the far more virtuous Catholic branch whom we have already met at Spetchley, Worcestershire.

The keep of **Berkeley Castle** was begun in 1153 around a central mound: the original entrance door survives, with its worn dogtooth-moulded arch. Both outer and inner courtyards on either side of this keep offer eloquent evidence of successive alterations – notice, for example, the Tudor chimneystacks and the much-restored main entrance to the house. Inside the keep is the room where Edward II was murdered by his gaolers, Maltravers and Gurney, using a red-hot poker and a table – enough said. We can still see the twenty-eight-foot-deep hole in the corner where the fumes of putrefying carcasses were intended to poison the king, though Edward, far from being the effeminate fawner on Gaveston portrayed by Marlowe, would certainly have survived such treatment.

The Picture Gallery has a first-rate Stubbs of a groom feeding horses, and some bustling Van de Velde sea-pieces of actions in the Dutch wars featuring Berkeley captains. In the Dining Room, by contrast, hang various bad modern likenesses of more recent members of the family. The Kitchen preserves its exposed Tudor roof timbers and many of its old impedimenta, including a splendid round table with four deep drawers. The Housekeeper's Room, with its choice Dutch pictures (one is an early Ruysdael) and lacquer cabinet, is for some superior châtelaine, and everything is almost more than it should be in the Great Hall, with its tremendous statement of medieval roofing (1340 renewed in 1497), Flemish tapestries, oak tables and Tudor screen, one of a very few in England to retain its painting.

On the Grand Stairs hang the two best of an excellent array of family portraits – George Cranfield Berkeley as a midshipman, leaning on a cannon, his look of nervous inexperience beautifully captured by Francis Cotes, and one of those mistily romantic female portraits (of Elizabeth, fourth Countess Berkeley) which give the lie to the Blake-inspired notion of Reynolds as a mere blustering dauber. In the Morning Room, a former chapel, look up at the roof timbers; their Norman-French inscriptions are taken from a translation of the Revelation made in 1387 by the family chaplain, John de Trevisa, a Cornish Lollard and pioneer English prose writer. More good woodwork of the period is found in the Long Drawing Room, where the late Perpendicular royal pew, galleried and carrying Henry VII's arms, once stood in the chapel. A smaller drawing room has been expertly fitted up to combine Brussels hangings, tall porcelain vases and one of De Hondecoeter's typical bird extravaganzas over the fireplace.

Outside we can look across from the garden terraces to the kennels of the Berkeley hunt, whose servants wear canary yellow coats. Several of them were buried in the graveyard of the big parish church, begun on the site of a Saxon monastery in the twelfth century, from which the font and parts of the west wall remain. A century later the present nave was built, with clustered shafts and carved heads above, rising, on the south side, towards a clerestory which may once have been matched on the opposite wall. At the north-west end notice the mysterious steps cut into the turn of the arcade, with the faces of a lady, a priest and a knight: on the south-east corner, a Roman tile is fixed into the wall.

Through the Perpendicular screen, below traces of a Doom on the arch, is the Berkeley Chapel, holding memorials to James, Lord Berkeley, who built it at some time before his death in 1463, and to his descendant, Henry, lying next to his wife, Lady Katherine Howard, under an alabaster canopy. This is of 1615, by Samuel Baldwin of Stroud, and makes a powerful stylistic contrast to James's effigy, placed next to his son's, in Yorkist collars of suns and roses, above a tombchest with saints in ogee-headed niches.

In the churchyard the bell-tower, rebuilt in 1753 from late-medieval elements, is freestanding. On the same side is the grave of Dicky Pearce, killed at a castle banquet in 1725. As the Earl of Suffolk's fool, he was probably the last private jester in England, and is commemorated in not especially deathless verses by Swift, inscribed on the tomb. Further to the north-east, adjoining the vicarage, is the thatched hut where in 1796 Edward Jenner succeeded in his earliest vaccination experiment of transferring cowpox matter to a smallpox-infected patient.

Berkeley, by the way, maintains strong links with the United States. Berkeley Plantation, Virginia, was established on the James River in 1619, the colonists having held, on landing in America on 4 December, the earliest recorded Thanksgiving service in American history. The early Virginians, sponsored by Richard Berkeley, may have been a less highminded group than the Pilgrim Fathers, but they were quite as tenacious in tilling the land and surviving Indian attack.

The B4509 runs south of Berkeley until the right turn on to the broad riverside flats towards Hill. The road actually passes close enough to the village cricket ground for motorists in summer almost to field a catch. The court and church lie side by side up parallel drives on a green hillside. The former, quite well restored in mid-

Victorian times from Caroline and Georgian elements, belonged to the Fust family, whose mortuary chapel, still in use, adjoins the church. This is a genuinely successful piece of Georgian refurbishing, done in 1759 by Sir Francis Fust, which retains its big canopied family pew, black and white chequered pavement, and the seats and pulpit of an earlier building to which the chancel and tower belonged. The whole interior, very well looked after, is enhanced by the brilliance of natural light through plain windows. Among the memorials, notice the tablet to Lancelot Law, who, the Latin epitaph tell us, was killed in a shooting accident: the word 'scloppus', incidentally, means a gun – it is obviously not original, so who was its inventor?

Across the motorway, it is worth making a diversion to **Tortworth**. Here the church, apart from its tall Perpendicular tower, was practically all rebuilt in 1872 by R. H. Carpenter and W. Slater, who created a most satisfying ensemble, free from the worst sorts of Victorian pedantry and nicely glazed by Powell (east window and south aisle) and Clayton and Bell (nave, north side). The monuments to the Throckmortons are substantially damaged, but the Ducies, bankers to Charles I and purchasers of the estate, have fared rather better. Their tremendous house, built in 1848–53, next to the church, was designed by the audacious S. S. Teulon in a massive ranting rhetoric of Gothic gone wild, more French or German than English, and exhaling the spirit of Viollet-Le-Duc and Dumas's *La Tour de Nesle*. Art, with its oriels, onion domes and crenellations, is rivalled at Tortworth by nature, which had a geological fling here, running through everything from oolite to lower Silurian. On the south side of the church, what is more, stands the colossal, gnarled, many-times-sundered trunk of the Tortworth Chestnut, England's oldest tree, supposed to have been growing since the reign of Egbert and certainly mentioned as a boundary mark in the twelfth century.

South of Cromhall is **Iron Acton**, the last really interesting village before the grim suburbs of Bristol are reached. Its houses spread out along a dip below the junction of two B-roads, and feature much colour-washing and pebble-dashing over Georgian and seventeenth-century fabric. The manor belonged to the Poyntz family until the Civil War at least, and Leland found, beside Iron Acton Court, 'two parks, one of redde dere, another of fallow'. These have both gone, as has much of the glory of the present house, shamefully neglected by its current occupants. Begun in Elizabeth's reign, it fronts a courtyard entered through what must once have been an ornate archway. Local legend marks it as the place where Sir Walter Raleigh smoked his first pipe of tobacco.

Down in the village the parish church has survived more success-fully. The Poyntzes were devout and benevolent, and proof of this is manifest in the tall Perpendicular churchyard cross of four arches centred on a panelled shaft, and in Robert Poyntz's contemporary rebuilding of the tower (note the little parish lock-up at the bottom). Practically the whole fabric belongs, in fact, to this early fifteenth-century period, and makes a surprisingly harmonious composition for a Vale church. There is the usual gleaming brass Georgian chandelier (1725) and a Jacobean pulpit with its tester. The monu-ments include a recumbent medieval knight, and an anonymous Poyntz lady, as well as her relative, Robert, who 'this stepyl here maked', and his two wives, Anne and Katherine, on carved slabs.

To the north-west, the B4461 leads to Aust and the M4's crossing of the **Severn Bridge**, designed by Sir Gilbert Roberts and opened in 1966. For once this justifies all the superlatives coined for it at the time. Between its 400-foot towers it is undeniably striking in the context of the bleak, brown mudflats which it spans, communicating a certain inevitable sense of excitement at leaping across from England towards Wales. Roads northwards converge on **Thornbury,** a large and, despite good individual buildings, slightly depressing town, whose *raison d'être* is clearly the castle and parish church at its western edge.

Thornbury Castle is now a restaurant, but enough of the exterior can be seen to gauge the extent of what would have been one of the biggest castles in England. Its building, begun in 1511 by Edward Stafford, Duke of Buckingham, was checked by his execution in 1521 on trumped-up treason charges by Wolsey. He 'was brought to the barre sorre chafyng and swette mervaillously' and it is probable that the grandiose scope of Thornbury reflected the secret ambitions which gave him so much guilty embarrassment in court. It was to be a huge quadrangle, but only the south range is complete, more domestic than defensive, and restored by Anthony Salvin in 1854 for the Howard family, to whom it had passed in 1727. Pugin, as highly enthusiastic as Horace Walpole had been when he visited Thornbury with his Swiss valet, published drawings of it in 1832, which doubtless influenced later architects. The west front remains unfinished, as does the garden wall, suggesting some unrealized building scheme.

The church belongs almost exclusively to dates after 1340 when the chancel was built, to which Hugh, Lord Stafford, added a chantry some fifty years later. The nave was reconstructed at the close of the fifteenth century and the tower ended the Perpendicular overhaul. Buckingham, it seems, intended to make Thornbury collegiate and had obtained a licence to that effect. Notice, by the way, that the clerestory windows on either side of the nave do not directly meet the arches below and that the mouldings differ. Outside, there is the expected complement of gargoyles and crockets, and we can also survey the magnificently flamboyant turrets of the tower, with their ogival cupolas. The general inspiration is, apparently, drawn from similar work at Gloucester Cathedral.

CHAPTER FIFTEEN

The Forest of Dean

❧

Leaving Gloucester by the A40 we are immediately aware of a change. The road crosses the Severn by a new bridge, parallel to the dourly neo-classical Over Bridge, 1825, by Telford, based on a design by Perronet for a single-arch structure at Neuilly-sur-Seine. Now we are in a foreign land, a place which has nothing whatever to do with Cotswold manorhouses or Tewkesbury Vale pastures or the cheese meadows on the other side of the estuary.

Highnam is as good a spot as any to prepare us for surprises, though its manorhouse, Highnam Court, need not altogether astonish. The design is pioneering, the work of Edward Carter, surveyor of works to Oliver Cromwell and an associate of John Webb, thus an important link between Inigo Jones and the later seventeenth century. A contemporary describes the house, begun in 1658 for William Cooke (his stepmother, Jane Danvers, 'a handsome bona-roba and ingeniose', was George Herbert's widow) as 'built quadrangular after the new fashion'. Its novelties include bracketed cornices, carved fruit-and-flower festoons, and a niche presumably meant to hold the shock-headed Hercules now in the garden. In 1755 Sir John Guise refitted the interiors. William Stocking of Bistol may have plastered the music room, with its wonderfully practicable violin and bow; in the slightly vulgar ceiling reliefs of the drawing room are an eagle, dolphin, wyvern and lion; the staircase balusters have delicate ironwork, and the Bossi fireplace in an upstairs sitting room was made in Georgian Dublin for export to Venice.

In 1838 Highnam passed from the Guises to Thomas Gambier Parry, whose discreet alterations were effected by Lewis Vulliamy, son of clockmaker Benjamin and an adaptable pupil of Smirke, who could turn his hand to anything from a smallpox hospital to a cathedral transept. Gambier Parry (1816–88) was a stupendous Victorian, a conscientious landlord, patron of Gloucester orphanages and schools and creator of the pinetum which can be seen north-west of the house. Heir to a nabob fortune, he spent some of it on his favourite enthusiasm, Italian Gothic art. He was not content to acquire this in the form of the picture collection now at the Courtauld Institute, but actually learned and applied its techniques.

The results can be seen in the parish church, whose bold plan (1847–51) by Henry Woodyer, Butterfield's pupil, he may well have influenced. The building (key at new vicarage) provides a perfect case for a Victorian decorative scheme – Clayton and Bell east window, south aisle lights to Pugin designs, lamps by Hardman and wrought-iron radiator grilles. These are all subservient to Gambier Parry's superbly handled polychrome frescoes, among the best things in mid-Victorian art, and based on his study of Italian examples. Over the chancel arch, for instance, look up at the trumpeting angels framing Christ in a mandorla, with apostles and evangelists ranged below, each with his gilded halo. The effect, increased by the height of the nave and the dim interior light, is almost Byzantine.

Past Minsterworth (the church also by Woodyer) the road hugs the widening Severn, then cuts across the Stantway peninsula to reach **Westbury-on-Severn**, whose fourteenth-century shingled spire is all of wood and was twice repaired in the seventeenth century with old cider casks. On the left-hand side, just past the Cleeve turn, is Westbury Water Garden, a remarkable survivor from that briefest of moments in English taste, the fad for Dutch pond gardens. Between 1696 and 1705 Sir Maynard Colchester (a founder of both the SPCK and the SPG) laid out his two long canals, fed by the Westbury brook, as an adjunct to his now demolished house. At the end of the western canal a pavilion, based on a model by a Mr Pyke, has a pediment holding the arms of Colchester and his wife, Jane Clarke. The National Trust's restoration of the gardens has restocked them with many of their former plants. A 1702 inventory lists tulip, iris, hyacinth, narcissus, anemone, bay and asparagus, as well as nectarines and grapes, amid yew and holly hedges.

At **Broadoak**, a favoured place for viewing the regular tidal wave known as the Severn Bore, shipbuilding was carried on throughout the eighteenth century. Sloops and barges were the speciality – we read of the *Sally*, later raised and decked at Brockweir, the *Unity*, the *Eleanor* and the *Hope*, a 149-ton snow, given a 'woeman' figure-head and finally sunk at Belfast in 1838. Most ambitious was another *Sally*, a 263-ton West Indiaman, armed with four-pounders and carronades. Some of these Broadoak boats must lie in the eerie marine graveyard on the east bank at Purton.

Newnham was a thriving port from the earliest Middle Ages, trading in timber, oak bark and forest coal, with tanneries and glassworks. Here, in 1171, Richard de Clare, 'Baron Strongbow', set sail on his momentous voyage to invade Ireland. Sixteen years later the town became a borough, electing mayors from 1542 till 1775, though it was never represented in Parliament. All this industry and consequence has gone, leaving an agreeable little place whose main street sweeps grandly up off the waterside in a pattern of variegated Georgian and William-and-Mary fronts, many of them hiding older timber structures behind. The grassy bank in the middle of the street formerly had houses on it. At the top is the handsome white portico of the Victoria Hotel, a Georgian private house which only became a coaching inn in 1836, containing some spacious downstairs rooms. Opposite this is the slightly drab parish church, with an interesting late Norman font showing the Twelve Apostles. This, and the Norman castle mound over the road, were the scene of a furious skirmish in 1644 between Sir Edward Massey's Parliamentarians and the entrenched Royalists led by Sir John Wintour, the local power-in-the-land. Beaten back into the church, Wintour's men prepared to make a stand, until 'one Tipper, a most virulent Papist' touched off a keg of gunpowder, which blew them all out of the building but killed nobody. The tree-shadowed turf banks and alleys behind the hotel are perhaps relics of Royalist trenches, built on an earlier town wall. Now, with their friendly benches and views down the fields, they make a charming rampart walk.

Leaving Newnham, the road swerves inland somewhat, and we can take the first left turn off it to reach **Awre**, one of the most beautifully sequestered spots on the estuary. Silence is the wonder of the place, and weary jokes about 'Awre-inspiring' are inevitable. To gaze out across the mudflats at low tide with the gentle line of Berkeley Vale beyond, or to stand in the churchyard looking into the well-kept cottage vegetable plots and chicken runs (there was a Gloucester cow somewhere over the hedge at my last visit) can provide the traveller with a dreadfully moralizing experience. The church (locked) has a Perpendicular tower and very good Early English masonry inside and out. Its glazing is plain, its walls properly plastered, and it holds two worthwhile pieces of woodwork, an early Tudor oak screen and a colossal three-foot dugout chest, apparently Saxon and known as 'the Mortuary', since it was used for corpses fished out of the river.

There is more estuary walking to be had by turning down the left-hand lane past the corner house at the village crossroads. Here, staked in the mud, you can see the traps for càtching eel and salmon. The season for the former runs from June to December, and they are caught in 'putcheons', wicker funnels baited with pieces of lamprey or rabbit and plugged at the narrow end with turf. Salmon are taken by a similar arrangement in even bigger affairs known as 'putts', as well as being netted in the river.

Beyond Awre there is little to hold us save the incidental beauties of the estuary, beckoning us off the road by a score of turnings. South of Blakeney, at **Gatcombe** and **Purton** lived, so they say, Drake and Raleigh, prospecting in the Forest. Drake's house was the white cottage beside the railway line, and Sir Walter lived in the gabled manor at Purton. **Lydney** is wholly charmless, but just outside the town on a hill above Aylburton in Lydney Park is the site of a temple to the Celtic river god Nodens, dating from as late as AD 350. Excavated foundations prove that paganism flourished here in the form of a healing centre, its temple fitted with chapels and a guest house and retreat close by, as well as baths. Lydney also welcomed, during the early nineteenth century, a most distinguished refugee in the shape of the Marquesa de Alorna, the Sappho of the Portuguese Enlightenment. Early married to a distinguished diplomat, she had spent profitable years in pre-revolutionary France, and now whiled away her exile in England (during the Miguelist troubles of the 1820s) by translating Pope and Klopstock into Portuguese and writing a long poem on botany, full of laudatory references to her host 'o generoso Bathurst' and with one or two asides on the dismal weather.

Finally we reach **Tidenham**, on the peninsula formed as Severn and Wye start to converge at Beachley. Its big church tower was once used as a beacon. Inside the church is one of Gloucestershire's six twelfth-century lead fonts all cast from the same mould (others at Frampton and Siston) and showing twelve arches alternating deftly detailed figures in fringed robes and scrollwork panels. Lower down the parish, at Sedbury Cliffs, a noted fossil deposit, Offa's Dyke begins its phenomenal northward progress. Recently opened as a footpath, it more than merits its popularity with walkers. Sedbury Park, now a school, was remodelled by Smirke in 1825, with Doric colonnades and a domed central hall, for George Ormerod, the Cheshire antiquarian, and was the birthplace in 1828 of Eleanor Ormerod, the 'economic entomologist'. Miss Ormerod was a pioneer in harnessing entomology to the practical demands of agriculture, and became a national authority on every imaginable creeping thing, whether a potato beetle, a horse bot or a warble fly, appealed to by worried farmers including the Prince of Wales. In 1848 she was at Sedbury with her father when the house was attacked by an enraged mob of Welsh Chartists. Bullet-holes from the resulting affray can still apparently be seen on the house.

Beachley, too, on the spit between Wye and Severn, was the scene of violent action. In 1644 Prince Rupert tried to secure the Severn passage across to Aust, under protection of a Royalist flotilla, but Massey cunningly waited until low tide before driving the cavaliers away. Twice the desperate Royalists came back, led by Sir John Wintour, but the Parliamentarians were always in wait. In the days of the old ferry, dangerous owing to the swift tide, it was said that you could see discarded Civil War armour rusting in the river mud. The ferry, after a hundred years' extinction, was revived from 1931 and kept going till 1966.

Wintour's name is kept fresh at Wintour's Leap, the spectacular cliff on the B 4228 down which he and his horse are supposed to have plunged to safety. Here the Wye coils like an adder through the woods, where footpaths give excellent walking along the line of the meanders. This was not achieved without years of experiment by Vaga herself, crossing a bewildering variety of rocks – carboniferous limestone here by Chepstow, old red sandstone around Tintern and Monmouth, limestone again at Symonds Yat and then shale before a loop back into sandstone. The resulting flat peninsulas offer strong scenic contrast with the sudden wooded cliffs and hills around them. This is very much Gilpin, Egerton and Fosbroke country, ripe for the sketching pencil and the Claude-glass. **Lancaut,** with its ruined church and patchwork of wheatfields and watermeadows, is probably the prettiest place to pause at for an exclamation.

So skirting Tidenham Chase, one of the last stretches of heath in the county, and the Devil's Pulpit, where the Black Gentleman is said to have harangued the Tintern Cistercians, the road takes us to **St Briavels** and the edges of the Forest of Dean. St Briavels (pronounced St Brevvles – he was the Breton St Brieuc) grew up as a woodland hamlet around the castle built here in 1130 by Milo Fitzwalter and reconstructed in the late thirteenth century by John de Monmouth. He it was who added the big curved gatehouse towers, whose modern conical roofs smack of some Angevin château, and these may have been used as a defensive rallying point, though there was a keep, which fell down in the eighteenth century. Since this was the seat of the Forest court, under supervision of the Constable of St Briavels Castle, there was also a prison in the gatehouse. Royal visitors, including an enthusiastic King John, would have stayed in the hall range behind. This is now a Youth Hostel. Fitzwalter and de Monmouth perhaps also built the rather grim parish church, heavily blending late Norman and Early English.

The royal **Forest of Dean** had been a hunting ground since Saxon times, extending from Ross and Newent in the north across the whole of the spur of land between the two rivers. Gradually, through assarting and other encroachments, it was reduced to its present area, which has been more or less the same since the thirteenth century. Everything green or moving in the Forest is supervised by the Verderers, four officers who meet for their 'Court of Speech' at the Speech House, roughly in the middle of the woods.

Besides timber, which made the ships which defeated the Armada and formed the line at Trafalgar, the Forest held stocks of iron and coal. The Celtic tribesmen had worked pockets of iron ore in the limestone surrounding the coal measures of the central forest, and the Romans made of Dean a sort of Black Country, with Ariconium (Weston-under-Penyard) as their chief depot. Out of the slag and cinders left by these extensive workings, whose pits can best be seen at the Scowles, south of the B4231 near Bream, the Middle Ages forged bar iron for marketing in Gloucester and Bristol, felling forest timber for its furnace fires. The early seventeenth century saw furnaces at Cannop, Parkend, Soudley and Lydbrook, turning out two hundred tons of pig iron per year, but the industry never really grew as it should have done, since Charles II, continually embarrassed for cash, needed timber for his navy and turned a deaf ear to the ambitious and exciting projects of our Worcestershire genius, Andrew Yarranton.

The ore was calcined in kilns, then carried to furnaces and forges called 'fineries' or 'chafers', powered by waterwheels. A 1635 inventory includes details of equipment, '1 Grindstone, 19 longe Ringers, one Constable, 7 Sinder Shovells, 1 moulding Ship, 2 casting ladles, 1 Plackett, 2 buck staves, 1 dame plate'. Ringers were used to clear furnace clinker, a constable was a heavy iron lever, a plackett was a trowel, and buckstaves and dame plates formed parts of the furnace itself.

In the middle of the Forest lie workable coal seams, open from time immemorial to the Free Miners, whose rights still stand. Any man living in St Briavels' Hundred, who had worked the mines for a year and a day, could claim his own 'gale' or pit from the royal gaveller (one of the four Verderers) and the Dean coalfields, mainly opencast, were being worked from the Conquest onwards. Miners, dressed in leather aprons and leggings, carried hods on their backs and candle-stands stuck between their teeth. The nineteenth century brought larger collieries, but nationalization spelt the end of pits too small to be run by modern methods.

This unique mixture of hunting, tree-felling, smelting and mining created a remarkable community, whose intensely individual qualities are still felt today by visitors and 'stranger' settlers in the thick woodlands tamed by the Forestry Commission and criss-crossed by rambler routes and scenic drives. 'A sort of robustic wild people, that must be civilized by good discipline and government,' said a seventeenth-century clergyman. His modern counterpart told me: 'They're fierce and tough, these people. You must never let them think that you're trying to tell them what to do.' Free they have always been, though freedom often went hand in hand with starvation and violence. Any tour of the Forest ought to start with a drive eastwards along the edges of the big woods from **Bream** through **Whitecroft, Pillowell** and **Yorkley.** This scatter of industrial settlement grew up from the squatter hamlets of the free miners and ironworkers. Like the little towns of **Coleford** and **Cinderford** to the north, they are compellingly charmless, depressed and depressing, eloquent of a life whose uncompromising poverty offered none of the specious *ouvrieriste* romance of northern mining towns or Tyne-side shipyards, endlessly sentimentalized by today's television dramatists.

Disturbed by the godless condition of miners 'following the corrupt dictates of their untutored minds', the Reverend Henry Poole, evangelical and amateur architect, built St Paul's, **Parkend,** to Richard James's designs in 1822. In recent years much has been done to reveal the originality of the octagonal plan – three galleries on cast-iron columns with alternating windows around a big stone-flagged open space. The Gothic reredos has an ungainly picture of Our Lord between the Commandments. The monstrous organ, mostly unplayable, came from a cinema in Southport, and of the other fittings only the handsome grey pulpit on its column is original. To the north across the field is Poole's rectory of 1829, ingeniously Gothic in all its decoration from staircase vault and drawing room ceiling bosses to the bedroom fireplaces, like the setting for a Peacock novel.

From Parkend we can follow a so-called 'scenic drive' through the heart of the Forest. It is to be hoped that somebody will soon re-open the old railway line, so that the Dean Forest Railway Society, whose smart green engine is shown off on open days on the track below the church, will be able to run a steam-train through the woods. The principal growths here are oak, beech and sweet chestnut, with conifers planted a good deal more judiciously than elsewhere in England. On the high waste tips of the old collieries, birch, alder and rowan have been set, and in the rides and clearings grow foxglove, speedwell, heather, sorrel and St John's wort. There is rich birdlife, both here and down on the estuary flats, and other local fauna include shrews, voles and weasels, as well as six varieties of bat. In this part of the Forest one of Dean's two fallow-deer herds browses near the **Speech House**, a big, strikingly lonely building on the corner of the B 4226 and a minor road to Moseley Green. This is the old Forest Courthouse, scene of the Verderers' annual meeting and markedly Restoration in style, with a heavy cornice, big chimneys and expansively hipped roof.

Another route from Bream, westwards towards the Wye by the B4231, takes us to **Clearwell**. This is a valley village typical of the area, with a mixture of houses scattered up the roadside. To our left stands the gateway to Clearwell Castle, set back from a triangular green at the top of the village. The house is an extremely interesting architectural casualty. It may well be the earliest Gothic building of its size in England, having been begun in the 1740s by Thomas Wyndham, whose descendants became Earls of Dunraven. We approach through a courtyard with crenellated stables and an arched gateway sporting the Wyndham crest. This is in fact the back of the house, and we have to go round to the garden front to obtain some idea of the true grandeur of the design (but who was the architect?), with its flanking turrets and pointed arches. In 1929 the interior was burnt out, and the place left to fall into disrepair until its present owners, from a family formerly working on the estate, began a laborious and dedicated restoration. Now several state rooms, with fine fireplaces and plasterwork, are on view, as well as a dining room made from a former chapel. The taste of the restorers is frankly debatable; their devotion is not.

Lady Dunraven built the somewhat fancy layer-cake church facing the gates in 1866, using John Middleton of Cheltenham as architect. No expense was spared, and the triumphantly High Church furnishings, a showy Hardman reredos, encaustic floor-tiles, painted roofs and a kaleidoscope of marbles in the chancel, give an oddly overdressed effect for a Forest church.

Fond as I am of Victorian architecture I cannot help preferring something altogether less fussy, such as All Saints, **Newland**. For a start there is the setting. This was indeed the 'new land' (the name is still so pronounced) cleared from the Forest in the early Middle Ages, and it may be that the village layout, of medieval farmsteads (the buildings mostly Stuart and Georgian, the sites much older) surrounding a vast three-acre churchyard, owes something to the founder's expectations of planting a town here as the Mortimers were doing in the southern March. He was Robert de Wakering, who began this tremendous building, known as 'the Cathedral of the Forest' some time before 1219.

Originally it consisted of a long chancel, a porch and tower, and an almost wildly spacious nave like that of some Italian Renaissance basilica, its twenty-six-foot-wide side aisles missing the breadth of the central aisle by only three feet. In 1305 Edward I, to whom Newland's fifth rector, John of London, was historian, added the chantry chapel on the south side known as 'King Edward's Service'. This was later used by the Probyn family, among them Sir Edmund, Lord Chief Baron of the Exchequer, commemorated in an excellent bust of 1742 by Ricketts of Gloucester, and Sir Dighton, rather tendentiously described by encyclopedias as 'courtier', but really a conscientious equerry to Queen Victoria and King Edward VII. A hundred and fifty years afterwards came Robert Greyndour's chantry, endowed with £12 to maintain a chaplain who was also to be schoolmaster of a 'half free' school, which still survives at Coleford. Robert and his wife, Joan, have memorial brasses in this chapel, and here, too, is the famous Miner's Brass, uniquely representational in church art of this kind, showing a free miner with hod, pick and candlestick, as the crest on a mantled helm. The two effigies of priests date from 1250 to 1320: the less sophisticated of them is perhaps Robert de Wakering himself, while the other, accompanied by his dog, is probably the vicar, Richard de Lodebrok.

In the south aisle are big, sumptuous effigies to Sir John and Lady Joce, he in armour, she in the height of fashion, both from the mid-fourteenth century. Here also is Jenkin Wyrall, a forester who died in 1457. He is dressed in his hunting costume – a looped cap, a bugle horn and a sword and knife on a baldric. 'Here lythe Jn Wyrall Forster of Fee' begins the inscription on the tomb chest. Leaving the church by the south porch, notice on the west side of the entrance a tastefully coloured glass panel showing an English man-o'-war in full sail. This is to Charles Brickdale, killed in a naval action off Point Obligado in the Paranà river in Brazil in 1845.

Outside in the meadow of the churchyard are some delightful Jacobean almshouses, a long ten-bay range, founded by William Jones, a London merchant, in 1615. At the west end of the churchyard, below the idiosyncratic late Decorated pinnacles of the tower, lies the grammar school, a Caroline building with big windows, to house the scholars of the Greyndours' medieval foundation. Newland then must have epitomized seclusion. Can the boys really have wanted to study, or were they itching to be out in the woods like Jenkin Wyrall, or, more adventurously, like the deerstealers he had to round up?

The deer grazing in **Highmeadow Woods**, in the Wye bend to the north, are less likely to be descendants of Jenkin's prickets or brockets than of fugitives from parks across the river in Monmouthshire. These woods are among the fairest in England, with some of Dean's handsomest oaks, wild-growing yew trees, lime and ash. The Duke of Wellington refused to live here because it reminded him too much of the Pyrenees, though Pyreneans could scarcely devise anything more extravagantly English than the fall of these woodlands to the Wye. **Staunton**, in a broad clearing, has a hilltop church, with Norman work in the lower tower stages and two of the nave arches, as well as a font of the same period, probably hacked from a Roman altar. A second font is Perpendicular, like the pulpit entered from the rood-loft stairs. In the churchyard lies David Mushet, pioneer Forest industrialist, whose first attempts to resume the iron manufacture at Coleford in the 1820s failed spectacularly (his abandoned forge was described as 'a monument over the grave of departed thousands') but showed the way to others.

Just out of Staunton, high up on Staunton Meend common, south of the A4136, is the twelve-foot sandstone mass of the Buckstone, with staggering vistas into Wales. To the north-west of the same road is the Suckstone, which I suspect got its name for the sheer hell of rhyming. This is a twelve-thousand-tonner, a giant among exposed sandstone fragments hereabouts. Superlatives, however, have always been reserved for **Symonds Yat** (Yat is Old English for 'gate' or 'gorge'), the classic viewpoint for the lower Wye, on whichever side of the river you choose. Herefordshire limestone here confronts Gloucestershire sandstone, and the plunge to narrow margins from wooded cliffs is exhilarating to the eye. The tourist becomes like one of those tiny gesticulators in an eighteenth-century landscape.

The road east from Staunton soon joins the B 4228 running north to **English Bicknor**, where Jenkin the Forster of Fee lived at Bicknor Court, now mostly Georgian, with one or two Elizabethan details. Bicknor Castle was probably part of the rash of fortresses referred to so indignantly by the Peterborough monk in that matchless description of Stephen's reign as a time 'when Christ and his saints slept'. Its walls have gone, and in the outer bailey stands a church

Upleadon church

whose fifteenth-century masonry encases a Norman nave worthy of a cathedral, with massive scooped decoration on the capitals. The two stone female effigies belong less to Gloucestershire than to a mid-Herefordian tradition, though they can scarcely compare for grace with Blanche Grandison at Much Marcle. Hawisia de Muchegros carries her heart in her hands, and the other woman is her relative, Cecilia. Near the village is a hill with the irresistible name of Rosemary Topping, sounding like some jolly girl at a gymkhana.

The road bends with the river to reach **Ruardean**, a big village impressively sited on the edge of a slope falling away towards the Wye and the woods of Penyard. It is said to stand on a Roman road, and this presumably accounts for the presence outside the porch of a Roman altar, maybe indicating the site of a former temple. The south aisle is Norman, incorporating an extraordinarily good tympanum over the doorway. This is plainly Herefordshire School in inspiration, probably influenced by French art of the mid-twelfth century and comparable to similar work at Brinsop. St George, in a wide-skirted surcoat, rides a trampling destrier almost into the mouth of a scaly worm into which he jabs a spear. Everything in the composition works and coheres – the saint's breeze-blown cloak, his slightly nervous grip on the reins, the heavily planted horse hooves and the dragon's wild eye. Inside the church are a font, dated with remarkable defiance of Puritanism 1657, and a pulpit given eighteen years earlier by 'Elizabeth Ale at her own cost and charge'. The earthwork in the field at the back was apparently the site of a fortified medieval house.

We rejoin the main road below **Drybrook**, probably the most consistently horrible village in the Forest, and move north-eastwards towards **Mitcheldean**, scarcely much prettier now, though the village streets have one or two pleasantish features, especially in the half-timbered cottages of Mill End Street. Rank Xerox, however, have recently established a plant here, in an effort to bring work to a depressed area, and this has inevitably added a rash of new housing. St Michael's church is well worth visiting. The spire, like those at Ross and Ledbury, is by Nathaniel Wilkinson, that master of graceful line, and this makes undeniably the best feature of the fabric. Inside is a massive fifteenth-century wagon roof, whose bosses, together with those in the aisles, merit craning a neck at. Over the chancel screen are big painted panels, early Tudor perhaps, showing the

Gloucester Cathedral cloisters

Last Judgement and scenes from Our Lord's life. The colours here are predominantly green, pink and beige, and the work has faint Flemish overtones. Beyond this is a compulsively hideous twelve-foot-high pile of grey marble, W. G. Storr-Barber's Edwardian reredos, whose life-size figures enact 'Come unto me'. The effect is precisely the opposite: what attracts is the thing's sheer monstrous awfulness.

South-east of Mitcheldean lie Flaxley woods, and east of these, in the hills above Westbury, is **Flaxley Abbey**, a manor built from the remains of a Cistercian monastery founded in 1148 by Roger, Earl of Hereford, in memory of his father, Milo Fitzwalter, killed by a misfired arrow while hunting here on Christmas Eve, 1143. It was a mitred abbey, with all the customary agricultural and industrial perks which made Walter Map (vicar, incidentally, of nearby West-bury) so savagely critical of the order. Dissolved in 1541, it was given to Sir William Kingston, one of Wolsey's men, who had attended the Cardinal's deathbed. From his family it passed in 1682 to William Boevey, and it is at this point that we meet with one of Dean's great characters, 'the Widow'.

Catharine Boevey, born Riches, was left a widow by William in 1691, aged twenty-two. She was what was then called 'a black beauty', raven-haired, ivory-skinned, and fair game for the fortune-hunting squires of Hereford and Gloucester. A widow, however, she remained, dedicating herself to charitable work among the Forest folk and offering shelter to nonjuring clergymen, including Bishop Frampton of Gloucester and Dean Hicks, who calls her *honestissima matrona*. For this she became a kind of High Tory emblem of beauty joined to virtue, and Steele, whose politics were nobody's business but his own, became her friend and immortalized her in the *Spectator* as Sir Roger de Coverley's flame, 'the Perverse Widow'.

Here lifelong companion was her cousin, Mrs Pope, 'who came for a visit of a month and stayed nearly forty years'. Between them, they fed, clothed and schooled the neighbourhood, female counter-parts of John Kyrle over at Ross (see chapter 18). Her death in 1726 was appropriately impressive, an episode from an unwritten Anglican hagiography. At Christmas she invited the thirty poor children educated at her expense to a treat of beef and plum pudding, followed by a dance to a fiddler and a Welsh harper strumming away in the hall. Catharine herself wore a splendid white and silver gown, of which she had earlier said to her maid, Mrs Vergo: 'Rachel, you will be surprised that I put such fine clothes on today; but I think these poor children will remember me the longer for it.' Within a fortnight she was dead.

Traces of the original conventual building at Flaxley survive most clearly on the west side, where the Guesten Hall, with its big arch-braced roof, stands above the reredorter and refectory. The remainder of the house belongs to the epoch of the Widow and to the late 1770s, when Anthony Keck, ubiquitous in the west Midlands, built the south wing.

CHAPTER SIXTEEN

The City of Hereford

꙰

Of all the Three Choirs cities, Hereford has most successfully come to terms with twentieth-century demands upon a medieval town. Lying down in the Wye river-plain, it effectively mingles industry and agriculture with sedate suburbs, a grandiose Georgian corner near the cathedral, and that central urban core of a Marcher capital, with an eye cocked warily towards Wales and a lingering atmosphere of alien cultures uneasily meeting, as in some trading post or fortress town of the American West.

Until the Civil War it was nearly always on the defensive. The very name 'Hereford' means an army river crossing, though despite so many converging Roman roads, the nearest garrison was some miles away at Kenchester. King Wulfhere of Mercia settled Saxon rule here, Bishop Putta, driven from Rochester, made the city diocesan, and the town, as a border fortress, saw King Athelstan's meeting with the Welsh client princes in 926. It was to keep out the Welsh a century later that Harold Godwinson rebuilt the walls and threw up a castle in what is now Castle Green and Redcliffe Gardens.

An even stronger impress was made by the Norman lord, William FitzOsbern, earliest of the great Marcher barons of medieval England, who, as well as fortifying the territory (castles at Chepstow, Clifford and Wigmore), gave Hereford special privileges and liberties which formed the nucleus of Marcher independence from the Crown. Over the next three centuries it became one of the thriving cities of medieval England, with fourteen guilds and thirty-two chantries, fairs and markets and a community of Jews. Its cathedral became a major centre of pilgrimage and scholarship: among its canons were Walter Map, author of the witty, satirical *De Nugis Curialium*, and Giraldus Cambrensis (Gerald de Barry), a prolific and genuinely gifted writer.

The **Cathedral of St Mary the Virgin and St Ethelbert the King** was begun on Saxon foundations in the late eleventh century. Bishop Robert de Losinga, who, as William of Malmesbury tells us, designed a two-storeyed basilica on the same pattern as the church at Aachen, was a brother of the more famous William whose cathedral still stands at Norwich. This basilica was probably used for services, while the more traditional cruciform church which now survives was still under construction. More Norman work survives at Hereford than at Worcester or Gloucester, and even given the greater extent of overall restoration, this interior homogeneity of style is to its advantage. After the city had provided a focus for the anarchic squabbles of Stephen and Matilda, it was left to the splendidly forceful Bishop Roger Bethune to cleanse, repair and rededicate the completed minster in 1148.

Bethune was deeply conscious of the need to establish Hereford as a fully equipped cathedral, and we find him writing desperately to his friend, Abbot Suger of St Denis, for some relics. Ultimately he fell back on the hitherto vague claims to sanctity of Ethelbert, King of East Anglia, murdered on a visit to Offa at his palace outside the city in 794. The assassin, a certain Wintbert, who pushed the King through a trapdoor into a pit where he was stifled, had apparently been suborned by Queen Cynefrith, piqued by Ethelbert's scorn of her. 'He detested the queen's unlawful embraces,' says an anonymous Latin poet, 'so she, despised for forbidden love, plotted his death.' Giraldus Cambrensis churned out a full-blown *Vita Sancti Ethelberti*, and meanwhile masses were actually said for the discovery of Ethelbertine relics. A shrine was eventually established, the saint's feast was celebrated on 20 May, and the church still carries his name. He was particularly associated with the cure of sick animals, and King Edward I sent two favourite falcons to be healed at the shrine.

Later building continued during the rule of the Foliots and their protégés, extending from Becket's enemy, Gilbert, in 1148 to Hugh in 1234. This period saw the construction of the ambulatory, the Lady Chapel and the tremendous timber-framed hall of the Bishop's Palace. The north transept was begun in *c*. 1240 by Bishop Aquablanca, the central tower fifty years later, and the aisles were rebuilt throughout. Later still, the College of Vicars Choral was added, the Stanbury and Audley chantries founded, and in 1519 the ample north porch, carrying a chapel in its upper storey, marked the last significant piece of pre-Reformation building.

The seventeenth and eighteenth centuries were an aesthetic and structural climax of disaster for the cathedral. In the first Civil War siege (1643) the Chapter-House was wrecked by Lord Leven's Scotch guns, and after Hereford's fall in 1645 to Colonel Birch's Parliament force the library was plundered, the College turned into

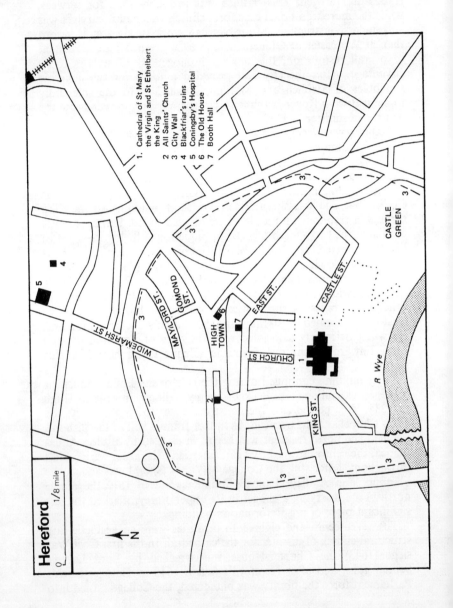

Hereford

0   1/8 mile

N

1. Cathedral of St Mary
   the Virgin and St Ethelbert
   the King
2. All Saints' Church
3. City Wall
4. Blackfriar's ruins
5. Coningsby's Hospital
6. The Old House
7. Booth Hall

WIDEMARSH ST.

MAYLORD ST.

GOMOND ST.

HIGH TOWN

EAST ST.

CHURCH ST.

KING ST.

CASTLE ST.

CASTLE GREEN

R Wye

a poor-house and the interior stripped of ornaments. Relevant to the ejected canons' sense of injustice is the expressive epitaph, on the south side, to James Read, which, translated, runs: 'he fought faithfully, in the field for the monarchy against the perfidious rebels, in the church for the hierarchical rule against the newfangled Puritans, in both against the satellites of Hell.' Worse was to follow when Bishop Bisse (1713–21) set about 'beautifying' the east end with a huge wooden reredos and tried to prop up the weakened central tower. Finally, in 1786, the west tower collapsed, and with it the western end of the nave.

What we now see is therefore a truncated nave and an almost wholly restored fabric, the work of James Wyatt and Gilbert Scott, and though both have been mercilessly criticized, Wyatt for over-much Gothicizing of Norman work, and Scott for his somewhat too detailed approach, the two, together with L. N. Cottingham, who overhauled the four tower arches, ensured the cathedral's survival – which, given the notorious examples of clerical apathy at Hereford during this period, is surely something! Much more hideous, to my mind, than anything Gilbert Scott or Wyatt ever did is Oldrid Scott's vile, municipal-looking red sandstone west front.

Much of the most interesting interior work can be seen in the **transepts** and up in the shaft of the tower. The latter represents the apparently endless resourcefulness of medieval masons in seeking fresh solutions to a structural problem: the groined cage of inner walling shelters a walkway between it and the outer walls, and the whole modern-looking ensemble belongs to 1295, during Swinfield's momentous episcopate. The south transept has a magnificent layered arrangement of Norman arcading in different heights and styles. In the north transept is a series of sharply-pointed Early English arches, with Purbeck marble shafts and a highly ornate triforium above. The allusion to similar work in Westminster Abbey is no accident, since Odo le Orfevre, father of an architect perhaps employed here by Bishop Aquablanca, had worked on rebuilding at West-minster.

This transept shelters the **shrine of St Thomas Cantelupe**, bishop from 1275 to 1282. A hair-shirted ascetic, who hated women and Jews, he was canonized in 1320 (presumably owing to Swinfield's efforts) the last English saint for some five hundred years. He was rich, learned and immensely litigious, and it was while on his way to wrangle before the Pope that he died at Montefiascone, where the flesh was carefully boiled off his bones before their despatch to England. His coat-of-arms became that of the see. His predecessor,

Aquablanca (Pierre de Aigueblanche), was even less likeable. Firm almost to physical violence, he came into England with a horde of other Provençal and Savoyard relatives of Queen Eleanor, wife of Henry III, overhauled the diocesan administration and filled the county with foreign clergy. At length he grew monstrously obese, suffering from gout and a disfiguring nasal polyp – '*Deo percutiente, merito deformatur*', says Matthew Paris, gleefully malicious. Paradoxically his tomb, complete with its original carved crucifix, is the most beautiful single piece of medieval carving in the cathedral.

The **choir** has a recently restored organ by Renatus Harris, presented by Charles II, original late fourteenth-century carved stalls, with exquisitely fluid detail in the misericords, and a sumptuous medieval episcopal throne. Behind it, the Early English Lady Chapel (much restored in the nineteenth century) is a feast of clustered columns and filigree carving in the arches of its stepped lancets. On the north side is the painted tomb of Peter de Grandison, shown wearing a cyclass, the forerunner of the surcoat, and to the south the Audley Chantry (1500) divided from the main chapel by a stone screen. Hereford's two distinctive treasures, however, are not architectural. In the north choir aisle the unique map made in about 1300 by prebendary Richard of Haldingham, and known as the **Mappa Mundi**, is displayed. This is a huge parchment sheet, scrambling together the sum of medieval knowledge and belief as to the nature of the world (both round and flat). Most of the European and Near Eastern geography is highly accurate, and the topography shows the social and economic importance Richard clearly attached to certain places. For the rest, imagine a cartoon conflation of Bible stories, classical mythology, monkish bestiaries and Sir John Mandeville (manticores, griffins and sciapods are clearly visible) and you have the 'Mappemounde' spoken of by Chaucer.

Almost immediately opposite is the entrance to the **Chained Library**, above the north transept. Besides its 227 manuscripts, among them the Hereford Breviary, with music, and the eighth-century Anglo-Saxon gospels on which Hereford's bishops are sworn in, the cathedral library has a notable collection of printed books, many of whose early volumes were kept in special presses built in the Lady Chapel by Dr Thomas Thornton, precentor, in 1611. These presses, of 'good and well-seasoned oke', were constructed on a pattern familiar from the Bodleian Library (Thornton was also a Christ Church canon) with chains to each volume shackled to a long single bolt which could then be locked at the end of the shelf. Some of the presses were re-erected here in the nineteenth century, and others accompanied the muniments to the library in the bishops' cloister.

This cloister is not nearly as rewarding as the **College of Vicars Choral**, all too easily missed by visitors to the cathedral. A door in the south-east transept leads to a long passage, its medieval roof rafters carved with angels and birds. Then a doorway. Then a double quadrangle of the college, all timber-framed, dating from the late fifteenth century, with arcaded cloisters surrounding gardens. Sometimes it is possible to walk through a passage in the far corner and look out on to clerical garden-plots falling to the Wye. The vicars who staffed the cathedral and sang or said its services were not always what they might have been. By 1832, when Samuel Sebastian Wesley became organist, their absenteeism from Sunday service was flagrant, and one Easter Day the irascible composer angrily took two trebles and the Dean's butler singing bass through an *ad hoc* anthem: it was *Blessed Be the God and Father*. As well as this sterling choral piece, Wesley also wrote his classic, *The Wilderness*, at Hereford, apparently inspired by the Black Mountains.

Outside the cathedral is a broad green precinct, with the expected crop of comfortable Georgian clergy houses at its eastern end blending into the august sophistication of Castle Street. To the west King Street presents an extraordinary prospect of clustered estate agents' offices, and to the south lies the gateway to the medieval bishop's palace. It was through here that Bishop Percival, 1895 to 1917, rode as Hereford's last mitred equestrian, dressed in topper, apron and gaiters. In the little lane to the right, a plaque marks the site of Nell Gwynne's birthplace (1650). The local girl made good with a vengeance when in 1746 Lord James Beauclerk, grandchild of her union with Charles II, began his stormy forty-year episcopate. Running northwards, Broad Street begins with the French Gothic-style City Library, its small and wholly unspectacular museum featuring a handful of interesting exhibits, beside the premises of the Woolhope Club, Hereford's local and natural history society. On the same side is the Green Dragon, biggest and best of the city's comparatively few hotels. Opposite is the handsome neo-classical Catholic church of St Francis Xavier, 1838, by Charles Day, and the cast-iron balcony above the bank building further along preserves a memory of its former use as the Mitre hotel, once the Duke of Norfolk's town house, and before that the Falcon Inn.

The prospect closes attractively with the church of **All Saints**.

Rebuilt after 1250, it was given its tower and spire (slightly cockeyed owing to subsidence) by 1330. The advowson was appropriated in 1249 by the Master and Brethren of the Hospital of St Anthony, near Vienne in southern France, and this explains the extreme grandeur of the ten carved stalls in the chancel, each with its canopy and misericord. Traces of fresco have recently been uncovered, including an Annunciation on the east wall, showing the Virgin in a blue cloak, the Dove of the Holy Spirit, and the outstretched hand of God. Besides the stalls, the church has other outstanding pieces of carving: an enriched Jacobean pulpit of 1621 (costing £7) on a plinth with moulded brackets, under a tester inscribed 'Howe beutyful are the feete of them that bring glad tidings of peace', fine late medieval roofing in north and south aisles, and a tremendous baroque reredos in the south chapel, topped with urns and high mitred finials. The chained library of 326 books in this chapel (second largest in England after the cathedral's) was the bequest, in 1715, of Dr William Brewster (no apparent connection with the *Mayflower* family). David Garrick was christened in the font.

Garrick was born here in 1717, while his father, an army officer, was on a recruiting drive in the Marches. The Raven Inn, his actual birthplace, stood half-way down Widemarsh Street, to the east of All Saints, but was later pulled down. For a town without a theatre, Hereford has more than its share of theatrical associations. Apart from poor Nelly and Garrick, it also produced his early leading lady, Kitty Clive, as well as Roger Kemble, Sarah Siddons's father. On the right at the end of Widemarsh Street is part of a medieval gateway in the old **city wall**. Hereford has more of its walls left than many another English town, and careful planning and renovation has exposed stretches of them along the ring road running round the city centre. With their fifteen stone bastions they were finally thrown up in 1298, during Edward I's reign.

Edward himself, while still crown prince, was held captive here after the battle of Lewes in 1264. In May, 1265, while exercising his horses in the company of his guards on Widemarsh Common, he persuaded them to a race, tired out their mounts, then, leaping on to a fresh one, spurred away to Wigmore to join the Montfort-hating Mortimers. The common later provided a site for a Dominican friary, begun in 1322 and consecrated in the presence of Edward III. The ruins of the Blackfriars refectory and part of the cloister can be seen behind **Coningsby's Hospital**, on the right of Widemarsh Street in its continuation beyond the traffic lights, together with the sole surviving English example of a friar's preaching cross, a tall late Decorated hexagon mounted on steps.

Coningsby's Hospital, taking in the Blackfriars and a former hostelry of Knights Hospitallers, was founded in 1614 for retired soldiers and superannuated servants by Sir Thomas Coningsby of Hope-under-Dinmore. The Jacobean quadrangle (now an alms-house) was made up from fragments of the friary, and incorporates the Hospitallers' chapel. Its eleven inmates wore 'a fustian suit of ginger colour, of a soldier-like fashion, seemly laced, an hat with a band of white, red slippers, with a moncado or Spanish cap, a soldierlike sword and a cloak of red cloth'. Their Spanish motto meant 'Be soldiers, doers not talkers.' Coningsby himself accom-panied the Earl of Essex to the siege of Rouen, of which he wrote a lively, detailed and absorbing memoir. Later he was a butt for Ben Jonson, who portrays him as Puntarvolo in *Every Man Out of His Humour* – 'a vainglorious knight wholly consecrated to singularity, a Sir that hath lived to see the revolution of the time in most of his apparel.' Apparently the role was first acted in a suit of Coningsby's clothes specially brought up from Dinmore, and the knight, who was among the audience, distractedly cried out: 'Is that Sir Thomas, or am I?'

Back along part of our route, we turn into Maylord Street, with Gomond Street at the further end marking the site of Hereford's medieval Jewry. The Jews of the city were notably prosperous and hospitable, and on the eve of their expulsion in 1290, Bishop Swin-field wrote anxiously to his clergy, urging them to dissuade their parishioners from attending Jewish weddings. The small covered Butter Market was established in 1817, and we can walk through this and out under its neo-Georgian entrance, sporting a clock tower, on to the broad triangular piazza of **High Town**, now mercifully dedicated to pedestrians. Here, where the town's hiring fairs took place, an entire row of timber-framed houses once complemented the vast Tudor market hall. The hall itself, an architectural phenomenon, and the whole row were destroyed in 1861, with the exception of the **Old House**, built in 1621 and now arranged as a museum of seventeenth-century domestic life. There is a comprehensive display in the various rooms of that pleasantly squat, bulbous Jacobean and Caroline farmhouse furniture, long tables, big beds and chairs made up like bacon flitches and legs of mutton. Equally appealing are the daybed, the walking-frame for exercising growing babies, and the fragments of mural decoration.

Through a passage opposite the Old House, we reach a pub enclosing the medieval **Booth Hall**, the 'bothalle' where pleas were heard and in whose cellars offending freemen were imprisoned. This was built between 1390 and 1400 as a series of twenty-two-foot oak posts supporting a fine traceried hammerbeam roof. From here we follow East Street into the attractive pedestrian alley known as Church Street or Capuchin Lane, formerly Cabbage Lane, suggestively medieval in its secretive plunge out of High Town, and full of good shops. At the top on the right, just before we come out opposite the cathedral again, is a house whose upper room, often open for local art exhibitions, has a good patterned Jacobean ceiling.

Finally, Hereford is as good a place as any at which to recall the unique event which has taken place annually, with only two significant breaks, in each of the three west Midland cathedral cities in turn since 1717. The Three Choirs Festival is the world's oldest surviving musical celebration. Begun with the aim of relieving clergy widows and orphans, it was given the necessary impetus by Thomas Bisse, chancellor of Hereford diocese and brother of the bishop whose 'beautifying' of the cathedral has since caused so many retrospective shudders. Festivals were known then, and still are, as 'music meetings' and were lively mixtures of oratorio and anthem performance with secular music and social events (nowadays rather sadly reduced to a single episcopal garden party). Most of Handel's major works were given, and all the leading contemporary English masters, Boyce, Greene, Stanley, Pepusch and Roseingrave, figured as directors or soloists.

The Victorian festivals had to weather increasing disapproval from the pious. Big operatic names drew the crowds – it comes as a surprise to find Pasta, Malibran, Alboni, Persiani and Lablache among the decent musical Mendelssohn-and-water dominating the programmes. In 1875, when Lord Dudley actually offered to stop it altogether with a substitute payment, the festival was banned from Worcester Cathedral amid bitter resentment, symbolized by the city cabmen draping their whips in mourning crêpe. But back it came three years later, with the young Edward Elgar playing second fiddle in the orchestra.

Ever since it has proved a worthy nursery of English music and musicians. Elgar became doyen of meetings in the years before and after the Great War, as Vaughan Williams and Holst rose to fame and the young Britten and Walton began composing. Every year new works are commissioned and others given their first English performances, while the big choral standards, such as *Messiah*, *Elijah*, Beethoven's *Missa Solemnis* and Verdi's *Requiem*, remain as cornerstones. The music is of the best, ticket prices are commendably low, audiences are discerning and dedicated and the enthusiasm is electric. There is really nothing like it in the world.

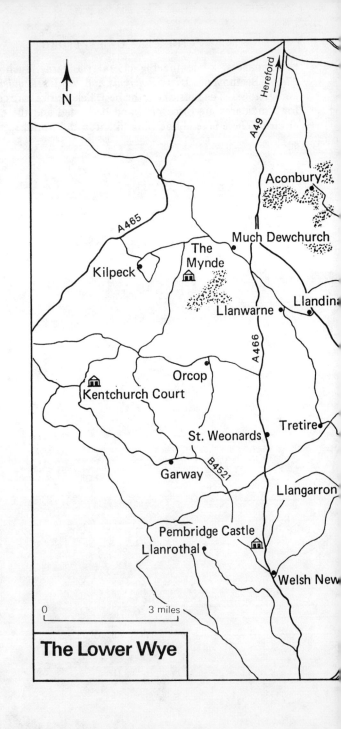

CHAPTER SEVENTEEN

The Lower Wye

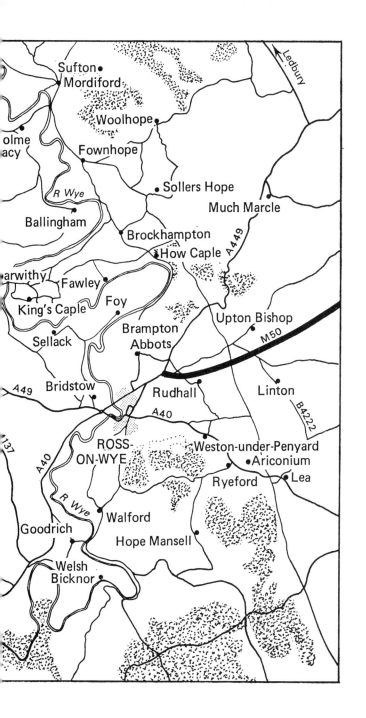

The Lower Wye: Right Bank

❧

Part at least of lower Herefordshire formed the small independent territory of Ergyng, later to become Archenfield, a Welsh enclave in the English domains, which retained separate laws and customs, such as payment of rents in honey, tenure by gavelkind and rights of free fishing and pasture, some of which prevailed until the present century. Leaving Hereford by the A49 on our way towards the frontiers of Archenfield, we take a sharp left at Lower Bullingham to follow the road towards **Holme Lacy**. Dinedor Hill, to the south, was formerly an Iron-Age camp. The road comes down quite suddenly into the flat river-plain, passes the Bower Farm Agricultural School, and finally brings us to one of the grandest and most haunting sights in a county not significantly rich in great houses – Hugh May's long red sandstone palace built in 1674 for John, second Lord Scudamore. Unlike other Herefordshire mansions it does not quite integrate with the gloomy park landscape and rolling turf banks, nor, I suspect, was it ever intended to. Its impact is that of something put there to surprise, which is what it invariably does.

Once the house boasted an amazing array of Gibbons carving, most of which is now at Kentchurch Court or in the Metropolitan Museum. Its florid plasterwork, best Restoration froth, incorporates the arms of Scudamore and Cecil (Lady Frances, a daughter of the fourth Earl of Exeter, later eloped with one of the Conyngsbys) but getting inside the house is almost impossible since it has become a mental hospital.

This is Scudamore-land as much as ever the left bank is a preserve of Kyrles and Rudhalls. The Scudamores have been in the county since Edward III's reign, and were lords of Holme Lacy from early in the fifteenth century. An Elizabethan Sir James was the original of Spenser's Sir Scudamore in the *Faerie Queene*, but it is his son

---

Romanesque fonts – Chaddesley Corbett
Castle Frome

John who, of all Herefordshire's worthies, best deserves immortalizing. A protégé of Buckingham and friend of Laud, he lived the life of a devout, versatile and discriminating Caroline gentleman, breeding sturdy horses, supposedly responsible for improving Hereford cattle with imported French stock, and certainly the father of good cider with his introduction of the redstreak pippin, 'the Scudamorean plant' as poet Philips calls it. We owe much to him, too, in the way of church building, since his pious attempts to atone for his great-grandfather's greed as receiver of augmentations at Henry VIII's dissolution of the monasteries brought him to restore all his family's impropriated tithes to the various livings, and to repair and beautify Abbey Dore and Holme Lacy.

His wealth, however, seems to have been proof against everything. An embassy to Paris in 1634, during which he introduced Milton to Hugo Grotius, cost him £6422 3s, and his loyalty to the crown during the Civil Wars was punished with £37,690 in fines and sequestrations. Perhaps it was owing to the good stewardship of Thomas Webb that he was able to survive, for Webb was one of those meticulous beavers whose records of expenses intrigue by the minuteness of their detail. There are entries for 'lineing yr. Ldship's drawers', 'nutmegs for yor hayre' and '1 laced Ruff & 2 peyer of Cuffs'. A forty-pound pie is sent to London at 3/4d and a funeral is billed at the staggering cost of £79 3s. We see Scudamore's magnificent open-handedness in action: 'to a souldier', 'to a poore woman at Hoarwithy', 'to the prisonors of the comon gaole of heref.', 'to 2 criples at the gate', 'to a man that brought goates', 'to a lewne at Hentland', and 'to a payer of shoes for the foole'. A trip to London takes in £3/6/6d at cards and shovelboard, an inn breakfast of butter, eggs, mutton, woodcocks, sauce, wine and sugar, bread and beer, fodder for fourteen horses, money to the smith, hostler, drawer, chamberlains, 'musick' and 'the poore by the way'.

Scudamore is buried humbly enough under the chancel of the parish church, down a muddy lane by the river. He it was who tunnelvaulted the nave and chancel, most of which is of the fourteenth century, though the south chapel is of 1280, when the original church was built. Both the font, with swags and putti, and some of the benches in the nave belong to the seventeenth-century refurbishing. There is more good carving on the Perpendicular chancel stalls, whose

West Midland barns – Leigh (Worcestershire)
Sufton (Herefordshire)

misericords include a grotesque face, a kneeling man and a horned demon. Here also are the best memorials, the cream, indeed, of Herefordshire baroque. Dedicatee of John Philips's *Cider* (see p. 254), Lord Scudamore of Sligo enjoys a confection of cherubs, wreathed skulls and curtains based on James II's tomb in the Scotch College in Paris. James Scudamore, who died in 1668 after 'a fall from his horse in riding hastily to Hereford about some electioneering business, which impaired his understanding', is a gorgeous wigged and armoured figure, reclining, hand outstretched, on a tasselled cushion under a tall pilastered arch. His widow Jane's tomb, though without effigy, is hardly less extravagant, with its ruched drapes, flame-spouting urns, flowery obelisk and camp-gesturing cherubs. From an earlier period there is an excellent Tudor tombchest with alabaster effigies of John Scudamore and Sibell Vaughan, their shield held by kneeling angels. As you leave the church, note, over the inner arcade of the south aisle, a tablet to a Regency land steward who seems to have been that rare bird, a bailiff popular with the tenants.

Aconbury lies below one of those typically sudden Herefordshire wooded knolls crowned with an Iron Age fort – this one occupied during the Civil Wars. Its little church of St John Baptist is now redundant, but for those keen on rooting out monastic remains it is worth a visit. Several blockings, brickings-in and old arch-springers show the building's relationship with a former Priory of Augustinian canonesses founded by the pious Margaret de Lacy in about 1230. There are few traces of the conventual buildings and none of the house incorporating 'the Lady Abbess's Room' which looked right into the church, though the blocked doorways presumably gave on to the cloister.

Place names hereabouts – Cwmcraig, Altwent, Altbough – show us the way into Archenfield, and though the hill near Much Birch is called Wormelow Tump, straight from the Saxon folklore which filled every mound (law) with a gold-guarding dragon (wyrm), the church at **Ballingham** is the first of several we shall find dedicated to the Welsh saint Dubricius. Dyfrig (Dubricius) means 'water baby' and he is said to have been born immediately after his mother was miraculously saved from drowning in the Wye. He was most active during the early decades of the sixth century, when, as a pillar of the Welsh church, he ordained St Samson and St Deiniol, and founded schools and monasteries all over Archenfield, taking Hentland ('henllan', old church) as his centre of operations. After years as a hermit on Bardsey Island he died in 546, and it is in large part due to him that southern Herefordshire became early so godly.

Keeping close to the river we come to another visual treat, the village and church of **Hoarwithy**, on a ridge facing flat meadows on the opposite bank. St Catherine's is, by any standards, a remarkable village church, built as it is in the style of an Italian Romanesque abbey, complete with campanile and a small round-arched cloister cum porch on the west side, through which the roofs of Hoarwithy look deliciously odd. Inside (key in vicarage at bottom of church path) there is, sadly vandalized, a gold Pantokrator in its Byzantine apse, an ambo of Cosmati work and a mosaic pavement. This decoration is by G. E. Fox, and the building itself, dating from 1880 to 1885, is by J. P. Seddon.

Another Welsh saint, one of Dubricius's disciples, is remembered at **Llandinabo**, a neat little church in a well-kept farm, where St Inabwy founded a monastery under the aegis of Pepiau, King of Ergyng. Here, on 28 May 1629, poor little Thomas Tompkins, the vicar's son, was drowned, aged three. The last two lines of the Latin elegiac inscription on his brass on the chancel north wall tell us: 'Thus twice washed I was yet foul, but now, purified in Christ's blood, I shall be forever unspotted.' The oak rood-screen is pure Renaissance in spirit, a pagan riot of dolphins, mermaids and grotesques in the frieze above its fussily ornamented arch, trefoils and shafts. This is all very Welsh in tradition, though the Llandinabo screen represents part of a mere handful of survivors from what must have been a rich crop of such furnishings all over the southern March.

Alders still grow in the hollow at **Llanwarne**, 'the church of the alders', now a poetic ruin, abandoned for the flood-proof Victorian building above. On Palm Sunday at **Sellack** the church wardens still distribute buns known as Pax cakes, uttering the words 'Peace and good neighbourhood'. The custom, said to have been instituted by the Scudamores, was perhaps merely a reinstituted rite dating back to the days of St Tysilio, to whom the church is dedicated ('Sellack' is a corruption). Son of Brochwel Ysgythrog, King of Powis, he became abbot of Meifod before fleeing to Brittany to escape the advances of his widowed sister-in-law, Haiarnwedd. He is buried there, at St Suliac: his day is 8 November.

The dark church down a no-through-road by the river is essentially one for Metaphysical poets. There are big, brawny Jacobean posts to uphold the west gallery, a tester over the pulpit, a lovely tablet of 1680 with flying cherubs pulling back baldacchino curtains to show Sir William Powell's urn, and, best of all, the Caroline glazing of the east window. Colours here are predominantly yellow, brown and blue. The gawky medievalism of the figures in the Nativity scene is belied by a Roman apron on one of the three Kings in the north light.

Roads now become gloriously minor as we follow them through the quiet meadows and sloping hillsides to the river. This is archetypal Hereford cattle country, and at Baysham Court, east of Sellack, lived Thomas Duckham, county MP and compiler of its first herd book. Down one of these typically muddy lanes we come to **Foy**, my favourite place on the Wye, an utterly rural solitude unmatched anywhere else. St Mary's church, in what is more like a garden than a churchyard, has one of the best-kept interiors hereabouts. Its stolidly primitive woodwork, including screen, stalls and communion rail, was the gift of the Abrahall family, as was the east window, done, according to John Abrahall's will 'after the same manner as such a window is placed in the church of Sellack'. Other Abrahalls have rather frumpish monuments in the chancel: note the very buxom caryatids and positively dropsical putti attending George Abrahall, 1673. The two battered medieval figures in tomb recesses may be members of the Tregoze family, Wiltshire barons who married into the county in King John's reign and lived across the river at Hill of Eaton. Robert de Tregoze was a standard-bearer at the battle of Evesham, but his castle of Eaton Tregoze, crenellated in 1309 by William Grandison, has gone.

A mere bridge separates **Bridstow** from Ross on the other bank. A very fine structure it is, too, completed in 1599 but much knocked about in the Civil Wars, as you can see from the nearest arch on the Bridstow side, which also has a seventeenth-century stone lock-up nearby. The obvious attraction here is what looks at first like a very successful piece of ivy-mantled folly-making, but is actually Wilton Castle, which came into the hands of the Brydges family in Queen Elizabeth's reign through the marriage of John Brydges to Elizabeth Grey. The castle, an oblong with angle towers, was kept out of King's and Parliament's hands by Sir John Brydges, 'one yt meddled not with the royall quarrell', until set afire through the desperate orders of the Royalists Lingen and Scudamore.

His son, James, as Lord Chandos of Sudeley, went as ambassador to Turkey in 1680, and married Elizabeth Barnard, daughter of a Levant merchant. 'Hearing Miss Barnard was engaged with a party to a fashionable conjurer, who showed the ladies their future husbands in a glass, he, by a proper application to the cunning man beforehand, and by a proper position at the time, was exhibited in a glass to Miss Barnard: clapping her hands, she cried: 'Then Mr Brydges is my destination, and such he shall be.' Their son was, of course, the famous 'Princely Chandos', who lived at Canons Park, Middlesex, in the style of a German margrave, with Handel for his *kapellmeister*.

There are almost as many 'Tre-' prefixed names here as in Cornwall. Besides Trebandy, Trebumfrey, Trevase and Treworgan, there is **Tretire** – 'pigs in the mire, say the bells of Tretire' – where John Webb, the county's greatest Victorian antiquary and author of one of the best works on the Civil War, was vicar, and Treribble, one of a trio of interesting William and Mary houses in **Llangarron** parish. All these houses have a common denominator of tall gatepiers decorated with extravagant finials. Others at Langstone Court and Bernithan. The former, built for the Gwillym family, incorporates an earlier house under a hipped roof with dormers and has flowery plaster festoons in the hall over a conservatively muscular staircase of 1670. Bernithan, dated 1695 on one of its barns, belonged to the Hoskyns family and appears more or less similar to Langstone.

Intermarriage between Gwillyms and Hoskynses is said to have inspired the rebuilding of Langstone in Bernithan style. A tablet to William Gwillym and Benedicta Hoskyns in Llangarron church is encrusted with foliage, arms, putti, cartouches and death's heads and looks like barnacled driftwood. Their houses, behind their wrought-iron gates, were centres for the strong local recusancy, more defiant here than elsewhere in the Midlands, even in mid-Worcestershire.

An excuse for recusant assembly seems to have been offered by the siege of **Goodrich Castle** in 1646, when the garrison, described as 'a nest of Papists and rigid Malignants', included the Catholic Pyes, Lochards, Vaughans and Berringtons, and was led by Sir Henry Lingen. Romance has it that Alice, niece of Parliamentary commander Colonel Birch, had taken refuge in the castle with her lover, Charles Clifford, and that in trying to escape they were drowned in the Wye, where, on stormy nights, her shrieks can still be heard. Birch slighted the pile in 1647, destroying the huge great hall roof timbers 'withoute knott or knarle sixty-six feet long and two feet square', and leaving a most impressive ruin.

The enormous rust-brown fortress lies between the A40 and the river and is approached up a track from the river. Probably begun by William Marshall in the thirteenth century, it consisted of a sizeable barbican, with a causeway leading over the dry, rocky moat to a gatehouse with a small chapel on its right. The heavy, tall keep is Norman work, and to the west of this there are visible traces of the kitchen and great hall. On the north-west side lay the solar and through the yawning arches we can look down to the bastions of the outer ward before climbing up to teeter along the ramparts, with superb vistas of woodland to the north and east, and Goodrich village and Coppet hill behind it to the south.

Don't miss, if you leave the castle and turn right opposite the school and general stores (Goodrich is a scattered place) Ye Olde Hostellerie, 1830 Gothic revival, said to have been copied from an illustration in a missal, though it might just as well have been dreamed up in an afternoon reading *Anne of Geierstein* or *The Betrothed*. Wordsworth, as well as Scott, visited Goodrich, and it was in the churchyard here, during the same trip that produced *Tintern Abbey*, that he met the little cottage child who gave him the notion for *We Are Seven*. Goodrich church, on a hill opposite the castle and entered across a field, has another literary association, for here during the Civil Wars Thomas Swift, the great Dean's great-grandpapa, was vicar, and is buried in the chancel. Noted for his loyalty, he once presented himself to the King at Raglan offering his old coat as a gift: sewn into the lining were the 300 gold pieces for which he had mortgaged his little Goodrich property. Plundered as it was by Captain Kyrle, along whose Parliament troopers' path Swift had strewn caltrops, his odd Y-shaped parsonage still survives, north-west of the village, as Newhouse Farm. His initials are over the porch.

Buried in Goodrich churchyard by the north aisle, though the grave is sadly derelict, is Joshua Christall, son of a Scotch ship-breaker and first president of the Water Colour Society. All this country is still much as it was when he and others painted it, and we can catch something of the excitement of Fosbroke, Gilpin and Gray at the ever-increasing beauty of the river, as the cliffs grow higher, the woods hang thicker and the Wye frolics in meander, by going down past Whitchurch (where, by the way, two consecutive Victorian rectors were named William Dry and F. Fitzroy Lofty) across the Dowards, where iron ore was worked, to the promontory of Symonds Yat, with its breathtaking prospects of the broadening Wye.

Above Kerne Bridge, replacing Goodrich ferry, where, in 1388, Henry Bolingbroke (then Earl of Hereford) received news of the birth of the future Henry V, is all that survives of Flanesford Priory, a late medieval Augustinian house valued at £200 at the Dissolution. Its refectory is now a barn, with traces of cloister to the north and the monks' fishpond on the south-west. **Welsh Bicknor**, a church and manorhouse (now a youth hostel) right over the river, was the early home, at Courtfield, of Cardinal Vaughan, one of the seminal figures of the Catholic revival in Victorian England. His mother, Louisa Rolls of Llangattock, a convert more zealous than sensible, used to pray that all her sons and daughters would become priests and nuns. The family had already produced Dame Clare Vaughan, mistress of novices at the English nunnery at Pontoise, and the Jacobite, Richard Vaughan, who followed Bonnie Prince Charlie into exile after Culloden and became a Spanish grandee.

Anglican alternatives here can hardly have been very inspiring: in 1628 the parish clerk, Morice Edwards, was fined 3/4d 'for calling his Neighbors whores, drabbs, queanes & the men Rogues & other unseemly termes' and 'for castinge noysom things in the Church waye'. He did the same in 1631, failed to ring his pigs' snouts and kept mangy horses on the common.

Welsh Newton has the grave, by the churchyard cross, of the last of Herefordshire's many saints and the venue of a yearly pilgrimage. On 22 August 1679, the Blessed John Kemble was executed at Hereford for complicity in the Popish Plot. Born at St Weonards in 1599 he had ministered for years to local Catholics, among them the wife and daughters of the Captain Scudamore who had arrested him. Though even Titus Oates declined to implicate him, he was sentenced to be hanged, drawn and quartered. For many years after his death the story of his smoking a last pipe with the under-sheriff before his execution was kept alive in the local phrase, 'a Kemble pipe'. He was beatified in 1929.

To the west, deep in the hills overlooking the Monnow, **Llanrothal** held the very heart of recusant activity at the Cwm, a fully operative Jesuit college with twenty-seven priests and two lay brothers, which flourished from 1622 until Bishop Croft of Hereford raided the college in 1678 with a posse and broke it up, carrying away books, papers and 'massing trash'. North of this is **Pembridge Castle**, where Father Kemble used to say mass in the chapel during the 1644 siege, when Sir Walter Pye held out against Colonel Kyrle. Built by Ralph de Pembrugge in about 1200, it is moated, with a round west keep and a gatehouse and curtain walls. The hall range is principally Jacobean, but the whole castle was substantially restored in the present century.

The road from Pembridge crosses the B4521, leading north towards **Garway** across a high, bracken-strewn common. This is the unmistakable Welsh border country, and the transition from the cow-meadows of the Wye to upland sheep-pastures is sudden and surprising. It is worth noting that in this part of Herefordshire there are no villages. A parish will have a church, an inn, a post office. Otherwise it will often as not be a scatter of mountain farms, crooked into the slopes up paths and under woodshores as if still cocking a defensive eye at Wales. Notice, too, the local church towers, big, squat, menacingly graceless, touched only by the beauty of age.

Garway's is one such, thirty-three feet square, angles on to the nave, and clearly meant for a refuge or a prison, by which name it was once known. As a preceptory of the Knights Templar it originally fitted a round nave, traces of which can be seen on the north side of the church. The astonishing Norman chancel arch, frankly oriental in feeling and resting on waterleaf capitals, formed a part of this, and the Templars' Chapel occupied the south side of the chancel, built in *c.* 1220.

The church is one of only six surviving Templar foundations in England. Its gift to the order was confirmed by King John in 1199, and in 1312, when royal covetousness forced dissolution on the Knights, Philip de Mewes, Garway's preceptor, was one of those prosecuted. Like so much Templar property it passed to the Knights Hospitallers, who must have rebuilt the nave as it now stands. Pink-washed and clear-glazed, it holds wonderfully rough-hewn Jacobean benches. Well carved, too, is the fifteenth-century chancel roof.

In 1326, as an almost obliterated inscription over its doorway tells us, the nearby Columbarium was made '*per Ricardum*'. Richard's dovecote, six yards across, with walls four feet thick honeycombed with 666 nesting-holes and capped with tufa, stands in the chicken runs of the farmyard south of the church. It is a splendid survival from the days when the Hospitallers' commandery needed the pigeons to exist, though it seems a pity that the hollow of the great drum is now silent.

Little **Orcop**, in the hills to the north, once had its castle like every other border hamlet, and traces of Sir Rhydderch Legros's motte and bailey survive at Moat Farm on the road to Bagwyllydiart, which is Welsh for 'gate of strength'. Orcop was once described as 'ten miles from everywhere', and its remoteness guaranteed a strong folk tradition. One Orcop tale depicts a mother returning from the fields to find her two children struck dumb. For a remedy, cunning man tells her to brew beer in an eggshell before them, then cast them into the brook on either side of the bridge. When she did this, they walked away down the stream – for they were fairy changelings – crying: 'We are old, ever so old, but we never saw beer brewed in an eggshell before.' When she got home again, she found her own babies returned to her.

The big, light, Perpendicular church of **St Weonards** is dedicated to Gwainerth, a minor saint. Its parclose screens are especially noteworthy, as also the highly distinguished Flemish glass panel of a north nave window, in beautiful browns and purples, showing St Peter walking on the water. This marine image is continued in the dignified epitaph, engraved on a brass plate, to Robert Minors Gouge (1765) in the north chapel. After speaking of death as 'A Common Port' and of 'life's uncertain Sea', the anonymous poet ends:

> *Would we but follow and that haven gain,*
> *Gouge and the Virtuous have not lived in vain.*

In the dip by the Garron Brook on the other side of the road stands Treago Castle, a *domus defensabilis* mixing architectural styles of every century from the thirteenth to the eighteenth. Its conical-roofed round towers give it a somewhat Frenchified air. It has belonged to the Mynors family, of Burghill, north of Hereford, since the reign of Edward II.

Kentchurch Court is the seat of a comparably ancient county clan, since this is the fountainhead of Scudamores. Sir John Scudamore married Alice, daughter of Owen Glendower, and the old Welsh rebel is said to have lived out his last days here in the tower that forms one of the oldest sections of the house, though Monnington, further up the Wye, offers a convincing candidature as well. Around a medieval core are grouped a Dining Room, Drawing Room, Library and Chapel Room added by John Nash, and containing much of the Gibbons carving retrieved from Holme Lacy. Among an extremely good collection of family portraits – the best, perhaps, in Herefordshire – is a small panel in the Chapel Room, dated to 1400 and ascribed to an anonymous Flemish artist. It represents Jack-of-Kent, a Welsh stable boy whom Sir John Scudamore sent to Oxford and then brought home as his domestic chaplain. His profound scholarship became a byword, and that peculiarly Welsh facility for making exaggerated legend soon created a whole series of wild 'Jack o' Kent' or 'Sion Cent' tales.

Thence, through a miraculously remote, roadless stretch of country, to **Kilpeck**, where a treasure awaits that is almost, though thank Heaven not quite, a celebrity. In its appropriate farmyard, in fact within a substantial Norman earthwork which once contained the whole of Kilpeck village, lies the church of Sts Mary and David. The juxtaposition of saints is worth remark – a place with a Welsh name but a resoundingly Norman church. This is indeed the sublime example of that 'Herefordshire School' of carving identified in recent decades by architectural historians. It seems to have flourished during the twelfth century, drawing powerful inspiration from Scandinavian sources, from Santiago de Compostela and from the Romanesque art of northern Italy. We cannot fail also to acknowledge a local influence: at the risk of becoming more misty-eyed and Celtic-Twilight-ish than ever, can we not find, in the swirling patterns of leaf and branch here, a certain sort of arcane Welsh feeling akin to that of the *Mabinogion*?

The newness of the stone is deceptive. In fact much of the tough red sandstone has survived intact from Norman days. The south doorway is immediately striking, with its very Norse dragons and warriors, beaks in the tympanum straight from a long-ship, and a profusion of thrusting leaves. Inside, the chancel arch has a comparably overpowering effect, though the carving is possibly of a later date, and certainly by another artist. Notice, running round the outside of the church, the consistently varied line of corbels, including the Lamb of God, a pair of wrestlers and the Celtic fertility figure known as 'sheila-na-gig'.

Behind the church is Kilpeck Castle, a more than usually substantial Norman tump, its layout plain beneath the bramble smother. Its history is a typical chivalric clangour of Walerans, Marmions, Plukenets and Fitz Warines. A frequent visitor here was King John, whom Joan de Kilpeck, a pretty widow, tried to bribe with fifty marks and a palfrey to let her marry whom she pleased. Whether he took them we don't know, but in 1207 she accepted his choice for her of William FitzWarine.

By 1600 Kilpeck had passed to Herefordshire's richest family (at £25,000 a year), the Pyes, one of whose branches lived at **The Mynde**, between Kilpeck and Much Dewchurch. This is an absorbing architectural fusion of a medieval hall and crosswings with an ambitious Georgian rebuilding, which takes in a Corinthian pilastered hall with a coved ceiling and a decorative scheme of plaster still-lives (music, sculpture, painting and architecture) and medallion portraits of English monarchs. The Kilpeck Pyes were recusant: one of them went into exile with James II and was rewarded with the title of Baron Pye of Kilpeck, but his family, as a pathetic letter from Paris reminds us, fell on hard times: 'excuse me Dr Mama if I desire you to send me, if possible, a little Mony; I am in terrible want of all necessarys and soon I shant be able to shew my head; if it had not been for GrandMama & Uncle Rudhalls goodness I should be this day upon ye pavement.'

A livelier image of prosperity is shown in the big tomb of Sir Walter Pye and his wife, Joan, stuck into the east end of the dark nave at **Much Dewchurch**. Both given markedly characterful faces, they kneel above their thirteen children, all named, and at right angles to them two Tudor Pyes, stiff, squinny-eyed and primitive, lie at prayer. Sir Walter was a rival of that other great Jacobean Herefordian, John Hoskyns. Aubrey tells the following story: 'Sir Robert [sic] Pye, attorney of the court of wardes, was his [Hoskyns's] neighbour, but there was no great goodwill between them. Sir Robert was haughty. He happened to dye on Christmas day: the newes being brought to the serjeant, said he "The devill haz a Christmas pye." ' The chancel arch at Much Dewchurch is Norman, so, too, the font, but I prefer the detailing of the head-stops on the Decorated windows outside. The place proudly proclaims itself Best Kept Village for 1976, though its visual charms are somewhat mixed, and the contrast between the church and the modern bungalow next to it, looking for all the world like a slice of Battenberg cake, is pretty eloquent.

CHAPTER EIGHTEEN

The Lower Wye: Left Bank

❧

The landscape of the lower Wye, on its left bank especially, has been a favourite ever since the mania for the picturesque encouraged droves of eighteenth-century tourists to follow Gray and Gilpin along its banks or to negotiate its often treacherous currents by boat. The Wye – the *Gwy* or White Stream of Celtic times – was always a capricious creature, full of twists, sudden and violent in flood, and claiming with sinister regularity her yearly tribute of the drowned. Pope's 'pleased Vaga' and Wordsworth's 'O sylvan Wye' are addresses paid with caution, and the virgin river has triumphantly resisted all but the slightest attempts (and those for only about a quarter of its length) to make her an industrial waterway like the Severn.

Though Gilpin and Gray are essential reading, it was Thomas Dudley Fosbroke (1770–1842), vicar of Walford, who wrote the most enjoyably personal tribute to the river scenery in his *Wye Tour*. Like Gilpin, he had followed the example set by Dr John Egerton, later Bishop of Durham, who, as incumbent at Ross, had first explored the Wye by boat. Besides observations on local history and folklore and detailed accounts of famous prospects between Ross and Chepstow, Fosbroke makes some pertinent comments on scenery and tourists in general, testily remarking of the latter: 'during summer and autumn they poke about the Wye like snipes and wood-cocks, and after rummaging through everything, re-emigrate to London.' For closer appreciation, he recommends 'a well-known small yellow pocket glass called a *Claude*, which gives a sunrise view at full day, without the obscuration of the morning mist.'

Leaving Ledbury by the A449 and turning right at Preston Cross, we can first explore the isolated villages of the Woolhope Dome, a sequence of shale valleys and limestone scarps, with a sandstone cap. Claudian indeed is this exquisite landscape, feathery with beech and chestnut woods and wonderful rolls of hillside. Left beyond Little Marcle, the road climbs up towards Marcle Hill, one end of which is rightly called 'the Wonder', for here in 1575 the entire hill 'roused

236

itself out of sleep . . . shoving its prodigious body forwards with a horrible roaring noise' from Saturday evening till Monday at noon, carrying its burden of sheep and trees with it and crushing the chapel at Kynaston as it moved. Since that alarming Elizabethan weekend, the Woolhope Dome has stayed still, though Herefordshire is earthquake-prone and Hereford itself has suffered some notable tremors.

Woolhope itself is perhaps 'the wolf's cliff', or more likely Wulviva's, since, with her more famous sister, Godiva, she held extensive property in the area and gave the manor to Hereford Cathedral. Both ladies are featured in a modern window in the church, which is restored Norman with a thirteenth-century tower. A number of interesting coffin lids here includes, on the north aisle wall, a thirteenth-century relief of a woman in a chinstrapped cap, though I find it impossible to account for the weird objects surrounding her, still less for what she has in her hand.

The way to **Mordiford** runs through big Haugh Wood, one roadside section of which belongs to the National Trust. One can see why local legend made it the home of a fire-breathing dragon, which subsisted on a diet of male villagers. It was finally slain by a criminal called Garson, who, on promise of a pardon, hid himself in a cider barrel and spiked the brute with an arrow shot through the bunghole. Stern morality, however, killed poor Garson with the last dying snort of the dragon's poisonous breath. Until restoration in 1811, the dragon, twelve feet long, green, with a red mouth and tongue, adorned the church tower, accompanied by the inscription:

This is the true Effigies of that Strange
Prodigious monster which our Woods did range,
In East Wood it was by Garson's hand slaine
A truth which old Mythologists maintaine.

Dedicated to the Holy Rood, the church has an eminently tasteful monument to Margaret Brydges (d. 1655). Within a niche with volutes and a pedimental curve kneels the lady in ruff and veil 'who dyed at her prayers in ye form as you see her porttrature'.

In 1786 Mordiford passed to the Caldecott family, who built, at **Sufton**, a house to rival Holland's Berrington as the finest neoclassical mansion in the county. Often attributed to Smirke (who was nine or ten at the time!) it is in fact by James Wyatt and typical of the architect at his best. A remarkably complete ensemble, it preserves, besides a profusion of deftly varied ornament in friezes, overmantels and doorcases, its servants' quarters, built separately from the house, and its original drainage system. The grounds were laid out by Humphrey Repton in 1795 (the Red Book survives) with characteristically imaginative use of conifer plantations and contrasting flat and hilly terrain.

Fownhope's chief glory is the tympanum of its Norman church, now kept inside, showing the Virgin and Child raising their hands in blessing, and stylistically close, in the folds of drapery and the carved eagle and winged lion to left and right, to the so-called Herefordshire School of sculpture. Several tablets in the church commemorate members of the Lechmere family, a branch of Worcestershire's Hanley Castle clan.

Sollers Hope, with its seventeenth-century church pulpit and modern timber bell-turret carrying a spire, is a tiny hamlet on the way over to **Much Marcle**, which, though not much larger in village terms, has two of Herefordshire's most rewarding buildings. The first is St Bartholomew's church, a big building of thirteenth-century nave arcades with lanceted clerestories and one of those three-light east windows which architectural historians love to point out as a typical local feature. The short central tower is Perpendicular, and the Laudian altar rail shelters a reredos entitled *Musica Celestis*, carved in the style of Desiderio da Settignano by Queen Victoria's great-niece, Lady Feodora Gleichen. She was a talented sculptress, and her works are found as far apart as Derby and Khartoum.

On the left-hand side of the chancel, on an arcaded tombchest in a recess, lies Blanche Mortimer, wife of Sir Peter Grandison, who died in 1347. The breathing delicacy of her face and hands and the fall of her mantle over the edge of the chest make this one of the pure jewels of English medieval sculpture.

To the north, iron railings enclose the Kyrle Chapel, taken over by the family in 1628. Another medieval tomb, almost as finely detailed, shows a husband and wife of the Audley family, of about 1400: notice the puppies pulling at the lady's chic dress. Near them lies what may be my favourite monument anywhere, the indescribably sophisticated and elegant effigies to Sir John Kyrle and his wife, Sybil Scudamore, dating (though he died in 1650) from before the Civil Wars, and if not by Nicholas Stone, then at any rate in his same Anglo-Flemish tradition. Everything tells here, the contrasting use of black and white marble, the lettering of the inscription, the facial features, and especially the styling of the clothes and the splendidly bristly porcupine on which Sybil has her feet.

Three more curiosities before we leave the church precincts: one is the painted oak effigy in the north aisle to a member of the Helyon family, his feet on what looks like a cow, but is in fact a lion. Until

1870 it was customary to carry this into the church at the head of every funeral. Then, outside and south-east, Much Marcle Castle, a Mortimer motte-and-bailey, stones from which were used to shore up the church. On the other side, a colossal yew tree, thirty feet broad, sheltering a seat in its open trunk. Behind, a delightful view, across the track leading to the Kyrle's house of Homme, of pastures falling and rising to the wooded hills.

Down a long drive opposite the church is Hellens, a Jacobean rebuilding of a medieval house, named after its medieval seneschal, Helyon. Baluns and Audleys lived here originally (St Katharine of Ledbury was one of them) and when the estate passed to the Walwyns Mary Tudor, as princess, was a visitor. Expecting her return as queen in 1554, the family fitted up the Queen's Room, complete with the royal arms supported by a lion and Welsh dragon over the fireplace and a plume-tufted four-post bed. The masonry of the house, built around a cobbled courtyard, is as intriguingly diverse as its history, much of it involving lost causes such as Royalism and Recusancy, and none of it altogether firmly grounded in fact.

Lanes from Marcle lead towards a broad peninsula in the Wye meanders, holding four noteworthy villages, the first of which, **How Caple**, nestles, impossibly romantic, immediately over the river, embowered in woods. How Caple Court, a much altered seventeenth-century house with an extensive stable range, once belonged to the Gregory family. Sir William Gregory, a noted Whig judge who quarrelled with James II, restored the nave, transept and tower of the church in 1693-5, and presumably contributed the astonishing screen, whose columns and arches coil like pieces of rope to centre on the royal arms of William of Orange. There are also a geometrically patterned Norman font and a Jacobean pulpit.

At **Brockhampton** (by Ross) we can pause to admire the singular Arts and Crafts church designed in 1902 by W. R. Lethaby and without contemporary parallels in the county. The thatched roof and jagged vaulting shelter William Morris tapestries created to Burne-Jones designs. With an increasing sense of aimless remoteness the road pushes on to **Fawley**, whose manorhouse, Fawley Court, is a superb essay in Caroline grandeur on a reduced scale, with its broadly mullioned bay windows on a pink sandstone façade. The door knocker carries the initials I.K. 1635, presumably for Sir John Kyrle, who died here and is buried in such state at Much Marcle.

After a stretch of open pasture, with gates and grids, and a bridge across the old Hereford–Ross railway, we reach **King's Caple** – Caple, by the way, is a contraction of 'Capitularius', when all this was part of the Hereford Chapter's manor of Woolhope. Here is a splendid church, with a tall spire on its Decorated tower, and a Perpendicular north chapel containing some rather recherché bosses (king, bishop, jack-in-the-green) where the vault ribs, springing from a central rose, meet the wall. As well as a Jacobean pulpit and pews, there is monumental work by Flaxman and Westmacott: the former's, to Mrs Holcombe Ferguson, shows a widow teaching a child, and Westmacott's has Eliza Woodhouse kneeling beside an urn.

At this point we can either cross the Wye to Hoarwithy, or follow the road back to How Caple and thence down to **Brampton Abbots** and Ross. St Michael, Brampton Abbots, has a Norman nave and chancel, a timber bell-turret, and a fourteenth-century timbered south porch. Here the A 449 and the Ross Spur Motorway converge at an extraordinary building which deserves consecration by any guidebook for its flamboyant, almost operatic hideousness. I mean, of course, the service station and motel known as the Travellers' Rest – indeed worth coming miles to see.

Signs in the neighbourhood to **Rudhall** remind us that this territory belonged as much to the Rudhalls as it did to the Kyrles. Pronounced as 'Ruddles', they lived at Rudhall House, which has a fourteenth-century core, but is mostly of Tudor workmanship, L-shaped with timbered gables, a Jacobean stone porch with Tuscan columns and a Georgian south front.

They also held property at **Upton Bishop**, where poor Mr John Rudhall died of a gaol fever caught while attending the 1635 spring assizes as Sheriff of Hereford. The parish register records a licence granted to him by the Vicar 'for eating some flesh upon fishe days and in Lent' because of his illness, of which two daughters also died. The church of St John Baptist has a late-Norman south arcade and a chancel rebuilt not long after King John had stopped here on his way into Devonshire. The Roman tombstone here probably came from Weston-under-Penyard. In the south aisle is an ogival canopy sheltering a medieval civilian holding a book.

Hence on to **Ross**, or Ross-on-Wye, its Welsh name *ros* meaning a spit of land. The spit here is more vertical than horizontal, a tall cliff overlooking the river, with the oldest part of the town perched on top. The eyecatching barge-boarded gables of the riverside houses give a somewhat misleading impression of some bijou salmon-fisher's paradise of the 1830s, but the town is altogether older, developed during the Middle Ages, but given its greatest impetus in the seventeenth century, following an attack of plague in 1637 and Civil War depredations. A long main street curves up the hill towards the worn sandstone Market Hall, resting on columns, with a medallion of King Charles II on the east gable. This was built between 1660 and 1674 for Frances, Duchess of Somerset, one of the most philanthropic women of her time, who endowed schools, colleges and almshouses as well.

Something in the bracing air of Ross seems to bring out philanthropy like nothing else, for in the town's plague year of 1637 was born the good genius later to be immortalized as 'The Man of Ross'. John Kyrle (1637–1724) actually came from Dymock, where the well-landed Kyrles had property, and was educated at Gloucester grammar school and Balliol, Oxford, before settling here as the universal benefactor of the town and its people. It was Jacob Tonson, the publisher, retired to Ledbury, who supplied Pope with the relevant information in the *Epistle to Bathurst*, which recent criticism has tried to align with fashionable views of the poet as a deep-dyed cynic. Though the Kyrles had been Parliamentarians, and John Kyrle himself was a Whig, I find it hard not to see Pope's lines as a genuine tribute by a Tory Catholic to the highest impulses of common humanity.

Kyrle himself lived in the big, half-timbered Kyrle House opposite the Market Hall, built as the family town house in about 1620: in the garden is a stone summerhouse. This part of the town is full of good building, especially in such features as the quaint medievalisms of the magnificently-sited Royal Hotel, built in 1837, and the Rudhall Almshouses of 1575. These lie close to the enormous churchyard, the logical focus of any walk round Ross. Inevitably it was Kyrle who enlarged it to make what was probably the first public garden in an English provincial town, a place still known as Kyrle's Prospect, whose marvellous views across to Wilton Castle and Bridstow are best seen in the crisp clarity of a morning in winter or early spring. One of Kyrle's original gates to the prospect remains, on the south side, with pilasters and pediment.

St Mary's Church itself received the Kyrle touch when, under his patronage, the spire was rebuilt in 1721 by Nathaniel Wilkinson, whose spires, heretical assertion as it may be, always seem bolder and more imaginatively agile than any medieval steeple. The interior arcades were refashioned in 1743, but the church remains basically a sister building, in its expansive grandeur, to those at Newent and Ledbury. The big east window contains four extremely good fifteenth-century panels from the Bishop's house at Stretton Sugwas, showing St Ethelbert, St Anne with the Virgin and a kneeling bishop, St Joachim and St Thomas Cantilupe. Close by is the monument to the

Man of Ross, tastefully restrained in its allusion to his good works. On the south-east side of the nave is a sort of open mausoleum to the Rudhall family. William Rudhall was attorney to Prince Arthur and died in 1530. He is shown next to his wife on a tomb surrounded by rows of saints with, at either end, kneelers before the Trinity and the Annunciation, all in the best workmanship of the period. Quite as good is a tomb from exactly a hundred years later, to John Rudhall and his wife, Mary Pitt. This, with its subtly highlighted effigies and the children scattered around the tomb sides with almost sinister casualness, suggests a similar hand to the Kyrle monument at Much Marcle – the same, perhaps, since Kyrles and Rudhalls intermarried. Altogether *sui generis*, however, is the standing figure of Colonel William Rudhall, a kilted and buskined Roman on a pedestal hung with martial trophies. The colonel was a noted and valiant Royalist, who died in 1651, and it would be interesting to know whether this was erected at once or whether the family had to await the Restoration to put up what seems as much something from a baroque opera as a memorial in a Herefordshire church. Outside in the churchyard a tall cross commemorates victims of the 1637 plague.

Ross marks the ancient boundary of the Forest of Dean, which begins in a very pronounced manner as soon as the ground starts to rise in Penyard Park on the outskirts of the town. **Weston-under-Penyard** has a fine Jacobean manorhouse, built up around an Elizabethan shell, with sandstone facing, by Walter Nourse, of Woodeaton, Oxfordshire, who is commemorated by a brass in the church. This has some good medieval woodwork in the porch and the scissor-braced nave roof, but ecclesiologically more interesting is the Baptist chapel down the road at **Ryeford**. Built in red and grey stone it has a front of giant pilasters and an arched doorway, with the remains of an earlier chapel, dating from 1662, incorporated into a schoolroom.

Both villages stand near the site of one of Herefordshire's two most important Roman settlements. **Ariconium** was, indeed, something quite special, a 250-acre complex of iron-smelting works, linked to the Forest mineral deposits, and excavation here has contributed much to the industrial archaeology of the area. Ariconium may have given its name to the district across the Wye known as Archenfield (more likely, perhaps, that Welsh 'Ergyng' became 'Ariconium', thence Archenfield). Tradition always took the area, appropriately called Bury Hill, between Bromsash and Penyard as the site, and when Mr Hopkins Merrick levelled the hill in the 1800s he found 'fibulae, lares, lacrymatories, lamps, rings, a bronze figure of

Diana, several skeletons and two rectangular buildings, one with a hypocaust, as well as, of course, large quantities of scoria.' 'That the town was a Roman Birmingham cannot be doubted', says Fosbroke, and it was clearly an important source of supply for garrison towns such as Gloucester and smaller places like Lydney and Kenchester.

Behind Penyard and almost into Gloucestershire lie **Walford** and **Hope Mansell**. The former has a thirteenth-century church, with a Perpendicular east window and a handsome font of the same period. The altar rails are Georgian, and over the chancel-arch hangs a funeral helm, perhaps of one of the Kyrles, who lived at Walford Court. Partial local historians like to portray Herefordshire as staunchly loyal in the Civil Wars, but the Kyrles did great things for Parliament – all, that is, except for Robert, a feckless turncoat to either side. His brother, Richard, became Governor of South Carolina, and his uncle by marriage was the poet Edmund Waller. Over the chancel south wall a tablet commemorates T. D. Fosbroke, curate and vicar here from 1810 to 1842.

North-west of Walford, Hill Court is an exceptionally beautiful William and Mary house built for the Clarke family between 1698 and 1708. Its main front was probably given its present form, with two projecting wings with Venetian windows, just before 1750, and the original staircase, ceilings and panelling remain. A delightful conversation piece by Arthur Devis still exists, showing Alicia and Jane Clarke sitting in the garden at Hill Court, with a view across to Walford Church.

Hope Mansell perches on the very borders of the county, high over the typical outlying wooded dingles of the Forest. Though the church has some eighteenth-century windows and a highly distinguished Latin elegiac epitaph of 1663 to Elizabeth Skynner, one of its rectors, Henry Bisse, ripped out the font, painted rood-loft and Caroline pulpit as 'relics of Popery'. **Lea**, to the north, is worthier of a visit for its late Romanesque font from southern Italy, given to the church in 1907, the bowl borne on an elephant. Following the B4222 almost to the motorway we reach **Linton**, where there has been a settlement of some sort since the Bronze Age. Whoever designed the tower of St Mary's church seems to have taken a hint from King's Caple, for the rib-vaults converging on the bell-opening spring from corbels of almost pagan exuberance, showing a cudgel-wielding figure, a hooded man, and two grotesque heads. In the churchyard are a number of vigorously carved headstones from the late seventeenth century.

Vicar here from 1703 to 1760 was Peter Senhouse, one of the founders of the Three Choirs music meetings, and preacher at Gloucester in 1727 of *On the Right Use and Improvement of Sensitive Pleasures, and more particularly of Music.* His unfortunate predecessor, Charles Hoskyns, incumbent for one year only, is commemorated in Bath Abbey by an inscription telling us that his gravestone covers his 'complicated dust'.

CHAPTER NINETEEN

Ledbury to Bromyard

❧

Hops, fruit and cattle make the wealth of Herefordshire and are all carefully localized within the county. The hop country is roughly that square formed by Hereford, Leominster, Bromyard and Ledbury, watered by the Frome, the Lugg and the Leadon, and as yielding a soil as any in England. Apart from the familiar tall avenues of strung poles, each with its dark green garland of 'North Down', 'Challenger' or 'Bullion' (the good old 'Fuggle' is now being phased out) the mark of hop growing is, or at any rate was, in the conical brick oasthouses, like the towers of a château, on farm after farm. Herefordshire farm buildings are nearly always worth a closer look, and though many of the oasthouses, with their pigeon-grey ventilators, have disappeared, and the Common Market's agricultural policy has restricted hop-growing, there are still enough to give a singularity to this landscape of distant prospects and long vistas.

From Ledbury we can strike north along the B4214 under Stephen Ballard's great railway viaduct of 1859–61, still carrying a track to Hereford, but shamefully neglected. The road runs up the Leadon valley towards the three Frome villages. **Canon Frome**, belonging to the canons of Llanthony Abbey, has a church whose west tower was rebuilt in brick in 1680, possibly part of a scheme begun sixteen years earlier by Dame Deborah Hopton, whose family lived at the court. Her husband, Sir Edward, had garrisoned the place for the King, to whom he was Yeoman of the Stirrup, but after fierce fighting Lord Leven's Scots took it on 22 July 1645, holding off two counterattacks by Sir Barnabas Scudamore, Leven himself being awarded by Parliament a jewel worth £500. The present house, built in 1786 and now a school, has a remarkable Tudor overmantel, with allegorical figures of Justice, Wisdom and Prudence framing architectural perspectives.

The church at **Castle Frome** stands well above the road and deserves visiting for its splendid font, described by Pevsner as 'one of the masterpieces of Romanesque sculpture in England'. As a sculptural ensemble it holds a mesmeric power, the earthy decoration

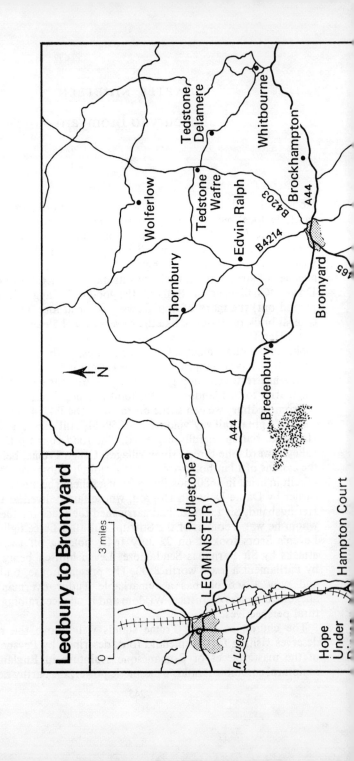

Ledbury to Bromyard

N

0 ——— 3 miles

Tedstone Delamere

Whitbourne

Brockhampton

A44

Tedstone Wafre

Edvin Ralph

B4203

Wolferlow

B4214

Bromyard

A465

Thornbury

Bredenbury

A44

Pudlestone

LEOMINSTER

R Lugg

Hope Under

Hampton Court

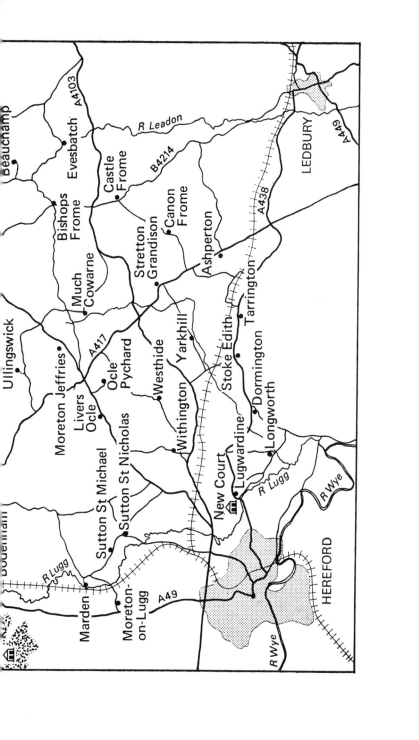

on the top of the bowl vigorously complemented by a moving Baptism of Christ and the crouching figures below. Norman work elsewhere can be seen in west and south doorways and the chancel arch, though the ribs and bosses of the ceiling beyond it are perhaps very early Tudor. Note here, by the way, the little surcoated heart-holding knight in the south-east window. There is also an exquisite Caroline monument to two anonymous members of the Unett or Devereux families: smartly dressed, they lie on tasselled cushions, with a pall drooping gracefully over the tombchest.

Little remains of the eponymous castle, belonging to the Lacys and Devereuxes, so let us climb Fromes Hill for one of my favourite Herefordshire prospects, of the hills and valleys stretching away westwards into Wales. **Bishops Frome**, apart from a medieval tower, is Victorian neo-Norman by F. R. Kempson of Hereford, who took his cue from a south doorway. There are two good monuments, one of them to an unnamed cross-legged knight in the act of drawing his sword, the other to Margery de la Downes, a member of the Pychard family who died in 1598, kneeling above her recumbent skeleton. Of the three distinguished fifteenth-century Italian paintings discovered behind the altar in 1974, two are given to Antonello da Messina.

A lane winds eastwards, to **Evesbatch**, whose Jacobean font-cover was probably given by one of the Dobyns family. Margaret Dobyns (d. 1658) has a pretty, chubby memorial, showing her holding her baby, and flanked by allegories. Earlier tenants of the manor, the Pembrugges, paid rent of a red rose on St John the Baptist's day. **Acton Beauchamp** church is, rarely for Herefordshire, Regency, of 1819, but incorporating, on the lowest stage of the tower, a Saxon cross carved with animals and birds.

We can join the main road again just outside **Bromyard**, spectacularly sited on the sides of a bowl. The original layout of its burgage plots is still marked in the curious scythe-shaped curve of its main streets. It has never developed to anything of great importance, despite the grandeur of some of its inns and houses, and comes upon the traveller as a charming urban surprise below its gorsy downs. There are several good coaching inns (the timber-framed Falcon and the Hop Pole are the best) and the main thoroughfares have good black and white: turn a deaf ear, however, to the local tradition which gives Tower House as a 'Charles-I-stayed-here'. Though the King really did lead the royal army through the town in 1645, the house he stopped at was long ago demolished.

Up on the hill, St Peter's church, in its expansive yard, has big profuse Norman doorways, with three orders of shafts, the south doorway carrying a carved panel of the saint with his two keys. The fourteenth-century tower has a round castellated stair-turret, but internally the church, its two nave arcades stylistically divided by twenty years (1190–1210) is dull, though it is worth inspecting the big lead bowl made in 1670 for the town's bushel measure, and also a Victorian oddity, Deacon's *Synchronological Chart of World Events since the Flood.*

North of Bromyard stretches a wooded border country formed by the western escarpments of the Teme valley. The main A 44 to Worcester takes us past some splendid old brick-and-tile works and over the rolling downland to **Brockhampton,** in woods belonging to the National Trust. The Trust also manages the fine medieval manorhouse reached down a drive to the left of the road. This was built during the reign of Edward III, and though added to in the sixteenth and seventeenth centuries, manages to preserve the sort of flavour associated with Chaucer's jolly Franklin:

> *It snewed in his hous of mete and drinke,*
> *Of all deyntees that men coude thinke.*

The timbered gatehouse, with its vine-trail bargeboards, is the gem of the ensemble, prettily encircled with a moat. Also in the park is a chapel built in 1798 by George Byfield, who built Graycombe in the Vale of Evesham, and Worcester gaol. Grey Gothic, with a pinnacled tower, it has some good neo-classical tombs, dating mostly from the early 1800s, including one, to Lydia Bulkeley, signed by John Bacon, jnr.

Crossing the broad Sapey brook and turning left, we reach **Whitbourne,** a favourite manor of the Bishops of Hereford. The last of them to live here was Dr Bisse, but the court with its big moat had already welcomed Swinfield and seen the death, in 1585, of the unpopular ex-Dominican Scory. Its most famous resident was surely Francis Godwin, talented, mercurial and 'a very great Symoniack', who died here in 1633. I like to think that he wrote his delightful little science fiction romance *The Man in the Moone* at Whitbourne, and so to claim him among Herefordshire's comparatively few good writers. On his tomb in the church was written 'Win God, Win All'. The church itself has nave, chancel and tower successively of twelfth to fourteenth centuries, a Tudor lychgate, and a richly embroidered late medieval cope. Its Norman font carries an Agnus Dei.

Passing Whitbourne Hall, built with powerful allusions to the

Erectheum by E. W. Elmslie for a wealthy vinegar merchant, for £21,500 in 1861, we cross the hill to **Tedstone Delamere** and **Tedstone Wafre**, named after medieval knightly tenants. At the former, St James's church mingles masonry in sandstone and Teme valley tufa. Its nave east end has Saxon work, meeting a chancel by Scott (1856–7) with a charming Perpendicular screen between, and a Hardman east window. In the porch is an iron hourglass stand, and by the churchyard gate a cross head, amazingly unscathed, preserves a fourteenth-century Crucifixus and Madonna and Child.

The local historian Dr Duncumbe, stunningly zeugmatic, observes: 'Through this parish also flows the brook from Sapey, remarkable for its finely flavoured trout and its romantic beauties.' Worried by the stream's lack of an adequate name, a local Orpheus was moved to verse. He was Dr Luke Booker, vicar 1806–12, who, besides making £9000 as a preacher of charity sermons, wrote turgidly and at some length such poetical works as *The Hop-Garden*, *Euthanasia*, *The Springs of Plynlimmon* and *Mandane, A Drama*. He ends a shorter effusion, to the brook, as follows:

> *Yet tho' no verse of mine may live,*
> *A name to thee thy bard will give,*
> *Through Tedstone Delamere's rich plains,*
> *Where crown'd with hops Pomona reigns,*
> *Thou musically flowst along,*
> *In concord with the woodman's song;*
> *Still flowing, grace these plains so fair,*
> *And hence be called,* THE DELAMERE.

Booker, poor fellow, was bang right. His verse has not lived, and Sapey, like Moscow and Parma, stands on a river carrying its name.

To the left of the B4203, a Roman fort was discovered in 1954. North of this, **Wolferlow** church, whose list of incumbents includes Egidius Rawlins and Laus-Deo Malden, has one of those poetically conceived effigies of medieval ladies in which Herefordshire abounds. She is, perhaps, Joan de Geneville, and she is shown with her coifed and wimpled head resting on angels, her feet on a dog, and her mantle caught up over her arm.

At **Edvin Ralph**, on the parallel B-road, the church contains effigies of comparable grace, now placed below the tower but presumably accommodated earlier in the two vacant recesses in the chancel. In both sets, a mailed husband of Edward I's time beside his wife, and a man of a later generation between two spouses, it is the styling of the hands, the blissfully calm features and the falling female drapery which arrest us.

Thornbury, or, to be more precise, Netherwood, down isolated cart tracks, was the birthplace of two of the stormiest figures of English history, Roger Mortimer and the Earl of Essex. Of the former, more will be said at his castle of Wigmore. Thornbury manor was given to Walter Devereux in 1552 and his son, Robert, was born fifteen years later. Cultivated, articulate and charming, his pride and high spirits inevitably brought him into the forefront of late-Elizabethan public life. Between piratical expeditions with Drake to Spain, he married Sidney's widow, Frances Walsingham, and thereafter his story, as the jealous old Queen's last attachment and a patron of Shakespeare's company, is part of English historical legend. What remains of his family house is one south-west wing incorporated in an eighteenth-century rebuilding.

From here to Leominster we can take two ways: the main road from Bromyard, interestingly dotted with bed-and-breakfast places, takes us through **Bredenbury,** whose village shop has good home-made fudge: just past Steen's Bridge, to right and left, runs a Roman road, with its inevitable Stretford hamlet, which can be walked as part lane, part footpath, right down to Bowley, after which it disappears. The other way, a good deal more meandering and all on minor roads, takes in **Pudlestone.** Pevsner convincingly suggests Anglo-Saxon origins for certain features of the church tower windows (it has a spire) and the nave, a Regency rebuilding of 1813, has stained-glass Apostles and angels by Pugin (1850–1). Elias Chadwick, who commissioned him, was responsible for the castellated lodges to Pudlestone Court.

South of Leominster, on the right bank of the Lugg, is the huge cornstone mass of Dinmore Hill, shaped like a turtle shell, with typical wooded sides. **Dinmore Manor,** tucked into its southern edge, is a house on the site of two earlier buildings, the first of which was a Commandery of the Knights Hospitallers, whose small fourteenth-century chapel (one of only three in England dedicated to St John of Jerusalem) remains. The present owner, son of the inventor of 'cat's eyes' for motorists, has added a Music Room, Cloister and Grotto, in markedly individual style, giving on to ornamental gardens open to the public. On the hill's north-eastern side, **Hope Under Dinmore's** Victorian church contains a font with exquisite thirteenth-century panels, showing Christ, St John the Baptist and Sts Peter and Paul. In the north-west chapel is a splendid monument, without inscription, showing Earl and Countess Conyngsby and their infant son, Richard. The two-year-old boy is holding the cherry on whose stone he choked to death. Pevsner hints at 1760 for this, though there is no reason why it should not be earlier, since the Earl died in 1729 and his son in 1708.

The Conyngsbys lived at **Hampton Court** across the river, an impressive fifteenth-century pile originally crenellated by Sir Rowland Lenthall, using ransom money from French prisoners at Agincourt. The gatehouse and chapel both belong to this period, but further gothicizing, by Wyattville, took place when Sir Richard Arkwright, the cotton-spinner's son, bought it in 1817. Inside, the main staircase and a big grey and white marble fireplace have been attributed to Talman.

Bodenham, in the river bend, has a village green, with its church down a dead-end lane. This contains a fine medieval effigy of a lady (Bohun, Lacy or Devereux) holding her child, her feet upon a greyhound, her face still highly characterful. To the south, **Marden, Moreton-on-Lugg** and the **Suttons**, St Nicholas and St Michael, form an attractive riverside group. At Marden, Laystone Bridge is seventeenth-century, its central arch heightened a hundred years later. From the west wall of the church nave gushes St Ethelbert's Well: the saint was murdered over the river at Sutton Walls. Moreton has another good bridge, Elizabethan, with cutwater piers. Both its church and that at Sutton St Nicholas have interesting screens. Moreton's is a sumptuous, eight-bay, ogee-headed example, Sutton's a hodge-podge of Tudor and modern. Sutton St Michael has two fonts, a simple Norman tub on lions, like an opened boiled egg, and a classical mid-seventeenth-century urn upon an angel with a book. The great earthwork of Sutton Walls, possibly an Iron Age tribal capital, was inhabited until the fourth century AD and once again in Saxon times by King Offa of Mercia. Numbers of headless and wounded skeletons found in the ditch here suggest a massacre during the Roman invasion.

On the higher ground south-east of Leominster, keeping the Lugg and the A 417 on our right, is **Ullingswick**. The church here is without dedication, though the presence of a Virgin and Child in the fifteenth-century east window glass may provide a clue. On the nave south wall a painted rectangular tablet shows John Hill (d. 1591) lying on an altar tomb, surrounded by his three surviving children, two shrouded infants and his wife, Elizabeth Brooke. The Hills lived at the big timber-framed farmhouse east of the church.

From Ullingswick it is worth pressing on, as if towards Little

Cowarne and then turning right to meet the main road and doubling back for the turn to **Moreton Jeffries**. Like all the villages in this part of Herefordshire it is down a lane to nowhere, a parish of farmsteads and muddy roadways, whose church, like several others in the county, preserves a tangible atmosphere of the Caroline Anglicanism reflected in the work of Marcher poets like Vaughan and Traherne. I like to imagine Herbert, himself from a Marcher family, preaching from the flamboyant pulpit, with its marvellous strapworked sounding board and spiky finials, and some flowing scrollwork on the reading desk below.

Much Cowarne, too, lies off the roads. Its church has great structural interest – a sturdy Norman tower joins a nave whose vanished thirteenth-century north aisle can be traced in a series of blocked arches, matched on the south side by another aisle added a century later. In the chancel is a Perpendicular east window. Visitors and parishioners have not been kind to Much Cowarne's tombs: the much mutilated effigy of Grimbald de Pauncefote in the south aisle was formerly accompanied by his wife, Constance de Lingen, who is said to have cut off her right hand as the stipulated ransom for her husband, taken prisoner in 1270 at the siege of Tunis by Louis IX. Comparable tales are told of Pauncefotes at Crickhowell, Breconshire, and Hasfield, Gloucestershire. Nor has Jacobean Edmund Fox of nearby Leighton Court done much better, lying next his wife, Anne Aberford, and kneeling children, but minus his stone feet. Notice, though, the three funny babies shown peeping over the cradle blankets. Childbed killed their neighbour, poor Mistress Reed of Lugwardine, commemorated in an unusually good Latin quatrain on a wall plaque.

To the west **Ocle Pychard** preserves the name of one of a set of Herefordshire clans like the Edvins, Baggards and Pembrugges who died out with the Middle Ages and the rise of the Scudamores and Devereuxes. Little **Livers Ocle**, close by, recalls the Norman abbey of Lire, which kept a Benedictine cell here until Henry V's dissolution of alien houses in 1413. **Westhide**'s church of St Bartholomew is of interest for its traces of fourteenth-century painted decoration around the south aisle east window. There are faint marks of painting, too, on the medieval effigy in the same aisle, probably to some local yeoman, his feet on a dog, his hands cradling a heart. At the west end is an alabaster slab of 1524 depicting Richard and Alice Monyngton and their sixteen children, the figures incised with a lumpy ineptitude.

Passing a hill called Poll Noddy and the long shore of Westhide wood, we reach **Withington**, a landmark in this countryside, with its lovely recessed church spire decorated with rolled mouldings. Inside, the carved screen has trefoiled ogee heads and a moulded cornice, and the churchyard is entered through a Tudor lychgate with wide and narrow entrances. The village is really a group of hamlets, two others being, as their names, Eau Withington and Withington Marsh suggest, down by a stream flowing into the Lugg. Timber-framed Eau Withington Court has its original Caroline staircase and was once the home of the minor poet, William Broome (1689–1745), who cobbled together eight books of 'Pope's' *Odyssey* for £500. Nothing if not acid, the master thanks him in the *Dunciad*:

> *Hibernian politics, O Swift, thy doom,*
> *And Pope's – translating three whole years with Broome.*

Broome was the great friend of my favourite Herefordshire poet, John Philips (1676–1709). Educated at Winchester and Christ Church, where he used to enjoy reading Milton while having his long hair combed, Philips set up as a sort of official Tory muse, but, readable as parts of his *Blenheim* are, it was in the affectionate burlesque Miltonic that his true talents lay, and in 1708 he published that minor masterpiece, *Cider*, a Wye valley Georgic of such remarkable wit and vitality as to attract French and Italian translations.

The Danes must have liked this marshy mesopotamia if the name Thinghill and the presence of two hills here called Daneshill are anything to go by. The slope above Shucknall produces fuller's earth, and in Victorian times, near the now vanished Withington station, Godwin's Mediaeval Encaustic Tile Works designed 'pavements for the decoration of cathedrals and other public buildings . . . manufactured with much taste and success'.

There seem to be more stretches of Roman road here than anywhere else in the west Midlands, and certainly the criss-cross of straights around Hereford suggests, if it does not prove, an importance and activity out of all proportion to the size of the county's various Roman sites. Just below one of these roads **Lugwardine** stands on a hill overlooking the broad watermeadows on either side of the river. St Peter's church jumbles Norman with Early English (note the chancel lancets) and a stolid Perpendicular tower, one of whose contemporary bells carries the rhyme: '*In multis annis resonet campana Johannis*'. There are several good Caroline tombs, including a coloured bust of parson John Best in ruff and beard, a brass in the south aisle showing his wife, Jane, kneeling in a church, and the reclining figure of William Reed, rather dashingly got up in a sash and rhinegrave boots.

Lugwardine is encircled with pleasant small Georgian country houses, built with an eye to the soft, gratifying prospects in this green, well-watered country. North-west of the church, near the newer of the two bridges (the one on the Withington road is medieval) New Court in its big park was gothicized, 1809–10, by H. H. Seward, a pupil of Soane, for Archdeacon Lilly. To the south-east, above the confluence of Frome and Lugg, Longworth was built in 1788 by Anthony Keck, who gave it a grandiose introduction of big lodges. Its owner was James Walwyn, MP for Hereford, member of a family supposedly descended from King Arthur's sister.

Home across the Frome through Dormington, where the big white farmhouse is now a hotel. The church has a remarkable Norman door-knocker showing a pop-eyed cat, and inside, the author of the epitaph (1669) to John Brydges seems to have had Donne in mind with his poignant forcing of the accent. Further along between the hopyards, Stoke Edith is the ghost of an estate belonging to the Foley family. Elegant, pink-veined sandstone gate lodges are there, so are parts of the Brownized grounds, but the fine William and Mary house was destroyed by fire in 1927. The church is a magnificent piece of 1740–2, with characteristic fittings, including simulated marbling in the apsidal shell. The railed-off alabaster figure at the west end is a late medieval member of the Walwyn family.

At the handsome Georgian Foley Arms at Tarrington, the geologist, Sir Roderick Murchison, after whom the Nile falls were named, stayed while studying the local strata and wrote up notes here for his epoch-making survey, The Silurian System (1838). Behind, and quite spectacularly placed above the road, is the Norman church, with some delicate patterned carving on the chancel arch responds, though the man and horse on the right-hand capital of the south doorway may simply be inspired faking. There is a chastely refined medieval font and an ornate recess of the same period shelters a stone lady, perhaps one of the De La Barres.

The parish registers contain much of interest, including a burial entry for the centenarian, Jane Gallett: 'She often said she remembered Oliver's Wind, as she called it, very well, being a good big girl, 14 or 15 at least when it [the storm on the night of Cromwell's death] happened, which was September 3rd, 1658, so that she was 105 or upwards . . . She had her faculties to the last, and died as if going to sleep.' She must have been at least a year old when the vicar of Tarrington, John Praulph, was murdered, as the register says, on 3 May 1644, 'by some of the Parliament soldiers near the

Well at Stoke Edith', with whom he had been forced into an argument.

Detours from the main Ledbury road can be made to **Yarkhill**, **Ashperton** and **Stretton Grandison**. The first, sometimes called Yarkle, has an interestingly composite church tower, basically Norman but finished off with that rarity in Herefordshire, a full set of Perpendicular battlements and gargoyles. Inside are no less than three fonts. At Ashperton, an oval moated island behind the church marks the site of a house of William de Grandison, crenellated in 1292. Grandison was the father of John de Grandison, the great Bishop of Exeter (1327–69). Another son, Peter, lies in Hereford Cathedral Lady Chapel.

This is *par excellence* Grandison country. The family came from Burgundy, and gave its name to the village on the Roman road, Stretton Grandison. By the time Celia Fiennes travelled it in 1698 to visit her cousins, the road had sadly declined: 'its allwayes a deep sand and soe in the winter and with muck is bad way', she somewhat incoherently observes. William and John Fiennes lived at timber-framed New House, east of the church where they are commemorated. This last is, for Herefordshire, remarkably homogeneous, all more or less of the Decorated period. In the chancel north wall is an Easter Sepulchre, the pulpit is Perpendicular, and also in the chancel hang a knight's sleeve and gauntlet belonging to the Hopton family.

CHAPTER TWENTY

Northern Herefordshire: Part One

✧

If Herefordshire has a show district comparable to, say, the Vale of Evesham or the Shakespeare villages, then it must be the north-west quarter of the county. The landscape, to begin with, is much the most rewarding, the broad valleys of Lugg and Arrow alternating dramatically with the sudden thrust, towards the Shropshire border, of the high ridges of the Wigmore Dome, a series of thickly wooded limestone outcrops between the Lugg and the Teme. Those comparable rarities in south Herefordshire, real villages with streets and cottages, are found here, there are two outstanding country houses and a score of almost equally good smaller mansions, and several of the finest late examples of English timber-framing. This is sometimes called the John Abel country after the great master of the genre (indeed perhaps the only named artist of any fame in this kind of work) who is buried in the churchyard at Sarnesfield, near Weobley. Born in 1577, he built market-houses up and down the country, of which only Leominster survives, carved the screen at Abbey Dore, and devised powder and corn mills during the siege of Hereford, for which he was named King's Carpenter. Judging by his inscriptions at Abbey Dore and Leominster, he must have been a diehard Royalist, grateful to the Cavalier gentry who supported him. He died in 1674, and promptly became a sort of local Inigo Jones to whom everything 'ye olde' got ascribed.

Leominster (pronounced Lemster) has his masterpiece at the Grange, near the priory church. This is the old Town Hall, built in 1633 from contributions by local squires. Its lower arches would naturally have been open, and over these runs a frieze of proverbial sentences, including 'Like as Collumns doo upprop the Fabrik of a Building, So noble Gentri doo support the Honor of a Kingdom'. The uppropped fabric is noble indeed, ornamented with fanciful ogee work in the timbering of the gables above the mullioned windows. Notice, below the transoms of each, the little caryatids. Though this now houses council offices, it was formerly considered useless and put up for auction in 1855: 'To all Lovers of such curious antiquated

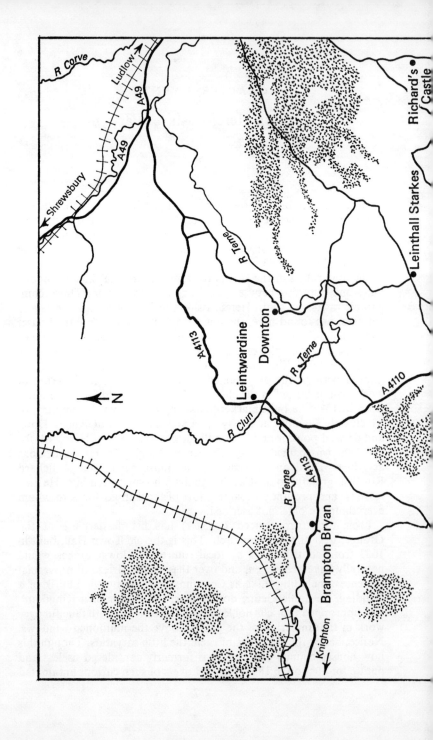

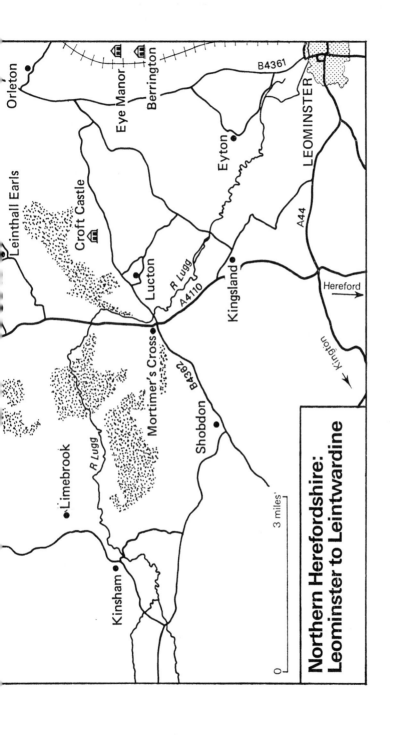

**Northern Herefordshire:
Leominster to Leintwardine**

Orleton

Eye Manor

Berrington

B4361

LEOMINSTER

Eyton

Leinthall Earls

Croft Castle

A44

Lucton

R Lugg

A4110

Kingsland

Hereford

Kington

Mortimer's Cross

B4362

Shobdon

Limebrook

R Lugg

Kinsham

3 miles'

0

Buildings, an opportunity of gratifying their tastes now presents itself which may never occur again, and which should not be lost sight of.' Mr Arkwright of Hampton Court bought it for £95 from a Mr Davis, and had it moved from Broad Street to its present site.

The Grange, as its name suggests, was formerly a big farmyard for **Leominster Priory**, a Saxon foundation around which the town grew up as part of a westward push by the kingdom of Mercia during the seventh century. The legend of its foundation owes something to Leominster's name. Apparently Ealfred, the first prior, sitting down to eat, was surprised by a hungry lion who calmly took the bread offered to him. This was an omen of success for Ealfred's missionary work. In fact 'Leominster' probably means 'the church in Lene', the old name for the Arrow valley. A nunnery was also founded here, but both houses had declined by the Conquest, and it was not until 1123 that the monastery's fortunes revived when Henry I attached it to Reading Abbey. Thereafter its history was more or less similar to those of Tewkesbury, Evesham and Malvern, though it is worth mentioning that Leominster's collection of saintly relics included the body of St Edward, one of St Luke's teeth, a piece of the Crucifixion sponge, a fragment of Moses' rod and one of the stones which killed St Stephen.

Bishop Robert de Bethune consecrated the (northernmost) nave in 1130, the central nave was added for parochial worship in 1239 and the south nave was built in 1320. We enter this western end of the church through the Decorated south-west porch, enclosing two earlier archways which may have formed part of the original porch before the building of the south aisle. Note the highly characteristic Herefordian ballflower ornament on the aisle windows. The eastern end contains the present Lady Chapel. The arcading on this southern side offers an eloquent contrast with the chunky columns of the surviving Norman portions, over which run the arches of a simple clerestory and triforium.

A disastrous fire in 1699 ravaged much of the interior, and the east end had in any case been torn down at the Dissolution. The chancel now occupies what was formerly the crossing into a vanished presbytery with its transepts and chevet of chapels. The Elizabethan altar table in this chancel is one of the few original furnishings to survive the fire. In the north aisle is the parish ducking stool, whose last recorded use (and the last recorded in England, incidentally) was on a woman named Jenny Pipes, ducked in the Arrow in 1809. Sarah Leeke, another town shrew, escaped similar punishment in 1817 since the river was too low.

The western end has a splendid Perpendicular window, its two central ribs buttressed, the gift of Lady Matilda Mowbray. To the right of this is the tower, its two lower stages Norman, and two further storeys added in the fourteenth century, with decorated pinnacles and discreet buttressing. The columns of the huge west portal, three deep, have individually carved capitals – the monk and lion on the north side are variously supposed to be Ealfred and the the lion, or the story of Samson.

Leominster was once celebrated for its wool, from the now almost extinct Ryeland breed, pastured on the rich meadows of Arrow and Lugg. It was known as 'Lemster Ore' and Fuller, writing in the 1640s, thought it 'equalling, if not exceeding, the Apulian or Tarentine in the south of Italy, though it cost not so much charge and curiosity in the careful keeping thereof'. Some of the resultant prosperity is reflected in the substantial stretches of good Jacobean and Georgian building of which the townscape is mostly a fusion – best understood in Etnam Street and Church Street. The first wool carding machine, by the way, was invented at Leominster in 1748 by Daniel Bourn.

Leaving Leominster by the B4361, we soon reach the turn to **Eyton**, whose timber manorhouse was probably the birthplace, in 1551, of Richard Hakluyt. Member of one of the older county clans, he was the inspired compiler of one of the most fascinating works ever written in English, *Voyages, Traffics and Discoveries of the English Nation*. With Sidney's *Arcadia*, Spenser's *Faerie Queene*, Bacon's *Essays* and the King James Bible, Hakluyt's *Voyages* is a classic of Shakespeare's age. The issue of authorship is slightly complicated by the existence of two Richard Hakluyts, one a lawyer, the other a cleric, both deeply involved with trade and exploration. The churchman seems the more likely candidate, since he was in touch with mapmakers and geographers, who named after him a headland in Spitzbergen, a river on the Russian coast and an island off Greenland.

The road north-west from Eyton crosses the Lugg to **Kingsland**, a considerable village with some stately Georgian houses and a nice-looking half-timbered ensemble taking in the Angel Inn. Opposite this is the path down to the church, a most impressive structure, with a big aisled nave entered through a fourteenth-century porch with a small chapel containing a tomb recess, known as the Volka Chapel (the un-English-sounding name remains obscure). This end of the church, probably built by one of the Mortimers, belongs to the early 1300s, and its high clerestory is punctured by round windows below the medieval roof trusses. Bodley painted the chancel roof in 1866–8, to harmonize with the fourteenth-century east window glass. Notice here the figure of Tobias, dangling the fish in one hand while listening intently to the Angel. The arms displayed are those of De Braose and the See of Hereford. In the south aisle hangs a cartoon of Christ Carrying The Cross, by Frank Brangwyn.

The crossroads of the A4110 and the B4362 face us with a difficult choice – west to Shobdon or east to Lucton. While we pause to see which way our walking sticks fall, we can note that the name of this place in the river valley is **Mortimer's Cross**. Here in 1461 Edward, Duke of York (himself half a Mortimer), having rounded up fighting men from his family estates around Wigmore, defeated the Lancastrian forces under Owen Tudor, thereby clinching his bid for the English crown as Edward IV. Shakespeare's presentation of the battle in *Henry VI, pt III* reminds us of the quasi-miraculous appearance of three suns in the sky, actually caused by the refraction of light through ice in the atmosphere and known to scientists as a parhelion. The Yorkists took these as symbolizing Edward, Richard, Duke of Gloucester, and George, Duke of Clarence, and adopted them as a badge.

It was a steward to an earlier Mortimer who founded **Shobdon** priory in *c.* 1140. Oliver de Merlimond had made the pilgrimage to Santiago de Compostela, but this is now thought not to have influenced the vigorous Kilpeck-style carving of the three arches surviving from the priory and moved to the top of the hill above the church as an eighteenth-century eyecatcher (the carving has, in any case, weathered to near-invisibility). The Shobdon estate passed in 1705 to Sir James Bateman, son of a Flemish merchant and former Lord Mayor of London. When his son, William, was made a viscount, George I remarked: 'I could not make him a gentleman, so I made him a lord.' William's wife, Anne, incidentally, was grand-daughter of the virago, Sarah, Duchess of Marlborough, who deliberately blackened the face of her portrait and wrote underneath: 'She is much blacker within'.

Their son, Richard, friend of Horace Walpole, rebuilt court and church at Shobdon, reached up a drive through the grounds. The house, of stone-dressed brick, was demolished in 1933, and only the big stables survive. The church is, to put it mildly, another matter. The cool white-painted porch with its brass doorknobs prepares us a little for the absolute surprise of a complete white and blue Gothic interior, like an expertly iced birthday cake, wittily detailed in bench ends, tiered pulpit, pendant ogee arches across the chancel and big pews for the house servants to the north, and for the squire, with handsome contemporary chairs, to the south. To say any more would spoil the fun. Shobdon has to be seen to be believed.

In the opposite direction lies **Lucton**, whose school was founded in 1708 by John Pierrepont, a London vintner with Herefordshire roots. The school building, the grandest in the county, is a fine piece of Queen Anne brick, with the periwig-pated statue of Pierrepont himself occupying a niche in the central pediment.

From Shobdon the road climbs up into the wooded hills of Deerfold Forest, with, to the east, the Wigmore Dome and Bringewood Chase. North of Byton, at **Kinsham**, Lord Byron rented a dowerhouse of the Harley family from Lord Oxford in 1812, and seems to have cherished it for a time as a rustic refuge from the importunate Caroline Lamb. Eng. Lit. associations cling, too, at **Limebrook**, with its ruins of a priory founded in the last decade of the twelfth century by Robert de Lingen. Its six Augustinian canonesses are supposed to have been the recipients of the advice given, not without a trace of bitchery here and there, in the Middle English classic, *The Ancrene Wisse*.

Roads north from Lingen lead us finally to the Shropshire border marked by the Teme and **Brampton Bryan**. The village itself is noteworthy for having a green, rare enough in the Marches, and at one end of this stands the manorhouse, a Restoration and Georgian synthesis, next to the ruined castle. This was begun in the early 1100s by Sir Barnard de Brampton, and subsequently renovated and rebuilt after 1400 by the Harley family. Staunch Yorkists and steadfast recusants, the family shifted to Puritanism in the person of Sir Robert Harley, iconoclast and hammer of Royalist 'malignants' in the Civil Wars. He built the plain, square parish church in 1656, a case to hold congregations listening to the preachers of whom he was so discerning a patron.

His wife was a Cromwellian counterpart to Cavalier châtelaines like Lady Derby and Lady Bankes, stout defenders of their absent husbands' strongholds. Clever, energetic and learned, she was born at Brill in the Netherlands, where her father, Sir Edward Conway (of Ragley, see ch. 2) was governor. Always enterprising in his choice of names, he called her Brilliana after his fortress: her sister, for reasons I cannot discover, he christened Helengenwagh. Brilliana's letters testify to her intelligence and charm. They are full of news, heavily flavoured with religion, erudition (she quotes from Seneca and French authors) and good sense, whether in counselling her 'deare sonne Ned' to wear inexpensive clothes or in softening up his

Oxford tutor with a gift of preserved plums.

As early as the winter of 1642, Lady Harley prepared for a siege by laying in stores and flooding the dry moat. Helped by one of the Hakluyts, a Thirty Years War veteran, she drilled her little household garrison to hold out for a leaguer of sixteen weeks, June to September 1643. When the Royalists drew off, they had burnt the village, poisoned the common stream and driven away the cattle. Brave to the last, Brilliana made ready for their return, but died from cold and exhaustion some months before a second siege, led by the sadistic Sir Michael Woodhouse, reduced the castle to rubble. By the war's end, the Harleys had suffered losses amounting to a modern equivalent of £70,000.

North-east of Brampton Bryan the A4113 carries us over the junction of Teme and Clun (poetic echoes here of Housman's 'valley of springs of rivers') into the attractively sited village of **Leintwardine**. It stands on the Roman road joining Wroxeter (Viroconium) to Kenchester (Magnis) and was once the military posting station of Bravonium, whose line of walls can still be traced around the village, though not much else survives. These ramparts run right under the parish church, raising the chancel appreciably higher than the nave. Later soldierly associations are recalled in the monument to Sir Banastre Tarleton (1745–1833). Familiar from Reynolds's wonderfully dashing National Gallery portrait, Tarleton, after a brilliant career in the American War of Independence, where he captured Philadelphia and Charleston, became MP for Liverpool and protector of Mary 'Perdita' Robinson, actress friend of 'Prinny', and it was she who ghost-wrote the general's military memoirs. Leintwardine also has a set of exceptionally good misericord stalls, with canopies and carved scenes of the Resurrection and Annunciation, perhaps from nearby Wigmore Abbey.

The Hereford-Salop border here rises up on to the ridge of romantically steep and wooded hills preparing the traveller for the suddenness and high drama of Clun Forest, the Strettons and the Long Mynd, all in the next county. Richard Payne Knight's acute sensitivity to these landscape possibilities resulted, in 1772, in the creation of **Downton**, an eighteenth-century re-ordering of an undistinguished village around an asymmetrically designed 'medieval' mansion, perfectly fused with the sandstone gorge made by the curve of the Teme below Bringewood Chase opposite. Bringewood, Burrington and Elton all belonged to the Knight family, leading ironmasters from Bridgnorth, who made everything from army cannon to the wonderful cast-iron tomb slabs in Burrington church-yard.

While his brother, Thomas, lived happily at Elton as an expert gardener, publishing the lavish *Pomona Herefordiensis* in 1811, writing energetically on blight and greenfly and raising new varieties of practically every familiar fruit and vegetable, Richard became one of the great pioneers of the shift in Georgian taste towards the wild and natural. Downton, uniting picturesque on the outside with severe classicism in its interiors, is an outstanding moment in English aesthetics, its aims and effects best summarized in Knight's own poem, *The Landscape*, dedicated to Sir Uvedale Price and printed, significantly, by a certain W. Bulmer. This extraordinary work, owing a good deal to such omnium-gatherum affairs as Erasmus Darwin's *The Botanic Garden*, takes in everything. Salvator Rosa, Hobbema and Claude are invoked, Brown is damned and the Amazon unfavourably compared with 'wide-wand'ring Wye, or rapid Teme'. There is an account of the progress of Art, long passages on plantation of woodlands ('Curse on the shrubbery's insipid scenes!') and the development of landscape is finally compared to the progress of the French Revolution.

From Downton the roads run south across the edge of the hills to the Leinthalls, Starkes and Earls. **Leinthall Starkes**, named after tenants of the Mortimers, has a nice remote church, mixing Norman with later work, and an honest simple roof and rood screen. **Leinthall Earls** belonged, of course, directly to the Mortimers, and has a smaller church, with comparably fine roofing. In the village is the building which, until 1962, when it was closed down, was one of the county's oldest schools. Its founder, Sir Sampson Ewer, lived at Gatley Park, up in the woods to the north. Herefordshire is not specially rich in Tudor and Stuart brick structures, and Gatley, which Ewer, Serjeant-at-Law and MP for Leominster, built in the 1630s, has a consequent importance. The antiquarian, Silas Taylor, adds that in Ewer's time the Gatley stud bred the best horses hereabouts.

Across the magnificent valley to the west, with broad flat fields beautifully contained between the outspread arms of wooded hills, lies one of the most strikingly placed of Marcher villages. Hardened Londoners will simply know Harley Street, Mortimer Street and Wigmore Street as Marylebone thoroughfares, but to me their names invariably strike a nostalgic Herefordshire echo. **Wigmore**, with other Mortimer lands, passed to the Harleys in 1601 and its castle was dismanted by Parliament troops forty years later. The ivied ruin (some of the overgrowth has recently been cleared) is spectacularly gaunt and stern amid the softening green of surrounding woods, and the whole mass of half-buried stonework and walls hidden under bramble thickets, a haven for big freckled toads, is a splendid place for the amateur moralist.

The name Mortimer Forest given to neighbouring plantations reminds us that this is the nerve-centre of the great Mortimer territory, which, at its most extensive, stretched from Hereford to Shrewsbury and formed an unofficial palatinate on the medieval English frontier, a concrete expression of Marcher independence. From the Conquest to the Wars of the Roses the Mortimers, ruthless and astute, kept up a wavering allegiance between the crown and whatever rebel power might be on foot (Sir Edmund Mortimer's change of loyalties to Glyndwr in a fit of pique at Henry IV's failure to pay his ransom is characteristic). Here at Wigmore Henry II reduced Hugh de Mortimer to submission, a savage Lady Mortimer of a later generation spat at the bleeding head of Simon de Montfort carried to her on a pole from Evesham fight, and Edmund Mortimer welcomed Edward I with a splendid tournament.

Greatest of the whole high-stomached tribe was Roger, lover of Edward II's Queen Isabella and effective ruler of England for five years. Violent and greedy as he was, there is yet something admirable in the disdainful courage with which he pursued his ends. His career, a tissue of battles, conspiracies, hair-breadth escapes and wild ambitions, culminating in his horrific execution at Smithfield, has an imperishably grim romance about it.

If Wigmore Castle is now only 'a melancholy dejected prospect of stately ruins', then the church at the hill's foot has fared little better. Over-restored (Bodley, 1864) with a rather dull interior, it is mostly interesting as featuring traces of nearly every medieval building style – notice especially the Norman nave walls and the Hereford triple lancets. As for Wigmore Abbey, half a mile away in fields by the Teme, founded by Hugh de Mortimer in 1179 for Augustinian canons originally at Shobdon, barely a wall of it remains, save the range of the abbot's lodgings as part of a private house.

Over the hill, east from Wigmore and the Leinthalls, are two villages with further Mortimer connections. **Richard's Castle** is a fascinating example of the family's attempt to influence local politics by planting new boroughs throughout their estates. At Richard's Castle, named after Richard Scrope, a Norman strong-arm man crushing local Saxon resistance by the half-legendary Wild Edric, we can still trace the boundaries of the township and mark the open space by the church, where King John granted Robert de Mortimer licence to hold a fair and markets. Scrope's castle, rebuilt by Mortimers and Talbots, was derelict by Henry VIII's reign, and the redundant church has a bluff-looking detached bell-tower, some elegant Decorated work in nave and chancel and – something of a treasure – seventeenth-century box pews.

Orleton church has an exceptionally good font, of local Norman workmanship, its row of nine apostles in an arcade recalling similar patterns on the Gloucestershire lead tub fonts. One of the best of the county's Jacobean and Caroline pulpits is here besides, and there is more fine woodwork in the timber-framing of the village itself. Pope is held to have stayed at the manorhouse, which belonged to a branch of the Blount family, though the link between these and his beloved 'Mrs M.B.' of Mapledurham, Berkshire, is rather tenuous.

Orleton's most notorious figure was undeniably Adam Orleton, a local-boy-made-good under Mortimer patronage during the early fourteenth century, when he became successively bishop of Worcester, Hereford and Winchester. During Edward II's reign he showed due gratitude by backing Roger and the rebel barons and distinguished himself by cruelty, worldliness and general unpopularity. It was he who gave religious sanction to Edward's murder in the wondrous ambiguity, '*Eduardum regem occidere nolite timere bonum est*', which, depending on how you punctuate it, comes out either as 'Fear not to kill King Edward: it is a good thing' 'Do not kill King Edward: it is good to be fearful'.

Finally a trio of great houses, laid almost end to end between the Lugg and the main A49 to Ludlow, so close indeed as to make the area a kind of textbook for students of the smaller types of English country mansion. **Eye Manor**, to take the smallest first, lies on the B-road beyond the railway line south of Orleton. Its exterior is unremarkable, an inoffensive Restoration box of pink brick, finished in 1680 for Sir Ferdinando Gorges, a Barbados trader in slaves and sugar known as the King of the Black Market, a very distant connection of the Elizabethan courtier poet after whom he was christened. His gains, however ill-gotten, were well laid out here on a series of exquisite ceilings through most of the main rooms, designed in the form of decorated panels in varying shapes. Tradition ascribes these to Italian plasterers, but the lavish swags of fruit, flowers and leaves, often surrounding family escutcheons, seem to me more in the well-established English vein with which Gorges may have been familiar from a visit to the Scudamores' new house at Holme Lacy.

Eye now belongs to Mr and Mrs Christopher Sandford, whose personal interests are reflected in detailed displays inside the house. His was the guiding spirit behind the Golden Cockerel Press, which did so much to improve artistic standards of book production during the 1930s and 40s, and his wife is the world authority on corn-dollies, those pagan enigmas of plaited straw without which no harvest was assured. Eye church, approached across the garden, has an immensely sophisticated Early English nave, with niched clerestory windows of a century later. The pulpit and benches are probably Sir Ferdinando's refurbishing, and there are two good alabaster effigies to Rowland and Richard Cornewall, early Tudor members of a family descended from a bastard of King Henry III's brother, the vacillating Richard, Earl of Cornwall and 'Emperor of Almain'.

The Cornewalls once owned **Berrington**, whose estate adjoins Eye over the stream east of the house. They sold it to the Harleys in 1775, and Thomas Harley immediately commissioned Capability Brown to reshape the grounds. Brown's assistant, Spyers, surveyed the park and the architect himself submitted what was to be one of his last landscape plans, a work costing some £1600. Meanwhile his son-in-law, Henry Holland, whose favoured style is epitomized in the architecture of the Scottish Office at Dover House, Whitehall, created what is surely one of the most practical and precise country houses ever built. The entire design rests, in a way which is strikingly anticipatory of later architectural trends, on the inter-relationship of contrasting shapes and volumes – a square rose sandstone shell containing an infinity of hollows, concave ovals, circles and semicircles, the curve of arches and ceilings offset by the lines of tall doors and long friezes, the whole to be centred on Holland's *coup-de-théâtre* of a domed staircase hall, a triumphant piece of neo-classical abstract, instinct with that sense of mass and depth which we find in the contemporary work of Boullée and Ledoux.

The decoration, including scagliola columns, white-and-gold curtain boxes, and painted medallions by the Venetian Biagio Rebecca (he had also worked for the Adams) is uniformly inspired, and if we add to it the skill of the disposition of domestic offices (bakery, laundry, steward's office, stables) around the broad northern courtyard, we can easily accept Berrington, within its carefully naturalized landscape, as a late Georgian artistic paradigm.

Jane Austen's Mansfield Park was in Northamptonshire, but Berrington would have done quite as well. **Croft Castle** is like Northanger Abbey or Donwell in *Emma* in seeming more self-effacing than it actually should be. There is in fact a thrilling quality in the house's very situation, on an eminence under the big Celtic hill-fort of Croft Ambrey, nine acres, and a thriving Iron Age settlement, with streets of huts, for three centuries. Looking southwards, there are tremendous prospects of the emerald, pink, turquoise and yellow folds of north Herefordshire, and to the south-west the dim Welsh mountain shapes. Something which could only have happened here took place in 1649, when some mowers in a field found a child wrapped in swaddling bands lying in the long grass. The infant, having forecast the restoration of Charles II and bloody deaths for the regicides, promptly disappeared.

With one significant break, there have been Crofts at Croft since the thirteenth century, when Hugo de Croft held the castle of the honour of Dilwyn. Several of the family figure in Tudor and Stuart history. James Croft, for example, tried to raise Herefordshire for Lady Jane Grey in 1554, but seems to have hedged his bets in Elizabeth's reign by courting the Queen's favour while secretly corresponding with the Spaniards. He died a Catholic, but his grandson, Herbert, was converted 'from the darkness of Popish errors and gross superstitions' to become a notably zealous, if somewhat dictatorial, Bishop of Hereford. While he risked his life preaching in the cathedral, where a Parliament soldier took a pot-shot at him, his brother William was killed in an ambush at Wistanton in Shropshire in 1643.

Through a 'ruined' Gothic gateway we cross the lawn to the compact, four-square castle with angle turrets, belonging probably to the late fourteenth century and thus one of the last Marcher strongholds. Originally the eastern side was open to the courtyard, but a new range closed it in during ownership by the Knights of Downton in the mid-eighteenth century. The Gothic look (the Knights were connected by marriage to the Johneses of Hafod) softens the grandeur of towers and Tudor mullions into something rather provincial, and this feeling prevails throughout the ground-floor rooms, with their agreeable mélange of styles, like some unimaginable meeting between Richardson and Mrs Radcliffe. Nothing here is too grand or crushing, and the cool suavities of Berrington seem far distant. The Jacobean gravity of the Oak Room, looking on to a western avenue of young trees, falls neatly between Gothic cake-icing in small rooms beyond and the bizarre Blue Room, with its rosette panels and crimped and curled rococo chimney-piece framing a Gainsborough portrait.

The church, too, is amusing in the best and truest sense of the term. Its bell-turret has delicately turned balusters half-way up, and inside is good plain Restoration Anglican, with box pews, a west gallery and a 'sky' over the altar. The finest early Tudor monument in Herefordshire is here, 1509, to Sir Richard Croft, a Yorkist who went over to Henry Richmond and was knighted by him (as Henry VII) after the defeat of Lambert Simnel's rabble at Stoke. He and his wife, Catherine Herbert, lie in a tombchest under figures of four saints – St Margaret, St Anthony with his pigs, St Roche with an angel pointing to his plague sore and St Sitha, patroness of housewives, holding her châtelaine's keys. The church organ makes a dulcet noise, and I am told that Croft occasionally rustles up a gallery band for church services, on approved Hardyesque lines.

CHAPTER TWENTY-ONE

Northern Herefordshire: Part Two

❧

On our way westwards from Leominster along the A4112, it is worth turning off to the left at Bainstree Cross to visit the redundant church at **Stretford**. This is quite well kept, and its design of two naves, with Perpendicular screens, and a chancel covered by a huge Tudor roof is unique to the county. Norman work shows in the north wall, and the southern side has Early English lancets. The roof, of arched and cusped braces, has shields of arms on the wallplates – Baskerville and Devereux facing Delabere. The Delaberes held the manor in the early fourteenth century and two sets of ungainly effigies in the church are probably those of Robert and John Delabere and their wives. Under the building there is said to be a curative spring dedicated to the physician saints Cosmas and Damian, Stretford's patrons.

These watery vales are rich in big, prosperous-looking, half-timbered farmhouses, a far cry from the unpretentious homesteads of the Monmouthshire border and something which, as well as saying much about the solidity of Saxon settlement here, bears out the old adage, 'Herefordshire farmers live rich, Monmouthshire farmers die rich.' Some of the farms occasionally offer refreshment to the traveller in summer, though when I last had tea in a farm near Weobley a blazing row was going on between the farmer's wife and her mother-in-law, both of them in a state of near speechless fury.

Dilwyn, lying in a dip just below the main road, is a good example of a north Herefordshire village in its collection of handsome farms and cottages. 'Very fayre for a country village' was how the Cromwellian antiquary, Silas Taylor, described St Mary's church, whose size and grandeur must owe something to its being under the tutelage of the Augustinian priory due south at Wormsley. The Wormsley canons rebuilt the chancel in 1305 and were perhaps also responsible for raising the height of the nave and remodelling the clerestory, though its windows, like those in the grand porch outside, are early Perpendicular. The tower is a Norman base with a Georgian spire – Nathaniel Wilkinson again? It is tempting to suppose so. Nave and chancel are divided by a tall, flamboyant screen, throwing out miniature fan vaults and displaying, at the base of each column, a farouche carved head in a fifteenth-century cap. Almost equally well-carved are the parcloses in the north transept and south aisle.

Further down the road from Dilwyn lies the village which for many is the county paradigm, its church spire beckoning for miles across the fields. **Weobley** began as one of the planted towns of the March. Its castle, quadrangular with six turrets, now an overgrown tump at the southern town-end, was garrisoned by Geoffrey fitz Scrope against King Stephen in 1139 and was later the scene of the surrender to King John of that grizzled old Marcher mastiff, William de Braose. It held out against the Welsh in 1262, and three centuries later was still 'a goodly castle but somewhat in decay'. As a thriving medieval community, with merchants and Jewish moneylenders, it sent burgesses to Parliament (until 1832). During the eighteenth century it was a pocket borough of the Marquess of Bath, who used to send his Shropshire tenants to vote in the elections, which they were eligible to do if they boiled a kettle in Weobley the night before – hence the name 'pot-wallopers' for those who set up their cooking fires in the main street. At least one prime minister, the Duke of Portland, was MP for Weobley. Lord Eldon, in his memoirs, tells us of his experience as a callow young candidate being advised on the best canvassing techniques, which seem to have involved kissing as many of the freeholders' wives and daughters as possible.

The main street originally held an island of houses in the middle, like those of so many other western English towns. These buildings, including a fine old market hall, were destroyed by an apathetic Lord Bath in the 1840s. What now survives is the classic broad black-and-white village street. One of the county's comparatively few cream teas can be had next door to the post office, half-way down. At the church end is the inevitable sophistication of two antique shops, and the Red Lion hotel is a sixteenth-century shell to a medieval nut.

Next to this is the turn down to the church, a big Early English and Decorated building, most of which can be dated to before 1325, when the altars were dedicated. The tower, set at angles on to the north aisle, has an octagonal spire on squinches, rebuilt after a seventeenth-century lightning attack. Inside is very bright and spacious, with some comic Tudor corbels, among them a monkey, in the south aisle. There are two medieval effigies in the chancel,

Kilpeck church: the south porch

both rather beaten about: Sir John Marbury, on the south side, was keeper of Henry V's jewels. The best memorial (apart from the Victorian tablet on the north wall to someone who died 'suddenly at Florence') is the standing full-length of 1691 to Colonel John Birch. In the midst of some rather inept local Civil War commanders, Birch, a Parliamentarian, emerges as a thoroughly resourceful character. He it was who reduced Goodrich and Hereford and enriched himself with sequestered estates. Sullen Royalists gave him out the son of a Lancashire pedlar, which he wasn't, but by the Restoration, when he had shrewdly changed sides, he was the local mafioso boss, MP for Weobley, and later, at the Revolution, in cahoots with Lord Conyngsby to ensure a Whig power in Herefordshire. Here he stands, defiantly flourishing a baton, between military trophies.

Up at Weobley's southern end are more fine village houses, among them the Unicorn Inn (also serving teas) which contends with a house called The Throne in Hereford Street as the place where Charles I stopped to dine in 1645 on his forlorn ramble after support in the west, and the old Grammar School. Just out of the town, off the B4230, are two notable houses. The Ley, up a track to the right, was built in 1589 by James Brydges, and his arms and initials are set in panels over the doorway beneath the vine-trailed bargeboards of the gables. Garnstone belonged to Colonel Birch: it was on this estate that, according to some rather muddled records, the Tomkins family began breeding Hereford cattle in 1720, the best strain coming from a cow called Silver and her calf left to Benjamin Tomkins in his father's will.

Hardy Herefords, dark red with white face, bellies and hocks, are the world's most widely distributed cattle, standing up to the driest and dampest terrains. The breed's fortunes are now supervised by its own Herd Book Society, though paradoxically local breeders are not many and the juicy, marbly Hereford beef on the county's tables is now more likely to come from Ireland, New Zealand or Argentina.

South of Weobley are the Pyons (Pyon is Welsh 'pen' – slope), **King's Pyon** and **Canon Pyon**. Music lovers will know that the little region between here, Weobley and Dilwyn contributed some of the richest of Ralph Vaughan Williams's folksong harvest. With the help of the folklorist, Mrs E. M. Leather, he collected a mass of them, between 1907 and 1909. Their singers were mostly old gypsies, and

---

Ross-on-Wye

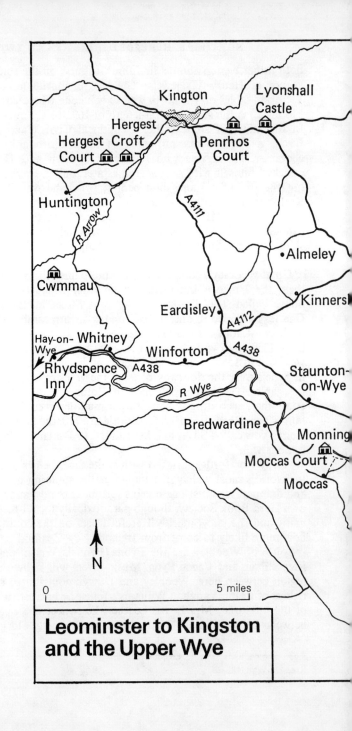

**Leominster to Kingston
and the Upper Wye**

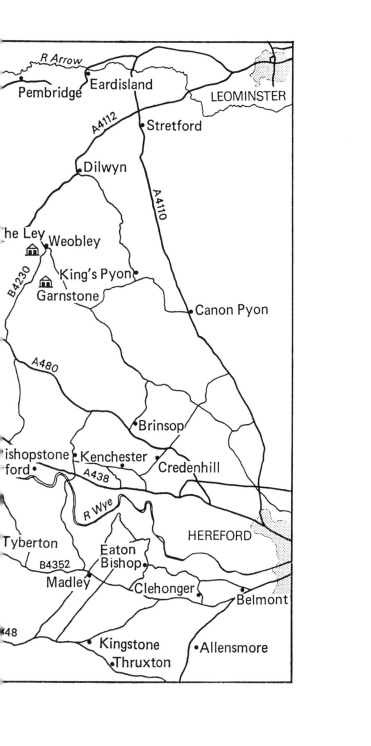

they include versions of *The Unquiet Grave*, *The Wife of Usher's Well*, *Dives and Lazarus* (later the source of the composer's *Five Variants*) and the classic carol, *This Is The Truth Sent From Above*. Gypsies, incidentally, are an integral part of the Herefordshire scene, now as for centuries. Traditionally employed as hop-pickers, some have settled in the various villages, and a strong gypsy strain can be seen in many of the country faces.

King's Pyon church has mixed sandstone and tufa in its Norman masonry. There is an imposing nave roof, with tie beams, collars and windbraces, probably of the fourteenth century, and a typical local-style tomb recess with mutilated Mortimer effigies. Canon Pyon has rare misericords, perhaps by the same carver as the chancel screen's, a man with a sense of fun and fond of animals if the two bishops between two monkeys are anything to go by. The marble urn to Major Sawyer is a late Roubiliac of 1753.

West past Sarnesfield on the Hay road is **Kinnersley**, whose so-called 'castle', now an old people's home, is a pretty, rather quirky piece of Elizabethan brick, with stepped gables and mullioned windows, built by Roger Vaughan in 1585 on the site of a medieval fort. The upper drawing room of the L-shaped house has a fine plastered overmantel. A gate from the garden leads into the church-yard, up whose mellow brick wall grow rambler roses. The church, with its rather old-fashioned Perpendicular saddleback roof and timber porch, has extravagant mid-Victorian decoration by Bodley, executed by a talented incumbent, Mr Andrews, as well as some most passable fake medieval glass of 1850. In the pulpit are four superb carved panels, probably Flemish sixteenth-century, showing the Virgin and Child amid virtues.

Francis Smallman bought the manor in 1620 and his lively monument is up on the north wall. With his wife, Susan Clarke, he kneels under a little pavilion, its curtains upheld by putti. Husband wears rhinegrave boots, wife a Paris hood, and their children kneel in the frieze, one of the sons balancing a skull upon his knee. At the far end of the nave, Lady Anne Morgan, a striking ensemble of angel and medallion, is by Roubiliac's assistant, Nicholas Read.

Almeley, to the north, may have been the birthplace of the Lollard martyr, Sir John Oldcastle, burnt in 1417, and supposed to have been an original for Shakespeare's Falstaff. In his time there was certainly a castle on the tump south of the church, where Simon de Montfort had done homage to Henry III. Apart from its ceiling painted with Tudor roses, the church itself has little of interest, though beleaguered Protestantism seems to be a local theme, for in the churchyard are the gravestones of a refugee community of Latvian Lutherans. What is more, in the hamlet of Almeley Wootton is a half-timbered Friends' Meeting House of 1672, one of England's oldest, given to the Quakers by a local yeoman, Roger Prichard.

Eardisley has that Herefordshire rarity, a long village street, with a church, mill and castle motte at its southern end. In the big barn of a church, which grew with the centuries from nave to aisles and chancel, is an exceptional Norman font, perhaps by the Canon Frome master, writhing and knotty in all its figures, a flurry of fighting warriors, the Harrowing of Hell, a sphinx-like evangelist and a swishtailed lion. The castle, belonging to the Baskervilles, was burnt out in the Civil Wars. In the village the Tram Inn recalls the Kington–Hay railway, a tramway opened in 1820 and kept going, despite competition from steam, during the mid-nineteenth century, when it carried lime, guano, lead and bar iron. Its course can be followed out of Eardisley, just north of the junctions of the A4111 and A4112, up to Kington and the Dolyhir quarries in Radnorshire.

Winforton and **Whitney** hang above loops in the Wye on its gradual bend towards Hay. Winforton sprawls lazily along the main road. The upper part of its church tower is timber, overlooking a thirteenth-century body. There is a sort of cottage baroque altar rail, and a Jacobean pulpit inscribed, 'Be not afraide of their faces, for I am with thee, saithe the Lord. This pulpit was given by Thomas Higgins gent. Anno Domini 1613.' The organ case is early Georgian. Uncomfortable closeness to the Wye meant that a flood washed away Whitney church in 1720, so that its look is scrambled Augustan-medieval, complete with a west gallery. Vicar here from 1632 to 1640 was Christopher Harvey, a friend of Izaak Walton. His religious poetry collection, *The Synagogue*, was printed as an appendage to the 1640 edition of Herbert's *The Temple*, and the influence, though Harvey seldom rises above the pedestrian, is fairly obvious.

The Welsh border is well marked by the **Rhydspence Inn**, a last trumpet blast of timber-framing before we take off into the tatty mountain pebbledash of mid-Wales villages. Set back from the road and well looked after, this was once a halting place for Welsh cattle drovers, whose beasts presumably browsed on the riverside slopes; the room above the porch is still called the Head Drover's Room. The whole building is said to rest on medieval foundations, and the meaning of Rhydspence – 'a river-crossing where provisions are kept' – suggests that there has been some sort of hostelry here for generations.

To the north, up the lanes and into the hills, we are very plainly in

Wales: a landscape of leaping streams, hidden farms and scraggy-fleeced sheep. Local historians remark on the way in which this north-western edge of the county has been settled by Radnorshire farmers, coming down from the forests and glens to the fatter pastures below. The spirit of the Elizabethan rhyme still holds good:

> *Poor Radnor shire, poor Radnor shire,*
> *Never a park, never a deer,*
> *Never a knight with five thousand a year*
> *Save Sir Richard Fowler of Abbey Cwmhir.*

A drive up from Brilley to Huntington across the Arrow valley takes us briefly into Wales. The border in fact runs along the left turn of the crossroads to Michaelchurch, and just off this road is the track down to **Cwmmau**, a typical Welsh frontier farmhouse, owned by the National Trust. The whole is a very solidly built seventeenth-century construction, conforming to a much older pattern of a hall with big rafters and screens, and indeed traditionally occupying the site of a royal hunting lodge. Notice the pigeon cote attached to the outside wall.

On the right of the track to Cwmmau is the tump of a castle possibly built by William de Braose, Marcher lord of Brecknock. De Braose, of the same family as Robert Bruce, King of Scots, was a defiant border boss in the best traditions of a county which produced Mortimer and Essex. Originally King John's favourite, he fell out with his master after failing to pay up the necessary sums for the vast number of castles given him by the King. Having fled to France after an unsuccessful rebellion, he died at Corbeil and was buried at the abbey of St Victor in Paris. His splendidly defiant wife, Maud de St Valery, a virago who passed into local folklore as Moll Wallbee, was finally imprisoned with her son at Windsor, where they were both left to die of hunger.

De Braose may well have erected two other castles in this part of the March, at Hengoed and south of Huntington, and almost certainly built the one whose ruined stump survives by the roadside at **Huntington** itself. This was another of the Norman planted towns which failed, like Pembridge, Weobley and Richard's Castle. As the centre of the lordship of Huntington, created for de Braose in 1173, it was given borough status, and we can still sketch out, in the rectangular lie of lanes between castle and church, what must have been the foundations of a town which never actually came into being. The large and impressively sited castle passed to the Bohuns, thence to the Staffords, providing a temporary refuge for Richard III's hapless 'cousin of Buckingham', and finally falling into decay in the sixteenth century.

The road to Kington crosses and re-crosses the Arrow, and here we reach **Hergest Court**, on the side of the great 400-foot bluff of Hergest ridge. The oldest part of the house is the long stone wing, which is probably part of the original fifteenth-century manor of the Vaughan family, with a shorter northern range, of close-studded timbering, added two hundred years later. Traces of a moat are to be found in the big pond below, for the building, now a farmhouse, was clearly made ready for defence during the last turbulent century of the independent March. Hergest was built in *c.* 1430 for Thomas Vaughan, one of the huge Welsh clan embracing everybody from a Metaphysical poet to a cardinal and a modern composer. Its founder, Moreiddig Warwyn, was born with a serpent around his neck, which gave the family its arms of three boys' heads proper, each snake-wreathed. Thomas Vaughan and his wife, Ellen Gethin, were fearsome enough to inspire local legends, including the story of Black Vaughan's ghost, eventually laid by twelve parsons who shut him into a snuffbox which they threw into a pool. His career was closely bound up with the Wars of the Roses, and he was killed at the battle of Banbury in 1469. One of the last great medieval Welsh poets, Lewis Glyn Cothi, was his household bard at Hergest. Though he celebrates the place and its owners in poignant verses, he is probably best known for his touching lament for the death of his own small son. Even more important for lovers of Celtic literature was the family's possession of the famous *Red Book of Hergest*, containing some of the *Mabinogion* stories and the wonderful riddling Welsh Triads.

Hergest Croft, further along the western approach to Kington, has fine rock gardens, rhododendrons and an arboretum, displayed to visitors on certain summer days. **Kington** itself I find the least attractive of Herefordshire's market towns. Its apologetic, down-at-heel look is distinctly southern Welsh, and though many of its buildings are individually interesting, it seems unconcerned with conservation. Best of them are the Oxford Arms, cradling some seventeenth-century fabric, the early Victorian classical Town Hall, and the Grammar School, founded from the will of Margaret Vaughan, widow of the seadog, John Hawkins. This is one of the rare survivals of John Abel's work in stone, begun in 1625. The parish church holds the tomb of Thomas and Ellen Vaughan: note his Yorkist collar of suns and roses. On the north nave wall is a brass to Albert Parker, who died aged twenty-one, along with seventy-eight others, in a shipwreck in the Bass Strait, Australia, in 1874.

Just outside the town, on the left of the Leominster road, is **Penrhos Court**, a medieval cruck frame building in a farmyard, now converted into a restaurant. **Lyonshall Castle**, whose mounds can be seen behind the church further along the road, was once a perk of various favourites of the unfortunate Richard II. Between here and Leominster lie two of the handsomest villages in the county. The first of these, **Pembridge**, is another failed medieval borough, still retaining images of former consequence in the early Tudor market hall at the village crossroads, the oak-beamed Greyhound and New Inn, and two sets of almshouses. The first of these, Duppa's in Bridge Street, were founded by Bryan Duppa, saintly and learned Laudian bishop of Winchester, in 1661. In East Street Alice Trafford, the vicar's wife and niece of Davenant, the poet, built Trafford's Almshouses in 1686. Elsewhere there is much good building to admire here, most of it in timber and some clearly medieval in origin.

Pembridge's unique feature is the striking late fourteenth-century octagonal belfry, freestanding on the north side of the big village church, which is set back behind the cottages across open lawns. This belfry has a plunging pyramid roof in three stages, covered with stone slates and timber shingles. Within, the supporting framework is of four sturdy uprights making a square, with subsidiary timbers rising around them. Next door the church is made up of tall six-bay Decorated arcades under round ogival clerestory windows, meeting lower pitched transepts and a chancel holding two sets of effigies. These, probably members of the Gower family, are suggestively Chaucerian: the man in cap and cloak is a knight, and his brother in coif and gown a serjeant-at-law. Disarmingly simple is the representation of the folds in his wife's long nun-like dress.

The parish church is the sole disappointment of **Eardisland**, a postcard gem if ever there was. Its site owes much to the watery nature of the surrounding terrain. The shallow-flowing Arrow joins a mill race, with lush banks, to form a kind of hummocky peninsula, carrying a fair dovecote in Queen Anne brick topped by a lantern and vane. Beside the bridge is the Old School House, and nearby is the Staick, a house made up from a medieval hall in which local justice was dispensed. Just outside the village, clearly signposted, is Burton Court, an even more interesting example of a house which has grown from an ancient nucleus of a great hall, with a typical big, high-pitched timber roof. Much altered during the Regency and especially by F. R. Kempson in the 1860s, its final addition came in 1912, when the young Clough Williams Ellis gave Burton its present entrance porch. The downstairs rooms are now given over to an exhibition of Victorian domestic life.

CHAPTER TWENTY-TWO

The Upper Wye

❧

Midland Herefordshire, the river plain of the upper Wye, has been favoured by settlers from Roman times onwards. Unlike those in the borderlands, the villages here are substantially spread and, for Herefordshire at any rate, there is a notable shortage of castle sites. This part of the county is among the most rewarding of interest, whether in landscape, houses or churches, though leaving Hereford by the Abergavenny road through a horrid grey blotch of post-war concrete-faced council houses is scarcely an encouragement.

At **Belmont**, however, things start changing for the better. The mid-nineteenth-century Romanist revival carried with it a local squire, F. R. Wegg-Prosser, who founded here a Benedictine abbey, commissioning the firm of Pugin and Pugin as builders, though Pugin himself was not the architect. Completed in 1882, the church became for a short while, during 1916 to 1920, a pro-cathedral. The overall effect, hardly subtle, suggests a Catholic fling at the dominant Anglican presence of Hereford cathedral down in the plain.

Pevsner tells us that Pugin designed the glass in the north-east nàve window of **Clehonger** church for Wegg-Prosser in 1850, but the current guide on sale there is doubtless more accurate in making Wegg-Prosser's gift the chancel east light, so intransigently Roman in its representation of the two St Francises and St Catherines as to flutter even the most ardent Tractarian. The big, well-kept church has a north transept built by Sir Richard Pembrugge in 1341 as a projected chantry, though the latter was not established until 1474 by his descendant, Sir John Barre. Both knights lie at rest here. Sir Richard has an altar tomb in the south arch of the chapel, and is shown in full armour, a bascinet on his head, a sword on his left hip, his right hand on a dagger, with a shield bearing his arms, *barry on a bend three leopards' faces*. The head is given a slight turn, and on his heels are finely carved spurs. Nearby is the exquisite little figure of his wife, Dame Petronilla, the details of her face emphasized with as much delicacy as her dress ornaments. The bird shown pulling at her skirt with its beak is either a goose or, given her name, a petrel.

Sir John Barre and his wife, Joan Greyndour, are represented by a pair of ornate brasses of *c.* 1480, he with a plumed tilting helm and she in daring décolletée, with a plucked forehead and monstrous wimple. Clehonger later passed from the Barres to the Aubreys, relatives of immortal John, who held the manor from 1596 to 1794, when the house was burnt down. The churchyard, facing a big pond and broad fields, contains several interesting graves, including those opposite the porch, of the Taylor brothers. The youngest, Thomas, was savagely clubbed over the head by a drunken coachman at Belmont in 1813, and the other three, John, William and James, all with children, were drowned in the Wye one March evening two years later.

The land to the south of Clehonger was once a wild stretch of marsh and scrubland on the edge of Haywood Forest, fragments of which survive to the east. It was reclaimed in the Middle Ages by Allan de Plukenet, Lord of Kilpeck, whose efforts gave **Allensmore** its name. The church, with its squat Perpendicular tower and gargoyles, has a sophisticated Jacobean pulpit enriched with pairs of Doric columns, and in the chancel floor a cement-inlaid stone slab shows Sir Andrew Herl in full armour next to his wife, Joan Pauncefote, with shields including Herl's own of a fesse between three sheldrakes.

Thruxton's church, like Allensmore's, has gargoyles on the tower, as well as some excellent fourteenth-century timbering in the bargeboards of the south porch and the roofs of its nave and chancel. Some glass fragments of the same period, including a Crucifixion and a border of crowns, castles and rosettes, decorate the chancel south window. The extremely sturdy, rough-hewn font is inscribed 'This fonte was made March the 16th 1677' with '*Baptismus est ablutio peccatorum*' on its base.

This is a countryside of superlative farm buildings, rich in good barns, several of them of the familiar local wattle and timber type, and in splendid courts and granges, many of which lie in the triangle of roads between Clehonger, Thruxton and Kingstone. North of this last, the name of Street House Farm denotes a Roman road running up to the former town of Magna at Kenchester. The Saxons seem to have abandoned this in favour of the almost parallel lane joining the B4348 to the B4352 at **Madley**. This large, prosperous-looking village is the scene of an annual summer music festival, when choral and orchestral concerts are given in the church. Dedicated to the Nativity of the Virgin, this is a colossal affair, basically cruciform Norman, remodelled in the thirteenth century. The chancel, rebuilt in the early 1300s, has a lanceted clerestory and a grand polygonal apse rising to a crown of pointed finials on the buttresses. For Herefordshire, always a bit shamefaced in this department, Madley's tower, soaring, massive, is unique. The Elizabethan tomb in the Chilstone Chapel to Richard and Anne Willison, much mutilated, is signed by John Gildon, author of the Harford monument at Bosbury.

The glories of Madley are rivalled by those of **Eaton Bishop**, a big village which has suffered architecturally from its closeness to Hereford. In the church, a spacious building with a triple-aisled thirteenth-century nave and lancets in the clerestory, is the county's finest medieval glass. To get in, you must first go down to the house called 'The Carpenters' below the new churchyard, where the Midwinter family keeps the key. The east window here was probably made for Adam de Murimonth, canon of Hereford, at some time before 1328 when he removed to Exeter. He is shown below another priest, kneeling to the Virgin and St John: other panels represent St Michael weighing souls, Christ and the Angel Gabriel, as well as a canopied Virgin and Child. The colours of the whole window, limited to brown, yellow and rich green, with patches of red, are highly reminiscent of contemporary glazing in the sanctuary at Tewkesbury, and may well be from the same workshop.

Unless we want to follow the not very rewarding riverside lanes in order to go north-west to **Tyberton** (pronounced Tibberton) we have to rejoin the B4352 at Madley. Tyberton has special associations with the great Brydges family, once such a power in the county and now, like their mansion here, vanished with completeness sufficient to satisfy the most stringent rustic moralist. The Georgian stables and a couple of fishponds give a tantalizing hint of what once was, but as so often with the surrounding villages, it is the church that offers most interest.

William Brydges, who came into the estate in 1711, was a cultivated lawyer, and seems to have supervised every aspect of the building work, which took approximately two years (1719–20). The walls of locally-made brick incorporated a Norman south doorway from the old church, and the mason in charge of this and of raising the urn-pinnacled west tower was Robert Pritchard of Clehonger. Inside, all is clear, bright and graceful in a harmony of Augustan furnishings, with a font by another local man, Stephen Reeves, painted to simulate marble, a double-decker pulpit, box pews, an angel lectern and the arms of George I.

Tyberton's treasure is the apsidal reredos (the end wall is actually flat) designed as a series of panels in 1728–30 by John Wood of Bath, protégé of Brydges's relative, the 'Princely' Duke of Chandos. Executed in Bath and thence shipped up the river from Chepstow to Sugwas opposite Eaton Bishop, these illustrate symbols of Christ's Passion and Resurrection, and were probably selected by Brydges himself. Notice the holy lance and, on the inner left-hand panel, the pair of swords, one of them carrying Malchus's ear. Highly baroque in feeling, they brilliantly suggest, despite their sacred allusions, some fragment of a stage set for a Handel opera.

The road now runs closer to the beautiful ridge of wooded hills dividing the river plain from the Dore, their summits thickly feathered with oak groves. It was the oldest of these that must have helped to give **Moccas** its name – 'Moch-rhos' means swine pasture, and we can imagine the hairy Welsh pigs rootling for acorns here before the Saxons came. Hugh de Fresnes crenellated his manorhouse as a castle in 1294 and the Normans built the delectably lonely little church of St Michael and All Angels, crouched in the great park of Moccas Court like a brooding anchoress. Its stonework is mostly of tufa, brought, presumably, from Teme Valley deposits, with worn sandstone doorways and Decorated windows in the chancel. In the north window canopied, yellow-robed figures sport the escutcheons of the Fresnes family, one of whom was presumably the fourteenth-century knight lying on the altar-tomb nearby. There is a good organ here, with an elegant High Art case in the Morris vein.

To the north-east is **Moccas Court**. This is a small jewel of late Georgian design, built in restrained local brick with Bath stone dressings to plans by Robert and James Adam for Sir George Cornewall in 1775. The work, under the supervision of Anthony Keck, was completed eight years later and the Cornewalls, once installed, could look out from the west front on to grounds laid out by Brown and later modified by Repton.

The west porch, sweeping up to the mezzanine inside, was added in 1792, and from here we can follow the cunningly calculated visual effect implicit in the shape and placing of the first-floor rooms. First comes a drawing room no doubt used for music, for which the Cornewalls had a passion. On the east wall is an excellent double portrait of Mrs Robert Master, wife of the Governor of Tobago, and Mrs Saladin, painted by a highly talented late eighteenth-century amateur, Ariana Egerton. The full length of Velters Cornewall, champion of Hereford cider-makers, is clearly not, even hypothetically, by Gainsborough.

Hence the library, once lined with seven bookcases, of which five were removed in 1972. As well as a display of seventeenth-century portraits of the present owner's family, this has a magnificent prospect of the Wye, sliding under red cliffs to the north-west. The surprise, however, awaits us behind the curved mahogany doors leading into the circular drawing room. This is like a little temple to the neo-classical principles enshrined in Adam's designs, now preserved in Sir John Soane's Museum. His work is to be found in the doorcases, the frieze and the chimneypiece above a steel grate in which no fires were actually lit for fear of spoiling the Parisian Reveillon *papier peint* on the walls, with its rich reds and blues. The drum shape of the room and the coved ceiling produce strange acoustic effects.

Now the supreme aesthetic point of the whole scheme is grasped, for this room is the only one in the house from which the Wye can be seen flowing in both directions, silvery and sinuous between woods and shaggy meadows. We can imagine the Cornewalls' delighted guests, their heads full of Gilpin and Egerton, congratulating Sir George on the novelty of it all. They could step out on to a small terrace and down grassy banks to the river itself: the gardens have since been substantially enlarged and make, with their mixture of lawn and wilderness, an agreeable walk after we have passed through the oval hall with its splendid flying staircase under a skylight.

Leaving the park through gates with lodges designed by G. S. Repton, Nash's pupil, we follow the main road on past the old wooden palings of Moccas Deer Park, a big stretch of woodland climbing to some 270 feet, and reach **Bredwardine**, on the very edge of the Kilvert country. Francis Kilvert should be well enough known to users of this guide for me not to have to point out that he was a Victorian curate of Clyro, Radnorshire, who happened to be an excellent diarist. An Englishman, he belongs as much to the Saesnaeg side of the March as he does to the Welsh, and who in any case, on this hotly contested frontier, will say where England ends and Wales begins? He was vicar of Bredwardine from 1877 until 1879, when he died of peritonitis contracted on his honeymoon. His church of St Andrew has a projecting tower built in 1790, and a Norman nave of white tufa with some easily visible herringbone work. In the north doorway are two carved rosettes containing bird- and monkey-headed figures. The chancel was rebuilt at the turn of the thirteenth and fourteenth centuries at a northward slant to the body of the church. Nearby are the earthworks of the old castle, with a series of ditches beyond it, presumably flooded from the river for additional defence.

Opposite the crossroads stands a fine late seventeenth-century inn, the Red Lion, and here we turn down, past church and castle and some well prettified cottages, to the old bridge. On the other side, from the hill above Brobury, there is a stupendous view over the Scar cliff down to the oak and chestnut groves of Moccas. At Staunton-on-Wye we rejoin the A438 as a stretch of Roman road, and opposite the freehouse significantly called Portway (a Roman road name as common in England as Stretton) we turn down the lane amid Messrs Bulmers' fruit farms, home of all those gallons of sweet fizzy 'Woodpecker', to reach the world's most sublime dead end at **Monnington.** Walkers (and it is worth footing it for the sheer quietness) can reach the court and church from various routes, but motorists will have to drive through the farm and park at the court gate. Thence across the front lawn of the house, which ends by a broad stream going down to the river, and through the churchyard to one of the lovelier small west Midland churches.

Apart from the Perpendicular west tower, all of St Mary's church was built in 1679 for Uvedall Tomkyns, who is buried in the chancel. Though materials and ground-plan from an older building may have been used, the present interior, plastered, with plain-glazed, round-arched windows, belongs ideally to the Latitudinarian world. All the fittings are consonant: the screen, like the ropework one at How Caple, the panelled balustered pulpit, the font of 1680. On the north wall is the bust of Robert Perrott, who died, after an adventurous career, in 1667. Part of the rhyming inscription runs:

> *Here Perrott ly's whose great capaceous mind*
> *In's Native Limitts scorn'd to be confin'd*
> *To th'unknown dangers of inraged Seas*
> *And forreigne enimys more feirce then thess,*
> *His valor him expos'd Venice may boast*
> *The aid he lent her to defend her coast*
> *Gainst unbelieving Turks.*

Monnington Court, an interesting mixture of fragments from every architectural period after 1400, is the conjectural scene of the death of Owen Glendower. The old patriot's daughter, Margaret, had married Roger Monnington, and her father's body is said to rest near the north porch. His ghost is said still to ride along the avenue north of the church. There are those in Wales, however, who say that the place of his death is not known, and that perhaps he never died at all . . .

Back on the main road we move south-east past the long shadow of Garnons Hill. The hill itself is an integral part of the exceedingly well preserved grounds by Humphrey Repton (1791) enclosing the big castellated mansion of Garnons, built in 1815 by William Atkinson for Sir John Cotterell. Atkinson (1773–1839) completed Abbotsford for Sir Walter Scott and excelled in Regency baronial. The Cotterell family church is at **Byford**, the turn to which faces the park gate. The nave, extended east and west during the late thirteenth century, is a decidedly grand affair, and the south transept, added at the same period, has its original collar-beam roof and a gracefully posed St Margaret painted on the wall. She wears a russet-coloured dress and is framed in a border of leaves. Nearly opposite the church, Byford Court, built for the Gomond family, whose arms are over the central doorway, is a sturdy, three-bay timber-framed structure.

The Roman road peters out between Monnington and Byford, and resumes as a parallel lane north of Bridge Sollers. Its inevitable destination is **Kenchester**, which, apart from Weston-under-Penyard and Leintwardine, is the county's only major Roman site. To examine it, you will need permission from Magna Castra farm, on the left of the turn to Credenhill. This was once the small town of Magna, surrounded by hexagonal, four-gated walls, built in the second century AD and reinforced during the later empire. Excavations here revealed the sophistications of painted plaster and mosaic floors, and fragments of these and other finds can be seen in the Hereford museum.

Aerial photography has disclosed several buildings beyond the walls, and in 1812, on the site of **Bishopstone** rectory, the Reverend A. J. Walker discovered a Roman house, with an amazing thirty-foot mosaic floor, full of beautifully varied patterns, which has since disappeared. Bishopstone Court was the home of the Berington family, noted recusants, who are said to have conducted Catholic worship in the church's north transept concurrently with the Protestant parishioners in the nave. Humphrey Berington 'raised a company of foote at his own expense for the use of the royal martyr, King Charles I,

---

Brockhampton Manor, Herefordshire
Croft Castle, Herefordshire

by whose cruel and bloody fate he and his children came to ruin'. His father, John, robed as a sheriff, is commemorated by a very old-fangled effigy beside his wife, Joyce Ketilby, holding prayer-books and lying on a rolled pillow.

The poet Thomas Traherne would probably not have recognized modern **Credenhill**, where he was vicar from 1661 to 1669. Closeness to Hereford and its status as an RAF base have made it spread hideously, almost wholly smothering some good houses in the village centre. Among these is Credenhill Court, built in 1760 by the guardians of Richard Eckley, heir to the estate. Richard's grandfather, James, had purchased it against strong competition from a Mr Geers of Bridge Sollers. On the day before the sale they both rode independently to London, but Geers's horse cast a shoe on the road, and by the time he reached his destination Eckley had collared the property.

Opposite this is the parish church, which I find unprepossessing, especially in its bald, triple-arched thirteenth-century stone screen, and in its muddled fenestration – lancets in the nave, Decorated chancel windows, and a Herefordshire triple east light. At least one of the chancel windows has good glass, a north-west panel showing St Thomas à Becket and St Thomas Cantelupe blessing. This was probably given by Bishop Swinfield and despite its primitive cast must be later than 1320, when Cantelupe was canonized. The elegant font, fluted like a blancmange mould, has an inscription round the bowl telling us that it was the 'giuft of John Squier who liveed at Colford 1667'.

Perhaps he was a friend of Traherne, who had succeeded the contumacious Cromwellian incumbent, Edmund Quarrell, in 1661. 'He gave God thanks,' says the report on Quarrell, 'in this ch. for his Mty's overthrow at Worcs., causing bonfires to be made, and music and dancing in the churchyard, and other expressions of delight openly and offensively; he preached against both sacraments, that all kings were tyrants, that there was a causeway in hell paved with kings' sculls, and the Bk. of Common Prayer was composed by the devil.'

Traherne's father was a Hereford shoemaker, originally from Lugwardine, and the fledgling poet, born in 1637, was probably educated at Ledbury Grammar School, from whence he went to Brasenose, Oxford. During his eight Credenhill years he was a

Mrs Fallows and her grandchildren, Herefordshire gypsies from Dilwyn member of the Anglican religious circle associated with Susannah Hopton at Kington. He describes the time as follows, in his *Centuries of Meditation*: 'When I came into the Country, and being seated among silent Trees and Meads and Hills, had all my Time in mine own Hands, I resolved to Spend it all, whatever it cost me, in Search of Happiness, and to Satiate that burning Thirst which Nature had Enkindled in me from my Youth. In which I was so resolute, that I chose rather to liv upon 10 pounds a yeer, and to go in Lether Clothes, and feed upon Bread and Water, so that I might hav all my time clearly to my self.'

His poetry and meditations, those of a modest, quiet and utterly assured Christian spirit, were only rescued from oblivion in the last century, and to anyone with the least sensitivity to the subtle colours and shadings and bursts of light on these border hillsides, they are as much of the landscape as his older contemporary, Henry Vaughan's. It is not too romantic to see both men, with George Herbert, also from a Marcher family, as belonging to a tradition almost more Welsh than English, mingling the ecstatic silences of the west Herefordshire uplands with rhapsodic, visionary outpourings as free-flowing as any Black Mountain torrent. A pity, I say, that Traherne should be buried anywhere as tame as Teddington, Middlesex.

An even greater apprehension of the mysteries of landscape was Wordsworth's, who used to visit his wife's relatives, the Hutchinsons, at **Brinsop**. Their house was the extremely imposing stone and timber manor standing in a moat amid gardens along the lane past the turn to the church. It was begun in the fourteenth century, and has a spectacular hall roof, with moulded tie beams and wallplates, and kingposts fanning out into struts to hold up the collars and purlin. The poet came here first in 1827, with Mrs Wordsworth and Southey's daughter. On a second visit in 1835 he wrote three bad sonnets and in 1841 he helped to lay out the garden. 'Ah, that Mister Wordsworth,' said an old gardener years later, 'he were one to go moonin' about the lanes.'

He is recalled in a window in Brinsop church, approached through a farmyard and standing in a strange ring of earthworks – what, indeed, were they? This is an immensely rewarding church, very well cared for. First of all comes the surprise of a Comper interior – Comper, what is more, at his finest, windows full of clean colours and lines, rich without the least trace of vulgarity. The blues and greens are especially subtle. He worked on Brinsop from 1920 to 1928, providing a resplendent gilded reredos, with a canopy flourishing the figure of St George, which can also be seen in one of the two medieval panels in the central east window light. Apart from the plain Perpendicular rood screen and traces of medieval painting in the nave and chancel, the church's other treasure is the Norman tympanum now preserved in the north aisle. This is pure Herefordshire School, showing St George in a flared and pleated tunic, his cloak flowing out over his shoulder as his horse tramples down a writhing worm. Above is an arcaded frieze of birds and animals.

CHAPTER TWENTY-THREE

Black Mountain and Golden Valley

❧

Black Mountain is the greatest single fact in the Marcher landscape. From the Malverns, the highest point to the east, it can be seen ridging the horizon in a straight grey bar which breaks off, dramatically sudden, at Hay Bluff, round whose wooded skirts run the borders of Brecon, Radnor and Hereford counties. All over the Wye vale you glimpse it, brooding, heavy, sinister on the skyline, an affirmation, if any be needed, of England's ending and the numinous presence of Wales closing in. Black, indeed it is in thundery weather, which lends in addition bluish and purplish tinges: on clear March days, with the snow still lying up in the highest clefts, it lies brindled brown and white like the long, sheer back of some pasturing heifer. Folklore, respectful of its dominance, has given it an evil spirit, the Old Woman of the Mountain who leads benighted travellers astray – though Offa's Dyke Path, running along its top to Hay, is now mostly travelled in daylight. Curlew breed up here and buzzard as well (I once saw three flying round a dead tree near Craswall) while above Longtown is a small annual colony of red grouse – the more common black variety is now extinct in Herefordshire.

From the Pontrilas crossroads we can approach the southern end of Black Mountain by various roads, all enchantingly minor, leafy and steep-banked among the wooded dingles. The road up to **Rowlstone** brings us to a parish church whose tympanum and chancel arch are both excitingly conceived Norman pieces. The former, in the south porch, has a big haloed Christ in Glory with boldly splayed feet, and swooping angels on each side. The latter is decorated with a frieze of birds above capitals showing deeply incised figures of saints and angels. Notice, too, the long, jagged late medieval candle brackets in the chancel itself, ornamented with rows of swans and cocks.

Walterstone, to the south, has a special place in history, for here at the old farmhouse of Allt-yr-Ynys by an island in the Monnow lived a family which was to rule England – the Cecils. As Seisyllts they had held it since Henry I's reign, and it was from here that

David Cecil followed Henry Richmond to Bosworth in 1485. The house, at the junction of the roads from Walterstone and Upper Goytre, is now a fairly simple Jacobean farm, with little trace of the ox-house for twelve oxen and twenty kine, the gatehouse and stable 'with standinge for a duzzen horses at leaste', reported in 1647. Place it side by side with Hatfield and the contrast in itself encapsulates a quintessentially English success story.

The Monnow is, if possible, even lovelier in its Herefordshire stretch than the Lugg or the Teme, 'a pleasant clere water, full of troutes, were there any order to preserve them from the annoyance of the otter, and ill-demeaning persons'. Fishing in the river is good, trout are preserved, and in 1882 Dr Matthews of Pontrilas Court added grayling, already found in other county rivers. From Walterstone the road runs up above its alder-hung shores, past **Clodock,** with its full complement of Restoration church furnishings and an ancient Welsh funerary slab behind the pulpit, commemorating the *'membra pudica'* of the wife of a certain Gwyndda, to **Longtown,** a fascinating relic of the old March.

Longtown, like Richard's Castle to the north, is the ghost of a piece of thirteenth-century urban development. In their efforts to keep the border in check, as well as to stress their own king-defying grip, the omnipotent Mortimers planted towns up and down the March, marking out burgage plots and granting tolls, fairs and markets. Longtown was a distinguished failure, but you can still follow the demarcation line of the turf rampart on the shaggy patch of common opposite the village primary school. More substantial evidence is given by the Angevin castle keep (currently under repair) pierced with fourteenth-century windows and with a section of its girdling bailey. The building material is, rather unusually, of hard, tile-shaped stones and thus looks more Roman than Marcher in character. As 'Ewyas Lacy' castle it was the chief fortress of the hundred, temporarily captured with siege-engines by the Welsh in 1146. The old approach to it, now a rutted cart-track between earth banks, is called, by the way, 'Jews' Lane': intriguing to think of some adventurous member of the Hereford community following the Mortimers out into these wild hills.

Right under the louring mountain, with the Monnow plashing and bouncing in pools and falls to the east, we turn off some two miles beyond to **Michaelchurch Escley,** on the opposite side of the valley, to visit the drab-looking church by the brook. Here is a strange, haunting late medieval mural of Christ of the Trades, a big, oafish figure, surrounded by the tools of carpentry, shearing, spinning

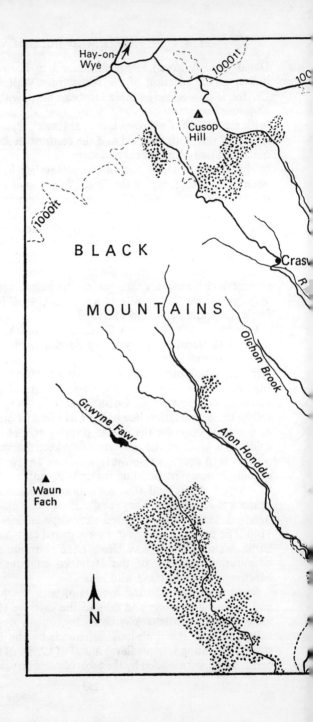

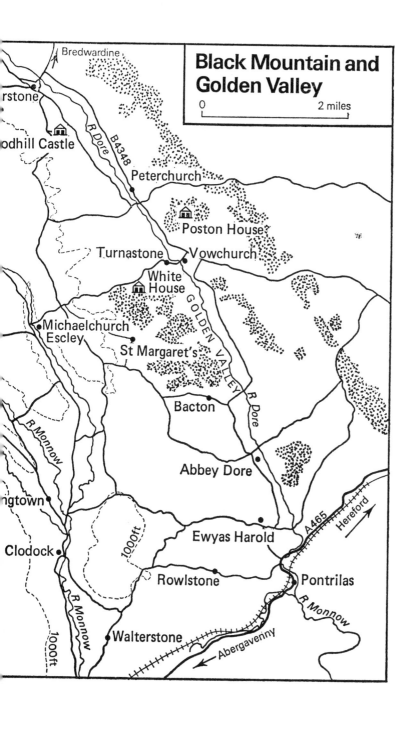

Black Mountain and Golden Valley

0   2 miles

Bredwardine

rstone

odhill Castle

R Dore

B4348

Peterchurch

Poston House

Turnastone

Vowchurch

White House

GOLDEN VALLEY

Michaelchurch Escley

St Margaret's

Bacton

R Dore

Abbey Dore

R Monnow

ngtown

Clodock

1000ft

Ewyas Harold

A465

Hereford

Rowlstone

Pontrilas

R Monnow

1000ft

R Monnow

Walterstone

Abergavenny

and cooking, painted in black, white and yellow.

Back on the mountainside we come to **Craswall**, formerly in far-flung Clodock parish. After two sharpish bends at the crossing of the Monnow, a track and a footpath lead off to the right to Abbey Farm and the ruins of a Grandmontine priory. This was founded by Walter de Lacy some time before 1231, for ten priests, three clerks and thirteen lay brothers, and was one of four such monastic houses in England. The order, founded as a Cistercian offshoot by Stephen of Muret and established at Grandmont near Limoges soon after his death in 1124, was noted for its severe rule, reliant on alms and agricultural labour by the lay brothers. It enjoyed particular favour from English monarchs (Henry II, for example, sent eight hundred cartloads of English lead for the building of the Grandmont church) but was suppressed, with other alien houses, in 1438, some three hundred years before its final dissolution in France.

Both site and design of the priory are interesting. The rugged terrain is perfect for an order favouring seclusion. Since the Grandmontines had no parochial responsibility, the nave of the 108-foot church is perceptibly narrower than the choir. Though only the south wall now stands, you can still pick out an apse, cloister, chapter-house and frater. Excavation during the 1930s hinted at a dour, ponderously detailed building in dark stone, with no ornate carving and doubtless deliberately gloomy. It also uncovered a lead-lapped arm-bone, which, it is suggested, was a relic of one of the eleven thousand virgins of Cologne of whom all the Grandmontine houses held souvenirs.

From Craswall we can either push on to Hay, a boom town for secondhand books, and thence into the Kilvert country, or turn off to the right just below Cusop Hill and make for Dorstone. Here it is worth making the detour to **Clifford** to inspect the overgrown ruins of the castle, hung high over a shallow bend in the Wye. Its builder was William Fitz Osbern, from whom it passed to Ralph de Todeni and Richard Fitz Ponz, whose son Walter took the name of de Clifford. His daughter, 'Fair Rosamund', born here, became mistress of Henry II, who kept her hidden from jealous Queen Eleanor in a labyrinthine bower at Woodstock. The Queen managed to find her way in and forced Rosamund to drink poison. She was buried in conditions of near-sanctity at Godstow Priory. Fuller transcribes and translates her epitaph:

Hic jacet in tumulo Rosa mundi non Rosa munda;
Non redolet sed olet quae redolere solet.

(This tomb doth inclose the world's fair rose, so sweet and full of favour;
And smell she doth now, but you may guess how, with none of the sweetest savour.)

The castle was probably never lived in after its attack by Owain Glyndwr in 1402, but we can still make out the square keep and round towers of the original rectangle, with its two baileys, moated to the river.

The road to **Dorstone** lies through a country pitted with castle sites. There are tumps at Mynyddbrydd, Newton and Dorstone itself, which belonged to the Sollers family. St Faith's church is alleged to have been founded by William de Brito in 1171 in expiation of his part in Thomas à Becket's murder at Canterbury. Most interesting here, however, is Arthur's Stone, clearly signposted on the road over Dorstone Hill to Bredwardine. This is that rarity hereabouts, a megalithic chamber tomb, of c. 3000 BC. The oval mound supports a hexagonal capstone on six (formerly nine) verticals, and the false door and part of the chamber are exposed. It was here that Charles I made a rendezvous with the Scots on 17 September 1645, commemorated at nearby Scotland Bank.

There are wonderful eastern prospects of the gradually softening Wye valley, but at Dorstone we stand in any case at the head of one of England's most Elysian stretches, the so-called Golden Valley, running down for some ten miles to Ewyas Harold and Pontrilas between typical wooded Herefordshire knolls. Golden, of course, it never was – the name comes from its little river, the Dore, Welsh dwr (water), which the Norman lords mistook for 'D'or', thus golden. It conforms beautifully to a Marcher stereotype, with an east side perceptibly English and a steeper west side, with dodging hamlets and sheep pastures, markedly Welsh, with the customary rash of castles. The most substantial among them was probably **Snodhill Castle**, just off the parallel road to the B4348, on the west side of the stream. There are clear traces here of a polygonal keep, gateways and round bastions, and remains of a curtain wall, mostly dating from the fourteenth century, when it was held by the Chandoses.

Peterchurch is said to have been a Saxon missionary outpost, which apparently explains the grandeur of the church, with its two chancels finished off with an apse. Village funerals always used to involve a procession with the coffin around both chancels before the service began. To the south, **Turnastone** and **Vowchurch** are subjects of a legend claiming that one devout sister remarked to the other: 'I vow I will build my church before you can turn a stone of yours', and there indeed they both are, face to face across the stream. The former has, against the chancel wall, a nice incised slab to Thomas ApHarry and his wife, Agnes Bodenham. He is in full armour, his head on a mantled helm, but the little piping satyr to his left and the date 1522 warn of the approach of an age when such splendid plating was to become worse than useless.

ApHarry left money to build the timber bell-turret of St Bartholomew, Vowchurch, the rest of whose fabric is basically fourteenth-century. In 1348 Bishop Trillek gave forty days' indulgence to visitors to the church on the feasts of the sixteen saints in whose names its two altars were consecrated, with similar benefits for contribution towards painting the holy images. Inside, the woodwork is ferociously good. The roof, a mishmash of timbers from three centuries resting on sharp posts set into the walls, bears the arms, on the third pair of posts from the east, of the Parrys and Vaughans, with the date 1613 and the initials R.V. for Rowland Vaughan, of whom more anon. The Jacobean screen, with a Norse looking Adam and Eve and curly monsters, is of the same date, with a lozenge-shaped panel saying: 'Heare below ly the body of Thomas Hill ande Margaret his wife whose children made this skryne.' Outside is an old half-timbered vicarage, perhaps contemporaneous with the tower.

Almost wholly surrounded by woods to the north is Poston House, a shooting box built for Sir Edward Boughton in 1780 by William Chambers, who provided a Tuscan portico, entrance hall and domed inner room. It is probably best to look at it from the path linking the B4348 to the road down to Vowchurch Common.

We have to go back to Turnastone in order to get to the sharp left turn to Upper Maes-coed and St Margaret's. Some way up the hill is White House, an absorbing mixture of late Tudor, Jacobean and early Georgian, with barge-boarded gables, a staircase with decorated newels and a curious fireplace featuring a painted bust of a man against a landscape background with a globe in the sky.

St Margaret's, a church beside a farm, is wholly captivating within and without. Its churchyard is a green velvet pasture full of bee-browsed flowers, sheep's-bit scabious, yarrow, and the 'brown' knapweed whose petals are a light purple. The building is of shaly rubble, dressed with sandstone, with a splotch of whitish plastering which makes it look, with its low weatherboarded bell-turret, a bit like a shorthorn cow. Thank providence for an interior of plain windows, wainscoting and whitewashed walls.

The boast of the church is its magnificent rood loft, dating from the early sixteenth century and one of a series of such fine pieces of carving to be found all along the Welsh border from Llangwm in Denbighshire to Llanvilo in Breconshire. Two pillars, with crocketed niches at the top for figures of the Virgin and St John, support decorated rails enriched with vine-trail frieze and brattishing. On the soffit, or underside, of the loft, note the bosses, carved in a multitude of lively forms, and the cornice dotted with fleur-de-lys and oak leaves. The composite effect of the whole piece is one of budding and flowering, as if the wood, by some perhaps not altogether Christian miracle, had retained its life even when cut from the tree. In fact a very Welsh affair indeed.

There are other good things in the church, including the original eighteenth-century wall texts (by the pulpit, appropriately, 'Cry aloud and spare not') recently refurbished with their green and pink surrounds. Outside, over the road from the churchyard, across the field gate, is a marvellous view over a diorama of Herefordshire hills, hedgy valleys and cornfields.

Out of sight on the slopes by the Dore is Newcourt Farm, scene, in Jacobean times, of one of those advanced technological experiments which foreshadowed the Industrial Revolution. Rowland Vaughan of Bredwardine married his kinswoman, Elizabeth Vaughan, of Newcourt and settled here in what was then one of the most depressed and backward areas of England. Obsessed with the idea of harnessing the valley waters, he started by improving the Newcourt estate with drainage and irrigation, raising its value from £40 to £300, and went on to make a complete system of locks and sluices which he called his 'Trench Royal'. At Newcourt itself he organized and maintained a 'commonwealth of mechanicals', designed to relieve local poverty and entirely self-sufficient, its members working in Vaughan's gloving, tanning and weaving mills.

Bacton, above Newcourt, shelters in its church of St Faith a wonderful monument to Vaughan's aunt, Blanche Parry, one of those loyal virgin maids-in-waiting with whom Queen Elizabeth surrounded herself like settings for a diamond. Her alabaster figure, against the chancel north wall, kneels to a little bell-tent Elizabeth, her face 'remarkably like'. Since the Parrys had recusant affiliations, Pevsner's detection of a hint of medieval Virgin-worship is perhaps not so far-fetched. A big piece of Blanche's needlework hangs on the nave wall: full of primitive exuberance, it carries at the same time the sense of a hankering, in its vision of a forest full of deer, bears and greyhounds, for somewhere more innocent and less contentious than the Elizabethan Court, a nostalgically envisaged Golden Valley perhaps.

The modern altar frontal, in rich red, green and gold, is in good enough taste to please a modern Blanche Parry. The chancel also has some medieval stalls and a set of little angels along the fifteenth-century wall plates of the roof.

Bacton parish includes Morehampton, once a mansion of the Hoskyns family and scene of one of the most remarkable events ever to have taken place in the county. Serjeant Hoskyns was a friend of Raleigh, Donne and Jonson, and possibly of Shakespeare, too, a choice enough Jacobean spirit to appeal to the Herefordian atavism of John Aubrey, who portrays him in the *Lives* as an incomparably versatile figure, poet, lawyer, Latinist, horseman and politician. Sent to the Tower for criticizing King James's liberality to his Scots henchman, he was kept 'close prisoner', in solitary confinement with boarded windows, but allowed conversation with his friend, Raleigh, to whose prose style he helped to give some expert polish.

Legend brings Hoskyns's angry king to Morehampton on a far happier occasion, that of the wondrous geriatric morris dance whose performers' ages added up to 1200. Besides the Maid Marian, 120-year-old Meg Goodwin, who could recall the death of Prince Arthur at Ludlow, there was gaffer Tompkins of Llangarron, footing it at 107, Thomas Winney of Holmer, a springheeled Methusaleh at 100, and a 'hobbyhorse' of 97. All went smoothly save when one old boy fell over and couldn't rise without help.

Hoskyns died in 1638, from a gangrened toe which had been trodden on by 'a massive countrey fellowe' at Hereford assizes. Morehampton house and gardens have long since gone, and so, too, has the old valley railway which ran from Pontrilas to Hay along what must have been the loveliest and most inefficiently-run line in England. In 1892 Timmins in his *Nooks and Corners of Herefordshire* called it 'that most eccentric of lines . . . where we have seen *the* linesman, when not engaged in haymaking, deeply engrossed in his occupation of weeding between the rails, as we waited for the train which, if we are to believe the tongue of rumour, sometimes fails to put in an appearance, the company's only locomotive having been seized for distraint of rent.'

Enthusiasts can follow its course best between Vowchurch and **Abbey Dore**, which has one of the most celebrated of Marcher churches. We can imagine Golden Valley, at the time when the Normans rode up it from Ewyas to Clifford, as a much wilder place, in short ideal for the Cistercian order, who could make sheep-runs here and relish the solitude. Their abbey was founded by Robert Fitz Harold in 1147, but the present building was started some thirty years later, with a long aisled nave, presbytery and transepts. Work probably continued over the next eight decades, and the church was consecrated in the late thirteenth century by St Thomas Cantelupe.

Its decay might have been allowed to continue after the Dissolution if the great Lord Scudamore had not supervised a thoroughgoing programme of repairs. The nave, past hope, was entirely blocked off and a tower was built by Addams, a Ross mason, in the angle of the south transept. The presbytery was given a wooden vault, a font and poor-box were installed and a music-gallery added. Scudamore's restoration is all the more interesting historically for its uncanny truth to the spirit of the original building: he even put back the stone altar-table, which had been used in Tudor times as 'hard top' for cheese-making.

The best of his additions are the florid wooden screen, carved by John Abel and flourishing the royal arms of Charles I flanked by those of Archbishop Laud and the Scudamores, and the magnificent glazing of the east window (1634) showing, in the centre, an Ascension, with eleven apostles, Moses and St John the Baptist, in the north light Sts Matthew, Mark, Peter and Andrew, and in the south St Luke, St James and both Sts John.

Despite Giraldus Cambrensis's merciless portrayal of the Cistercians as hypocritical, landgrabbing gluttons, their architecture is always distinguished by a grandeur touched with simplicity. So carefully restrained is the design of the medieval columns and capitals that the church always seems much higher than it actually is. The presbytery, perhaps the finest expression of that Herefordshire cliché, the triple-light east end, has two tiers of arches, long lancets above a deeply layered Early English arcade. Notice the glazed tiles on the floor (those with the arms of Leon and Castile an allusion to Edward I's Spanish queen Eleanor) and the two knightly effigies in the north and south ambulatories. The former is Roger de Clifford, grandson of the latter, the abbey's founder, Robert, one of whose stone arms, Aubrey tells us, was carried off by a mower to whet his scythe with.

Robert's father, Harold, gave his name to **Ewyas Harold** (pronounced Yewas) which in its turn got given to the whole Norman lordship of this part of the March, called by the Welsh 'one of the two sleeves of Ergyng'. The Norman castle, however, its ditch and tump surviving west of the church, was built by William Fitz Osbern, who was nothing if not enterprising. Having supplied sixty ships for the Conqueror's invasion, he received the Earldom of Hereford and ruled as viceroy in William's absence. In 1071 he went to the help of Richildis, widowed countess of Flanders, who had offered him her hand in marriage as a reward, but he was killed fighting at Cassel and buried in Normandy.

The church itself is up the village, well off the main road and, apart from a thirteenth-century west tower, is mostly a Victorian rebuilding. There is a curious reredos, featuring pieces of sixteenth-century German woodcarving with scenes from the Passion, showing Christ before Caiaphas and Pilate. It was here that the composer, Samuel Sebastian Wesley, was married in secret to the daughter of a Hereford canon. He had probably got to know the vicar while sampling the excellent fishing which had originally attracted him to the otherwise not very rewarding job as Hereford cathedral organist.

The village – and for once in the southern March it is a village – abounds in freehouses, most of them appealing to the growing interest in obtaining 'real' beer. As you leave for the Pontrilas crossroads, notice the spiny little Catholic church, recently built to a design by Nigel Deas of Hereford. Unassumingly effective, it fits in well with the surrounding cottages, and is one of the few really adequate modern buildings in the West Midlands.

Bibliography

❧

The two best books on Worcestershire are now more or less generally unobtainable: William Habington's Jacobean survey deserves to be kept in print, as does George Turberville's splendidly compendious *Worcestershire in the Nineteenth Century*. Modern readers will have to be contented with Maxwell Fraser's *Companion into Worcestershire*, P. J. N. Havins's *Portrait of Worcestershire* and Canon Leatherbarrow's *Worcestershire* in the Batsford County series.

Herefordshire has done rather better. Mrs E. M. Leather's *Herefordshire Folklore* has recently been reissued, and can be read as a substantial and enjoyable chapter of local history. An outstanding recent survey of the county by someone who knows every inch of it has been written by E. W. Tonkin in his *Herefordshire* for the Batsford series.

Few good modern books have been written on Gloucestershire. The best is David Verey's volume in the Shell Guide series. An interesting conspectus of county history is offered in the collection of centenary essays published by the Bristol and Gloucestershire Archaeological Society.

Warwickshire has been most worthily served in three recent works, Lyndon F. Cave's *Warwickshire Villages*, Vivian Bird's *Warwickshire* and J. C. Trewin's highly entertaining *Portrait of the Shakespeare Country*.

It goes without saying that the appropriate volumes in Pevsner's *Buildings of England* series will be found indispensable, as will the Victoria County History. In the case of Worcestershire this is now in need of revision: in the case of Herefordshire, beyond a single introductory volume, it does not even exist. The Warwickshire and Gloucestershire sections are excellent, and I am, of course, indebted to them, as well as to the other books mentioned, for much useful information.

APPENDIX 1

Opening times of museums etc.

❧

Unless otherwise stated, the following general rules apply: all municipal museums are open during daytime hours on weekdays; all country houses and museums mentioned below are open on Bank Holiday Mondays.

At other times the following hours apply:

WARWICKSHIRE

Anne Hathaway's Cottage, Stratford-upon-Avon
April–October: weekdays 9–6 (9–7 in June, July, August and September); Sun 10–6
November–March: weekdays 9–4.30; Sun 1.30–4.30

Charlecote Park
May–September: daily except Mon, 11.15–5.45
April–October: Sat and Sun only 11.15–5.45

Coughton Court
April and October: Sat and Sun 2–6
May–September: Wed, Thur, Sat, Sun 2–6

Hall's Croft, Stratford-upon-Avon
April–October: weekdays 9–6; Sun 2–6
November–March: weekdays only 10–1, 2–4

Harvard House, Stratford-upon-Avon
April–October: weekdays 9–1, 2–6; Sun 2–6
November–March: weekdays only 10–1, 2–4

Lord Leycester Hospital, Warwick
All year: weekdays 10–5.30 (summer); 10–4 (winter); closed Sun

Mary Arden's House, Wilmcote
April–October: weekdays 9–6; Sun 2–6
November–March: weekdays only 9–12.45, 2–4

New Place, Stratford-upon-Avon
April–October: weekdays 9–6; Sun 2–6
November–March: weekdays only 1–12.45, 2–4

Ragley Hall and Park
House and Park, March–October: daily, except Mon and Fri 1.30–5.30
Park only, May–September: daily 11–7

Shakespeare's Birthplace, Stratford-upon-Avon
April–October: weekdays 9–6 (9–7 in June, July, August and September); Sun 10–6
November–March: weekdays 9–4.30; Sun 1.30–4.30

Warwick Castle, Warwick (currently under reorganization, 1979)
March–October: daily 10–5.30
November–February: 10–4.30

WORCESTERSHIRE

Avoncroft Museum, Bromsgrove
March–November: 10.30–5.30

Greyfriars, Worcester
May–September: first Wed in every month, 2–6

Hanbury Hall
March 25–Sept 30: daily, except Mon and Tues, 2–6

Harvington Hall
Daily, except Mon and Fri after Bank Holiday, 2–6
Easter–September: 11.30–10

Little Malvern Court
May–September: Wed 2.30–5.30

Spetchley Park
(gardens only) April–October: daily, except Sat, 11–5; Sun 2–6

HEREFORDSHIRE

Berrington Hall
April–September: Wed and Sat 2–6

Brilley, Cwmmau
Bank Holiday Sat, Sun and Mon 2–6

Brockhampton Manor
February–December: Mon, Wed, Fri, Sat 10–1, 2–6; Sun 10–1

Burton Court
Whitsun–mid-September: Wed, Thur, Sat, Sun 2.30–6

Croft Castle
April–September: Wed, Thur, Sat, Sun 2.15–6

Dinmore Manor
All year: daily 2–6

Eastnor Castle
  Sun, May–September: 2.15–6; also Easter Monday, Spring Bank
  Holiday Sun, Mon, Summer Bank Holiday

Eye Manor
  Easter–June: Wed, Thur, Sat, Sun 2.30–6
  July–October: daily 2.30–5.30
  Bank Holiday Mon and Tues 2.30–5.30

Hellens, Much Marcle
  (guided tours) Easter–October: Wed, Sat, Sun 2–6

Hergest Croft Gardens
  May–August: daily 11–7

Kentchurch Court
  May–September: by appointment only

Moccas Court
  (house and gardens) April–September: Thurs 2–6

Pembridge Castle
  May–September: Thurs 10–7

GLOUCESTERSHIRE

Berkeley Castle
  Daily, except Mon, April: 2–5; May–August: 11–5; Sun 2–5; September:
  2–5; October: Sun only 2–4.30

Clearwell Castle
  April–May: Sun 11–6
  May–September: weekdays 2–6; Sun 11–6

Lydney Park
  (gardens and park) March–October: Wed 2–4; certain Suns 2–6

Westbury Water Garden
  April and October: Sat and Sun; May to September: daily, except
  Mon and Tues, 11–1, 2–6

APPENDIX 2

Select list of hotels, etc.

✤

The following is in no way intended as an exhaustive list. In each case I have added the telephone number in preference to an address as, practically speaking, more desirable. The places have been chosen principally with the idea of their being used as bases for exploring the surrounding region.

Hotels

WORCESTERSHIRE: Abberley: The Elms, 029 921 666
Broadway: Lygon Arms, 038 681 2255
Evesham: Evesham Hotel, 0386 6344
Pershore: Angel, 038 65 2046
Malvern: Abbey Hotel, 068 45 3325
Foley Arms, 068 45 3397
Cottage In The Wood, 068 45 3487
Essington, 068 45 61177
Bewdley: Black Boy, 0299 402119
Worcester: Giffard, 0905 27155
Star, 0905 24308

HEREFORDSHIRE: Bromyard: Hop Pole, 08852 2449
Hereford: Green Dragon, 0432 2506
Castle Pool, 0432 56321
How Caple: How Caple Grange, 098 986 208
Ledbury: Feathers, 0531 2600
Symonds Yat: Wye Rapids, 060 081 366
Weston-under-Penyard: Wye, 0989 3541
Weobley: Red Lion, 054 45 220
Unicorn, 054 45 230

GLOUCESTERSHIRE: Berkeley: Berkeley Arms, 045 381 291
Gloucester: Fleece, 0452 22760
New County, 0452 24977
New Inn, 0452 22177
Tewkesbury: Royal Hop Pole, 0684 293236
Tudor House, 0684 293129

APPENDICES

WARWICKSHIRE: Stratford-upon-Avon: Alveston Manor, 0789 4581
Falcon, 0789 5777
Red Horse, 0789 3211
Royal Shakespeare,
0789 3631
Swan's Nest, 0789 66761
Welcombe, 0789 3611
White Swan, 0789 3606
Warwick: Lord Leycester, 0926 41481
Tudor House, 0926 45447
Warwick Arms, 0926 42759
Woolpack, 0926 41684
Wilmcote: The Swan House, 0789 67030

Restaurants

Thornbury, Gloucs: Thornbury Castle, 0454 412647
Newent, Gloucs: Bistro One, 0531 820896
Great Witley, Worcs: Hundred House, 029 921 215 & 565
Worcester: King Charles II, 0905 22449
Stratford-upon-Avon: Ashburton House, 0789 2444
Marianne, 0789 3563

APPENDIX 3

A select list of architects, etc.

꙳

THOMAS ARCHER, 1668–1743, was a Warwickshire squire who worked as an amateur architect, mainly for fellow gentry. His work shows the influence of Bernini and Borromini, and is seen at its best in St John's, Smith Square, Westminster, in St Philip's, Birmingham, and in work at Cliveden and Chatsworth.

JOHN BACON jr., 1777–1859, was a son of the sculptor John Bacon, and became one of the leading monumental artists of his period. Examples of his work can be found all over England, as well as in India and the West Indies.

EDWARD BLORE, 1787–1879, was a topographical artist and architect. His reputation for working cheaply earned him a commission to redesign Buckingham Palace after Nash had been sacked for extravagance. He later specialized in mock Tudor designs of a dull but competent variety.

LANCELOT BROWN, 1715–83, is better known as 'Capability' Brown, through his declared intention to inspect the 'capabilities' of whatever landscape he was set to improve. As a gardener at Stowe he followed William Kent's lead in redesigning the grounds of country houses by using natural means to hand, such as turf banks, scattered trees and sheets of water. He became the acknowledged master of his art, though he was never without critics.

GEORGE BYFIELD, 1756–1813, was probably a pupil of Sir Robert Taylor. He specialized in institutional buildings, but designed a number of country houses, mainly in the West Midlands.

WILLIAM CHAMBERS, 1723–96, son of a Scotch merchant, journeyed to China with his father's Swedish East India Company ships, where he developed a taste for Chinese design which was to bear fruit in such works as the Pagoda in Kew Gardens. Learned and enthusiastic, he published various books, and as Surveyor-General and Comptroller of Works he displayed an eclecticism of taste in designs for Buckingham Palace, Somerset House and the royal State Coach.

FRANCIS CHANTREY, 1781–1841, was the last great monumental artist in the classical tradition begun by Evesham and Stone in the late sixteenth and early seventeenth centuries. He built up a large practice and was personally very popular. A famous story tells of his shooting a brace of woodcock at Holkham, Norfolk, with a single shot, carving them in marble and offering the result to his host.

JOHN FLAXMAN, 1775–1826, worked originally for Wedgwood, designing cameos, portrait medallions and friezes. In 1787 he went to Rome and seven years later returned to England to become one of the most refined exponents of distilled Hellenism in neo-classical sculpture.

WILLIAM & DAVID HIORN, 1712–76, ?–1758, were brother stonemasons from Great Tew in Oxfordshire. As assistants to Francis Smith they worked at Coventry, Warwick and on various country houses.

ANTHONY KECK, 1726–97, specialized in country houses and institutional buildings, mainly in the West Midlands. His work can be seen to effect at Upton, Moccas and in the two Gloucester markets.

HUGH MAY, 1621–84, son of a Sussex squire, was Charles II's Paymaster and Comptroller of Works, employed as one of the three surveyors for the rebuilding of London after the Great Fire of 1666. Holme Lacy is one of only four to survive of the country houses on which he worked with the painter Antonio Verrio and the carver Grinling Gibbons.

SANDERSON MILLER, 1716–80, was another Warwickshire gentleman architect, from Radway on Edgehill. Much admired for his gothicizing, he worked with professional assistants at Croome, Hagley and at the Warwick Shire Hall.

HUMPHREY REPTON, 1752–1818, died the year after Jane Austen, who mentions him in *Mansfield Park*. A successor to Brown in the landscape tradition, he prepared his garden designs with a series of watercolour panoramas in the famous Red Books. His landscapes are notable for the use of evergreens and for their stress on the gradual transition from the house to the surrounding country.

THOMAS RICKMAN, 1776–1841, developed his interest in medieval architecture during country walks to cure depression following his wife's death. He set up offices in Liverpool and Birmingham, and was the first Gothic revivalist with a good knowledge of medieval detail.

LOUIS FRANCOIS ROUBILIAC, 1695–1762, was born in Lyons and came to London in 1732. His first important work was the statue of Handel in Vauxhall Gardens. His style, always dignified and dramatic, is probably seen at its best in the monument to Lady Elizabeth Nightingale in Westminster Abbey.

JOHN MICHAEL RYSBRACK, 1694–1770, a Fleming, studied at Antwerp and then worked at Copenhagen, Paris and Rome, before coming to London in 1732. His monuments are notable for their stress on pyramidal composition, and he was justly considered Roubiliac's rival in the art.

GEORGE GILBERT SCOTT, 1811–78, was the most successful Gothic revivalist of his day. The fruits of his study of Pugin are shown in such works as the Oxford Martyrs' Memorial, St Pancras Station frontage (the Midland Hotel) and the Albert Memorial. At the head of a huge firm, he was responsible for cathedral restoration throughout England. So busy indeed was he that he is said once to have telegraphed his London office, on arrival in Manchester, with the words 'Why am I here?'

ROBERT SMIRKE, 1780–1867, is famous as the designer of the British Museum. With Soane and Nash he is one of a fine triumvirate of neoclassical architects. His work in the West Midlands was concentrated principally in Herefordshire and Gloucestershire.

FRANCIS SMITH, 1672–1738, the son of a Staffordshire bricklayer, was a master builder, mason and architect. Nearly all his houses, with those of his brother William, fall within a fifty-mile radius of Warwick. Uniform and serviceable, they lack distinction, though ideally representative of the average late Baroque country mansion. Good examples are at Kinlet and Mawley, on the Shropshire-Worcestershire border.

JAMES STUART, 1713–88, acquired his soubriquet 'Athenian' after a visit to Athens in 1751, following years in Rome where he may have acted as a tourist guide. Having toured the Greek islands he returned to England to publish *The Antiquities of Athens* and to introduce a revival of Hellenic principles in the temples built at Hagley for Lord Lyttelton and at Shugborough for Lord Anson.

THOMAS TELFORD, 1757–1834, is well known as one of the super-technologists of the Industrial Revolution, building roads, making canals, draining fens and improving harbours. Three of his bridges, at Bewdley, Tewkesbury and Over, are to be seen in the West Midlands.

JAMES THORNHILL, 1675–1734, was the greatest English fresco painter of the Baroque. His work, effusive and colourful, can be seen at its best in the Painted Hall at Greenwich Hospital, but he also produced handsome grisaille panels for the dome of St Paul's.

THOMAS WHITE, 1674–1748, was an architect and monumental mason,

311

whose work is nearly all concentrated in the Worcester area. His art shows itself best in the marble cartouches of memorial tablets, where the sprigs of fruit and blossom show an undeniable affinity to Worcestershire orchards.

JOHN WOOD, 1704–54, 'the Elder', was born in Bath, where his romantic-historical imagination created the great urban complexes of Queen Square, Gay Street and the Circus, laying the foundations of the city's primacy as a paradigm of Georgian design.

EDWARD WOODWARD, 1697–1766, and Thomas his brother, were masons from Chipping Campden, Gloucestershire, whose speciality was a series of tidy, elegant parish churches, best seen in St Swithun's, Worcester, and St John Baptist, Gloucester.

Index

❧

Bredwardine, 286
Bretforton, 69–70
Bricklehampton, 62
Bridstow, 228
Brinsop, 290–1
Broadheath, 127
Broadoak, 200
Broadwas, 127
Broadway, 71
Brockhampton (Ross), 239
Brockhampton (Bromyard), 249
Bromyard, 248–9
Broome, 103
Broome, William, 254
Brown, 'Capability', 29, 152, 268
Browning, Elizabeth Barrett, 148
Burne-Jones, Edward, 35, 117
Burton Court, 280–1
Bushell, Thomas, 71
Bushley, 163
Butler, Samuel, 159
Butterfield, William, 61
Byfield, George, 66, 249
Byford, 288

Canon Frome, 245
Canon Pyon, 273
Cantelupe family, 36
Cantelupe, Thomas, 124, 148
Cantelupe, William, 123
Castle Frome, 245
Castlemorton, 164–5
Chaddesley Corbett, 111
Chafy, W. K. W., 68
Chantrey, Francis, 108
Charlecote Park, 29–34
  church, 34
Charles I, King, 143
Charles II, King, 75, 83, 122
Château Impney, 92
Claines, 122
Clearwell, 206
Cleeve Prior, 71
Clehonger, 282
Clementi, Muzio, 65
Clent, 104–5
Clifford, 296
Cliffords Mesne, 175
Clifton-on-Teme, 136
Clodock, 293
Clopton, 26

Coddington, 148
Cofton Hackett, 106
Colwall, 147
Combertons, The, 58
Comper, Ninian, 290
Coningsby Wall, 118
Conway family, 38–40, 41
Cookes, Thomas, 64, 108, 110
Cookhill, 95
Corbett, John, 92
Corelli, Marie, 23
Cotheridge, 126
Coughton Court, 23–40
Coventry family, 152–6
Craik, Mrs, 170
Craswall, 296
Craycombe, 66
Credenhill, 289
Croft Castle, 268–70
  family, 269
Croome, 152–6
Cropthorne, 63
Crowle, 96
Cwmmau, 278

Dallam, Thomas, 172
Dean, William, 155
Deerhurst, 173
Defford, 157
Despenser, Hugh Le, 171
Deykes, J. and S., 145–6
Dilwyn, 271
Dingley family, 63–8
Dinmore, 251
Dodd, Charles, 112
Dodderhill, 92
Doddridge, Philip, 161
Dodford, 110
Dormington, 255
Dormston, 96
Dorstone, 297
Dowdeswell, William, 163
Dowles, 113
Downton, 264
Droitwich Spa, 90–1
Dubricius, 226
Dunkley, Samuel, 48
Dymock, 176
Dymock Poets, 176–7

Eadburh, St, 56

314

315